Lecture Notes of the Institute
for Computer Sciences, Social-Informatics
and Telecommunications Engineering

Xiao Jun Hei   Lawrence Cheung (Eds.)

Access Networks

4th International Conference, AccessNets 2009
Hong Kong, China, November 1-3, 2009
Revised Selected Papers

 Springer

Volume Editors

Xiao Jun Hei
Huazhong University of Science and Technology
1037 Luoyu Road, Wuhan, China
E-mail: heixj@hust.edu.cn

Lawrence Cheung
Hong Kong Polytechnic University
Hung Hom, Kowloon, Hong Kong, China
E-mail: lawrenceccccheung@yahoo.com.hk

Library of Congress Control Number: 2009943508

CR Subject Classification (1998): C.2, K.4.4, K.6.5, D.4.6

ISSN   1867-8211
ISBN-10   3-642-11663-9 Springer Berlin Heidelberg New York
ISBN-13   978-3-642-11663-6 Springer Berlin Heidelberg New York

springer.com

© ICST Institute for Computer Sciences, Social-Informatics and Telecommunications Engineering 2010
Printed in Germany

Typesetting: Camera-ready by author, data conversion by Scientific Publishing Services, Chennai, India
Printed on acid-free paper   SPIN: 12840373   06/3180   5 4 3 2 1 0

Preface

With the rapid growth of the Internet as well as the increasing demand for broadband services, access networks have been receiving growing investments in recent years. This has led to a massive network deployment with the goal of eliminating the bandwidth bottleneck between end-users and the network core. Today many diverse technologies are being used to provide broadband access to end users. The architecture and performance of the access segment (local loop, wired and wireless access networks, and even home networks) are getting increasing attention for ensuring quality of service of diverse broadband applications. Moreover, most access lines will no longer terminate on a single device, thus leading to the necessity of having a home network designed for applications that transcend simple Internet access sharing among multiple personal computers and enable multimedia support. Therefore, the access network and its home portion have become a hot investment pool from both a financial as well as a research perspective.

The aim of the annual International Conference on Access Networks (AccessNets) is to provide a forum that brings together scientists and researchers from academia as well as managers and engineers from the industry and government organizations to meet and exchange ideas and recent work on all aspects of access networks and how they integrate with their in-home counterparts. After Athens in 2006, Ottawa in 2007, and Las Vegas in 2008, this year AccessNets moved to Asia for the first time. AccessNets 2009 was the fourth edition of this exciting event, which was held in Hong Kong, China, during November 1–3, 2009. The conference program started with the International Workshop on Advanced Wireless Access Technologies for IMT-A (IWATA) comprising seven papers organized in two technical sessions in the afternoon of November 1. The technical program of AccessNets 2009 consisted of seven technical sessions distributed over the next two days on November 2 and 3 in a single-track format. The first talk of each day was delivered by an invited keynote speaker from either industry or academia.

The conference received approximately 22 submissions from different countries. After a thorough review process, 11 papers were accepted from the open call for presentation. The overall paper acceptance rate is 50%. In addition, several distinguished researchers were invited to contribute to the conference program. The IWATA workshop started with the first talk by Yiqing Zhou of the Hong Kong Applied Science and Technology Institute on the topic of recent standardization development on IMT-A. The keynote speaker of the first day of the conference was Jeffrey Yuen from PCCW and the title of his talk was "From Quad Play to Connected Living." The keynote speaker of the second day was Joseph Hui from Arizona State University and his topic was on "Beyond Access for Virtualization and Cloud Computing." The conference participants were from different countries including Norway, Spain, Belgium, Canada, USA, Korea, Japan, China, and Hong Kong.

We would like to express our sincere gratitude to all the authors and the invited speakers for their valuable contributions. We would also like to thank all members of the AccessNets 2009 Organizing Committee and Technical Program Committee in organizing the conference and putting together an excellent conference program. In addition, we would also like to thank all the reviewers for their efforts to accurately review the papers on time.

Finally, we would like to thank the staff of ICST for their support in making AccessNets 2009 successful. In particular, we would also like to thank Eszter Hajdu, Maria Morozova, and Diana Dobak for taking care of the conference preparation especially in the final stage.

Danny H.K. Tsang
Nirwan Ansari
Pin-Han Ho
Vincent K.N. Lau

Organization

ACCESSNETS 2009 Committee

Steering Committee

Imrich Chlamtac (Chair)	Create-Net Research
Jun Zheng	Italy Southeast University
Nirwan Ansari	China New Jersey Institute of Technology, USA

General Chair

Danny H.K. Tsang — Hong Kong University of Science and Technology, Hong Kong, China

TPC Co-chairs

Nirwan Ansari	New Jersey Institute of Technology, USA
Pin-Han Ho	University of Waterloo, Canada
Vincent K.N. Lau	Hong Kong University of Science and Technology, Hong Kong, China

Workshop Co-chairs

Chonggang Wang	NEC Laboratories America, Inc., USA
Nei Kato	Tohoku University, Japan

Panel Co-chairs

Martin Maier	INRS, Canada
Qinqing Zhang	Johns Hopkins University, USA

Publication Co-chairs

Lawrence Cheung	Hong Kong Polytechnic University, Hong Kong, China
Xiaojun Hei	Huazhong University of Science & Technology, China

Web Chair

Xiaojun Hei — Huazhong University of Science & Technology, China

Publicity Co-chairs

Chadi Assi   Concordia University, Canada
Rong Zhao   Detecon International GmbH, Bonn, Germany

Industry Sponsorship Chair

Carlson Chu   PCCW, Hong Kong, China

Conference Coordinator

Maria Morozova   ICST

Local Arrangements Chair

Wilson Chu   Open University of Hong Kong, Hong Kong, China

Technical Program Committee

Gee-Kung Chang   Georgia Institue of Technology, USA
Ruiran Chang   Northeastern University, China
Lin Dai   City University of Hong Kong, Hong Kong
Maurice GAGNAIRE   ENST (TELECOM ParisTech), France
Paolo Giacomazzi   Politecnico di Milano, Italy
Zhen Guo   Innovative Wireless Technologies, USA
Kaibin Huang   Hong Kong University of Science and Technology,
                                   Hong Kong
David K Hunter   ESE Department, University of Essex, UK
Raj Jain   University of Washington in St. Louis, USA
Meilong Jiang   NEC Laboratories America, USA
Ken Kerpez   Telcordia Technologies
Polychronis Koutsakis   Technical University of Crete, Greece
Chang-Hee Lee   KAIST, Korea
Helen-C Leligou   Technological Educational Institute of Chalkis, Greece
Kejie Lu   University of Puerto Rico at Mayaguez
Martin Maier   INRS Energie, Materiaux et Telecommunications
John Mitchell   University College London, UK
Enzo Mingozzi   University of Pisa, Italy
Djafar Mynbaev   New York City College of Technology, USA
Sagar Naik   University of Waterloo, Canada
Qiang Ni   Brunel University, UK
Martin Reisslein   Arizona State University, USA
Djamel Sadok   Federal University of Pernambuco (UFPE), Brazil
Gangxiang Shen   Ciena Corporation, USA
Driton Statovci   Telecommunications Research Center Vienna, Austria
Scott A Valcourt   University of New Hampshire, USA
Athanasios Vasilakos   University of Western Macedonia, Greece
Wei Wei   NEC Laboratories America, USA

Gaoxi Xiao	Nangyang Technological University, Singapore
Wei Yan	Trend Micro, USA
Kun Yang	University of Essex, UK
Panlong Yang	Nanjing Institute of Communications Engineering, China
Angela Zhang	The Chinese University of Hong Kong, Hong Kong
Dustin Zhang	University of California, Irvine, USA
Hong Zhao	Fairleigh Dickinson University, USA
Rong Zhao	Detecon International GmbH, Bonn, Germany
SiQing Zheng	University of Texas at Dallas, USA
Hua Zhu	San Diego Research Center, USA

IWATA Workshop 2009 Committee

Workshop Co-chairs

Tung-Sang Ng	University of Hong Kong, Hong Kong
Jiangzhou Wang	University of Kent, UK
Yiqing Zhou	Applied Science and Technology Research Institute Company, Hong Kong

Technical Program Committee

Heung-Gyoon Ryu	Chungbuk National University, Korea
Kai-kit Wong	University College London, UK
Lin Tian	Institute of Computing Technology, China Academy of Science, China
Shaodan Ma	University of Hong Kong, Hong Kong
Wei Peng	Tohoku University, Japan
Wen Chen	Shanghai Jiao Tong University, China
Xiangyang Wang	Southeast University, China
Xiaohui Lin	Shenzhen University, China
Xiaolong Zhu	Alcatel-Lucent Shanghai Bell Co., Ltd., China
Xiaoying Gan	University of California, San Diego, USA
Yafeng Wang	Beijing University of Posts and Telecommunications, China
Yonghong Zeng	Agency for Science Technology and Research, Singapore
Zaichen Zhang	Southeast University, China
Zhengang Pan	Applied Science and Technology Research Institute Company, Hong Kong
Zhen Kong	Colorado State University, USA
Zhendong Zhou	University of Sydney, Australia

Table of Contents

Session 5: Broadband Access Networks

Session 6: Cognitive Radios

Session 7: Cross-Layer Design & DSL Technologies

IWATA Workshop

Session 1

Session 2

Hybrid Dynamic Bandwidth and Wavelength Allocation Algorithm to Support Multi-Service Level Profiles in a WDM-EPON

Noemí Merayo[1], Rubén González[1], Ignacio de Miguel[1], Tamara Jiménez[2],
Ramón J. Durán[1], Patricia Fernández[1], Rubén M. Lorenzo[1], Juan C. Aguado[1],
and Evaristo J. Abril[1]

[1] Optical Communications Group Department of Signal Theory,
Communications and Telematic Engineering
E.T.S.I. Telecomunicación, University of Valladolid (Spain)
Campus Miguel Delibes, Camino del Cementerio s/n, 47011 Valladolid, Spain
Tel.: +34 983 423000 ext. 5549; Fax: +34 983 423667
noemer@tel.uva.es
[2] Center for the Development of Telecommunications (CEDETEL)
Edificio Solar, Parque Tecnológico de Boecillo, 47151, Boecillo, Valladolid, Spain
Tel.: +34 983 546502; Fax: +34 983 546696

Abstract. A novel bandwidth assignment algorithm in WDM Ethernet Passive Optical Networks, called DyWaS-SLA, is proposed not only to provide service differentiation but also to offer subscriber differentiation. Simulation results show that DyWaS-SLA outperforms other bandwidth allocation algorithms in WDM-EPONs as it makes fairer bandwidth distribution than those methods. Consequently, it always insures a guaranteed bandwidth for every priority subscriber. Furthermore, DyWaS-SLA obtains lower mean packet delay and packet loss rate for the highest priority subscribers when compared with other bandwidth distribution schemes in WDM-EPONs.

Keywords: Wavelength Division Multiplexing (WDM), Dynamic Bandwidth Allocation (DBA), Ethernet Passive Optical Network (EPON), Service Level Agreement (SLA), CoS (Class of Service).

1 Introduction

Passive Optical Networks (PONs) are an excellent technology to develop access networks, as they provide both high bandwidth and class of service differentiation [1-2]. The PON technology uses a single wavelength in each of the two directions and such wavelengths are multiplexed on the same fiber by means of Wavelength Division Multiplexing (WDM). Since all users share the same wavelength in the upstream direction, a Medium Access Control (MAC) is necessary to avoid collision between packets from different Optical Network Units (ONUs). Time Division Multiple Access (TDMA) is the most widespread control scheme in these networks. However, it

X. Jun Hei and L. Cheung (Eds.): AccessNets 2009, LNICST 37, pp. 1–13, 2010.
© Institute for Computer Sciences, Social-Informatics and Telecommunications Engineering 2010

is inefficient because the nature of network traffic is neither homogeneous nor continuous [3-4]. In this way, algorithms which distribute the available bandwidth in a dynamic way, called Dynamic Bandwidth Allocation algorithms (DBA), are necessary to adapt the network capacity to traffic conditions by changing the distribution of the bandwidth assigned to each ONU depending on the current requirements [3-8]. Therefore, the current MAC protocols are based on a dynamic distribution of the upstream bandwidth among the connected ONUs in the PON.

Although PON infrastructures are able to provide enough bandwidth for current applications, both the gradual increase of the number of users and the bandwidth requirements of the new emerging services, demand an upgrade of such access networks. The addition of new wavelengths to be shared in the upstream and downstream direction in PON infrastructures leads to the so-called Wavelength Division Multiplex PONs (WDM-PONs). The pure WDM-PON architecture assigns one dedicated wavelength per ONU, which implies more dedicated bandwidth and more security in the system. However, the related cost associated to such deployment makes pure WDM-PONs as the next-generation architectures. Hence, the combination of the WDM technology with Time Division Multiplexing (TDM) techniques is likely the best near future approach. These hybrid architectures exploit the advantages of wavelength assignment of WDM techniques and the power splitting of TDM techniques.

On the other hand, end users contract a Service Level Agreement (SLA) with a provider, which forces the access network to treat each SLA subscriber in a different way. Many studies are related to service providers, which offer multi-service levels according to subscribers' requirements [5-8]. The Bandwidth Guaranteed Polling (BGP) method proposed in [5] divides ONUs into two disjoint sets of bandwidth guaranteed ONUs and best effort ONUs. While the guaranteed ONUs receive the demanded bandwidth, the remaining bandwidth is delivered over the best effort ONUs. However, this scheme only differs between guaranteed ONUs and best effort ONUs, but it does not distinguish other profiles with specific restrictions. Hence, a typical way to offer customer differentiation is to use a fixed weighted factor assigned to each ONU associated to a specific SLA. Then, the bandwidth is allocated depending on these weights. In the method presented in [6], each ONU is assigned a minimum guaranteed bandwidth based on the associated weight, so that the upstream channel is divided among the ONUs in proportion to their SLAs. In the Dynamic Minimum Bandwidth algorithm (DMB) [7-8], the OLT distributes the available bandwidth by assigning different weights to each client depending on their SLA. Therefore, ONUs associated with a higher weight will be assigned more bandwidth.

In this paper, we present a novel DBA algorithm applied to a hybrid WDM-TDM EPON architecture for a gradual upgrade of the existing TDM EPON infrastructures. Unlike other DBA algorithms proposed in WDM-EPONs, the new algorithm is able to differ between service level profiles with the aim to distribute the available bandwidth conscious of the requirements of every profile. Then, the algorithm is designed to insure a guaranteed bandwidth to every subscriber when the available bandwidth is not enough to support every bandwidth demand. Furthermore, the Ethernet protocol has been considered because it is a well-known inexpensive technology and interoperable with a variety of legacy equipment [1-2].

The paper is organized as follows. Section 2 describes the related work focus on WDM-PON deployment. Section 3 explains the new WDM-TDM algorithm. In Section 4 the environment and results achieved from simulations carried out are presented. Finally, in section 5, the most relevant conclusions obtained in this study are shown.

2 Related Work in WDM-TDM PONs

Several WDM-TDM architectures have been proposed recently, although the deployment of the WDM technology in the access network is still in its first stages. One extended WDM-PON approach employs one separate wavelength for the transmission between the OLT to each ONU. In general, this architecture does not allow bandwidth redistribution and presents high deployment cost. In order to reduce costs, the authors in [9] proposes a hybrid WDM-TDM access architecture with reflective ONUs, an arrayed-waveguide-grating outside plant, and a tunable laser stack at the OLT. This architecture decreases a lot the number of lasers at the OLT and also improves highly the security at each ONU. However, dynamic wavelength assignment is not permitted and it can not take advantage of the inter-channel statistical multiplexing to fairly redistribute the available bandwidth.

On the contrary, the WDM-PON architecture called SUCCESS [10] permits a gradual migration from TDM-PON to WDM-PON by adding tunable transmitters at the OLT. It allows that multiple tunable transceivers can be shared among several independent PONs. Furthermore, the SUCCESS prototype was improved by deploying a ring topology in the so-called SUCCESS-HPON [11]. Then, the OLT communicates with users using several distribution starts. The authors developed in [12] a scheduling algorithm applying dynamic wavelength allocation to allow bandwidth sharing across multiple physical PONs, by means of sharing the tunable transceivers at the OLT. It enhances the architecture performance and reduces the related costs.

The hybrid novel WDM-TDM architecture proposed in [13] uses a transmitter without wavelength selectivity based on an uncooled Fabry-Pérot Laser Diode (FP-LD). The study demonstrated that a single FD-LD can be used in any wavelength channel without wavelength tuning in a temperature range from 0 to 60°C. The architecture has a double-star topology in a cascade of several arrayed-waveguide gratings (AWGs), and each of them is shared by a number of users by means of splitters via TDM techniques. However, no DBA algorithms were discussed for such architecture.

The architectures proposed in [14-16] consider a smooth upgrade of TDM-PONs, allowing several wavelengths for the upstream transmission. Authors in [14-15] proposed that the OLT consists of an array of fixed laser/receivers and the ONUs of either an array of fixed laser/receivers or one or more tunable laser/receivers. However, since the providers' point of view is more likely the utilization of either tunable laser/receivers or fixed laser/receiver arrays, but not both simultaneously. Moreover, the migration from TDM-PONs to WDM-PON would be upgraded gradually along the time depending on economical constrains.

In the prototype proposed in [16], every ONU employs one or more fixed transceivers, permitting a gradual upgrade depending on the traffic demand of the ONUs. Then, the OLT assigns the bandwidth to each ONU in those wavelengths they support. In addition, the fixed transceivers at the ONU can be interchanged by a fast tunable laser. In that case, the OLT only can transmit in one single wavelength at any given time, which may lead to poor bandwidth utilization due to the dead tuning time every time there is a wavelength switch.

Finally, there are other architectures which propose to divide ONUs into multiple subsets [17]. As each subset is allocated a fixed wavelength channel for the upstream transmission, each ONU is equipped with a fixed transceiver and the OLT with a stack of fixed transceivers. However, this architecture is limited flexible as it does not allow dynamic wavelength allocation.

Regarding DBA algorithms developed in WDM-PONs, the algorithm proposed in [16] presents three variants in order to allocate the excess bandwidth among ONUs with great traffic demand (high loaded ONUs). Among these three schemes, namely controlled, fair and uncontrolled methods, the former improves the bandwidth utilization and therefore the overall network performance. In the controlled variant, the OLT waits until all reports messages from one cycle are received in order to apply the allocation algorithm for the next cycle. However, in the other two approaches the OLT permits that ONUs with low traffic demand can transmit before the reception of every report. Moreover, the dynamic channel allocation is based on the first-fit technique (i.e. the first available free wavelength).

The algorithm proposed in [18] is an extension of the Interleaved Polling Adaptive Cycle Time (IPACT) for EPON access networks. Similar to the previous method [16], it also applies the first-fit technique to dynamically select each channel wavelength. Besides, it also provides Class of Service (CoS) differentiation by means of the extended strict priority queue scheme.

The algorithm proposed in [15] developed an extension to the Multi-Point Control Protocol (MPCP) for WDM-PONs in order to support dynamic bandwidth allocation. They implemented two scheduling paradigms for WDM-EPONs, namely online and offline. In the former, the OLT applies bandwidth and wavelength allocation based on the individual request of each ONU. However, in the offline policy the OLT applies scheduling decisions taking into account the bandwidth requirements of all ONUs. The simulations demonstrate that online scheduling obtains lower delays than offline scheduling, especially at high ONU loads.

Finally, the algorithm presented in [19] supports Quality of Service (QoS) in a differentiated services framework. The algorithm allows each ONU to simultaneously transmit at two channels, where each channel is dedicated to a different type of traffic.

The WDM-PON architectures and the WDM-DBA algorithms for such architectures are being strongly studied nowadays. However, it does not exist a predominant or imposed architecture. Therefore, the gradual WDM upgrade would be limited by technological costs and based on the necessity of service providers. It is preferable flexible WDM-PON architectures which could be upgraded in a cost-effective way. We agree with these flexible architectures which allow both time and wavelength dynamic allocation. In order to share several wavelengths for the upstream transmission, each ONU will be equipped with several fixed transceivers or a tunable transceiver. However, the utilization of a tunable transceiver may provide less bandwidth due to the dead tuning time necessary to switch wavelengths. Therefore, it is necessary to have transceivers with a tuning speed at least of microseconds.

3 DyWaS-SLA Algorithm

In order to distribute the available bandwidth among users there are two essential approaches which can be applied: the separate wavelength and time allocation, or the joint wavelength and time assignment. Most of the proposed studies [15, 18-19] consider the joint time and wavelength assignment as it permits multidimensional scheduling.

Furthermore, there are multiple schemes to assign wavelengths and some of them are extensively used in the transport network, such as the fixed, the random, the least assigned, the least loaded or the first fit allocation. Then, the OLT keeps track of the utilization of each wavelength and uses this information to decide on which ONUs the wavelength assignment changes. In the fixed scheme, once a wavelength has been assigned for the transmission of one ONU, this assignment is never changed. This makes the wavelength allocation very simple to implement but it lacks of the statistical wavelength-domain multiplexing advantages. On the other hand, the random, the least assigned and the least loaded methods tend to excessively overload certain wavelengths, as it is demonstrated in [15]. Therefore, the online scheduling wavelength scheme in which ONUs are able to transmit in the first free wavelength, leads to an efficient solution [18]. Then, in this simulation study it is assumed the first fit method to dynamically assign the wavelengths.

In order to allocate bandwidth at each separate wavelength channel, polling algorithms are a good choice as they can improve the channel utilization. Among the different bandwidth allocation schemes which may be used in polling methods, the limited scheme offers the best performance, as it is demonstrated in [19, 21]. In this scheme, the OLT gives the required bandwidth to each ONU as long as the demand is lower than a maximum bandwidth imposed. When the demand is higher than this bandwidth, the OLT gives this latter maximum. This behaviour makes the cycle time to be adaptive depending on the updated demand of each ONU. The cycle time is the total time in which all ONUs transmit in a round robin discipline.

As the network allows different service levels profiles, it is necessary to treat subscribers differently depending on their priority. In order to do that, it is applied the method based on assigning a fixed weight to each profile [9, 14-15] depending of its priority. Then, the OLT uses these weights to allocate the available bandwidth at each channel.

The new algorithm called Dynamic Wavelength aSsignment to support multi- Service Level Agreement (DyWaS-SLA) has been designed taking into account the previous ideas. In contrast to other existing DBA algorithms applied to WDM-PONs, the new algorithm distinguishes between profiles with different requirements, insuring a guaranteed bandwidth when every profile demand excesses the available bandwidth. Therefore, DyWaS-SLA sets different maximum bandwidths $\left(B_{max}^{sla_k}\right)$, one for each priority SLA. Therefore, the allocated bandwidth in one cycle time for each ONU ($B_{alloc}^{onu_i}$) can be defined by Eq. 1:

$$B_{alloc}^{onu_i} = \begin{cases} B_{demand}^{onu_i} & \text{if } B_{demand}^{onu_i} < B_{max}^{sla_k} \\ B_{max}^{sla_k} & \text{Otherwise} \end{cases} . \tag{1}$$

where $B_{demand}^{onu_i}$ is the aggregated bandwidth demand of all supported services in the ONU i. The term $Q_{i,j}$ is the demanded bandwidth for the class of service j in the ONU i (Eq. 2) reported in the last control message.

$$B_{demand}^{onu_i} = \sum_j Q_{i,j} \cdot \tag{2}$$

The maximum allocated bandwidth permitted for each ONU depending on its SLA at each cycle time, $B_{max}^{sla_k}$, is calculated using the Eq. 3. In this equation W^{sla_m} represents the weight associated to the SLA m, $B_{cycle\_available}$ the available bandwidth at each maximum cycle (i.e. maximum cycle time of 2 ms set by the EPON standard). The term $N_{onus}^{sla_m}$ is the number of ONUs associated to SLA m in the network and λ_n represents each supported wavelength.

$$B_{max}^{sla_k} = \frac{B_{cycle\_available} \cdot W^{sla_k} \cdot \sum_n \lambda_n}{\sum_m W^{sla_m} \cdot N_{onus}^{sla_m}} \cdot \tag{3}$$

4 Simulation Results

4.1 Simulation Scenario

Simulations were made considering an WDM-EPON with 32 ONUs and one user connected to each ONU using OPNET Modeler 14 [20]. The transmission rate of the upstream link between ONUs and the OLT is set to 1 Gbit/s and the access link from the user to each ONU to 100 Mbit/s [6, 22-23]. The distance between ONUs and the OLT is set to 20 km, which is near the maximum permitted distance for a typical PON [6, 23]. In order to avoid collisions between adjacent ONUs, a guard time of 1 µs is chosen, a value within the limits specified by the standard IEEE 802.3ah D1.414 [24].

Moreover, the WDM-EPON network copes with a variety of traffic streams with different requirements. Then, taking into consideration the ITU-T G.1010 [25] and G. 114 [26] Recommendations and other related works [3, 6, 23], it is assumed that three of these classes of service, P_0, P_1 and P_2 are supported by the network. They respectively represent Real-Time, Responsively and Best effort traffic. In addition, it is considered that the highest priority service P_0 represents 20% of the ONU load, while P_1 and P_2 priority services get equal shares of the remaining ONU load [3, 23]. Hence, each ONU is equipped with three queues, one for each class of service, all of them sharing the same buffer of capacity 10 MB like in [6, 22].

As the WDM-EPON network also contemplates subscriber differentiation, it is presented a scenario with three priority SLAs: SLA$_0$ for the highest priority service level, SLA$_1$ for the medium priority service level and SLA$_2$ for the lowest priority service level. In general, only very few conventional users contract high level agreement conditions, whereas users tend to contract medium or low priority service level profiles. As a consequence, it is assumed that one ONU contracts the highest priority service level agreement SLA_0, five ONUs contract the medium priority service level SLA_1 and ten ONUs the lowest priority service level SLA_2. Related to the assigned weights to each SLA (W^{sla_k}), it is set the values $W^{sla_0} = 4$, $W^{sla_1} = 3$ and $W^{sla_2} = 2$ as well as other other published studies [7-8]. These weights are considered to comply with the NTT DSL service plans (50/70/100 Mbit/s) [27], also used by the algorithms proposed in [7-8]. Therefore each SLA should be offered this guaranteed bandwidth when the bandwidth demand of every SLA exceeds the available bandwidth. Furthermore, it is considered 3 supported wavelengths in the WDM-PON in order to increase the total capacity of the shared upstream channel.

Packet generation follows a Pareto distribution with a Hurst parameter, H, equal to 0.8, considering them of fixed length (1500 bytes plus additional headers, i.e., 1538 bytes). This length was assumed because it is the MTU of the standard IEEE 802.3. Moreover, the maximum cycle time is set to 2 ms, limited by the standard IEEE 802.3ah D1.414 [24].

Related to the evaluation of algorithms, DyWaS-SLA is compared with WDM-IPACT [18] as the original algorithm IPACT [22] is a very efficient method even when it does not differentiate priority profiles. Finally, both algorithms support service differentiation by means of the strict priority queue method. This method achieves the best performance for the highest priority services and it is easy to implement.

4.2 Simulation Results

Fig. 1 represents the mean packet delay versus the ONU load, when WDM-IPACT and DyWaS-SLA algorithms are compared for the three service level agreements (SLA_0, SLA_1 and SLA_2) and for the highest priority service P_0. As it can be noticed, there are slight differences between both algorithms for every ONU load, obtaining all of them values under 1E-3 seconds. Furthermore, this value is under the maximum limited imposed in the access by the Recommendation ITU-T G. 114 [31] for such applications, that is 1.5 ms. However, DyWaS-SLA achieves lower delay than WDM-IPACT for every subscriber at high ONU loads, although the differences between them are very small. Regarding the packet loss rate, both algorithms do not permit packet losses for such priority service P_0, therefore it has not been represented in any graph.

Fig. 2 represents the mean packet delay versus the ONU load, when WDM-IPACT and DyWaS-SLA algorithms are compared for the three SLAs and the medium priority service P_1. It can be observed that WDM-IPACT does not differ between subscribers with different priority, achieving the same delay for every SLA. In contrast to WDM-IPACT, DyWaS-SLA obtains lower mean packet delay than WDM-IPACT for the two highest priority subscribers (SLA_0, SLA_1). It can be noticed that DyWaS-SLA keeps the mean packet delay for such priority subscribers near the values obtained for the highest priority service P_0. Regarding packet losses, these algorithms do not allow losses for such priority service and it has not been represented in any graph.

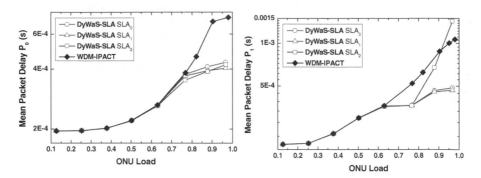

Fig. 1. Mean packet delay versus ONU load of WDM-IPACT and DyWaS-SLA algorithms for every SLA subscriber and class of service P_0

Fig. 2. Mean packet delay versus ONU load of WDM-IPACT and DyWaS-SLA algorithms for every SLA subscriber and class of service P_1

Related to the lowest priority service P_2, Fig. 3 represents the mean packet delay versus the ONU load, when WDM-IPACT and DyWaS-SLA are compared for the three SLAs. One more time, it can be seen how WDM-IPACT treats subscribers in the same way. On the contrary, DyWaS-SLA achieves a great reduction in the mean packet delay when compared with WDM-IPACT for the two highest priority subscribers (SLA_0, SLA_1). The most noticeable improvement appears for the highest priority subscribers (SLA_0), where DyWaS-SLA is able to keep their mean packet delay under or around 1E-3 seconds for every ONU load. Therefore, it has been demonstrated that this profile achieves very low delays for every supported service. Furthermore, differences between WDM-IPACT and DyWaS-SLA for SLA_0 and SLA_1 subscribers reach more than two orders of magnitude when the ONU load is higher than 0.8.

In order to analyze the packet losses of the service P_2, Fig. 4 represents the packet loss rate versus the ONU load, when WDM-IPACT and DyWaS-SLA are compared.

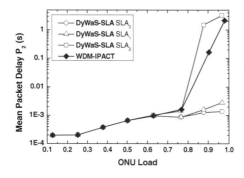

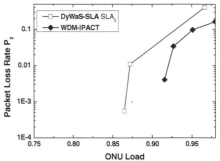

Fig. 3. Mean packet delay versus ONU load of WDM-IPACT and DyWaS-SLA algorithms for every SLA subscriber and class of service P_2

Fig. 4. Packet loss rate versus ONU load of WDM-IPACT and DyWaS-SLA algorithms for every SLA subscriber and class of service P_2

It can be observed that WDM-IPACT presents losses for every subscriber independently of its priority. However, DyWaS-SLA differs between SLAs and performs better for the two highest priority subscribers (SLA_0 and SLA_1), as it does not permit losses for such subscribers. Consequently, DyWaS-SLA presents packet losses for the lowest priority subscribers (SLA_2), in order to avoid losses for SLA_0 and SLA_1 profiles.

On the other hand, one important characteristic of DBA algorithms is the offered bandwidth to each priority subscriber. Then, Fig. 5 shows the offered bandwidth to one ONU of each SLA versus the ONU load when WDM-IPACT and DyWaS-SLA are compared for 32 ONUs. As all ONUs have the same traffic distribution, all of them demand the same bandwidth (B_{demand}), as it is shown in the figure. As it can be seen in Fig. 5 the demanded bandwidth follows a linear function until the maximum user transmission rate of 100 Mbit/s. In the same way, the represented offered bandwidth to one ONU of each SLA is the same for all ONUs belonging to such SLA.

It can be noticed that WDM-IPACT offers the same bandwidth to every SLA as it does not take into consideration the priority of the subscriber. On the contrary, DyWaS-SLA differs between profiles and it offers more bandwidth than WDM-IPACT for the two highest priority subscribers (SLA_0 and SLA_1). Then, DyWaS-SLA outperforms WDM-IPACT as it always insures the guaranteed bandwidth when the total capacity is not enough to cover the bandwidth demand of every profile. On the contrary, WDM-IPACT does not offer the guaranteed bandwidth to the highest priority subscribers SLA_0 (100 Mbit/s) when the ONU load is higher than 0.9.

The same behaviour can be observed in Fig. 6, when it is assumed that 48 ONUs are connected to the WDM-EPON. In the figure, it can be noticed that differences between both algorithms are much higher. DyWaS-SLA can offer the demanded bandwidth for the highest priority subscribers SLA_0 for every ONU load. Related to the SLA_1 priority profile, DyWaS-SLA offers the demanded bandwidth up to ONU loads around 0.75. Meanwhile, WDM-IPACT algorithm does not distinguish between priority SLAS and it only offers the demanded bandwidth for the two highest priority subscribers for lower ONU loads than DyWaS-SLA, that it is, loads lower than 0.6. This means that for the two highest priority profiles SLA_0 and SLA_1, DyWaS-SLA supports efficiently higher loads than WDM-IPACT does.

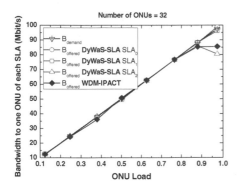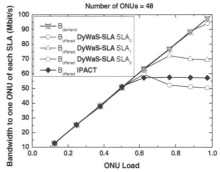

Fig. 5. Demanded and offered bandwidth to one ONU of each SLA versus ONU load for WDM-IPACT and DyWaS-SLA for 32 ONUs

Fig. 6. Demanded and offered bandwidth to one ONU of each SLA versus ONU load for WDM-IPACT and DyWaS-SLA for 48 ONUs

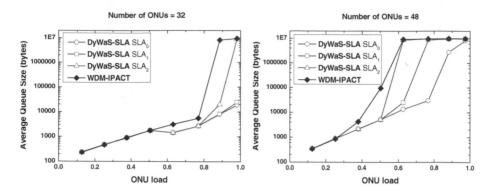

Fig. 7. Average queue size versus ONU load for WDM-IPACT and DyWaS-SLA for 32 ONUs

Fig. 8. Average queue size versus ONU load for WDM-IPACT and DyWaS-SLA for 48 ONUs

Regarding the guaranteed bandwidth to each profile, in Fig. 6 it is shown that Dy-WaS-SLA is able to insure the guaranteed bandwidth for every SLA and every ONU load. However, WDM-IPACT can not offer the guaranteed bandwidth for the most important priority subscribers SLA_0 (100 Mbit/s) and SLA_1 (70 Mbit/s). This behaviour means that DyWaS-SLA efficiently complies with the bandwidth restrictions imposed by the service provider.

In Fig. 7 and Fig. 8 it is represented the average queue size versus the ONU load in order to compared DyWas-SLA and WDM-IPACT for 32 and 48 ONUs. In both figures it can be seen how WDM-IPACT keeps the same queue size for every SLA. On the contrary, DyWas-SLA maintains lower queue size than WDM-IPACT for the two highest priority profiles SLA_0 and SLA_1.

In particular, in Fig, 7, when the number of ONUs is set to 32, WDM-IPACT keeps the queue of every profile nearly full (10 Mbytes) for ONU loads higher than 0.8. This behaviour provokes that the highest priority subscriber SLA_0, cannot comply with its guaranteed bandwidth for such loads, as it has been demonstrated in Fig. 5. When the number of ONUs is increased to 48, Fig. 8 shows how WDM-IPACT keeps the queue nearly full for every SLA when the ONU load is higher than 0.6. Therefore, it makes that SLA_0 and SLA_1 subscribers cannot have insured their guaranteed bandwidth for such loads, as it can be seen in Fig. 6.

On the contrary, DyWaS-SLA keeps lower queue size than WDM-IPACT for SLA_0 and SLA_1 subscribers, which allows these profiles to achieve their guaranteed bandwidth for every ONU load.

If we analize the wavelength utilization, Fig. 9 represents the percentage of the wavelength utilization along the time when WDM-IPACT and DyWaS-SLA are compared. As it can be seen, both algorithms use every wavelength in the same way. Also this figure demonstrates that the first fit method does not overload one particular wavelength, as it distributes the wavelength allocation fairly between every supported wavelength. This behaviour can be seen in Fig. 10, which represents the wavelength allocation at one particular ONU along the time for the DyWaS-SLA algorithm. It is shown that one ONU is assigned the three supported wavelengths in the same proportion along the simulation time.

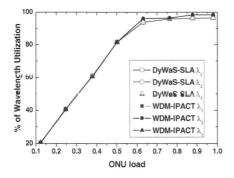

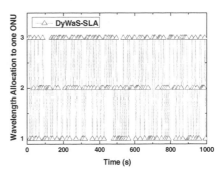

Fig. 9. Percentage of the wavelength utilization along the time when WDM-IPACT and DyWaS-SLA are compared

Fig. 10. Wavelength allocation at one particular ONU versus the time for DyWaS-SLA algorithm

5 Conclusions

A novel polling algorithm called DyWaS-SLA to provide service and subscriber differentiation in WDM-EPONs has been proposed. DyWaS-SLA distributes the bandwidth according to a set of weights in order to offer a guaranteed bandwidth to each priority profile when the available bandwidth is not enough to cover the demand of every subscriber.

DyWaS-SLA has been compared with WDM-IPACT as it is a very efficient method even when it does not differentiate service level profiles. Simulation results show that DyWaS-SLA makes subscriber differentiation as the delay and the packet loss rate for the highest priority subscribers are lower than methods which do not offer subscriber differentiation, such as WDM-IPACT.

Related to the mean packet delay, the differences between WDM-IPACT and DyWaS-SLA for SLA_0 and SLA_1 subscribers reach more than two orders of magnitude when the ONU load is very high. Furthermore, it is demonstrated that DyWaS-SLA achieves very low delays for every supported service, under or around 1E-3 seconds for the highest priority subscriber SLA_0.

Regarding packet losses, WDM-IPACT presents losses for every subscriber independently of its priority for the service P_2. In contrast to WDM-IPACT, for such service, DyWaS-SLA differs more efficiently between priority SLAs and it does not permit losses for the highest priority subscribers (SLA_0 and SLA_1).

DyWaS-SLA makes a more conscious bandwidth distribution when it is compared with WDM-IPACT, as DyWaS-SLA insures a predetermined guaranteed bandwidth to every subscriber (SLA_0, SLA_1 and SLA_2) even when the number of ONUs is highly increased to 48. On the contrary, WDM-IPACT always offers the same maximum bandwidth to every SLA independently of its priority. Then, WDM-IPACT does not insure the guaranteed bandwidth to the SLA_0 subscribers when the number of ONUs is 32 and for the two highest priority profiles SLA_0 and SLA_1 when the number of ONUs is increased to 48.

Acknowledgments. This work has been supported by the GR72 Excelence Group funding by the Regional Ministry of Castilla y León (Junta de Castilla y León).

References

1. Kramer, G., Mukherjee, B., Maislos, A.: Ethernet Passive Optical Networks. In: Dixit, S. (ed.) Multiprotocol over DWDM: Building the Next Generation Optical Internet, pp. 229–275. John Wiley & Sons, Chichester (2003)
2. Pesavento, M., Kelsey, A.: PONs for the Broadband Local Loop. Lightwave 16, 68–74 (1999)
3. Luo, Y., Ansari, N.: Bandwidth allocation for multiservice access on EPONs. IEEE Communications Magazine 43, 16–21 (2005)
4. Byun, H.-J., Nho, J.-M., Lim, J.-T.: Dynamic bandwidth allocation algorithm in ethernet passive optical networks. Electronics Letters 39, 1001–1002 (2003)
5. Ma, M., Zhu, Y., Cheng, T.-H.: A bandwidth guaranteed polling MAC protocol for ethernet passive optical networks. In: 22th Annual Joint Conference of the IEEE Computer and Communications Societies (INFOCOM 2003), San Francisco, pp. 22–31 (2003)
6. Assi, C., Ye, Y., Dixit, S., Ali, M.A.: Dynamic Bandwidth Allocation for Quality-of-Service over Ethernet PONs. IEEE Journal on Selected Areas in Communications 21, 1467–1477 (2003)
7. Chang, C.-H., Kourtessis, P., Senior, J.M.: GPON service level agreement based dynamic bandwidth assignment protocol. Electronics Letters 42, 1173–1174 (2006)
8. Chang, C.-H., Merayo, N., Kourtessis, P., Senior, J.M.: Dynamic Bandwidth assignment for Multi service access in long-reach GPONs. In: Proceedings of the 33rd European Conference and Exhibition on Optical Communications (ECOC 2007), Berlin, Germany (2007)
9. Segarra, J., Sales, V., Prat, J.: An All-Optical Access-Metro Interface for Hybrid WDM/TDM PON Based on OBS. Journal of Lightwave Technology 25, 1002–1016 (2007)
10. An, F., Kim, K.S., Gutierrez, D., Yam, S., Hu, E., Shrikhande, K., Kazovsky, L.G.: SUCCESS: A next-generation hybrid WDM/TDM optical access network architecture. Journal of Lightwave Technology 22, 2557–2569 (2004)
11. An, F., Kim, K.S., Gutierrez, D., Yam, S., Hu, E., Shrikhande, K., Kazovsky, L.G.: SUCESS-HPON: a next-generation optical access architecture for smooth migration from TDM-PON to WDM-PON. IEEE Communication Magazine 43, 40–47 (2005)
12. Kim, K.S., Gutierrez, D., An, F., Kazovsky, L.G.: Design and performance analysis of scheduling algorithms for WDM-PON under SUCESS-HPON architecture. Journal of Lightwave Technology 23, 3716–3731 (2005)
13. Shin, D.J., Jung, D.K., Shin, H.S., Kwon, J.W., Hwang, S., Oh, Y., Shim, C.: Hybrid WDM/TDM-PON with wavelength-selection-free transmitters. Journal of Lightwave Technology 23, 187–195 (2005)
14. McGarry, M.P., Maier, M., Reisslein, M.: WDM Ethernet Passive Optical Networks (EPONs). IEEE Communications Magazine 23, 187–195 (2005)
15. McGarry, M.P., Reisslein, M.: Bandwidth Management for WDM EPONs. Journal of Optical Networking 5, 627–654 (2006)
16. Dhaini, A.R., Assi, C.M., Maier, M., Shami, A.: Dynamic Bandwidth Allocation Schemes in Hybrid TDM/WDM Passive Optical networks. Journal of Lightwave Technology 5, 277–286 (2007)
17. Hsueh, Y.-L., Rogge, M.S., Yamamoto, S., Kazovsky, L.G.: A highly flexible and efficient passive optical network employing dynamic wavelength allocation. Journal of Lightwave Technology 23, 277–286 (2005)

18. Kwong, K.H., Harle, D., Andonovic, I.: Dynamic Bandwidth Allocation Algorithm for Differentiated Services over WDM EPONs. In: IEEE International Conference on Communications Systems (ICCS), Singapore, pp. 116–120 (2004)
19. Dhani, A.R., Assi, C.M., Shami, A.: Quality of service in TDM/WDM Ethernet Passive Optical Networks (EPONs). In: 11[th]IEEE Symposium on Computers and Communications (ISCC 2006), Sardinia, Italy, pp. 621–626 (2006)
20. Opnet Modeler Technologies, http://www.opnet.com
21. Kramer, G., Mukherjee, B., Ye, Y., Dixit, S., Hirth, R.: Supporting differentiated classes of service in Ethernet passive optical networks. Journal of Optical Networking 1, 280–298 (2002)
22. Kramer, G., Mukherjee, B., Pesavento, G.: Interleaved Polling with Adaptive Cycle Time (IPACT): A Dynamic Bandwidth Distribution Scheme in an Optical Access Network. Photonic Network Communications 4, 89–107 (2002)
23. Sherif, S.R., Hadjiantonis, A., Ellinas, G., Assi, C.M., Ali, M.: A novel decentralized Ethernet-Based PON Access Architecture for Provisioning Differentiated QoS. Journal of Lightwave Technologies 22, 2483–2497 (2004)
24. IEEE 802.3ah Ethernet in the First File Task Force, IEEE 802.3ah Ethernet in the First File Task Force home page, http://www.ieee802.org/3/efm/public/
25. ITU-T Recommendation G.1010, End-user multimedia QoS categories, Telecommunication Standardization Sector of ITU (2001),
http://www.itu.int/rec/T-REC-G.1010-200111-I/en
26. ITU T Recommendation G.114, One-way transmission time, in Series G: Transmission Systems and Media, Digital Systems and Networks, Telecommunication Standardization Sector of ITU (2000),
http://www.itu.int/rec/T-REC-G.114-200305-I/en
27. NTT, NTT VDSL service plan,
http://www.asist.co.jp/jensspinnet/bflets.html

Utility Max-Min Fair Resource Allocation for Diversified Applications in EPON

Jingjing Zhang and Nirwan Ansari

Advanced Networking laboratory
New Jersey Institute of Technology, Newark NJ 07102, USA
{jz58,nirwan.ansari}@njit.edu

Abstract. In EPONs, differentiated services enable higher quality of service (QoS) for some queues over others. However, owing to the coarse granularity of DiffServ, DiffServ in EPONs can hardly facilitate any particular QoS profile. This paper investigates an application-oriented bandwidth allocation scheme to ensure fairness among queues with diversified QoS requirements. We first define application utilities to quantify users' quality of experience (QoE) as a function of network layer QoS metrics. We then formulate the fair resource allocation issue into a max-min utility problem, which is quasi-concave over queues' delayed traffic and dropped traffic. We further employ the bisection method to obtain the optimal solution of the quasi-concave maximization problem. The optimal value can be achieved by proper bandwidth allocation and queue management schemes in EPONs.

Keywords: QoE, EPON, utility, fairness, optimization.

1 Introduction

Differentiated services (DiffServ) is widely employed in access networks for quality of service (QoS) provisioning. Specifically, it classifies the incoming traffic into three classes: expedited forwarding (EF), assured forwarding (AF), and best effort (BE). EF is applicable to delay sensitive applications that require a bounded end-to-end delay and jitter specifications; AF is tailored for services that are not delay sensitive but require bandwidth guarantees; BE is not delay sensitive and has no minimum guaranteed bandwidth. However, the coarse granularity of DiffServ can hardly meet any particular QoS requirement imposed by various applications. This is a critical issue for future access networks with the sprouting of new applications, such as IPTV, video conference, telemedicine, immersing interactive learning, and large file transfer among computing and data-handling infrastructures (e-science). These applications impose different QoS requirements as compared to those demanded by traditional video, voice, and data traffic. For example, large file transfer among e-science computing sites, on one hand, has strict throughput requirements, and hence possesses higher priority over traditional data traffic. On the other hand, traffic generated from these applications is not delay sensitive as compared to voice and video traffic. It is inappropriate to map these traffic into any of the three classes in DiffServ. Inappropriate QoS mapping leads to either QoS

X. Jun Hei and L. Cheung (Eds.): AccessNets 2009, LNICST 37, pp. 14–24, 2010.
© Institute for Computer Sciences, Social-Informatics and Telecommunications Engineering 2010

over-provisioning or QoS under-provisioning. The diversified QoS requirements of applications pose great challenges on resource allocation in access networks.

This paper focuses on ensuring fairness for queues with diversified QoS requirements in Ethernet Passive Optical Networks (EPONs), which have gained popularity among the access network technologies for their low cost, high bandwidth provisioning, and easy implementation. IEEE802.3ah standardized Multi-Point Control Protocol (MPCP) as a MAC layer control protocol for EPON. Specifically, MPCP defines two 64-byte control messages REPORT and GATE for the bandwidth arbitration in the upstream. Optical Network Units (ONUs) report its backlogged traffic to Optical Line Terminal (OLT) by sending REPORT. After collecting REPORT from ONUs, OLT dynamically allocates bandwidth to ONUs and informs its grant decisions to ONUs via GATE. Dynamic bandwidth allocation (DBA) has two major functions. One is to arbitrate bandwidth allocation among queues within the same ONU, referred to as intra-ONU scheduling. Another one is to arbitrate bandwidth allocation among different ONUs, referred to as inter-ONU scheduling. However, IEEE802.3ah does not specify any DBA algorithms for EPON. Fairness and QoS guarantee are usually regarded as objectives of DBA algorithms.

Generally, ensuring fairness among queues with diversified QoS requirements is equivalent to addressing the following problem: *under the heavy-load scenario, which of the queues' performance should be sacrificed and at what degree?*

To describe the diversified QoS requirements of applications, we adopt the concept of *application utility* to quantify users' quality of experience (QoE) as a function of received QoS of the specific application [1]. Specifically, application utility depends on the relationship between QoE and network-level QoS performances of the specific application. Large utility corresponds to high degree of user satisfaction degree at the user-level and high QoS performances at the network-level.

By virtue of application utility, we define fairness in terms of application utilities, and formulate the problem of ensuring fairness for requests as a utility max-min fairness optimization problem. From the optimization point of view, the single-objective utility max-min problem is a scalarization of the multi-objective max-min fairness optimization with respect to a set of QoS metrics, such as delay, loss ratio, and jitter. We also show that the utility max-min fairness optimization problem is quasi-linear over delayed traffic and dropped traffic of queues, in which the optimal solution can be obtained by employing the bisection method. To achieve the optimal value in the EPON system, proper bandwidth management and local queue management are required.

2   Related Works

DBA with fairness and QoS guarantee has received broad research attention during the past several years. As a seminal work in EPON DBA, IPACT interleaves polling messages with Ethernet frame transmission to maximize link utilization [2]. To provision QoS guarantees, the DiffServ framework was proposed to be incorporated into the DBA to address the intra-ONU scheduling issue [3, 4, 5, 6, 7]. Regarding fairness, the employed strict-priority discipline when incorporating the DiffServ framework into DBA raises the so-called *light-load penalty* problem [3]. To compensate for the light-load penalty, Kramer et al. [3] further proposed a two-stage queueing system, where a proper local queue management scheme and a priority-based scheduling algorithm are employed. Kim *et al.* [8] adopted weighted fair queuing to give queues with different weights for their priorities. Besides intra-ONU scheduling, inter-ONU scheduling is needed to arbitrate bandwidth among ONUs for fairness. IPACT-LS prevents ONUs from monopolizing the bandwidth by setting a predetermined maximum of the granted resources [2]. Assi *et al.* [4] proposed to satisfy requests from light-load ONUs first, while penalizing heavily-loaded ONUs. Naser *et al.* [5] combined inter-ONU scheduling and intra-ONU scheduling together. Specifically, they employed a credit pooling technique as well as a weighted-share policy to enable the OLT partition the upstream bandwidth among different classes in a fair fashion.

DBA is desired to facilitate any QoS profile for queues and ensure fairness among queues. To achieve a finer granularity of QoS control, we define application utility to describe QoS requirements of applications, and then make bandwidth allocation decisions based on application utilities. To ensure fairness among queues, we treat maximizing the minimum application utility as the DBA objective.

3   Application Utility

Here, we introduce the concept of *application utility* to quantify the relationship between users' degree of satisfaction and received network layer QoS performances. Formerly, Tashaka *et al.* [9] specified QoS at each level of the Internet protocol stack: physical level QoS, node level QoS, network level QoS, end-to-end level QoS, application level QoS, and user level QoS (or perceptual QoS). Typically, throughput, delay, delay jitter, and loss ratio are typical QoS parameters considered in a network. Mean opinion score (MOS) and subjective video quality are two subjective QoS measurements for voice and video at the user level [10]. Performances in these layers are interrelated. The QoS in the upper layer depends on the QoS in the lower layer. Both MOS and subjective video quality provide numerical indications of the perceived quality of received media after compression and/or transmission, and are related to the network layer QoS performances, such as throughput and delay. In this paper, we use application utility to describe the relationship between the user-level QoS and network-level QoS.

Determining the utility of an application needs to consider the application's specific QoS requirements; this is, however, beyond the scope of this paper. In this paper, we consider application utilities as a function of packet loss ratio, packet delay, and jitter. We further unify and normalize application utilities to the range from 0 to 1. Generally, application utility possesses the property that large utility implies small packet loss ratio, small packet delay, and low jitter. Mathematically,

$$\begin{cases} 0 \leq f_{i,j} \leq 1, \forall i, j \\ f_{i,j}(x_1 + \varepsilon, x_2, x_3) \leq f_{i,j}(x_1, x_2, x_3), \forall \varepsilon > 0 \\ f_{i,j}(x_1, x_2 + \varepsilon, x_3) \leq f_{i,j}(x_1, x_2, x_3), \forall \varepsilon > 0 \\ f_{i,j}(x_1, x_2, x_3 + \varepsilon) \leq f_{i,j}(x_1, x_2, x_3), \forall \varepsilon > 0 \end{cases}$$

where $f_{i,j}(x_1, x_2, x_3)$ is the application utility of queue j at ONU i, x_1 is the packet loss ratio, x_2 is the delay, and x_3 is the jitter. The application utility is a monotonic function with respect to loss, delay, and jitter. Hence, it is quasi-linear over these QoS metric. Some particular applications may be modeled by convex functions. Cao *et al.* [1] used convex bandwidth utility function to model elastic delay-tolerant traditional data applications such as email, remote terminal access, and file transfer.

By virtue of application utility, the problem of ensuring fairness among queues with diversified QoS requirements can be formulated as a utility max-min fairness optimization problem. From the optimization point of view, the single-objective max-min optimization with respect to application utility can be considered as a scalarization of the multi-objective max-min fairness optimization with respect to a set of criteria of delay, loss ratio, and jitter [11].

4 Utility Max-Min Fair Bandwidth Allocation and Queue Management

In EPON, after collecting reports from ONUs, OLT estimates the real-time QoS performances of queues at ONUs, and then tries to maximize the minimum utility received by queues. In this section, we first discuss the queue management scheme, and then estimate QoS performances of ONUs and present the scheme to address the utility max-min fair resource allocation problem.

4.1 Drop Head Queue Management

After a queue obtains the information of the amount of traffic of its queues to be dropped, it selects packets to be dropped if necessarily. Drop Tail is a typical queue management algorithm used by Internet routers. It drops the newly arrived packets when the buffer is filled to its maximum capacity. Instead of dropping packets from the tail of the queue, we drop packets from the head of the queue in this paper. For packets at the head of the queue, they experience a longer waiting time in the queue as compared to those at the tail of the queue. Rather than allocating the channel resource to those packets with larger delay, we drop packets from the head to allocate the precious channel resources to packets which have smaller delay, thus achieving high utility of the queue. So, in this paper, the backlogged traffic is dropped with higher priority over the newly arrived traffic for higher utility.

4.2 Estimating QoS Metric of Queues

OLT needs some information of queues at ONUs in order to estimate the QoS metric and calculate their utilities. Such information includes the amount of successfully transmitted traffic, the time stamp when the traffic is arrived, and the time stamp when the traffic is transmitted. However, OLT does not contain information with granularity as fine as the packet level. So, we estimate the average loss, delay, and jitter of packets in a queue. In addition, it is hard to predict the future network traffic, and estimate the time that the delayed traffic will be transmitted. In this paper, we make optimistic assumption that the delayed packets in the current cycle can be successfully transmitted in the next cycle. The following address the issue of estimating packet loss ratio, delay, and jitter.

Table 1 list the notations used in this section.

Table 1. Notation

Symbol	Definition
$cycle$	The upper bound of the cycle duration
$q_{i,j}$	The reported traffic of queue j at ONU i
$q_{i,j}^b$	The backlogged traffic of queue j at ONU i in the last cycle
$\Delta_{i,j}$	The time duration allocated to queue j at ONU i
$\delta_{i,j}$	The dropped traffic of queue j at ONU i in the current DBA cycle
$t_{i,j}^1$	The last time stamp that the status of queue j at ONU i is reported
$t_{i,j}^2$	The time before the last time stamp that the status of queue j at ONU i is reported
$l_{i,j}$	The data loss ratio of queue j at ONU i
$d_{i,j}$	The average delay of successfully transmitted packets at queue j at ONU i
$v_{i,j}$	The jitter of successfully transmitted packets at queue j at ONU i
$d_{i,j}^b$	The average time that the backlogged traffic $q_{i,j}^b$ of queue j at ONU i spent in the buffer before time $t_{i,j}^2$
$d_{i,j}^{mb}$	The longest time that the backlogged traffic $q_{i,j}^b$ of queue j at ONU i spent in the buffer before time $t_{i,j}^2$
$\alpha_{i,j}$	The beginning time assigned to queue j at ONU i

Average Loss Ratio of the $q_{i,j}$ Reported Traffic. For queue j at ONU i, $\delta_{i,j}$ traffic among the total $q_{i,j}$ traffic is dropped. With the assumption that the delayed traffic can be transmitted finally, $q_{i,j} - \delta_{i,j}$ among $q_{i,j}$ is successfully transmitted. The average loss ratio $l_{i,j}$ is $(q_{i,j} - \delta_{i,j})/q_{i,j}$.

Average Delay of the $q_{i,j}$ Reported Traffic. We analyze four scenarios as follows.

- For the newly arrived $q_{i,j} - q_{i,j}^b$ traffic of queue j at ONU i, the average arrival time is $(t_{i,j}^1 + t_{i,j}^2)/2$. If they are successfully transmitted in the current cycle, the average departure time is $\alpha_{i,j} + \Delta_{i,j}/2$. The average delay of the newly arrived traffic is $\alpha_{i,j} + \Delta_{i,j}/2 - (t_{i,j}^1 + t_{i,j}^2)/2$.
- For the newly arrived traffic in the current cycle, if they are further delayed to the next cycle, the average delay $d_{i,j}$ is $d_{i,j} = \alpha_{i,j} + \Delta_{i,j}/2 - (t_{i,j}^1 + t_{i,j}^2)/2 + cycle$.
- For the backlogged traffic $q_{i,j}^b$ who already spent on average $d_{i,j}^b$ in the buffer before time $t_{i,j}^2$, the average delay is $d_{i,j}^b + \alpha_{i,j} + \Delta_{i,j}/2 - t_{i,j}^2$ under the condition that they are successfully transmitted in the current cycle.
- For the backlogged traffic $q_{i,j}^b$, if they are further delayed to the next cycle, the average delay will be $d_{i,j}^b + \alpha_{i,j} + \Delta_{i,j}/2 - t_{i,j}^2 + cycle$.

Jitter of the $q_{i,j}$ Reported Traffic. We analyze four scenarios as follows.

- For the newly arrived traffic, if they are successfully transmitted in the current cycle, the maximum delay is $\alpha_{i,j} + \Delta_{i,j} - t_{i,j}^2$.

- For the newly arrival traffic, if some packets are delayed to the next cycle, the maximum delay of the $q_{i,j}$ reported traffic is $\alpha_{i,j} + \Delta_{i,j} - t^2_{i,j} + cycle$.
- For the backlogged traffic, if they are successfully transmitted in the current cycle, the maximum delay is $\alpha_{i,j} + \Delta_{i,j} - t^2_{i,j} + d^{mb}_{i,j}$.
- For the backlogged traffic, if some packets are further delayed to the next cycle, the maximum delay can be $\alpha_{i,j} + \Delta_{i,j} - t^2_{i,j} + d^{mb}_{i,j} + cycle$.

This optimization problem involves both sequencing and scheduling. We assume the ONU scheduling order remains the same as that in the last cycle, and focus on the scheduling problem in this paper. As shown before, $f_{i,j}$ is a quasi-linear function with respect to loss $l_{i,j}$, delay $d_{i,j}$, and jitter $v_{i,j}$. $l_{i,j}$, $d_{i,j}$, and $v_{i,j}$ are linear functions of granted bandwidth $\Delta_{i,j}$ and dropped traffic $\delta_{i,j}$. Therefore, the optimization problem is a quasi-concave maximization problem. We next present our scheme of obtaining an optimal solution to the problem.

4.3 Utility Max-Min Fair Bandwidth Allocation

With the estimation of QoS performances, OLT can perform bandwidth allocation for utility max-min fairness. We herein employ the bisection method to obtain the optimal solution of the quasiconcave utility max-min problem. The main idea is as follows: Let a be the lower bound of the utility, b be the upper bound of the utility, x be the utility to be achieved. Since we assume the application utility is normalized between 0 and 1, initially, a is set as 0, b is set as 1, and x is set as 1. We calculate the maximum dropped traffic $\delta_{i,j}$ and delayed traffic $\Delta_{i,j} - \delta_{i,j}$ which can guarantee x. If the sum of the minimum required bandwidth $\Delta_{i,j}$ is less than the available bandwidth $cycle$, the upper bound b is updated to be x, and x is decreased to the midpoint between a and b; otherwise the lower bound a is increased to x, and x is increased to the midpoint between a and b. The above process is performed recursively until a and b are close enough to each other. The pseudocode of the algorithm is presented below.

Algorithm 1. Determine $\Delta_{i,j}$ and $\delta_{i,j}$
___
1: Let $a = 0, b = 1, x = 1$
2: **while** $b - a < \varepsilon$ **do**
3:      calculate the maximum allowed loss ratio of each queue to ensure its corresponding utility to be above x
4:      calculate the maximum $\delta_{i,j}$ for each queue
5:      calculate the maximum delay and jitter of each queue to ensure its corresponding utility to be above x
6:      calculate the maximum $\Delta_{i,j} - \delta_{i,j}$ for each queue
7:      calculate the minimum required $\Delta_{i,j}$ for each queue
8:      **if** $\sum_{i,j} \Delta_{i,j} < cycle$ **then**
9:          $b = x, x = (a + b)/2$
10:     **else**
11:         $a = x, x = (a + b)/2$
12:     **end if**
13: **end while**

In Algorithm 1, line 4 and line 6 are calculated based on the estimation discussed in Section 4.2. Line 3 and line 5 are calculated based on the specific application utility function. Let function $f^1(x_1)$ describe the application utility function with respect to loss ratio, function $f^2(x_2)$ describe the application utility function with respect to packet delay, and function $f^3(x_3)$ describe the application utility function with respect to jitter. $f_{i,j}^1(x_1) = f_{i,j}(x_1, 0, 0)$, $f_{i,j}^2(x_2) = f_{i,j}(0, x_2, 0)$, $f_{i,j}^3(x_3) = f_{i,j}(0, 0, x_3)$, where $f_{i,j}(x_1, x_2, x_3)$ is the application utility function as defined in Section 3. The maximum allowed loss ratio, the maximum delay, and the maximum jitter are obtained from the inverse function of $f_{i,j}^1(x_1)$, $f_{i,j}^2(x_2)$, and $f_{i,j}^3(x_3)$, respectively.

5   Simulation Results and Analysis

In this section, we investigate the performance of our proposed utility max-min fair algorithm presented above. The simulation model is developed on the OPNET platform. The number of ONUs is set as 16. The round trip time between ONUs and OLT is set as $125\mu s$. The channel data rate is set as 1.25 Gb/s. The maximum cycle length is set as 2 ms. Since self-similarity is exhibited by many applications, we input the queues with self-similar traffic. The pareto parameter is set as 0.8. The packet length is uniformly distributed between 64 bytes to 1500 bytes. An ONU in a cycle is labeled as light-load when the total request of its queues is less than 1K bytes.

In the simulation, we want to show that our scheme can guarantee fairness among queues, each of which may exhibit any application utility. We assume each ONU has five queues corresponding to five kinds of applications. Our objective is to show that QoS profiles received by the five queues conform to the corresponding profiles derived from their application utilities. We claim that fairness is achieved if application utilities obtained by queues are similar with each other.

First, we consider the application utility as a function of packet loss ratio, i.e., $f_{i,j}(x_1, x_2, x_3) = f_{i,j}^1(x_1)$. For five queues in each ONU, $f_{i,j}^1(x_1)$ is defined as follows.

$$f_{i,0}^1(x_1) = \begin{cases} 1 & x_1 \le 0.01 \\ (1 - x_1)/0.99 & x_1 \in [0.01, 1] \end{cases}, \forall i$$

$$f_{i,1}^1(x_1) = \begin{cases} 1 & x_1 \le 0.1 \\ (1 - x_1)/0.9 & x_1 \in [0.1, 1] \end{cases}, \forall i$$

$$f_{i,2}^1(x_1) = \begin{cases} 1 & x_1 \le 0.2 \\ (1 - x_1)/0.8 & x_1 \in [0.2, 1] \end{cases}, \forall i$$

$$f_{i,3}^1(x_1) = \begin{cases} 1 & x_1 \le 0.3 \\ (1 - x_1)/0.7 & x_1 \in [0.3, 1] \end{cases}, \forall i$$

$$f_{i,4}^1(x_1) = \begin{cases} 1 & x_1 \le 0.4 \\ (1 - x_1)/0.6 & x_1 \in [0.4, 1] \end{cases}, \forall i$$

Fig. 1 shows the sampled packet loss ratio of queues with the above five different application utilities. The sampling is taken every 8 ms. From the application function $f_{i,0}^1(x_1)$, $f_{i,1}^1(x_1)$, $f_{i,2}^1(x_1)$, $f_{i,3}^1(x_1)$, and $f_{i,4}^1(x_1)$, we know that utilities of the five queues equal to the highest value of 1 when the packet loss ratios of queue 0, 1, 2, 3 and 4 are below 0.01, 0.1, 0.2, 0.3, and 0.4, respectively. Therefore, for fairness, if the packet loss ratio of queue 4 is lower than 0.4, packet loss ratio of queue 0, 1, 2, and

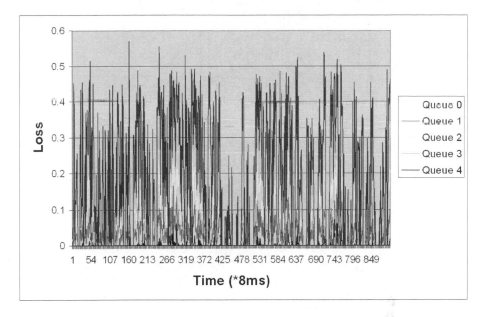

Fig. 1. Packet loss ratio vs. application utilities

3 should not exceed 0.01, 0.1, 0.2, and 0.3, respectively. From Fig. 1, we can see that almost all points comply with this rule. On the other hand, when the network is heavily loaded and the maximum utility cannot be guaranteed for queues, the packet loss ratio of queue 0, 1, 2, 3, and 4 will be increased to be higher than 0.01, 0.1, 0.2, 0.3, and 0.4, respectively. For fairness, this increase should enable the five queues achieve the same utility. For example, based on the application utilities, when the packet loss ratio of queue 2 equals to 0.24, queue 0, queue 1, queue 3, and queue 4 should experience packet loss ratio of 0.065, 0.15, 0.34 and 0.43, respectively, for the same utility. Simulation results show that when the packet loss ratio of queue 2 is increased to around 0.24, packet loss ratio of queue 0, queue 1, queue 2, and queue 3 are around 0.078, 0.166, 0.36, and 0.45, respectively. The minor discrepancy between the theoretical values and the simulation values is probably attributed to the disagreement between the number of dropped bits and the size of the packet to be dropped. Therefore, in terms of the packet loss ratio, our algorithm can guarantee fairness among the five queues.

Here, we consider application utility as a function of packet delay, i.e., $f_{i,j}(x_1, x_2, x_3) = f_{i,j}^2(x_2)$. $f_{i,j}^2(x_2)$ for the five queues are defined as follows.

$$f_{i,0}^2(x_2) = \begin{cases} 1 & x_2 \leq 3ms \\ e^{(x_2-3)/3} & x_2 > 3ms \end{cases}, \forall i$$

$$f_{i,1}^2(x_2) = \begin{cases} 1 & x_2 \leq 4ms \\ e^{(x_2-4)/4} & x_2 > 4ms \end{cases}, \forall i$$

$$f_{i,2}^2(x_2) = \begin{cases} 1 & x_2 \leq 5ms \\ e^{(x_2-5)/5} & x_2 > 5ms \end{cases}, \forall i$$

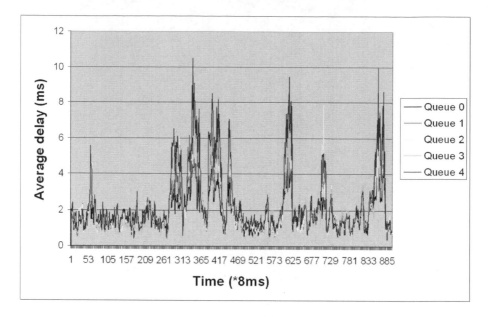

Fig. 2. Packet delay vs. application utilities

$$f_{i,3}^2(x_2) = \begin{cases} 1 & x_2 \le 6ms \\ e^{(x_2-6)/6} & x_2 > 6ms \end{cases}, \forall i$$

$$f_{i,4}^2(x_2) = \begin{cases} 1 & x_2 \le 7ms \\ e^{(x_2-7)/7} & x_2 > 7ms \end{cases}, \forall i$$

Fig. 2 shows the sampled average delay of packets arrived during each sampling period. Due to the bursty characteristic of the arriving traffic, the delay of traffic for all the five kinds of queues fluctuates. Under the light load scenario, requests from all queues can be satisfied, and delay of all queues are about 3/2 times of the DBA cycle. Under the heavy load scenario, delay of all queues increases but with different degrees, as determined by their own application utilities. Let u be the converged utility in Algorithm 1 under heavy load scenario, i.e., $u = a$ or b with $a \approx b$. Then, delays of queue 0, queue 1, queue 2, queue 3, and queue 4 are $3(1 - \ln u)$, $4(1 - \ln u)$, $5(1 - \ln u)$, $6(1 - \ln u)$, and $7(1 - \ln u)$, respectively. Simulation results show that the delay of queue 0 is the lowest, whereas the delay of queue 4 is the highest. The proportions between the delays of any two queues conform to around the theoretical values. So, the simulated delay performances of the five queues generally agree with the delay profiles derived from their respective application utilities, but with some slight discrepancy. The main reason of the discrepancy lies in the inaccurate estimation of the delay. We make optimistic assumption that delayed traffic can be successfully transmitted in the next cycle. However, the delayed traffic may not get a chance to be transmitted in the next cycle, but be further delayed. In this case, the queue with delayed traffic has smaller utility over others though Algorithm 1 guarantees the same utility for queues.

From the above, we can see that the QoS profiles obtained from the simulations conform to those derived from application utilities. When the network is heavily loaded, the queues can achieve nearly equal utilities. Hence, fairness is guaranteed for the queues. Our scheme is potentially able to accommodate any number of queue classes by properly designing their respective application utilities.

6   Conclusion

This paper has tackled the issue of ensuring fairness among applications with diversified QoS requirements in EPONs. We first employ application utility to describe the relationship between users' QoE and network-level QoS of each application. Application utility is a quasi-linear function over packet loss ratio, delay, and jitter. By virtue of application utility, we formulate the problem of ensuring fairness among applications with diversified QoS requirements into a utility max-min fairness problem. The maximization problem possesses quasi-concave property with respect to the delayed traffic and dropped traffic. We hence adopt the bisection method to obtain the optimal solution of the maximized minimum utility. The optimal value can be achieved via proper bandwidth management and queue management. As compared to schemes using DiffServ, our proposed scheme possesses finer granularity and is able to ensure fairness among diversified applications with proper design of application utilities and estimation of QoS metrics.

References

1. Cao, Z., Zegura, E.: Utility max-min: an Application-oriented Bandwidth Allocation Scheme. IEEE INFOCOM 2, 793–801 (1999)
2. Kramer, G., Mukherjee, B., Pesavento, G.: IPACT a Dynamic Protocol for an Ethernet PON (EPON). IEEE Communications Magazine 40(2), 74–80 (2002)
3. Kramer, G., Mukherjee, B., Dixit, S., Ye, Y., Hirth, R.: Supporting Differentiated Classes of Service in Ethernet passive optical networks. OSA Journal of Optical Networking 1(8), 280–298 (2002)
4. Assi, C., Ye, Y., Dixit, S., Ali, M.: Dynamic Bandwidth Allocation for Quality-of-Service over Ethernet PONs. IEEE Journal on Selected Areas in Communications 21(9), 1467–1477 (2003)
5. Naser, H., Mouftah, H.: A joint-ONU Interval-based Dynamic Scheduling Algorithm for Ethernet Passive Optical Networks. IEEE/ACM Transactions on Networking 14(4), 889–899 (2006)
6. Luo, Y., Ansari, N.: Bandwidth Allocation for Multiservice Access on EPONs. IEEE Communications Magazine 43(2), S16–S21 (2005)
7. Jiang, S., Xie, J.: A Frame Division Method for Prioritized DBA in EPON. IEEE Journal on Selected Areas in Communications 24(4), 83–94 (2006)
8. Kim, C., Yoo, T., Kim, B.: A Hierarchical Weighted Round Robin EPON DBA Scheme and Its Comparison with Cyclic Water-filling Algorithm. In: IEEE International Conference on Communications, pp. 2156–2161 (2007)

9. Tasaka, S., Ishibashi, Y.: Mutually Compensatory Property of Multimedia QoS. In: IEEE International Conference on Communications, vol. 2, pp. 1105–1111 (2002)
10. Takahashi, A., Yoshino, H., Kitawaki, N.: Perceptual QoS Assessment Technologies for VoIP. IEEE Communications Magazine 42(7), 28–34 (2004)
11. Nace, D., Pioro, M.: Max-min Fairness and its Applications to Routing and Load-balancing in Communication Networks: a Tutorial. IEEE Communications Surveys & Tutorials 10(4), 5–17 (2008)

Fairness Enhancement for 802.11 MAC

Caishi Huang, Chin-Tau Lea, and Albert Kai-Sun Wong

Department of Electronic and Computer Engineering,
HKUST, Clear Water Bay, Hong Kong
cshuang@ust.hk, eelea@ee.ust.hk, eealbert@ust.hk

Abstract. Location dependency and its associated exposed receiver problem create the most severe unfairness scenario of the CSMA/CA protocol. An analytical model is built up to study the success probabilities of RTS reception and RTS/CTS handshake of the typical disadvantaged link under the exposed receiver scenario. Derived from the analytical insights, we propose a receiver assistance feature (RcvAssist) for the CSMA/CA protocol which not only significantly enhances the fairness of disadvantaged links suffering from exposed receiver problem, but also increases the overall throughput without introducing other side effects, such as aggregating the hidden terminal problem.

Keywords: Fairness; CSMA/CA; Receiver assistance; Exposed receiver.

1 Introduction

The CSMA/CA (Carrier Sensing Multiple Access with Collision Avoidance) MAC protocol, adopted by the IEEE 802.11 standard, has been widely deployed in both wireless LANs and mobile ad hoc networks. It is well known that CSMA/CA's user treatment is location dependent: some links are treated more favorably than others, depending on their spatial locations. This property leads to unfair channel sharing among different links in media access. There are other elements in CSMA/CA that also contribute to its unfair behavior, like the binary exponential back-off scheme that always favors the latest channel contention winner succeeding user in channel contentions and EIFS (Extended Inter-Frame Space) that could make one sender defer much longer than another contender before counting down the residual back-off time. But the severity of these problems is much less than that created by the location dependent property of CAMA/CA.

Location dependency of CSMA/CA leads to the hidden and the exposed terminal problems and both have some intrinsic fairness issues. Recently new schemes have been proposed that can eliminate to a large extent the hidden terminal problem [28]. The focus of this paper is on the improvement of the fairness issue caused by the exposed terminal problem in CSMA/CA networks. There are two types of exposed terminal problems: exposed senders and exposed receivers. The former prohibits concurrent transmissions, while the latter leads to unfair channel access. An illustration of the two types is given in Fig. 1 that contains the two independent transmission links and each can correspond to a wireless LAN or an ad hoc wireless link. The 4-way RTS/CTS/DATA/ACK handshake [11] and the IEEE 802.11 DCF [22] are assumed in these networks.

X. Jun Hei and L. Cheung (Eds.): AccessNets 2009, LNICST 37, pp. 25–39, 2010
© Institute for Computer Sciences, Social-Informatics and Telecommunications Engineering 2010

- Exposed senders

  S3 and S4 in Fig. 1a are called exposed senders. Both are within their mutual carrier sensing range. Suppose S4 is transmitting. When S3 attempts to access the channel, it detects the channel busy and will defter its transmission. Although simultaneous transmissions from S3 and S4 will not interfere each other at their corresponding destinations, the protocol does not allow it. When S4 finishes its transmission, both S3 and S4 will compete for the channel in a fair manner. Thus fairness in the exposed sender case is not an issue. The main issue is throughput [8][9][12][13][14][15][16].

- Exposed receivers

  R1 is the exposed receiver in Fig. 1b, where S2 and S1 are out of their carrier sensing range,   S2 and R1 are within each other's carrier sensing range, but S2 is out of interference range of R1 (if S2 falls into R1's interference range, this would be the case of hidden terminal problem). Suppose there is an on-going transmission between S2 and R2 when S1 tries to initiate a transmission to R1. Because R1 is within the sensing range of S2, CSMA/CA protocol prevents R1 from replying to S1 even if it can receive RTS packets from S1. Thus R1 is called an *exposed receiver.* The lack of reply from R1 will force S1 into the back off mode. The problem is further aggravated by the MAC's binary exponential back-off algorithm, which always favors the latest winner in channel contentions. As a result, the chances of R1's acquiring the channel will be less and less over time.

The impact of unfairness at the MAC layer will get amplified in higher layer protocols. If node S1 fails several more times (the total number of retrial is limited to 7 in the IEEE 802.11 standard), the MAC protocol would treat the link between S1 and R1 as broken and reports a link failure to the routing layer. This triggers route failure recovery at the network layer and all packets routed through S1 with R1 as the next hop destination will be dropped. Thus no packets can reach the destination until a new route is established by the routing protocol. To complicate the issue further, TCP will treat the packet loss as network congestion and halve its congestion window size accordingly, leading to low efficiency in channel utilization [1][3].

In this paper, we tackle the fairness problem caused by exposed receiver problem as described in Fig. 1b. We will show, with both analysis and simulation, that often there is a good chance for R1 to receive RTS packets correctly from S1. By exploiting this property, we propose a simple **receiver assistance (not initiated)** feature added to CSMA/CA that can significantly improve the fairness of the protocol. Our main contributions are the following.

- We build up an analytical model to study the success probabilities of RTS receptions and RTS/CTS handshakes of the disadvantaged link under the exposed receiver scenario in Fig. 1b. The insights derived from the ·analysis lay the foundation for our proposed fairness enhancement feature.
- We propose a receiver assistance feature for CSMA/CA protocol. The proposed feature not only enhances significantly the fairness of disadvantaged links (like link S1-R1 in Fig. 1b) in the exposed receiver scenario, but also increases the

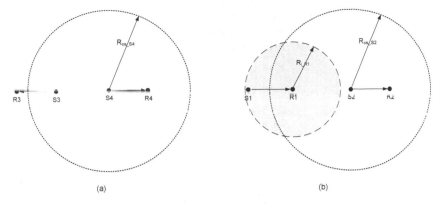

Fig. 1. Two typical cases of exposed terminal problem; (a) exposed sender S3 and S4 in R3-S3-S4-R4 scenario; (b) exposed receiver R1 in S1-R1-S2-R2 scenario; the dot circle represents the carrier sensing range; the dash circle denotes interference range. Although we use circle to represent the transmission, carrier sensing and interference ranges, the protocol does not assume circles for carrier sensing/interference areas and it works for any irregular shapes as well.

overall throughput without introducing other side effects, such as aggregating the hidden terminal problem. The resulting protocol retains the advantages of both sender-initiated and receiver- initiated MACs.

The rest of the paper is organized as follows. Section 2 presents the related work. Section 3 analyzes the success probabilities of RTS receptions and RTS/CTS handshakes of the disadvantaged link. Based on the results derived from Section 3, Section 4 presents the fairness enhancement feature. It also studies and compares performance of the protocol and 802.11 in terms of fairness and throughput via NS2-based simulations. Section 5 concludes our discussions.

2   Related Work

Both exposed and hidden terminal problems have severe negative impact on network performance and there exist many proposals addressing these problems. One issue is related to the relative frequency of the two events. Although major attention is given to the reduction of hidden terminals [2][4][7][8][9][11], Reference [17] has shown that the exposed terminal problem is actually much more severe than the hidden terminal problem. In their CMU campus-wide Wifi network measurement they studied, there were as many as 11438 exposed pairs, while there were only 406 hidden pairs. The focus of the paper will be on the exposed terminal problem. Another issue is the trade-off between the exposed and hidden terminal problems. The reduction of hidden terminal problems often comes at the cost of an increase of exposed terminal problems [2][7][8][9]. This, however, is not the case with the proposed scheme in this paper.

Several literatures have tried to address the exposed terminal problem. But most of them are focusing on increasing the concurrent transmissions [8][12][13][14][15], rather than solving the fairness issue in the presence of exposed terminals. Reference [8] studies the optimal carrier sensing threshold that can lead to maximum spatial reuse. MACA-P [12] introduces a control gap between the RTS/CTS exchange and the subsequent DATA/ACK exchange to facilitate other pairs to conduct potential concurrent transmission. References [13][14] exploit more concurrent transmission opportunities for exposed terminals via overhearing. DBTMA [15] proposes to use two busy tones to indentify and protect packet transmissions and receptions so that an exposed sender can launch concurrent transmissions if it does not hear reception busy tone.

In terms of the fairness, there exists a large amount of work on fairness improvement of the binary back-off scheme [1][23][24][25][26][27]. For example, Reference [1] presents a back-off copy scheme to manage the contention window size so as not to favor the terminal that has just won the contention in the subsequent transmission. References [23][24] suggest that by overhearing packets sent on the medium, each terminal can measure the rates of contending links and determine if its access rate is above or below its neighbors. [25][26] try to serialize transmissions among contending links based on their scheduling tags. Reference [27] proposes a general analytical model and MAC protocol to approach proportional fairness among the links. This type of research is independent of the work done in this paper, which focuses on solving the fairness issue caused by exposed terminal problem via improving the underlying MAC protocol.

As far as the latter is concerned, there is also some related work. MACA-BI [4] is a receiver initiated MAC protocol, while 802.11 DCF [22] a sender initiated MAC protocol. References [5][6] are hybrid protocols. A pure receiver initiated protocol, as exampled by [4], needs to have an effective polling scheme so that the receiver can predict the sending patterns of various potential senders. This is obviously difficult to achieve. References [5][6] propose to switch between sender-initiated and receiver-initiated mode. But this does not solve the fairness issue caused by exposed terminals, as receiver-initiated mode also suffers from exposed terminal problem. The proposed receiver assistance (not initiated) protocol keeps the simplicity of sender initiated MAC in packet delivery, and avoids its unfairness pitfall through a receiver assistance feature. As mentioned in [5][10], fairness enhancement schemes usually exhibit some form of tradeoff between throughput and fairness. This, however, is not the case with the proposed scheme. The results given later will show that the fairness improvement of the proposed scheme does not come at the cost of throughput.

3   Probabilities of Successful RTS Receptions and RTS/CTS Handshakes

Before proceeding with the new scheme proposal, an analytical model for studying the success probabilities of RTS receptions and RTS/CTS handshakes of the disadvantaged link S1-R1 under the exposed receiver scenario (see Fig. 1b) is given first. We will show that even under heavy traffic between S2 and R2, a large number of RTS packets that can still be received by R1. This fact is exploited later in Section 4.

In the analysis, both links are assumed to always have packets to send, and 802.11b standard parameter setting is used. The following summarize the notations appearing in the analysis:

$T_{backoff}$	The back-off time of S2
T_{4-way}	4-way handshake time of link S2-R2
T_{total}	The cycle time of link S2-R2 to finish a packet delivery process, which includes 4-way handshake T_{4-way}, the back off time $T_{backoff}$, and DIFS
T_{silent}	The silent time of S2 in T_{total}
T_{RTS}	The transmission time for RTS frame
T_{CTS}	The transmission time for CTS frame
T_{DATA}	The transmission time for DATA frame
T_{ACK}	The transmission time for ACK frame
CW_{S2}	The contention window size of S2
CW_{min}	The minimum contention window size (note that in 802.11b, $CW_{win} = 31$).
BO	the back off number picked by S2 from its contention window
IFS	SIFS =10us, DIFS =50us, and EIFS =SIFS+ T_{ACK}+DIFS [22].

In Fig. 1b, the degree of cooperation imposed by the 802.11 MAC between the two links is determined by the interaction between R1 and S2. Senders S1 and S2 are out of their mutual carrier sensing range, but R1 and S2 are still within the carrier sensing range of each other. So link S1-R1 has to compete for the channel with link S2-R2 through R1. As link S2-R2 is continuously back-logged, the transmission by link S2-R2 consists of cycles. An important observation from the discussion of Section 1 is that when link S2-R2 has an on-going flow, there is little chance for link S1-R1 to interrupt the transmission. This means that although the cycle and cycle time is occasionally interrupted by link S1-R1, we can ignore link S1-R1's scattered interruption, without sacrificing the accuracy of the results much.

Once we ignore link S1-R1's interruption, link S2-R2's cycle would be the one shown in Fig. 2. The cycle time, denoted by T_{total}, becomes

$$T_{total} = T_{4-way} + T_{backoff} + DIFS$$

Where $T_{backoff} = 20us \times BO$, BO is the back-off number selected from $[0, CW_{S2}]$. The successful reception of an S1's RTS packet at R1 can only occur if S1 starts to

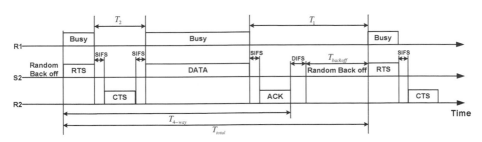

Fig. 2. Packet transmission cycles of the S2-R2 link

transmit the RTS packet when S2 is silent. If not, R1 is already locked to the signal from S2 and this prevents the correctly decoding the packet from S1 even if it is stronger than the signal with which R1 is already synchronized with [17][18][19][21]. The total length of S2's silent intervals, denoted by T_{silent}, is $T_1 + T_2$. Let A be the event that the RTS from S1 can be received correctly by R1. Since S1's attempt to access the channel can occur at any point within the cycle, we have the following conditional probability

$$P(A \,|BO = x) = \frac{T_{silent}}{T_{total}} = \frac{T_1 + T_2}{T_{total}} = \frac{3 \times SIFS + T_{CTS} + 20x + T_{ACK} + DIFS}{T_{4-way} + DIFS + 20x}$$

Let B be the event that an RTS/CTS handshake of link S1-R1 can be completed successfully. Event B can occur if (a) an RTS packet is received correctly and (b) R1 sees a clear channel in the immediate SIFS interval right after the reception of RTS. That means that S2 needs to be silent for a $(T_{RTS} + SIFS)$ duration. Only time slot T_1 allows this to happen and the transmission time of S1 must occur during the first $(T_1 - T_{RTS} - SIFS)$ second of T_1. This means

$$P(B \,|BO = x) = \max\left(\frac{T_1 - T_{RTS} - SIFS}{T_{total}}, 0\right)$$
$$= \max\left(\frac{20x + T_{ACK} + DIFS - T_{RTS} - SIFS}{T_{4-way} + DIFS + 20x}, 0\right)$$

It is rare that link S2-R2 experience collision, thus $CW_{S2} = CW_{min}$. The back off number BO is uniformly distributed within [0, CW_{win}]. Therefore,

$$P(A) = \sum_{x=0}^{x=CW_{win}} P(A \,|BO = x)P(C = x) = \sum_{x=0}^{x=CW_{win}} P(A \,|BO = x)\frac{1}{CW_{win} + 1}$$

$$P(B) = \sum_{x=0}^{x=CW_{win}} P(B \,|BO = x)P(C = x) = \sum_{x=0}^{x=CW_{win}} P(B \,|BO = x)\frac{1}{CW_{win} + 1}$$

Fig. 4a shows the analytical results of the success probabilities of RTS receptions and of RTS/CTS handshakes of link S1-R1, while Fig. 4b and 4c are the corresponding simulation results. It is noted that under the condition that R1 and S2 are within their mutual carrier sensing range in Fig. 1b, R1 and S2 can be within or outside their mutual transmission range (see Fig. 3a and Fig. 3b). The difference is that if they are within the mutual transmission range, S2 can decode the packet transmitted by R1. If outside the transmission range, it can only sense the packet. The difference will lead to different lengths of T_{total} and T_{silent} when an S2-R2 transmission cycle is interrupted by an S1-R1 transmission, thus the simulation results for both sub-cases are provided. Results in Fig. 4 show that the accuracy of the simplified analysis is pretty good.   Both analytical and simulation results indicate that a large number of RTS packets can still be received by R1. However, the number of successful RTS/CTS handshakes is much smaller— meaning that most successful RTS packets at R1 are wasted.

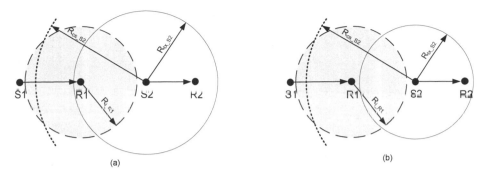

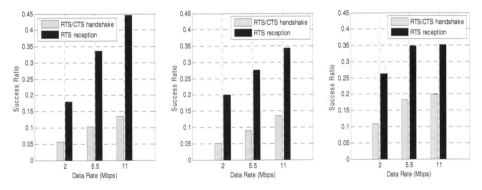

Fig. 3. (a) R1 and S2 are within the transmission range. (b) R1 and S2 are out of the transmission range. The dash circle is R1's interference range; the dot circle is S2's carrier sensing range.

Fig. 4. The probabilities of successful RTS reception and RTS/CTS handshake of link S1-R1; From left to right: (a) Analytical results (b) Simulation results of Fig. 4a. (c) Simulation results of Fig. 4b. Packet lengths = 1000 bytes.

4   Proposed Receiver Assistance MAC Protocol

The results of Section 3 indicate that there are many RTS packets that can arrive correctly at the R1 of the disadvantage link. To exploit this result, we propose a simple receiver assisted feature. The proposed protocol, called *RcvAssist* in the paper, can significantly improve the degree of fairness.

4.1   RcvAssist Protocol

RcvAssist is almost identical to 802.11, the only difference being a simple receiver assistance feature added to the sending and the receiving side of the MAC protocol. On the sending side, everything remains the same except that after a fixed number of failed RTS attempts (the value is determined later), the sender will turn on a "help" flag in subsequent RTS packets. This will activate the receiver assistance feature on the receiving side.

When the receiver receives an RTS packet and the channel is detected busy, the receiver will check if the "help" flag in RTS packet is set. If not, it simply drops the RTS packet, in the same way as defined in the 802.11 protocol. If yes, it will generate a CTS packet and contends the channel (for sending the CTS packet) once the channel is sensed idle. The channel contention follows the normal procedure defined in IEEE 802.11 MAC. But the receiver only makes one, not seven, attempt to acquire the channel. The receiver will get back to the normal mode once the attempt is done, regardless if it is a failure or success.

Note that in the four-way handshake RTS/CTS/DATA/ACK defined by 802.11, if the receiver assistance feature is turn on and the CTS reply is done through channel contention by the receiver, then there will be a gap between arrival of the RTS and the transmission time of the CTS packet by the receiver. This gap corresponds to the channel contention time. This gap is not included in the NAV (Network Allocation Vector) of sender's RTS. Thus the NAV setting in RTS might not be long enough to protect the ACK reception. This, however, is not a problem because on the sender side, in addition to RTS packets, all terminals still use carrier sensing and they thus still need to wait for a duration of an EIFS (EIFS = SIFS + ACK duration + DIFS) period before trying to access the channel again. This means that the ACK at sender side can be protected as before even if the NAV in the RTS packet is not accurate.

Another situation worth mentioning is that when receiver assistance MAC is activated, both the sender and the receiver will initiate packet transmissions to each other and their transmissions may collide. But the chance is slim as the probability that they transmit in the same time slot is no larger than $32 \times (1/32) \times (1/64) = 0.0156$ (sender's contention window size has doubled because of no reply for its previous RTS transmission before. 31 is the minimum contend window size defined in 802.11b MAC). Even in 802.11a, of which the minimum contend window size $=15$, the probability is no larger than $16 \times (1/16) \times (1/32) = 0.0313$.

Fig. 5 give an illustration of the proposed receiver assistance feature based on the scenario in Fig. 3a. As the number of failed RTS attempts exceeds the pre-set threshold, S1 turns on the help flag in its subsequent RTS transmissions to node R1. Once R1 can correctly receive a RTS packet with "help" flag on and channel becomes clear again, it will contend the channel for sending back the CTS packet. This contention between R1 and S2 does not favor S2, as in the traditional 802.11 protocol. So R1 will have an equal probability of seizing the channel.

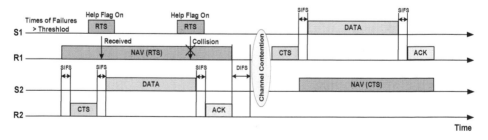

Fig. 5. A graphic illustration of receiver assistance MAC based on Fig. 3a

4.2   Performance of RcvAssist

NS2 (version 2.30) simulator [21] is used to evaluate and compare the performance of the proposed protocol and the IEEE 802.11 DCF. Performance evaluation is based on two metrics: network throughput at transport layer and fairness among different communication sender/receiver pairs. Network throughput measures the protocol's efficiency of channel utilization and fairness indicates how channel bandwidth is shared among different communication links. The degree of fairness is indicated by the instantaneous throughput of individual users versus the total channel capacity.

UDP flow is used in simulation. Data packets are generated by continuously-backlogged CBR (Constant Bit Rate) flows with a fixed packet size 1KB. Because the default setting of channel update in NS2 does not reflect the real situation when multiple packet transmissions occur simultaneously, one of our simulation efforts is to modify the current implementation and make it reflect the real channel conditions at each node.

Four cases are simulated. Two are the basic scenarios shown in Fig. 3, and the other two are shown in Fig. 6. IEEE 802.11b protocol parameters are adopted in the simulation. In addition, the following parameters, unless indicated otherwise, are chosen in the simulations:

(1) The number of failed RTS attempts for turning on the "help" feature in RcvAssist is set to 1.
(2) The transmission range and the carrier sensing range of each node are R_{tx}=250m and R_{cs}=550m respectively.
(3) The SINR threshold for capture requirement is 10dB.
(4) The propagation model is the two-ray ground reflection model.
(5) The default data rate is 11Mbps.
(6) Each simulation runs for 50 seconds.

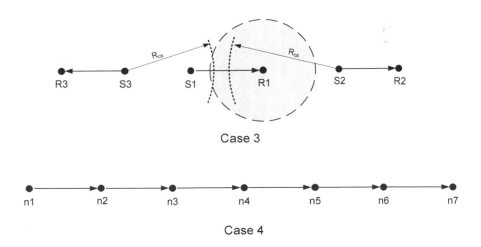

Fig. 6. Case 3 and Case 4; The dash circle is interference range of R1, the dot circles are carrier sensing range in Case 3.

4.2.1   Case 1

This case refers to the scenario in Fig. 3a. There are two communication flows: S1→R1 and S2→R2. The distances between S1 and R1, R1 and S2, S2 and R2 are 210m, 250m and 210m respectively. The simulation environment in NS2 simulator provides no walls and obstacles. We need to set the carrier sensing range and capture SINR threshold smaller (R_{cs}=450m and SINR threshold = 2) to simulate scenario 1. This is the only situation where the default R_{cs} and the SINR threshold are changed. Flow S1→R1 starts first and begin its transmission at t = 0. At time = 4s, flow S2→R2 starts.

Fig. 7a and 7b describe the instantaneous throughputs of two links under 802.11 and RcvAssist respectively. The throughput of flow S1→R1 under 802.11 drops quickly once flow S2→R2 starts; in contrast, it can still maintain a fair level of throughput flow in RcvAssist. The degree of fairness is improved significantly in the RcvAssist protocol. The S1→R1 link of the RcvAssist can grab around 33% total channel capacity; in contrast, it only gets 10% of the channel capacity if 802.11 is used. Fig. 7c compares the total throughput. It shows that RcvAssist can achieve higher network throughput than 802.11. One reason is that RcvAssist has a better spatial reuse factor. For example, flow S1→R1 in RcvAssist may finish their RTS transmission during the transmission of S2→R2. If the receiver assisted feature is turn on, R2 may seize the channel during the inter-frame period of S1→R1. This means that R1 only needs to finish the remaining phases (CTS/DATA/ACK). The overlapping of RTS transmission of the S1-R1 link with the transmissions of the S2→R2 is not possible in conventional 802.11.

Fig. 8 plots the throughput of flow S1→R1 under different threshold values that will trigger the receiver assisted feature in RcvAssist. As can be seen, different thresholds lead to different degrees of channel sharing for flow S1→R1. A lower threshold allows flow S1→R1 to grab a higher portion of the capacity. If the threshold is set to 8, the throughput of S1→R1 in RcvAssist is reduced to that in the 802.11 MAC protocol.

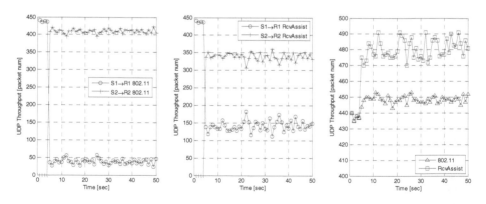

Fig. 7. Case 1 throughput performance; from left to right: (a) Throughput performance of two links in 802.11; (b) Throughput performance of two links in RcvAssist; (c) Network throughput comparison between 802.11 and RcvAssist

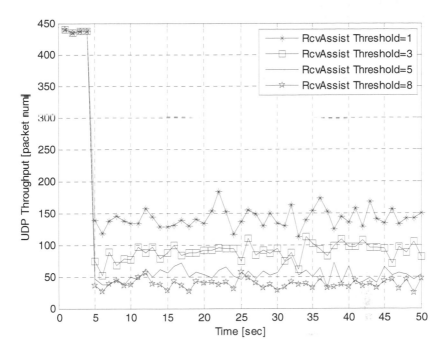

Fig. 8. RcvAssist throughput performance with different thresholds in Case 1

4.2.2 Case 2

This case refers to the scenario shown in Fig. 3b. The distances from S1 to R1, R1 to S2 and S2 to R2 are 220m, 400m and 220m respectively. Flow S1→R1 begins its transmission at t = 0. At time = 4s, flow S2→R2 starts. The performance of the two links and total network throughput are shown in Fig. 9. The interpretations for the

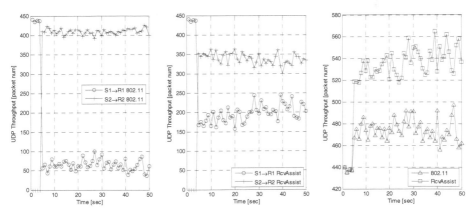

Fig. 9. Case 2 throughput performance; from left to right: (a) Throughput performance of two links in 802.11; (b) Throughput performance of two links in RcvAssist; (c) Network throughput comparison between 802.11 and RcvAssist

results are similar to that in Case 1. The main difference of Case 2 is that R1 and S2 are out of their mutual transmission range. Whenever R1 gets a chance of sending a packet, there is an additional EIFS (EIFS = SIFS+T_{ACK}+DIFS) back-off in S2's back-off period because S2 cannot decode CTS packets from R1. This leads to a better chance for flow S1-R1 to capture the channel. The performance for both protocols is better than Case 1. RcvAssist and 802.11 gets 11.3% and 3.4% more capacity in case 2.

4.2.3   Case 3

This case (Fig. 6) has three links and S1-R1 needs to compete with S2-R2 and S3-R3 simultaneously. In both contention cases, S1-R1 represents the disadvantageous link in an exposed receiver scenario. The distances from R3 to S3, S3 to S1, S1 to R1, R1 to S2, and S2 to R2 are set to be 220m, 350m, 220m, 400m, and 220m. Both flows S1→R1 and S2→R2 have continuously-backlogged packet to send. Flow S1→R1 begins its transmission at t = 0. At t= 4s, flow S2→R2 starts. At t = 15s, flow S3→R3 starts with rate = 0.4Mbps. It then increases the rate to 0.8Mbps at t = 30s, to 1.2Mbps at t= 45s, and to 1.6Mbps at t = 60s. The simulation ends at time =70s.   Again, Fig. 10 shows that RcvAssist outperforms 802.11 MAC and flow S1→R1 can maintain a decent throughput level even under this double jeopardy condition.

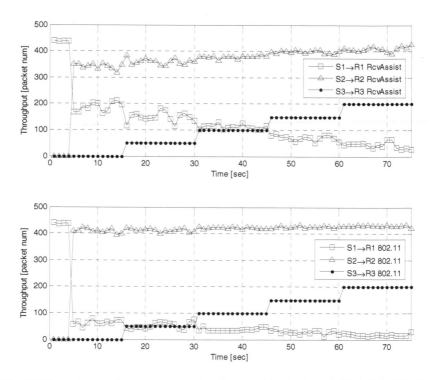

Fig. 10. Throughput performance comparison between RcvAssist and 802.11 MAC in Case 3

4.2.4 Case 4

This case refers to the multi-hop topology with 7 nodes shown in Fig. 6. Each node is 200m away from its immediate neighbors. Node 1 (n1) is the source node and the last node (n7) the sink. This is the same scenario used in [29] for studying ad hoc wireless networks. The packet generation rate at n1 is 1Mbps. Fig. 11 shows that the throughput of RcvAssist is 23.3% higher than that of 802.11.

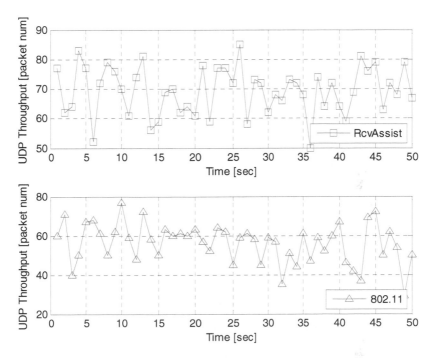

Fig. 11. Throughput performance comparison between RcvAssist and 802.11 MAC in Case 4 multihop environment (chain topology)

5   Conclusion

In this paper, we developed an analytical model to study the RTS reception and RTS/CTS handshake success rates of a typical disadvantaged link in the exposed receiver scenario. Derived from the analytical insights, we proposed a new protocol RcvAssist for fairness enhancement in CSMA/CA wireless networks. The simulation results of various scenarios indicate that the new protocol not only significantly improves the fairness of the CSMA/CA protocol, but also increases the overall throughput without introducing other side effects, such as aggregating the hidden terminal problem. The added feature is easy to implement and the concept is applicable to the design of future MAC protocols.

References

1. Bharghavan, V., Demers, A., Shenker, S., Zhang, L.: MACAW: A medium access protocol for wireless LANs. In: SIGCOMM 1994 (1994)
2. Xu, K., Gerla, M., Bae, S.: How effective is the IEEE 802.11 RTS/CTS handshake in ad hoc networks? In: Proc. IEEE GlobeCom (2002)
3. Xu, S., Saadawi, T.: Does the IEEE 802.11 MAC protocol work well in multihop wireless ad hoc networks? IEEE Commun. Mag., 130–137 (June 2001)
4. Talucci, F., Gerla, M., Fi-atta, L.: MACA-BI (MACA By Invitation): A Receiver Oriented Access Protocol for Wireless Multiple Networks. In: PIMRC 1997 (1997)
5. Wang, Y., Garcia-Luna-Aceves, J.J.: A hybrid collision avoidance scheme for ad hoc networks. In: ACM Wireless Networks (2004)
6. Chen, C., Luo, H.: The case for Heterogeneous Wireless MACs. In: HotNet 2005 (2005)
7. Zhai, H., Fang, Y.: Physical Carrier Sensing and Spatial Reuse in Multirate and Multihop Wireless Ad Hoc Networks. In: Proc. of the IEEE Infocom 2006 (2006)
8. Zhu, J., Guo, X., Yang, L.L., Conner, W.S.: Leveraging spatial reuse in 802.11 mesh networks with enhanced physical carrier sensing. In: IEEE ICC (2004)
9. Yang, X., Vaidya, N.: On Physical Carrier Sensing in Wireless Ad Hoc Networks. In: IEEE Infocom 2005 (2005)
10. Chaudet, C., Dhoutaut, D., Lassous, I.: Performance issues with IEEE 802.11 in ad hoc networking. IEEE Communication Magazine (2005)
11. Karn, P.: MACA—A new channel access method for packet radio. In: ARRL/CRRL Amateur Radio 9th Computer Networking Conf., pp. 134–140 (1990)
12. Acharya, A., Misra, A., Bansal, S.: MACA-P: a MAC for concurrent transmissions in multi-hop wireless networks. In: Proc. IEEE PerCom Conference, March 2003, pp. 505–508 (2003)
13. Shukla, D., Chandran-Wadia, L., Iyer, S.: Mitigating the exposed node problem in IEEE 802.11 adhoc networks. In: IEEE ICCCN 2003, Dallas (October 2003)
14. Vutukuru, M., Jamieson, K., Balakrishnan, H.: Harnessing exposed terminals in wireless networks. In: USENIX NSDI (2008)
15. Haas, Z.J., Deng, J.: Dual Busy Tone Multiple Access (DBTMA): A Multiple Access Control Scheme for Ad Hoc Networks. IEEE Trans. Commun. 50(6), 975–985 (2002)
16. Zhai, H., Wang, J., Fang, Y., Wu, D.: A dual-channel MAC protocol for mobile ad hoc networks. In: IEEE Workshop on Wireless Ad Hoc and Sensor Networks, in conjuction with IEEE Globecom 2004 (November 2004)
17. Judd, G., Steenkiste, P.: Understanding Link-level 802.11 Behavior: Replacing Convention with Measurement. In: Wireless Internet Conference 2007 (Wicon 2007) (2007)
18. Gummadi, R., Wetherall, D., Greenstein, B., Seshan, S.: Understanding and Mitigating the Impact of RF Interference on 802.11 Networks. In: ACM SIGCOMM 2007 (2007)
19. Kochut, A., Vasan, A., Shankar, A., Agrawala, A.: Sniffing out the correct physical layer capture model in 802.11 b. In: ICNP 2004 (2004)
20. Rappaport, T.S.: Wireless Communications: Principles and Practice. Prentice Hall, New Jersey (1996)
21. http://www.isi.edu/nsnam/ns/
22. IEEE-SA Standards Board, ANSI/IEEE Std 802.11,1999 Edition (R2003), IEEE, New York, NY, USA (1999)
23. Bensaou, B., Wang, Y., Ko, C.: Medium Access in 802.11 Based Wireless Ad Hoc Networks. In: ACM MobiHoc (2000)
24. Huang, X., Bensaou, B.: On max–min fairness and scheduling in wireless ad-hoc networks: Analytical framework and implementation. In: ACM MobiHoc (2001)
25. Luo, H., Cheng, J., Lu, S.: Self-Coordinating Localized Fair Queueing in Wireless Ad Hoc Networks. In: IEEE Trans. on Mobile Computing (2004)

26. Vaidya, N.H., Bahl, P., Gupta, S.: Distributed fair scheduling in a wireless LAN. In: ACM Mobicom (2000)
27. Nandagopal, T., Kim, T., Gao, X., Bharghavan, V.: Achieving MAC layer fairness in wireless packet networks. In: Proc. of ACM Mobicom 2000 (2000)
28. Huang, C., Lea, C.-T.: Rate Matching: A New Approach to Hidden-Terminal Problem in Ad Hoc Networks. To be appear in ACM Wireless Networks
29. Li, J., Blake, C., De Couto, D.S.J., Lee, H.I., Morris, R.: Capacity of ad hoc wireless networks. In: ACM Mobicom (2001)

SWIM: A Scheduler for Unsolicited Grant Service (UGS) in IEEE 802.16e Mobile WiMAX Networks*

Chakchai So-In, Raj Jain, and Abdel-Karim Al Tamimi

Department of Computer Science & Engineering, Washington University in St. Louis
One Brookings Drive, Box 1045, St. Louis, Missouri 63130 USA
{cs5,jain,aa7}@cse.wustl.edu

Abstract. Most of the IEEE 802.16e Mobile WiMAX scheduling proposals for real-time traffic using Unsolicited Grant Service (UGS) focus on the throughput and guaranteed latency. The delay jitter and the effect of burst overhead have not yet been investigated. This paper introduces a new technique called **Sw**apping **M**in-**M**ax (SWIM) for UGS scheduling that not only meets the delay constraint with optimal throughput, but also minimizes the delay jitter and burst overhead.

Keywords: Scheduling, Resource Allocation, Mobile WiMAX, IEEE 802.16e, Unsolicited Grant Service, UGS, QoS, Delay Jitter.

1 Introduction

One of the key features of the IEEE 802.16e Mobile WiMAX is its strong quality of service (QoS). The IEEE 802.16e Mobile WiMAX provides the multiple QoS classes for voice, video, and data applications [1]. To meet QoS requirements especially for voice and video transmissions with delay and delay jitter constraints, the key issue is how to allocate resources among contending users. That is why there are many papers on designing resource allocation algorithms for the IEEE 802.16e Mobile WiMAX [2].

The IEEE 802.16e Mobile WiMAX offers five classes of service: Unsolicited Grant Service (UGS), extended real-time Polling Service (ertPS), real-time Polling Service (rtPS), non-real-time Polling Service (nrtPS), and Best Effort (BE). UGS is designed for Constant Bit Rate (CBR) traffic with strict throughput, delay, and delay jitter constraints. ertPS is a modification of UGS for voice with silence suppression. rtPS is designed for variable bit rate voice, video, and gaming applications that have delay constraints. nrtPS is for streaming video and data applications that need throughput guarantees but do not have delay constraints (the packets can be buffered). BE is designed for data applications that do not need any throughput or delay guarantees.

---

* This work was sponsored in part by a grant from Application Working Group of WiMAX Forum. "WiMAX," "Mobile WiMAX," "Fixed WiMAX," "WiMAX Forum," "WiMAX Certified," "WiMAX Forum Certified," the WiMAX Forum logo and the WiMAX Forum Certified logo are trademarks of the WiMAX Forum.

X. Jun Hei and L. Cheung (Eds.): AccessNets 2009, LNICST 37, pp. 40–51, 2010.
©Institute for Computer Sciences, Social-Informatics and Telecommunications Engineering 2010

These five service classes can be divided in two main categories: non-real-time and real-time. nrtPS and BE are in the first category and UGS, rtPS, and ertPS are in the second category. For the first category, common schemes can directly apply such as Weighted Fair Queue (WFQ) and a variation of Round Robin (RR) since there are no hard constraints on delay and delay jitter [2]. On the other hand, real-time services have strict constraints on these parameters. This makes scheduling difficult in trying to meet the delay constraint and tolerate the delay jitter with optimal throughput.

UGS is one of the real-time services. Basically, UGS traffic provides a fixed periodic bandwidth allocation. Once the connection is setup, there is no need to send any other requests. UGS is designed and used commonly for Constant Bit Rate (CBR) real-time traffic such as leased-line digital connections (T1/E1) and Voice over IP (VoIP). The main QoS parameters are maximum sustained rate, maximum latency, and tolerated jitter (the maximum delay variation).

As indicated earlier, previous papers on the IEEE 802.16e Mobile WiMAX scheduling have ignored the effect of burst overhead and often ignored the delay and delay jitter constraints [2 to 5]. In this paper, we propose an algorithm for UGS scheduling that includes these features. Although, the discussion in this paper is limited to UGS service class only, we plan to extend this algorithm for other real-time services and for a mixture of users from different service classes.

Scheduling Factors

The scheduler for UGS needs to be designed to meet the four main QoS criteria for the IEEE 802.16e Mobile WiMAX [1, 2]. First, to optimize system throughput, that is, the scheduler should use all available UGS slots if there is traffic.

Second, the scheduler should guarantee the delay constraints or maximum latency guarantees. In this paper, we also use the term "deadline" to mean delay constraint because the allocation is made within the deadline.

Third, the scheduler should minimize delay jitter. The definition of delay jitter is the variability in inter-packet times from one inter-packet interval to the next.

Finally, the scheduler should minimize number of bursts in order to reduce Media Access Control (MAC) and MAP overheads that reduce system throughput.

2   Related Work

There has been some research on delay jitter control for real-time communication in ATM and packet data networks. One way is to introduce a delay jitter regulator or rate regulator at each hop. The regulator delays a packet in order to keep constant delay jitter over the end-to-end path [6, 7, 8]. This method minimizes delay jitter increasing the mean delay and possibly reducing the throughput.

As shown in our extensive survey of the IEEE 802.16e Mobile WiMAX schedulers [2], channel-unaware IEEE 802.16e schedulers have applied two techniques for UGS traffic: Weighted Round Robin (WRR), equally spread the allocation over all Mobile

WiMAX frames (we call this averaging or AVG algorithm) and Earliest Deadline First (EDF) [3, 4, 5]. With the admission control, these techniques can achieve optimal throughput and meet deadlines; however, the delay jitter is not considered. This parameter is one of the required QoS parameters for UGS, that is, the tolerated jitter [1].

In addition, most papers have ignored burst overhead, which directly depends on how many bursts a Base Station (BS) allocates in a Mobile WiMAX frame [2]. Therefore, the delay jitter and the number of bursts are investigated in this paper. In this paper, we introduce a new algorithm, called SWIM (**Sw**apping **M**in-**M**ax). This algorithm assures deadlines and delay jitter constraints, optimizes the throughput, and also minimizes the number of bursts. We show that along with zero delay jitter, a number of bursts with SWIM are comparable with those of EDF.

The paper is organized as follows: UGS allocation algorithm with assumptions of arrival traffic and parameters is described in Section 3. Then, the performance evaluation and examples are demonstrated in Section 4. Finally, the conclusions are discussed.

3   SWIM Algorithm

In this section, general assumptions are described first in subsection 3.1. Our algorithm can be used for both downlink allocation and uplink allocation. However, the problem is more difficult in the uplink since a Base Station (BS) has no information about the actual traffic at Mobile Stations (MSs), i.e., the arrival traffic process or queue length. The BS only knows about total demand and the period. Then, in subsection 3.2, SWIM algorithm is introduced. The SWIM algorithm basically can be divided into three basic steps that achieve optimal throughput while meeting the deadline, minimal delay jitter (in fact zero delay jitter), and minimal number of bursts.

3.1   Assumptions and Parameter Explanation

Basically for the IEEE 802.16e scheduler, all allocations are integer number of slots. In this paper, the definition of resource is fixed in terms of the number of slots per uplink (or downlink) subframe. This is denoted by the variable #*slots*. The number of bytes corresponding to a slot depends upon the modulation and coding which can vary among users. Without any loss of generality, we use a fixed number of bytes per slot and use bytes as the unit of resource allocation and demand.

For UGS traffic, at connection setup, MSs basically declare the total demand (denoted by *DataSize*) and a *period*. For example, *connection_1* asks 540 bytes every 3 frames. In other words, every 15 ms (WiMAX profiles specify a frame size of 5ms [9]). Due to the periodic nature of UGS traffic, the period is the same as deadline. We use these terms interchangeably; however, we show in Section 4.4 that if the deadline is less than the period, the throughput is not optimized.

MSs can dynamically join and leave the networks. For joining, in order for BS to admit a connection, the BS needs to verify if there are enough resources. Also, the

MS may request to change its service on the fly. Therefore, the scheduler needs to be aware of the quality assurance of all currently accepted connections.

In other words, there is an admission control mechanism. The BS can only admit a connection if and only if the sum of the total number of currently used resources per frame and the new demand divided by the deadline of the connection is less than the total available slots per frame for UGS.

The allocation algorithm is based on *DataSize* which is a MAC Service Data Unit (SDU) size for both deadline and delay jitter calculation. We do not explicitly consider any headers such as fragmentation and packing headers, MAC header, and ARQ retransmission overhead. However, the MS has to include these overheads in its demand at the connection setup time.

Finally, we assume that the MS has data available at the beginning of each period. In other words, the MS has enough buffer space at least for one period. This allows the BS to allocate the resources anytime within the deadline.

3.2 Algorithm Description

Our algorithm has two parts. First, an initialization procedure that starts with optimal throughput and delay. Second, a series of resource swapping steps that leads to optimization of all goals.

Given n users with i^{th} user demanding d_i over a period p_i, optimal throughput can be obtained by taking a Least Common Multiple (LCM) of periods p_i's and allocating resources over this cycle.

To achieve zero delay jitter, the algorithm initializes allocated resources (#slots or #bytes) for each connection by *DataSize/period*, i.e., d_i/p_i.

In each frame, the connection with the maximum resource allocation is called *max-res* connection and the one with the minimum allocation is called *min-res* connection.

To minimize the number of bursts, there is a swapping procedure between *max-res* and *min-res* connections that results in eliminating the *min-res* connection and thereby, reducing the number of connections served in that frame by one. In effect, this reduces the number of bursts in that frame by one. This will become more clear in Section 4, where we provide an example.

The swapping procedure is described as follows: first, the algorithm determines the *min-res* connection (say, ith connection) and the *max-res* connection (say, jth connection). The two connections swap their resources such that ith connection gives up its resources in the current frame while gaining an equal amount of resources in a future frame. Of course, the constraints are that jth connection still needs more resources in this frame and that ith connection's deadline will still be met.

The system manager can set a minimum burst size parameter, *MinBurstSize*. The swapping procedure ensures that each burst is at least this size. In our examples, we use a *MinBurstSize* of 1. However, the procedure can be easily applied for any other values of this parameter. The main effect of this parameter is that the connections whose deadline is in the current frame must have *MinBurstSize* allocation or more. If their allocation is equal to *MinBurstSize*, they are excluded from swapping. Leaving

MinBurstSize at a non-zero value ensures that all SDUs are delivered exactly at the deadline and the delay jitter is zero. Setting *MinBurstSize* to zero will result in a reduced number of bursts but non-zero delay jitter. The SWIM algorithm will then produce results similar to EDF.

The new *max-res* and *min-res* connections do the resource swapping. Note that the total allocated resources per frame do not change by this swapping procedure. Also, the total resources allocated to a connection over its period do not change.

```
Preallocation(flows)                              //1ˢᵗ step
Sorted_max_to_min = Sort (flows)
FOR each max_res in Sorted_max_to_min             //2ⁿᵈ step
    Sorted_min_to_max = Sort (flows)
    FOR each min_res in Sorted_min_to_max         //3ʳᵈ step
        Max_Min_Swapping (max_res, min_res);
    END FOR
END FOR
```

Fig. 1. Steps in SWIM Algorithm

There are a few special cases. First, a *max-res* connection cannot accept more resources than it needs and so the *min-res* connection may not get eliminated. In this case, the next *max-res* connection becomes the candidate for swapping for the remaining resources of the *min-res* connection.

Second, if there are more than one *max-res* connections (more than one connection with the same maximum resources allocated in the frame), we choose the connection whose resources are higher in the next frame.

Third, if there are more than one *max-res* connections with the same next frame resources, we select the connection whose deadline is longer. Of course, we exclude the connections whose deadline is in the current frame and which have allocation equal to *MinBurstSize*.

Fourth, if there are more than one *min-res* connections, we select the connection that has earlier deadline. Also, if there are more than one *min-res* connections with the same deadline, we choose the connection with lower resources in the next frame.

4 Performance Evaluation and Examples

In this section, we evaluate the performance of the proposed algorithm with other two commonly used algorithms: EDF and AVG (allocating *DataSize/period*, d_i/p_i in each frame to the ith user). For all three algorithms, the process is cyclic that repeats after LCM period. We show just one such cycle.

First, we evaluate the performance in terms of throughput, mean delay, mean delay jitter, and number of bursts for each algorithm. Then, the concept of flow admission is discussed. Finally, we show an alternative scenario in which the deadline is less than period. In that case, all resources cannot be allocated to UGS connections optimally. Some resources are left over and can be used by other service classes.

4.1 Throughput, Mean Delay, Mean Delay Jitter, and Number of Bursts

The throughput, mean delay, mean delay jitter, and number of bursts are investigated in this section. We start with a simple example (Table 1) of static flows by applying all three algorithms: AVG, EDF, and SWIM. The performance comparisons are summarized in Table 6.

Table 1. Example I: Static Flows

	C1	C2	C3	C4	C5
DataSize (bytes)	540	80	900	120	600
Period (frame)	3	4	6	6	12

Table 1 shows a simple example of 5 connections (C1 through C5) and their demands (*DataSize*) in bytes and period in terms of WiMAX frames. The total allocated UGS slots are 420 bytes per frame (540/3) + (80/4) + (900/6) + (120/6) + (600/12). With all three algorithms, within one LCM cycle (12 frames in this example), the throughput is optimal, that is, (540×4) + (80×3) + (900×2) + (120×2) + (600×1) = 5,040 bytes or it is equal to 420×12 = 5,040 bytes.

Tables 2 and 3 show the allocations using AVG and EDF algorithms respectively. In AVG, the resource is allocated equally in every frame, e.g., 180 bytes in every frame for C1, 20 bytes for C2, and so on.

Table 2. Example I: AVG Allocation

Time	C1	C2	C3	C4	C5	Sum
0	180	20	150	20	50	420
1	180	20	150	20	50	420
2	180	20	150	20	50	420
3	180	20	150	20	50	420
4	180	20	150	20	50	420
5	180	20	150	20	50	420

In EDF, the resource is allocated to the connection whose deadline is earliest. At the beginning, C1 has the earliest deadline, that is, 3 frames. In the first frame, the EDF scheduler allocates the entire available capacity of 420 bytes to C1. In the next frame, the scheduler allocates the remaining 120 bytes for C1 to meet C1's throughput guarantee (540 bytes). Of the left-over 300 bytes, 80 and 220 bytes are allocated for C3 and C2, respectively, because the deadlines of C3 and C2 are 4 and 6 frames.

Table 3. Example I: EDF Allocation

Time	C1	C2	C3	C4	C5	Sum
0	420					420
1	120	80	220			420
2			420			420
3	420					420
4	120		260	40		420
5		80		80	260	420
6	420					420
7	120		300			420
8			420			420
9	420					420
10			80		340	420
11	120	80	100	120		420

   In SWIM, we initialize the allocation table with equal allocation. This results in allocations shown in Table 2 for AVG. The swapping steps of SWIM are shown in Table 4. In the first frame, the *max-res* connection is C1 and the *min-res* connection is C2. Therefore, C2's allocation in the frame is given to C1 and taken back in the second frame. This results in C1 obtaining 180+20=200 and C2 obtaining 20-20=0 in the first frame. C1 obtains 180-20=160 and C2 obtains 20+20=40 in the second frame. The resulting allocations are shown in Table 4a. Thus, swapping has reduced the number of bursts by one (one less burst in the first frame while still meeting all the throughput and delay guarantees for all sources).

   In the next swapping step, C1 and C4 swap their allocations in frame 1 and 2 resulting in allocations shown in Table 4b. Next, C1 and C5 swap their allocations in frame 1 and 2 resulting in allocations shown in Table 4c. Next C1 and C3 swap in frames 1 and 2. However, in this case, C1 has only 90 units of allocations in 2nd frame and so the swap is done in two steps. In the first step, 90 units are swapped between C1 and C5 in frames 1 and 2. Then, the remaining 50 units are swapped in frames 1 and 3. This results in allocations shown in Table 4d. At this point, the allocation for the first frame is complete since there is only one burst left in this frame. Continuing these processes for the 2nd frame and other subsequent frames result in the final allocations shown in Table 5.

   The mean delays for both AVG and SWIM are the same. These delays are equals to the periods: 3, 4, 6, 6, and 12 frames for connection 1 through 5, respectively. For EDF, the mean delays are $\{(2+2+2+3)/4\}=9/4$, $\{(2+2+4)/3\}=8/3$, $\{(5+6)/2\}=11/2$, $\{(6+6)/2\}=6$, and 11 frames for connections 1 through 5, respectively.

   Both AVG and SWIM have zero mean delay jitter, i.e., all SDUs are received on the period. For EDF, the mean delay jitters are $\{(0+0+1)/3\}=1/3$, $\{(0+2)/2\}=1$, 1, 0, and 0 for connections 1 through 5, respectively.

Table 4. Example I: SWIM Initial Steps

(a)

Time	C1	C2	C3	C4	C5	Sum
0	**200**		150	20	50	420
1	**160**	40	150	20	50	420
2	180	20	150	20	50	420

....

(b)

Time	C1	C2	C3	C4	C5	Sum
0	**220**		150		50	420
1	**140**	40	150	40	50	420
2	180	20	150	20	50	420

....

(c)

Time	C1	C2	C3	C4	C5	Sum
0	**270**		150			420
1	**90**	40	150	40	100	420
2	180	20	150	20	50	420

....

(d)

Time	C1	C2	C3	C4	C5	Sum
0	**420**					420
1		40	**240**	40	100	420
2	**120**	20	**210**	20	50	420

....

Table 5. Example I: Final Allocations of SWIM

Time	C1	C2	C3	C4	C5	Sum
0	420					420
1			420			420
2	120	20			280	420
3	360	60				420
4			420			420
5	180	60	60	120		420
6	420					420
7		20	400			420
8	120				300	420
9	420					420
10			420			420
11	120	80	80	120	20	420

Consider the number of bursts: AVG gives 5 connections × 12 frames or 60 bursts, 24 bursts for SWIM, and 23 bursts for EDF. All four performance metrics are summarized comparatively in Table 6.

Table 6. Performance Comparisons of UGS scheduling disciplines

	Mean Delay	Mean Delay Jitter	#Bursts	Throughput
AVG	Period	Zero	High	Optimal
EDF	Low	**Variable**	Low	Optimal
SWIM	Period	Zero	Low	Optimal

4.2 Fractional Resource Demands

Since both AVG's final allocation and SWIM's initial allocation are obtained by dividing the resource demand by the period, this can result in fractional allocations. To show this, we change the resource demands of C1 and C4 in the previous example to 500 and 200, respectively. With a period of 3, C1 requires (500/3) bytes per frame. Similarly, C4 needs 200/6 bytes per frame. With fractional allocations, we simply round the allocations in a frame after the frame has been completely allocated. We find that two decimal digit representations (1/100th) are generally sufficient to avoid any truncation errors. Table 7 shows the final SWIM allocations for the example. The allocation is still feasible and results in 26 bursts.

Table 7. Example II: SWIM with DataSize/Period is prime

Time	C1	C2	C3	C4	C5	Sum
0	420					420
1			420			420
2	80	7		33	300	420
3		73	347			420
4	420					420
5	80	40	133	167		420
6	420					420
7		40	380			420
8	80			41	299	420
9			420			420
10	420					420
11	80	80	100	159	1	420

4.3 Dynamic Connections

It is common for flows to join or leave the network. For AVG, a newly admitted flow does not affect the current flows as long as the sum of the total pre-allocated resources and the resource demand per frame of the new connection is less than the total available resources per frame.

The above statement also holds for SWIM and EDF. However, the scheduler needs to maintain the flow states such as how many resources have already been allocated to each connection. We illustrate this with an example. Suppose a new connection C6 joins the network at time 15 with a resource demand of 500 bytes over a period of 4 frames. At 15th frame, the total resource demand changes from 420 to 545 bytes per frame. Table 8 shows the initial allocation process for SWIM. The allocations from time 0 to 10 are the same as that in Section 4.1, Table 5.

At the end of 14th frame, the allocations for the five connections are 540, 20, 420, 0, and 280 bytes. Also, a connection C2 has an allocation of 60 bytes in 15th frame. This was a result of previous swapping. In Table 8, this type of pre-allocation (which has changed from initial value due to swapping) is indicated by enclosing it in parentheses. The pre-allocations for other connections and other frames at the end of 14th frame are also shown in the table by enclosing the allocations in parentheses.

Table 8. Example III: SWIM Initial Steps

(a)

Time	C1	C2	C3	C4	C5	C6	Sum
.....							420
11	120	80	80	120	20		420
12	420						420
13			420				420
14	120	20			280		420
15	180	(60)	(180)	(0)	(0)	125	545
16	180	20	150	(70)	(0)	125	545
17	180	20	150	(50)	(20)	125	545

....

(b)

Time	C1	C2	C3	C4	C5	C6	Sum
15	305	60	180	0	0		545
16	55	20	150	70	0	250	545
17	180	20	150	50	20	125	545

....

(c)

Time	C1	C2	C3	C4	C5	C6	Sum
15	485	60		0	0		545
16		20	205	70	0	250	545
17	55	20	275	50	20	125	545

....

To meet their throughput guarantees, in their period containing 15th frame, connections C1 through C5 need 540, 40, 300, 0, and 0 bytes over and above their pre-allocations. So, the new initial allocations are made by equally dividing these remaining values by the remaining period. The final results after C6 joins in 15th frame are shown in Table 9.

Table 9. Example III: SWIM with a new admitted flow C6

Time	C1	C2	C3	C4	C5	**C6**	Sum
.....							420
11	120	80	80	120	20		420
12	420						420
13			420				420
14	120	20			280		420
15	485	60		0	0		545
16			170		0	375	545
17	55	60	310	120			545
18	420					125	545
19		20	525				545
20	120					425	545
21	539				6		545
22			374		96	75	545
23	1	80	1	120	218	125	545

4.4 Deadline Less Than the Period

If the deadline is less than the period, the total demand before and after a connection's deadline is different and it is possible that some frames may be under-allocated. In other words, it is not possible to achieve full throughput. The unallocated resource can easily be used for non-time critical service classes. If we try to achieve full throughput with UGS traffic only, we may not be able to meet the deadline. This is true for all three algorithms as shown by the examples below.

Table 10. Example IV: Deadline < Period

	C1	C2	C3	C4	C5
Data Size (bytes)	540	80	900	120	600
Period (frame)	**3**	4	**6**	**6**	**12**
Deadline (frame)	**2**	4	**4**	**4**	**6**

In Example IV shown in Table 10, the deadline for connections C1 through C5 has been set to 2, 4, 4, 4, and 6 frames, respectively. If we allocate equal resources over all frames before the period (resource demand divided by the period), the allocation per frame is 420. We have full throughput but are missing the deadlines. If we allocate equal resources over all frames before the deadline (resource demand divided by the deadline), we need (540/**2**) + (80/4) + (900/**4**) + (120/**4**) + (600/**6**) or 645. This is over the available capacity of 420. Of course, if the admission control ensures that no new connections will be admitted if the sum of resources per frame (using resource/deadline) is more than the available capacity, we have a feasible solution and can meet the deadlines in a straightforward manner.

5 Conclusions

In this paper, we have introduced a new algorithm for UGS scheduler for the IEEE 802.16e Mobile WiMAX networks. The algorithm tries to minimize the number of bursts and gives zero delay jitter. Compared to AVG, the number of bursts is much less. Compared to EDF, the delay jitter is zero and the number of bursts is comparable. Although this technique has been designed for UGS service, we believe a simple extension with a polling mechanism can be used for ertPS service.

There is a tradeoff between delay jitter and the number of bursts. Thus, further study is needed to relax the tight delay jitter constraints and reduce the number of bursts.

In this paper, we assumed "Partial Usage of Subcarrier Utilization" permutation. In this case, all slots have the same capacity. With other permutations, such as adaptive modulation and coding (band-AMC) permutation, the slot capacity for each slot is different. We are working on an extension to handle this case. Finally, we have assumed the uplink allocation. The same algorithm can be extended for the downlink allocation with further optimization using extra information such as the actual arrivals, packet sizes, and head of line delays.

References

1. IEEE P802.16Rev2/D2.: DRAFT Standard for Local and metropolitan area networks: Part 16: Air Interface for Broadband Wireless Access Systems, p. 2094 (December 2007)
2. So-In, C., Jain, R., Al-Tamimi, A.: Scheduling in IEEE 802.16e WiMAX Networks: Key Issues and a Survey. IEEE Journal on Selected Areas in Comm 27(2), 156–171 (2009)
3. Cicconetti, C., Lenzini, L., Mingozzi, E., Eklund, C.: Quality of service support in IEEE 802.16 networks. IEEE Network 20(2), 50–55 (2006)
4. Wongthavarawat, K., Ganz, A.: IEEE 802.16 based last mile broadband wireless military networks with quality of service support. In: Proc. Military Commun. Conf., vol. 2, pp. 779–784 (2003)
5. Sayenko, A., Alanen, O., Karhula, J., Hamalainen, T.: Ensuring the QoS Requirements in 802.16 Scheduling. In: Proc. Int. Conf. on Modeling Analysis and Simulation of Wireless and Mobile Systems, pp. 108–117 (2006)
6. Dong, L., Melhem, R., Mosse, D.: Effect of scheduling jitter on end-to-end delay in TDMA protocols. In: Proc. Int. Conf. on Real-Time Computing Systems and Applications, pp. 223–230 (2000)
7. Mansour, Y., Patt-Shamir, B.: Jitter control in QoS networks. IEEE/ACM Transactions on Networking 9(4), 492–502 (2001)
8. Verma, D.C., Zhang, H., Ferrari, D.: Delay jitter control for real-time communication in a packet switching network. In: Proc. Commun. for Distributed Application and Systems, pp. 35–43 (1991)
9. WiMAX Forum.: WiMAX System Evaluation Methodology V2.1, p. 230 (July 2008), http://www.wimaxforum.org/technology/documents

Influence of Technical Improvements on the Business Case for a Mobile WiMAX Network

Bart Lannoo, Jeffrey De Bruyne, Wout Joseph, Jan Van Ooteghem, Emmeric Tanghe, Didier Colle, Luc Martens, Mario Pickavet, and Piet Demeester

Dept. of Information Technology (INTEC), Ghent University – IBBT, Gaston Crommenlaan 8 box 201, 9050 Gent, Belgium
{bart.lannoo,jeffrey.debruyne,wout.joseph,jan.vanooteghem, emmeric.tanghe,didier.colle,luc.martens,mario.pickavet, piet.demeester}@intec.ugent.be

Abstract. From a technical point of view, Mobile WiMAX may offer an appropriate solution for delivering broadband wireless access. Two remaining questions, however, are whether the rollout of a WiMAX network is economically feasible or not, and how technical improvements like MIMO, beamforming and turbo-coding can influence the business case. In this paper different technical scenarios for a Mobile WiMAX rollout are defined and evaluated from an economic as well as a technical perspective. To obtain realistic figures, we have defined a business case for a Mobile WiMAX rollout in Belgium, a country with a high wired broadband penetration. Further, we give an indication about the feasibility of a Mobile WiMAX network related to the population density. Finally, as the introduction of a new technology involves a lot of uncertainties, a detailed sensitivity analysis on both the economic and technical input parameters is performed to determine the most influencing parameters.

Keywords: Broadband Wireless Communication, WiMAX, 802.16e-2005, Mobility, Business Case, Techno-economic Analysis.

1 Introduction

Ever-increasing bandwidth demands and recent mobility trends are two main challenges for the access communications network during the next years. Based on the booming markets of broadband connectivity and mobile phone usage, it may be clear that there exists a great potential for broadband services on mobile terminals. To enhance mobility in the access network, Mobile WiMAX may possibly offer an appropriate solution. Its bandwidth is high enough to be a competing technology for the currently available fixed access networks (like e.g., DSL, cable), and by its support for mobility, it can also be an alternative for mobile access networks (like e.g., UMTS, HSDPA). Note that WiMAX is a certification label, mainly based on the IEEE 802.16 standards [1-3] and promoted by the WiMAX Forum [4]. Today, two important WiMAX profiles are defined: a Fixed and Mobile version. Due to the addition of mobility, it is expected that mainly Mobile WiMAX (based on the IEEE 802.16e-2005 standard [3]) will be used in the future.

X. Jun Hei and L. Cheung (Eds.): AccessNets 2009, LNICST 37, pp. 52–66, 2010.

The performance of Mobile WiMAX systems has already been extensively investigated [5-7]. Coverage and performance of Mobile WiMAX have been analyzed via link and system simulations in [5-6], and [7] presents an overview of some multiple antenna technologies like Multiple Input Multiple Output (MIMO) and beamforming, which have gained a lot of interest the latest years because of their potential benefits in increasing coverage or capacity. Next to these technical studies, the economic feasibility of a Mobile WiMAX deployment has also already been investigated. In [8-9], results are given for a developed country (Belgium) with a high penetration of a wired infrastructure (DSL and cable). These two papers especially focus on the economic feasibility of Mobile WiMAX for outdoor reception and the sensitivity of the business case is only applied to uncertainties in the economic parameters (i.e. costs, revenues and user adoption). Technical parameters such as antenna heights, path loss, MIMO and beamforming gains, and penetration loss also include a high uncertainty, and, by our knowledge, no research up to now has been performed about the influence of this uncertainty on the economic viability of a Mobile WiMAX rollout. In this paper, we present the results of an extensive analysis about the rollout of Mobile WiMAX for both outdoor and indoor coverage in Belgium. For this analysis, we have developed a planning tool which incorporates all necessary economic and technical aspects. A thorough sensitivity analysis is also executed to compare the influence of technical and economic parameters.

The most important characteristics of a Mobile WiMAX system and the related business case are described in Section 2. Section 3 shows the results of the link budget calculations for Mobile WiMAX, which is necessary to obtain the number of required base station (BS) sites to cover a certain area. Different technical solutions and propagation models are compared to each other. Section 4 discusses the influence of different technical characteristics on the rollout of Mobile WiMAX (for outdoor and indoor coverage) in Belgium by means of a net present value (NPV) analysis. Section 5 presents a detailed sensitivity analysis to indicate the most influencing parameters within our model. Finally, conclusions are presented in Section 6.

2   Configuration

Mobile WiMAX typically uses a cellular approach, requiring the installation of several WiMAX cell sites or BSs through the covered area. The number of needed BSs is a determining cost factor in a WiMAX deployment. That is why it is very important to properly dimension the network. An accurate planning tool has been developed which incorporates all the necessary technical and economic aspects that will be discussed in the following sections.

2.1   Selection of Characteristics of Mobile WiMAX System

We describe the physical characteristics of a Mobile WiMAX system and motivate the selected parameter values of our reference Mobile WiMAX system. As some technologies will improve in the future, some additional gains are also considered.

These characteristics are vendor-specific, which indicates the importance of a sensitivity analysis including these technical parameters as well (discussed in Section 5).

WiMAX System Characteristics. Deployments of 802.16e are preferred in the frequency band between 2.3 GHz and 2.5 GHz [10]. In this paper we consider a Time Division Duplex (TDD) system (3:1 downlink (DL) / uplink (UL) ratio) with a carrier frequency of 2.5 GHz, channel bandwidth of 10 MHz and cyclic prefix of 1/8. The system also provides adaptive modulation from QPSK 1/2 to 64-QAM 3/4, which corresponds with bitrates ranging from 4 to 19 Mbps for DL, and 1 to 5 Mbps for UL (considering a protocol overhead of 20%).

A BS antenna height of 30 m, a BS transmit power of 35 dBm and a BS antenna gain of 16 dB are chosen for our analysis. For the subscriber station (SS), we consider a height of 2 m, a transmit power of 27 dBm, and an antenna gain of 2 dB, which is equal to the gain of a realistic dipole antenna (typically used for SSs such as laptops).

Receiver Sensitivity. The required receiver (Rx) sensitivity to detect the wireless signal at the SS (DL) or BS (UL) is an essential parameter for determining the range of the Mobile WiMAX system. This minimum Rx sensitivity is vendor-specific and can be calculated from the thermal noise (-174 dBm, at 290 K), the receiver Signal-to-Noise ratio (SNR), the receiver noise figure (5 dB in UL, 7 dB in DL) and the implementation loss (2 dB) [10]. The SNR depends on the modulation scheme and Forward Error Correction (FEC) algorithm. Two much used FEC algorithms are the Reed-Solomon Convolutional Code (RS-CC) and the Convolutional Turbo Code (CTC). RS-CC has higher SNR requirements than CTC, but CTC from its side requires a higher implementation cost.

Multiple Antenna Techniques. To improve radio performance, multiple antenna technologies are very often used in cellular systems. Currently, more advanced antenna techniques such as smart antenna technology with MIMO and beamforming antennas are proposed.

MIMO: MIMO systems refer to solutions where the same information is transmitted (after space-time coding) in space and time. The theoretical diversity gain of such a solution for both DL and UL is a function of the product of the transmit/receive antennas and is equal to $10\log(N_{Tx} \times N_{Rx})$ [11], with N_{Tx} the number of transmit antennas and N_{Rx} the number of receive antennas. Furthermore, the use of MIMO also includes a Cyclic Combining Gain of 3 dB in DL [5].

Beamforming or Adaptive Antenna System (AAS): The beamforming technology principle is to coherently combine the signals received from N antenna elements of an antenna array. Beamforming improves the link budget for the data transmission for both the DL and UL. Indeed, by concentrating the energy in one direction, the resulting antenna gain in one direction is significantly increased. This additional gain is beneficial for improving the coverage of the BS and/or reducing the power needed by the SS to transmit signals. Theoretical gains (in comparison to a conventional antenna) for an N-element antenna array are $20\log(N)$ for DL and $10\log(N)$ for UL [11].

Orthogonal Frequency Division Multiple Access (OFDMA). In an OFDMA system, resources are available in the time domain by means of OFDM symbols and in the frequency domain by means of sub-carriers. The time and frequency resources can then be organized into subchannels for allocation to individual users (as well in DL as in UL). This usage of subchannels causes a subchanneling gain which is equal to $-10\log$(Fraction of Number of Used Subchannels to total number of Available Subchannels) [12]. In this paper we consider only uplink subchanneling gain.

2.2 Selection of Characteristics of Business Case

Different business parameters (rollout, services, tariffs) are selected by the operator and others (equipment costs) are vendor-specific. Combined with a chosen rollout area and well-estimated market forecast, an economic feasibility study can be performed for a Mobile WiMAX rollout (see Section 4).

Possible Rollout Scenarios. The optimal rollout strategy of a new WiMAX network typically depends on the targeted market. In developing countries with a low penetration of fixed access networks, WiMAX can be a viable alternative for DSL or cable access. In developed countries, WiMAX can be a complementary technology with the current access networks, providing the advantage of portability or even mobility. In this paper, we especially focus on a Mobile WiMAX deployment in a developed country, starting in the urban areas since they have the largest potential customer base.

A second important part in the rollout strategy of an operator is the assumed rollout speed. Due to practical constraints and/or too high investments, it may be preferred to spread a full (e.g., nationwide) rollout over several years. Otherwise, for a booming market with a lot of strong competitors, it may be advantageous to adopt a faster rollout speed to gain a first-mover advantage. The preferred strategy however, is very case–specific, and in Section 4, we discuss a case in Belgium.

Offered Services. To reach as much customers as possible, an operator has to differentiate its offered products, each corresponding to a varying user profile or target group. In this way, we assume four service types for broadband Internet access (summarized in Table 2): '*Stand-alone wireless broadband*' (WiMAX used as broadband connection, instead of DSL or cable, especially suited for the residents of the covered area), '*Second residence*' (mainly intended for users that need a second connection, e.g., business people, students), '*Nomadicity*' (a light version of the previous product, comparable with the current subscriptions to a hotspot, suited for a varying target group) and '*Prepaid*' (a prepaid card grants the user a limited number of hours for using the WiMAX network, used by e.g., tourists).

We suppose that the 'Stand-alone' and 'Second residence' service offer a bandwidth of 3 Mbps downstream and 256 kbps upstream, and the other two services have a bandwidth of 512 kbps downstream and 128 kbps upstream. Furthermore, we assume an overbooking factor of 20 as it will never occur that every subscriber simultaneously uses its full WiMAX connection.

Tariff Setting. A good tariff setting is extremely important as it defines the final profits of an operator. If the tariffs are set too low, the operator will lose a lot of revenues, but on the other hand, a too high tariff will have a negative effect on the adoption. The assumed tariffs in our analysis are shown in Table 2, and are comparable to similar products, currently offered by diverse operators.

CapEx and OpEx. Capital Expenditures (CapEx) contain the rollout costs of the new WiMAX network. An important equipment cost originates from the WiMAX BSs, of which the antenna cost depends on the chosen multiple antenna technique. The BSs are installed on pylons or on rooftops of existing buildings. Reusing existing pylons is very often stimulated or even regulated, and then only a rental price is required, just as for placing an antenna on a rooftop. Building a new pylon on the other hand requires a high investment cost. In addition, costs for connecting the BSs to the backhaul network (e.g., fiber network or backhauling via WiMAX) and costs for core equipment in the central office are required. Equipment is renewed every five years (economic and technical lifetime) and a yearly cost erosion of 5% is taken into account.

Operational Expenditures (OpEx) contain the yearly returning costs and they can be divided between network and service related costs. The former consists of costs for operations & planning, maintenance, leasing of the sites (if applicable, e.g., pylons) and backhauling. The latter incorporate costs for marketing, sales & billing and helpdesk.

Regarding the WiMAX spectrum license costs, they can be considered as either CapEx or OpEx, but this is very country-specific and determined by the national telecom regulator.

2.3 Overview

Table 1 and Table 2 summarize the technical characteristics of a Mobile WiMAX network and the offered service types, respectively.

We define three main technical scenarios:

- *Reference scenario* (Table 1): Typical commercial systems currently available.
- *Extended scenario 1*: 'Reference scenario' extended with two more antennas for MIMO at BS side (so 4×2 in DL, and 1×4 in UL).
- *Extended scenario 2*: 'Reference scenario' extended with two more antennas for MIMO at BS side (so 4×2 in DL, and 1×4 in UL) and 4-antenna array AAS at BS side.

Each of the three above scenarios is separated in two subscenarios: one using RS-CC as FEC algorithm, the other using CTC (both are already available in commercial systems).

Table 1. Parameter values of Mobile WiMAX characteristics of reference scenario [5], [10-13]

Parameter	Value
Mobile WiMAX System	
Carrier Frequency	2.5 GHz
Channel Bandwidth	10 MHz
Duplexing	TDD
DL/UL ratio	3:1
FEC	RS-CC
Cyclic Prefix (CP)	1/8
BS Characteristics	
BS Height	30 m
Tx (DL) output power	35 dBm (3.2 W)
Tx (DL) / Rx (UL) antenna gain	16 dB
Tx (DL) / Rx (UL) feeder loss	0.5 dB
Noise Figure (UL)	5 dB
Implementation Loss (UL)	2 dB
Mobile SS Characteristics	
SS Height	2 m
Tx (UL) output power	27 dBm (0.5 W)
Tx (UL) / Rx (DL) antenna gain	2 dB
Tx (UL) / Rx (DL) feeder loss	0 dB
Noise Figure (DL)	7 dB
Implementation Loss (DL)	2 dB
Uplink Subchanneling	
Gain	$-10\log\left[\dfrac{used\ subchannels}{\max\left(\#\ subchannels\right)}\right]$
MIMO: Reference scenario (2x2 in DL, 1x2 in UL)	
MIMO gain DL /UL	6 dB / 3 dB
Cyclic combining gain (DL)	3 dB

Table 2. Parameter values of offered Mobile WiMAX services

Parameter		Value	
Offered service	**Tariff (incl. VAT)**	**Offered bit rate**	
		Downlink	*Uplink*
Nomadicity	13 €/month	512 kbps	128 kbps
Second residence	23 €/month	3 Mbps	256 kbps
Prepaid	9 €/3-hour card	512 kbps	128 kbps
Stand-alone wireless broadband	40 €/month	3 Mbps	256 kbps

3 Link Budget and Coverage Range

The calculation and tabulation of signal powers, gains, losses and SNR for a complete communication link is called a link budget, which is a useful approach for the basic design of a communication system. Using the link budget parameters, the coverage range of the Mobile WiMAX system can be obtained for different modulation schemes. These coverage ranges are necessary to obtain the required number of BSs for the rollout of a Mobile WiMAX network.

Next to the vendor-specific parameters described in Section 2.1, other technical parameters such as path loss, penetration loss (for indoor coverage) and several margins are also necessary for the link budget calculations. These parameters are described in the following paragraphs. Using the technical scenarios introduced in Section 2.3, the results of the coverage ranges for different modulation schemes are shown.

3.1 Path Loss Models

The path loss is defined as the transmit power times the antenna gains divided by the mean received power. Different path loss or propagation models have been defined, and a comparison of them can be found in [5], [13].

The first one is the COST-231 Hata model which is based on empirical results in the 2 GHz band and tends to make very conservative coverage predictions for 2.5 GHz. A second model is the COST-231 Walfisch-Ikegami (W-I) model matching extensive experimental data for flat suburban and urban areas with uniform building height. The COST-231 W-I model gives more precise path loss than the Hata model due to additional data parameters: building heights, street width, building separation and street orientation with respect to the direct radio path. The third one is the Erceg model, which is based on extensive experimental data collected at 1.9 GHz for suburban areas in the US [14], and which has been expanded with a correction factor to cover higher frequencies. The Erceg model has three variants (A, B, and C) based on the terrain type, varying from very hilly terrains with heavy tree density (type A) to flat terrains with low tree density (type C). This model is recommended for Fixed and Mobile WiMAX link budget calculations [5].

3.2 Building Penetration Loss

The received power at indoor locations is significantly attenuated depending on the materials and the construction of the buildings. Several measurements have been carried out to verify real values of attenuation. A large spread of building penetration losses have been obtained in [15] and the practical range varies from 7 dB to 15 dB. For our research, we assume an average building penetration loss of 11 dB with a standard deviation of 6 dB.

3.3 Shadowing, Fade and Interference Margin

Shadowing Margin. A service (offered by the network operator) should have to be provided at more than 90% of all locations within a cell with 99% reliability. To achieve this, a shadowing margin is necessary for accounting the temporary variations in signal strength caused by trees, buildings, etc. located on the signal path between transmitter and receiver. This shadowing margin depends on the used path loss model. For the Erceg model [14], shadowing margins of 13.6 dB (A), 12.3 dB (B), and 10.5 dB (C) are obtained for a coverage requirement of 90% at the edge of the cell. For the Hata and W-I model we use shadowing margins of 10 dB [13].

Note that the shadowing margin at indoor locations is the combined result of the outdoor variation and the variation due to building attenuation. As a consequence, the shadowing margin increases for indoor reception.

Fade Margin. The fade margin takes the yearly availability of the system into account. The link availability is affected by clear-air and rain multipath fading. We use the ITU-R P.530 model described in the ECC report [16] for the fade margin. A fade margin of 10 dB is used which results in a yearly availability of 99.995% for a cell radius of 10 km.

Interference Margin. The system's performance is limited by co-channel interference (CCI). The most common sources of CCI are due to frequency reuse: inter-cell interference (at the cell edges) and intra-cell interference (at the sector boundaries). [5] proposes maximum interference margins of 2 dB and 3 dB for DL and UL, respectively and are also used in our analysis.

3.4 Coverage Range Results

Fig. 1 shows the ranges in DL for different path loss models, outdoor and indoor environments, and BS heights in urban areas with gains and margins described in previous sections (see also Table 1). Note that we include an additional 3 dB margin for Erceg C in urban areas, as this is also used for the COST-231 Hata model in urban areas.

Fig. 1 shows that for the reference scenario (Table 1), the path loss model of Erceg type C delivers ranges of 1300 m and 600 m for QPSK 1/2 and 64-QAM 3/4, respectively. COST-231 Hata and W-I give significantly lower ranges than Erceg type C (e.g., only 500 m can be reached for QPSK 1/2). Upgrading the technology to 'Extended scenario 2 with CTC' improves considerably the ranges (e.g., from 1300 m to 3300 m for QPSK 1/2, using Erceg type C). This motivates the use of technologies such as MIMO and beamforming.

Indoor reception is also of great importance for the usage of Mobile WiMAX applications. Fig. 1 shows the results for indoor reception for 'Extended scenario 2 with CTC', and we observe a significant decrease in range (e.g., from 3300 m to 1500 m for QPSK 1/2). This will have a high influence on the business case of a Mobile WiMAX rollout, especially when the operator wants to guarantee mobile connection at any time at any place. A solution to enhance the coverage range is the use of more additional antennas and/or changing the BS antenna height. If we move the antenna from 30 m to 45 m, we can observe in Fig. 1 an increase in range from 1500 m to 1900 m for QPSK 1/2.

These results indicate the strong influence of the technical parameters on the range and by consequence on the minimum required base stations for a Mobile WiMAX deployment.

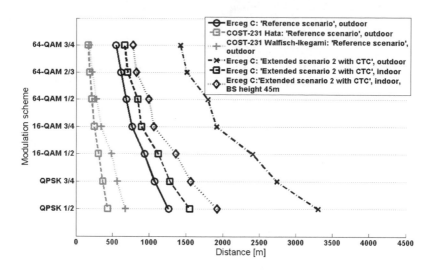

Fig. 1. Coverage range results in downlink for different technical scenarios in urban areas (outdoor and indoor)

4 Economic Feasibility of a Mobile WiMAX Rollout

In this section, we analyze the feasibility of a realistic business case for Mobile Wi-MAX in the period 2008-2017 in Belgium (counting 10.6 million inhabitants on an area of 30,528 km^2). The different technical scenarios (described in Section 2.3) are compared to each other, using Erceg C as path loss model, because of Belgian flat nature.

For our analysis, we assume an S-shaped adoption curve following the Gompertz model, with different input parameters for the four services. Because of the already high penetration of wired access networks in Belgium, Mobile WiMAX will probably not succeed as 'Stand-alone' service, but more as a complementary service ('Nomadicity' and 'Second residence'). We assume for the subscriptions to the 'Stand-alone', 'Nomadicity' and 'Second residence' services, final adoptions of ca. 0.5%, 8.5%, and 5.0% of the households, respectively. Besides, the number of yearly sold prepaid cards corresponds to ca. 3.5% of the Belgian inhabitants (inh). Note however that especially the 'Second residence' service is not only intended for covered house-holds, and that prepaid cards can also be bought by foreigners. So, the above numbers give only a rough indication about the adoption, more precise details are given in [9].

4.1 Determining the Optimal Rollout Area

For a first analysis, we suppose that the network rolled out is deployed in one year, and compare the impact of an increasing number of municipalities where the network is deployed. The rollout sequence is based on population density. In this way, it is possible to estimate the minimal required density to obtain a positive business case for both outdoor and indoor coverage.

Fig. 2 shows the NPV results after ten years (taking into account a discount rate of 15%) for the six technical scenarios, assuming outdoor coverage. The X_1-axis indicates the number of municipalities that is covered, and the X_2-axis represents the corresponding population density. We see that the reference scenario for outdoor coverage generates a positive NPV from a population density of 1000 inh/km^2. We also notice that it is most advantageous to extend the coverage area to all cities with a minimum of 1800 inh/km^2 (where a maximum NPV of 25 M€ is obtained). Further, an evolving technology has a very positive influence on the business case leading to a shift of the curves to the right, and the maximum NPV increases up to 50 M€ for the most optimistic scenario ('Extended scenario 2 with CTC' for a deployment in an area with a minimum population density of 1000 inh/km^2). For this scenario, a rollout in almost all suburban areas (i.e. up to 400 inh/km^2) is feasible.

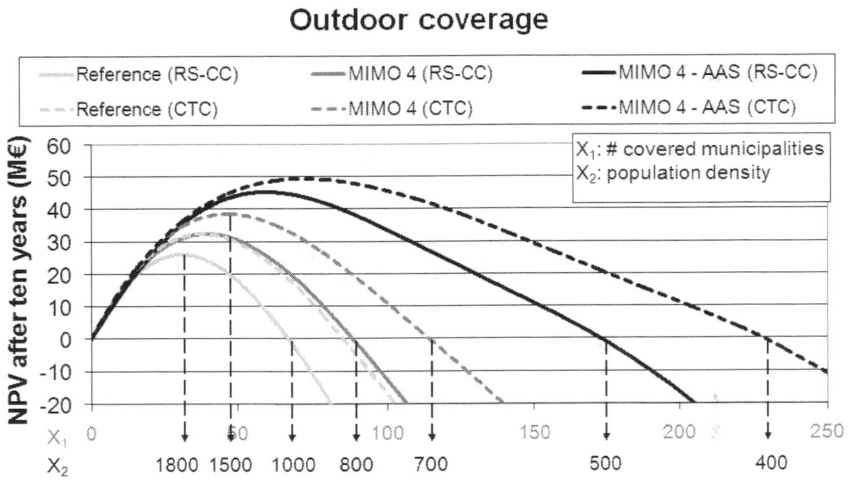

Outdoor coverage

Fig. 2. NPV results for outdoor coverage for six different technical scenarios

Fig. 3 shows that indoor coverage has a very high influence on the business case. With the assumed adoption, indoor coverage is only feasible for a rollout in very densely populated areas: above 5000 inh/km^2 for the reference scenario, and for minimum 1700 inh/km^2 for the most optimistic technical scenario. Most likely however, adoption will change if indoor coverage is guaranteed, but it turns out that the adoption has to be increased by a factor of 4 to 5 to obtain a business case comparable to outdoor coverage.

4.2 Detailed Analysis for a 5-Year Rollout

As mentioned in Section 2.2, a realistic rollout is typically spread over several years. More details about the most suited rollout speed are provided in [9]. Fig. 4 shows the

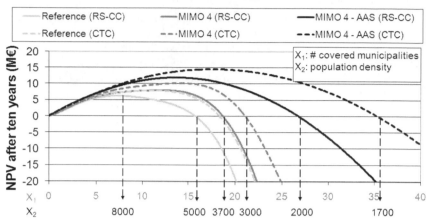

Fig. 3. NPV results for indoor coverage for six different technical scenarios

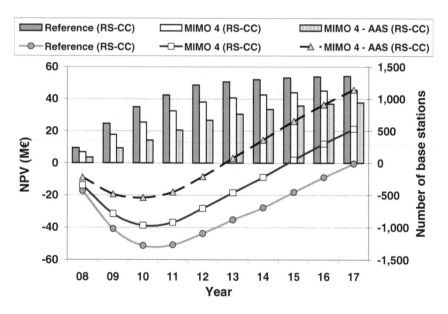

Fig. 4. NPV results (lines) and number of required base stations (columns) for a realistic 5-year rollout and outdoor coverage

outcome of a 5-year rollout in Belgium providing outdoor coverage in all areas with 1000 inh/km² or more (corresponding to 8% of the area and 36% of the population of Belgium). The three technical scenarios with RS-CC as FEC algorithm are compared to each other and the NPV in 2017 matches very well to the corresponding points on Fig. 2. Next to the NPV results, the number of required BSs after each year is also depicted, as this is the main factor responsible for the differences between the technical scenarios. Upgrading the technology from our reference scenario to the 'Extended scenario 2' leads to a 30% decrease of the number of required BSs.

5 Sensitivity Analysis

A detailed sensitivity analysis by using Monte Carlo simulations is performed to assess the potential impact of uncertainties on the project's outcome. The aim is to identify the impact of changes in both technical and economic assumptions.

5.1 Varying Parameters

This section discusses the considered input parameters.

Technical Parameters. A general parameter for link budget variations and the base station heights are two technical input parameters that are varied in our sensitivity analysis.

Link Budget Parameters. A lot of physical characteristics such as the admitted transmit power, antenna gains, additional gains caused by MIMO and AAS, and required SNR are vendor-specific, and can be improved in the future. We have varied the total link budget for our analysis according to a Gaussian distribution with a standard deviation of 1 dB.

Base Station Height. In Section 4 we consider a fixed BS height of 30 m, but this height will of course vary for different municipalities. For our sensitivity analysis, the base station height is varied according to a Gaussian distribution with a mean value of 30 m, and a standard deviation of 10%.

Economic parameters. Different economic input parameters like adoption, costs and revenues, together with the offered services are also considered in our sensitivity analysis.

Adoption, CapEx and OpEx, and Service Tariffs. These are the most important economic parameters and for our sensitivity analysis, we have varied them according to a Gaussian distribution, with a standard deviation of 10%. Note that especially the adoption can be very uncertain, but for a fair comparison we have equally varied the four parameters. In [9], the sensitivity analysis is limited to these four economic parameters.

Offered Bit Rates. Like the service tariff (see Section 2.2), the bit rate for each service is set by the operator. To compare its influence with the other parameters, we have varied it according to a Gaussian distribution, with a standard deviation of 1 Mbps for a 3 Mbps service (and proportionally for the other bit rates).

5.2 Results

Fig. 5 shows the sensitivity results of ten consecutive years for the 5-year rollout scenario. For each year the sensitivity results of different input parameters are analyzed.

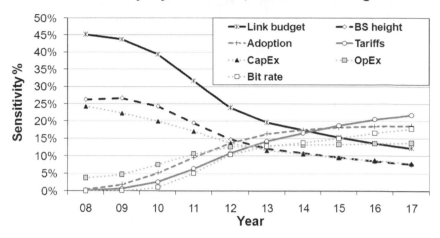

Fig. 5. NPV sensitivity results, taking into account technical as well as economic parameters

One very important conclusion from Fig. 5 is that, during the five rollout years (2008 to 2012), the NPV is more sensitive to both technical parameters than to the economic ones. The link budget and BS heights together experience a sensitivity of more than 50% during the network rollout, which is a consequence of their direct impact on the number of required base stations. On the other hand, after ten years, the adoption and tariff setting, determining the revenues for the operator, are the most influencing parameters (together about 40%). However, we still observe that the influence of the technical parameters remains significant at this time (together about 20%), even in case of a five-year completion of the WiMAX network. This clearly stresses the importance of the technical parameters. Furthermore, adoption and tariffs will certainly influence each other, limiting their common influence on the NPV.

6   Conclusions

In this paper, we have investigated the influence of technical improvements on the economic feasibility of a Mobile WiMAX deployment. Enhanced antenna technologies such as MIMO and beamforming lead to larger WiMAX ranges resulting in a reduction of the required number of base stations. In our business case for Belgium, we obtain a decrease of 30% of the number of base stations between our reference scenario and the most optimistic scenario taking into account MIMO as well as beamforming. Of course, this is very beneficial for the general feasibility of a Mobile Wi-MAX rollout. As we have assumed that the WiMAX network is gradually rolled out from dense urban areas to less populated ones, we can define an indication of the minimum required population density for making the business case feasible. For outdoor coverage in Belgium the most optimistic scenario reduces the required population density with 60%, taking into account an adoption of ca. 15% of the households. The feasibility of the rollout of Mobile WiMAX also strongly depends on whether outdoor or indoor coverage is considered. To guarantee indoor coverage, a much larger number of base stations is required to cope with the indoor penetration loss. This leads to an increase by a factor of 4 to 5 of the required number of subscribers for making the rollout as feasible as the outdoor coverage business case (possible by a higher population density or a higher user adoption).

Both technical and economic parameters greatly influence the business case for a Mobile WiMAX rollout. The sensitivity analysis shows that the technical parameters have a significant influence exceeding the economic parameters during the rollout years (more than 50%). After these years, economic parameters such as adoption and service tariffs are most determining, but the technical ones remain very important. When the feasibility of new technologies, such as Mobile WiMAX, is analyzed, one has to be very careful when selecting the values for technical parameters and especially the link budget parameters.

Acknowledgments. W. Joseph is a Post-Doctoral Fellow at the FWO-V (Research Foundation at Flanders).

References

1. IEEE Std. 802.16 - 2004, IEEE Standard for Local and Metropolitan area Networks: Part 16: Air Interface for fixed broadband wireless access systems (2004)
2. ETSI: ETSI Broadband Radio Access Networks (BRAN) HIPERMAN Physical (PHY) layer. Standards TS 102 177 (2003)
3. IEEE Std. 802.16e - 2005, Amendment to IEEE Standard for Local and Metropolitan area Networks: Part 16: Air Interface for fixed broadband wireless access systems – Physical and Medium Access Control Layers for Combined Fixed and Mobile Operations in Licensed Bands (2006)
4. WiMAX Forum, http://www.wimaxforum.org
5. WiMAX Forum White Paper: Mobile WiMAX-Part 1: A Technical Overview and Performance Evaluation (2006)
6. Wang, F., Ghosh, A., Love, R., Stewart, K., Ratasuk, R., Bachul, R., Sun, Y., Zhao, Q.: IEEE 802.16e System Performance: Analysis and Simulations. In: 2005 IEEE 16th International Symposium on Personal, Indoor and Mobile Radio Communications (PIMRC 2005), vol. 2, pp. 900–904 (2005)
7. Hottinen, A., Kuusela, M., Hugl, K., Zhang, J., Raghothaman, B.: Industrial Embrace of Smart Antennas and MIMO. IEEE Wireless Communications Magazine 13, 8–16 (2006)
8. Lannoo, B., et al.: Business scenarios for a WiMAX deployment in Belgium. In: Proceedings of IEEE Mobile WiMAX 2007 conference, Orlando, pp. 132–137 (2007)
9. Lannoo, B., et al.: Economic Feasibility Study of a Mobile WiMAX Rollout in Belgium: Sensitivity Analysis and Real Options Thinking. In: Proceedings of Broadband Europe, Antwerp (2007)
10. WiMAX Forum White Paper: WiMAX System Evaluation Methodology, V1.0 (2007)
11. Nuaymi, L.: WiMAX: Technology for Broadband Wireless Access. Wiley, Chichester (2007)
12. IEEE 802.16 Broadband Wireless Access Working Group: Simulation Results for Sub-channelization (2002)
13. Joseph, W., Martens, L.: Performance Evaluation of Broadband Fixed Wireless System based on IEEE 802.16. In: IEEE Wireless Communications and Networking Conference (WCNC 2006), Las Vegas, vol. 2, pp. 978–983 (2006)

14. Erceg, V., et al.: An empirically based path loss model for wireless channels in suburban environments. IEEE J. Sel. Areas Commun. 17(7), 1205–1211 (1999)
15. ETSI, TR 102 377 v1.1.1: Digital Video Broadcasting (DVB); DVB-H Implementation Guidelines (2005)
16. ECC report 33: The analysis of the coexistence of FWA cells in the 3.4 – 3.8 GHz band (2003)

Optimizing Energy and Modulation Selection in Multi-Resolution Modulation For Wireless Video Broadcast/Multicast

James She[1], Pin-Han Ho[1] and Basem Shihada[2]

[1] University of Waterloo, Waterloo, ON, N2L 3G1, Canada
{james,pinhan}@bbcr.uwaterloo.ca
http://bbcr.uwaterloo.ca/~james/
[2] King Abdullah University of Science and Technology, Thuwal 23955-6900,
Kingdom of Saudia Arabia

Abstract. Emerging technologies in Broadband Wireless Access (BWA) networks and video coding have enabled high-quality wireless video broadcast/multicast services in metropolitan areas. Joint source-channel coded wireless transmission, especially using hierarchical/superposition coded modulation at the channel, is recognized as an effective and scalable approach to increase the system scalability while tackling the multi-user channel diversity problem. The power allocation and modulation selection problem, however, is subject to a high computational complexity due to the nonlinear formulation and huge solution space. This paper introduces a dynamic programming framework with conditioned parsing, which significantly reduces the search space. The optimized result is further verified with experiments using real video content. The proposed approach effectively serves as a generalized and practical optimization framework that can gauge and optimize a scalable wireless video broadcast/multicast based on multi-resolution modulation in any BWA network.

Keywords: wireless video broadcast/multicast, energy allocation, scalable video coding, superposition coding, optimization.

1 Introduction

Unprecedented advancements in 3/4G Broadband Wireless Access (BWA) networks based on Long Term Evolution (LTE), IEEE 802.11n and IEEE 802.16 (WiMAX) standards as well as scalable video coding technologies, such as H.264/MPEG4 Advanced Video Coding (AVC), have made it possible in provisioning large-scale and high-quality wireless video broadcast/multicast applications, such as mobile/wireless Internet Protocol Television (IPTV), wireless digital signage, e-poster, etc. Adopting the use of wireless broadcast/multicast radio signals for these broadcasting/multicasting applications achieves the best scalable usage of transmission capacity at the base stations (BSs). Instead of the number of receivers, the system scalability is only determined by the number of

X. Jun Hei and L. Cheung (Eds.): AccessNets 2009, LNICST 37, pp. 67–79, 2010.
© Institute for Computer Sciences, Social-Informatics and Telecommunications Engineering 2010

video channels simultaneously provisioned along with their bandwidth requirements. This facilitates the possible largest-scale and highest-quality
wireless video broadcast/multicast, in which multiple receivers simultaneously
receive bandwidth-intensive data of the same video stream from the same broad-
cast/multicast radio signal. One of the legacy problems in the aforementioned
approach is the transmission rate selection under multi-user channel diversity. A
broadcast/multicast signal using monotonic modulation rate could under-utilize
the channel capacity of some receivers with good channel conditions, while being
not decodable by some receivers with bad channel conditions. A straightforward
yet dummy solution could be adopting the most conservative transmission rate
for satisfying as many receivers as possible. This results with the expense of a
much reduced number and quality of video channels that can be jointly provisioned, which certainly leads to a poor economic scale. To tackle such multi-user
channel diversity problem, efficient and robust cross-layer architectures for scalable wireless video broadcast/multicast are recently emerged [1-11], which will be
described in the following section. Among these skillfully engineered cross-layer
architectures, multi-resolution modulated broadcast/multicast radio signals are
commonly generated through hierarchical/superposition coded modulation at
the channel. Each resolution of such modulated signal embeds a successively
refinable quality layer of the original video data that is encoded by a scalable
video coding. Allocating optimal energies and modulation schemes for different
quality layers of video data are the common and critical operational decisions
in these cross-layer approaches. However, it is completely lack of a generalized
optimization framework that gives the global optimum in high computational
efficiency. This motivates the contributions of our work to introduce a generic
optimization framework for energy allocation and modulation selection for this
rapidly growing area in wireless video broadcast/multicast. For the simplicity,
only the word of "multicast" is referred in most of the following discussions,
since all the concepts, technical details and our proposed solution are basically
equivalent or interchangeable in both scenarios of wireless video broadcast and
multicast. The paper is organized as follows. Previous works and some back-
grounds are described in Section 2. Section 3 details a generic system model
and the proposed optimization framework. The section is divided into four sub-
sections to thoroughly detail the performance metric, optimization variables,
objective function and proposed optimization framework. Section 4 provides the
results of optimizations performed using the developed framework followed by
Section 5, where a conclusive discussion is summarized there.

2   Previous Works and Background

2.1   Previous Works

Novel cross-layer architectures of scalable wireless video multicast are actively
introduced in recent years to address the multi-user channel diversity problem
through multi-resolution modulated multicast signals coupled with successive
refinable source coding. One of our earliest works [1] presented the results from

the extensive simulations using real video trace files of High-definition Television (HDTV) content. It proved the effectiveness of this cross-layer approach not just in preserving the use of multicast for higher system scalability. A much better video quality is offered to all receivers all the time, while assuring the base video quality regardless of their average channel conditions. However, formulations and optimizations of energy allocation and modulation selection are not further discussed, which are critical to these kinds of cross-layer architectures. Initial effort on the energy allocation problem was made by Sesia et al. in [2], the optimization problem was formulated by discretizing the continuous fading states, and an algorithm was devised when the source coding layers are assumed with the same rate. This algorithm, however, does not directly yield the optimal energy allocation when the fading states are discrete and pre-specified, nor does it give a closed-form solution for the continuous case. Etemadi et al. also considered this problem in [3], and provided an iterative algorithm by separating the optimization problem into two sub-problems. However, explicit modulation schemes are not considered in their optimization algorithm. In two interesting recent works [4], [5], Ng et al. provided a recursive algorithm with the worst-time complexity of $O(2^M)$ to compute optimal energy allocations across quality layers under finite fading states, where M is the number of fading states. However, it minimizes the distortion in terms of mean-squared errors, which is based on a system model assuming a Gaussian source. Since a video content is never with a Gaussian distribution, such approach can only serve as an analytical purpose but not practically work for a real-world deployment and operation. One of our previous works [6] have developed a generic system model without any assumption of source distribution and incorporated practical modulation schemes for the optimization. The total received bitstreams of each wireless multicast signal is considered as the performance metric, which will be maximized by optimal energy and modulation scheme for achieving the highest video quality. A 3-fold iterative search is introduced to determine optimal allocations of energy and modulation scheme throughout the entire solution space. Some other recent works [7, 8, 9], including those from the industry such as Qualcomm [10, 11], also considered some additional parameters in their proposed cross-layer designs along with the multi-resolution modulations for scalable wireless video multicast. Up to our knowledge, however, there is no any previous attempt in this area to obtain the global optimum through the dynamic programming with a much reduced solution space at a linear complexity of $O(n)$. This paper is the first attempt to introduce such efficient optimization framework that generically applicable to many, if not all, cross-layer architectures for scalable wireless video multicast based on multi-resolution modulation.

2.2   Background - Superposition Coded Multicast

For the purpose of simplicity, the proposed optimization framework is based on a generic cross-layer designed wireless video multicast architecture - Superposition Coded Multicast (SCM) [1] shown in Fig. 1, in which a sample scenario of wireless video multicast with two quality layers is assumed. In fact, the optimization

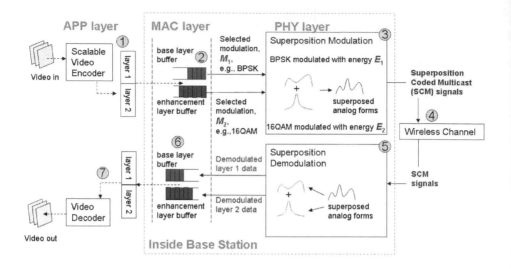

Fig. 1. An overview of SCM for wireless video multicast

framework is designed with a great flexibility to accommodate any arbitrary number of quality layers and even other integrated parameters. It is applicable to other similar architectures of the interests under any total energy transmit limit and collection of modulation schemes.

There are 7 major procedures in SCM to generate and decode a wireless video multicast signal, which has multi-resolution modulated data embedding multiple video quality layers:

(1) A video frame or group of frames (GoF) is encoded by a scalable video encoder into scalable bitstreams with multiple quality layers (e.g., base and enhancement layers).

(2) Video bitstreams of each quality layer is queued into individual buffer for the multi-resolution modulation.

(3) Hierarchical/superposition coded modulation [12, 13, 14] is adopted in this procedure to generate multi-resolution modulated signal. Both of them are well-studied modulation technique for broadcast in the community of information theory. Some background idea is described in the next sub-section. According to the selected modulation, M_i, for layer i, corresponding number of bits in buffer i is modulated individually with an allocated energy E_i. The modulated signal is then superimposed with another signal modulated with energy E_j from buffer j, where $i \neq j$. Note that the order of modulation scheme selected for layer i must not be higher than that for layer j due to the intrinsic mechanism of multi-resolution modulation, where $i < j$.

(4) SCM signals containing bitstreams of base and enhancement layers are multicasted over the wireless channel.

(5) A receiver obtains a SCM multicast signal, and decodes the signal according to its channel condition using the technique of signal-interference cancelation that will be described in the following.

(6) Depending on the receiver's channel condition, a receiver generally can decode the base layer bitstream for a basic video quality. If the receiver's channel condition is good enough, more bitstreams of the enhancement layer can be decoded from the same received SCM signal for a higher video quality.

(7) Decoded bitstreams from each layer are reassembled to reconstruct the video at the receiver's video output, as illustrated in Fig.1.

In summary, the procedure (3) involves the operational parameters, i.e., energy, E_i, and modulation schemes, M_i, to be optimized in each multi-resolution modulated multicast signal for maximizing the video quality.

2.3 Background - Hierarchical/Superposition Coded Modulation

The intrinsic goal of hierarchical/superposition coded (SPC) modulation is to facilitate a transmitter to send two or multiple independent receiver's information within a single wireless radio signal by superimposing two or multiple modulated signals at the channel level. The superposition of two modulated signals is analogous to the vector addition in a signal constellation diagram.

As shown in Fig. 2, x_1 with the information for receiver 1 is modulated using QPSK for a higher transmission rate yet weaker resistance to channel noises, and x_2 with the information for receiver 2 is modulated by BPSK (a lower order of modulation scheme) for stronger resistance to channel noises but slower transmission rate. The superimposed signal, x, is a vector sum of the two modulated signals governed by $x = x_1 + x_2$. In Fig. 2(c), vector x represents the superimposed signal, consisting of symbol '0' from Fig. 2(b) and symbol '01' from

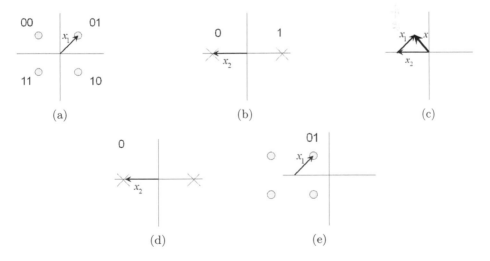

Fig. 2. (a-c) SPC modulation, and (d-e) SPC demodulation

Fig. 2(a). The signal x is then launched as a single wireless broadcast/multicast transmission signal and received by two receivers with diverse channel conditions within the same coverage.

The received signal is expressed as $y_i = x + z_i$, where z_i is the noise perceived by receiver i. The conventional technique to decode the SPC modulated multicast signals is known as Signal-Interference Cancelation (SIC), which is used at receiver i to identify the signal components meant for the noise and other receivers. Receiver i obtains its own information by subtracting those non-corresponding signal components from its received signal y_i. For example, for receiver 1 to decode its data from y_1, it must first use SIC to determine the data meant for receiver 2, x_2, and then subtract x_2 from the received signal y_1. The result of the subtraction using SIC is x_1, which is usually distorted by the noise experienced at receiver 1, i.e., z_1. Note that x_2 is completely decoded by receiver 1 during the process of obtaining x_1 using SIC. The information of x_2 in fact could be utilized by receiver 1, if it refers to the basic quality of video as discussed in this work.

3   The System Model and Optimization Framework

The system model is common in a number of ways to many related previous works, which requires optimized energy allocation and modulation selection under certain transmit energy limit.

3.1   Performance Metric - Total Received Bitstreams

Video quality is always challenging, if not impossible, to be measured quantitatively, due to the subjective importance of content perception in each video frame. According to the rate-distortion theory, a monotonically decreasing trend of the distortion, $D(b_i)$, with an increasing number of bits received is observed as shown in Fig. 3. The bit boundary, b_i, indicates the minimum amount of bitstreams required for the video quality corresponding to layer i.

It is proved in [6], the amount of total received bitstreams, T, of a frame or a GoF decodable by a receiver can serve as an objective and measurable approximation of the perceived video quality. Hence, it is used as the performance metric of the objective function in the optimization. With a sample scenario of two quality layers (i.e., $L = 2$) in this paper, the total received bitstreams, T,

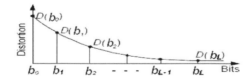

Fig. 3. Distortion vs. bitstream boundaries in a frame or a GoF

is accounted by the received bitstreams of base and enhancement layers, T_1 and T_2, which can be formulated as:

$$T = \sum_{i=1}^{L} T_i \tag{1}$$

3.2 B. Variables - Energy Allocation Ratio and Modulation Scheme

The performance metric, T, in a scalable wireless video multicast architecture based on SCM is subject to the channel conditions, in terms of signal-to-noise ratios (SNRs), for receiving associated SCM multicast signals. In fact, the SNR, γ_i, of the channel condition in receiving bitstream of layer i by a receiver, is determined by the following optimization variables.

Allocation ratio, β: The energy E_i allocated for modulating the bitstream of layer i in each SCM signal is defined with the following condition:

$$E_1(\beta) = (1 - \beta)E \tag{2a}$$
$$E_2(\beta) = \beta E \tag{2b}$$

where E is the total energy transmit limit, and β is the energy allocation ratio for E_1 and E_2. Note that a smaller β value allocates less energy to the enhancement layer. The SNR, γ_i, of the channel condition in receiving bitstream of layer i by a receiver relates to E_i as follows:

$$\gamma_i(\beta) = \frac{cd^{-\alpha}|h^2|\ 10log_{10}\frac{E_i(\beta)}{n_0}}{1 + cd^{-\alpha}|h^2|\sum_{j=i+1}^{L}\ 10log_{10}\frac{E_j(\beta)}{n_0}} \tag{3}$$

where the distance d of the receiver from the BS, α is a path loss exponent ($\alpha = 4$ for urban area, or 3 for rural area), c is some constant, h is a random number from a Rayleigh fading distribution, and the averaged background noise, n_0, towards each transmit symbol. The variables E_1 and E_2 are indeed jointly optimized through the allocation ratio, β.

Modulation scheme, M_i: the modulation/demodulation scheme selected for modulating/demodulating bitstreams in layer i by a receiver has the following conditions:

$$M_i(\gamma_i) = \left\{ \begin{array}{l} 2(BPSK),\ \ if\ \ 8dB \leq \gamma_i < 14dB \\ 4(QPSK),\ \ if\ \ 14dB \leq \gamma_i < 20dB \\ 16(16QAM),\ \ if\ \ 20dB \leq \gamma_i < 26dB \\ 64(64QAM),\ \ if\ \ 26db \leq \gamma_i \end{array} \right\} \tag{4}$$

By selecting a particular modulation M_i for layer i that fulfills the required SNR by a receiver channel, the symbol error, e_i, of decoding layer i in each SCM signal can be derived as below:

Table 1. Settings of a wireless video multicast network

Parameter	Setting
n_0	1
E	10000 (i.e., 40dB)
N	50
c	1

$$e_i(M_i, \gamma_i) = \begin{cases} Q(\sqrt{2\gamma_i}), & if \ M_i = 1 \\ 1 - (1 - 2(1 - 1/\sqrt{M})e^{-3\gamma_i/2(M-1)})^2, & if \ M_i = 2, 4, 6 \end{cases} \quad (5)$$

3.3 The Objective Function

Given the number of transmissions, N, required to multicast a GoF of a 2-layer video as well as other system parameters as shown in Table 1 for a wireless video multicast network, the amount of bitstreams, T_i, of layer i successfully received by a receiver is derived as:

$$T_i(M_i, \gamma_i) = N log_2(M_i) \prod_{j=1}^{i} (1 - e_i(M_i, \gamma_i))^N \quad (6)$$

Note that the existence of a product term in Eq. (6) is due to the decoding dependency of a higher layer on the lower layer required by the video decoder.

A multicast signal is shared by all receivers simultaneously within the coverage, and all receivers should able to decode some bitstreams from each multicast signal for the basic video quality. An objective function can be optimized for maximizing Eq. (1) (i.e., the video quality) subject to a multicast receiver with the worst-channel condition over the duration of a GoF or a reasonable long time-window. The optimization problem can be formulated through the variables, β and M_i below:

$$\max_{\beta, M_i} T = \sum_{i=1}^{L} T_i \quad (7)$$

with the constraints of Eqs. (2)-(5) and $L = 2$.

3.4 The Proposed Optimization Framework

Due to the discreteness and nonlinearity of Eqs. (4) and (5), it is intractable to solve the formulation optimally in Eq. (7) using simple optimization techniques. Note that a base layer have 4 discrete modulation schemes (M_i=1, 2, 4, 6) with a continuous value of energy allocation ratio (1-β), and the enhancement layer also have 4 possible modulation schemes to pair with another continuous value of its allocation ratio, β. A dynamic programming (DP) can assure to obtain the global optimum under each allocation ratio, β, but involve a cost of parsing through a huge search space repeatedly. A 3-fold heuristic search methodology is therefore designed with the following steps, which reduces the search space significantly by conditioned parsings:

(1) Discretizes the range of β values evenly through a fixed interval, δ, and take all discrete values to form a limited set with each of them denoted as β_t, where $t = [1, \ldots, 1/\delta]$. Under many practical total energy transmit limits, for example, $\delta = 0.001$ is already small enough to provide a BS generating a SPC multicast signal with the common SNR range from 0dB to 30dB. A smaller interval, δ, is only required when a smaller granularity of energy value is necessary by a BS system for energy allocations over more quality layers or other operational factors.

(2) For each discrete β_t value, a DP is conducted with the following definitions and conditioned parsings.

    (a) Each stage of DP is referred as a quality layer (i.e., only stage 1 and stage 2 needed in our sample scenario.)

    (b) Each state of stage i corresponds to a possible modulation scheme, M_i, to be selected under a SNR, γ_i, subject to a discrete energy ratio, β_t.

    (c) The benefit of each state is the received bitstream, $T_i(M_i, \gamma_i(\beta_t))$ under selected M_i and β_t.

    (d) Recall the rate-distortion theory discussed in Section 2, it is desirable to receive as many video bitstream as possible reliably when the channel fulfills the SNR requirement of a modulation scheme. The parsing in

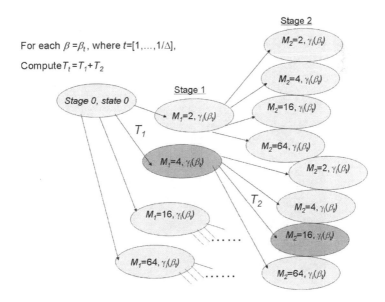

Fig. 4. Conditioned parsing of the DP graph for each value of β_t

each DP graph only considers the state with the highest value of M_i that the channel SNR, $\gamma_i(\beta_t)$ supports with the constraint $M_i \leq M_j$ (where $i < j$) required by SCM. Hence, only two states will be parsed along each graph as shown in Fig. 4.

(e) $T_t = T_1 + T_2$ is tracked and compared, where $t = [1, \dots, 1/\delta]$.

(3) The optimal energy allocation is given by the parse giving the maximum benefit $\{T_t\}$, where $t = [1, \dots, 1/\delta]$.

In summary, the search space for solving Eq. (7) is dramatically reduced to the complexity of $O(n)$, where $n = 1/\delta$ defined by a required granularity of energy values. The computation for optimal energy allocation and modulation selection is linearly efficient for a practical implementation.

4   Experimental Results

The optimal energy and modulation scheme allocations are optimized through the proposed optimization framework to maximize the video quality in a wireless video multicast network based on the settings in Table 1. A general trend is observed that the perceivable SNR in a layer is proportional to the allocated energy on that layer. Hence, SNR is naturally expected to increase as the energy allocated in that layer increases as shown in Fig. 5(a). As less energy is allocated to the base layer when β increases, a receiver only sustains a lower SNR that supports a lower order modulation with slower but more reliable transmission rate, and vice versa. Fig. 5(b) exhibits such dynamics of supportable modulation in each layer with respect to β.

Fig. 6 indicates that the optimal energy allocation ratio is located at $\beta_t^* = 0.134$ (i.e., $E_2 : E_1 = 0.134 : 0.866$) with optimal modulation selections as BPSK and 64QAM for the base and enhancement layers. These optimized settings give

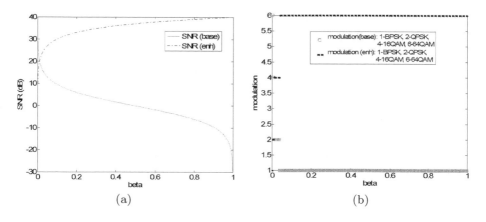

(a)   (b)

Fig. 5. Illustration of (a) SNR, and (b) optimal modulation selection, for each layer with respected to β

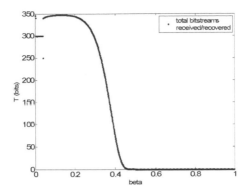

Fig. 6. Total received bitstream, T, vs. allocation ratio, β

the largest amount of receivable bitstreams, T, from both layers (i.e., the highest video quality) over N consecutive transmissions in a scalable wireless video multicast network using SCM signals.

There is no any similar optimization framework previously available at this moment for comparing the search complexity and its impact towards the video quality. However, experimental simulations are realistically conducted in this work with some standard video sequence (in CIF format) using the optimized energy and modulation scheme allocations under various granularity of δ values. The purpose is to evaluate the computational cost and impact of δ values on the visual perception due to the resulting discretized β_t^* values. As demonstrated in Fig. 7(a), a much better video quality is achieved with $\beta_t^*=0.134$ when $\delta=0.001$. Under the same optimized modulation selections as in Fig.7(a), the same video with a less perceptual quality is resulted in Fig. 7(b) with $\beta_t^*=0.25$ when $\delta=0.25$ that exhibits a much faster computation. For a PC running with a 3.2GHz

(a) $\beta_t^*=0.134$ when $\delta=0.001$ (b) $\beta_t^*=0.25$ when $\delta=0.25$

Fig. 7. Video qualities

Pentium CPU and 1G RAM, it only takes about 0.0003 seconds (timed in the Matlab platform) to search the optimized configuration for δ=0.25, but it is about 0.0623 seconds (i.e., $\approx$ 200 times more) for δ=0.001. This provides us an insight for the real-world deployment about the potential tradeoff of video quality with respect to the search complexity (i.e., the computational cost), which is determined by the δ value.

5   Discussions and Conclusions

It is demonstrated that the proposed DP optimization framework can find the global optimum configuration of energy and modulation scheme in a linear complexity of $O(n)$, which results with the highest amount of received bitstreams (i.e., the highest achievable video quality) even the optimization problem is discrete and nonlinear. Although it involves a certain number of graph parsings in multiple DP parsing processes, the optimization framework can efficiently determine the optimized variables by removing unnecessary search spaces through the conditioned parsing in each stage of every DP graph. The results from the optimization framework are further verified with the experiments on some real video sequence using optimized variables, which provided an useful and controllable insight on the tradeoff between the highest achievable video quality and computational cost. The current framework does not consider the sub-carriers assignment in each multicast/broadcast transmission, which are considerably useful and critical to 4G/BWA technologies. Up to our knowledge, this paper is the first attempt to develop such generalized framework for optimizing energy allocation and modulation selection that generically applicable to emerging cross-layer architectures for scalable wireless video broadcast/multicast in any coming BWA network.

References

1. She, J., Hou, F., Ho, P.-H., Xie, L.-L.: IPTV over WiMAX: Key Success Factors, Challenges, and Solutions. IEEE Commun. Magazine 45(8), 87–93 (2007)
2. Sesia, S., Caire, G., Vivier, G.: Lossy transmission over slow-fading AWGN channels: A comparison of progressive, superposition and hybrid approaches. In: Proc. IEEE Int. Symp. Info. Theory, Adelaide, Australia, September 2005, pp. 224–228 (2005)
3. Etemadi, F., Jafarkhani, H.: Optimal layered transmission over quasi-static fading channels. In: Proc. IEEE Int. Symp. Info. Theory, Seattle, WA, July 2006, pp. 1051–1055 (2006)
4. Ng, C., Gündüz, D., Goldsmith, A., Erkip, E.: Recursive power allocation in Gaussian layered broadcast coding with successive refinement. In: Proc. IEEE Int. Conf. Commun. (ICC), Glasgow, Scotland, U.K, June 2007, pp. 889–896 (2007)
5. Ng, C., Gündüz, D., Goldsmith, A., Erkip, E.: Minimum expected distortion in Gaussian layered broadcast coding with successive refinement. In: Proc. IEEE Int. Symp. Info. Theory, Nice, France, June 2007, pp. 2226–2230 (2007)

6. She, J., Yu, X.: A Cross-Layer Design Framework for Robust IPTV Services over IEEE 802.16 Networks. IEEE Journal of Selected Areas on Communications (JSAC) 27(2), 235–245 (2009)
7. Chan, Y.S., Modestino, J.W., Qu, Q., Fan, X.: An End-to-End Embedded Approach for Multicast/Broadcast of Scalable Video over Multiuser CDMA Wireless Networks. IEEE Trans. Multimedia 9(3), 655–667 (2007)
8. Cakareski, Z., Ahmed, N., Dhar, A., Aazhang, B.: Multilevel coding of broadcast video over wireless channels. In: Proc. of IEEE Int. Conf. on Acoustics, Speech, and Signal Processing (ICASSP 2002), August 2002, vol. 3, pp. I-2797– III-2800 (2002)
9. Tian, C., Steiner, A., Shamai (Shitz), S., Diggavi, S.N.: Successive Refinement Via Broadcast: Optimizing Expected Distortion of a Gaussian Source Over a Gaussian Fading Channel. IEEE Trans. Info. Theory 54(7), 2903–2918 (2008)
10. Chari, M.R., Ling, F., Mantravadi, A., Krishnamoorthi, R., Vijayan, R., Walker, G.K., Chandhok, R.: FLO Physical Layer: An Overview. IEEE Trans. Broadcasting 53(1), 145–160 (2007)
11. Qualcomm Incorporated, Hierarchical Coding With Multiple Antenna In A Wireless Communication System, WO/2005/032035, Patent Application, Patent Cooperation Treaty (September 2004)
12. Cover, T.M.: Broadcast channels. IEEE Trans. Info. Theory 18(1), 2–14 (1972)
13. Shamai (Shitz), S.: A broadcast strategy for the Gaussian slowly fading channel. In: Proc. IEEE Int. Symp. Info. Theory, June 1997, p. 150 (1997)
14. Shamai (Shitz), S., Steiner, A.: A broadcast approach for a single-user slowly fading MIMO channel. IEEE Trans. Info. Theory 49(10), 2617–2635 (2003)

System Evaluation of PMI Feedback Schemes for MU-MIMO Pairing

Yinggang Du, Jianfei Tong, Jing Zhang, and Sheng Liu

Wireless Research Department
Huawei Technology Co. Ltd.
Shenzhen, China
duyinggang@huawei.com

Abstract. A Best Companion Cluster (BCC) user terminal (UE) feedback scheme for Multi-User Multi-Input-Multi-Output (MU-MIMO) pairing is proposed in this paper. With this scheme, one UE should feedback both a preferred Precoding Matrix Index (PMI) and a cluster index with least interference to it. The system level simulation results show that this scheme can make a reasonable tradeoff between feedback overhead and throughput, especially when the system load is not so heavy.

Keywords: MU MIMO, pair, best companion cluster, PMI.

1 Introduction

In wireless communication systems, owing to the large overhead of feedback channel state information, the codebook based precoding is adopted for MIMO scenarios in FDD systems. With this scheme, the NodeB and the UE have some predefined common codebooks. In transmission process, one UE will normally feedback its preferred matrix index(PMI) to NodeB, named as Normal Feedback scheme here. With the reported PMI and the help of other system information, the NodeB will allocate one PMI to the UE if this UE is scheduled. It should be noted that the allocated PMI may or may not be same as the reported PMI.

On the way to improve the cell throughput interference among users and different cells has become a large obstacle. On the other hand, more deployed antennas have made MU MIMO possible. Then naturally the question comes: what is the information the UE can provide Node B to pair the users to efficiently control the interference level? Besides the traditional preferred PMI, can one UE feedback more information? Recently, the pairing issue in MU MIMO feedback and scheduling has attracted much attention in both academic and industrial field [1-7].

In [1][2], different scheduling and precoding matrix designs are suggested. To improve the pairing efficiency, more PMI feedbacks are suggested [3][4] for both single cell and multi-cell scenario. In IEEE 802.16m [5][6], the PMI for the interfering cell or interfering user is also similarly suggested.

X. Jun Hei and L. Cheung (Eds.): AccessNets 2009, LNICST 37, pp. 80–88, 2010.

In this paper, different PMI feedback schemes are evaluated for downlink FDD scenario. The first one is the Normal Feedback Scheme (NFS) as mentioned above. The second one[3][4] is that UE feeds back a best PMI with highest SNR(Signal to Noise Ratio) and one or a set of best interfering PMI(s) with least interference to it, named Best Companion PMI (BCP). Based on the second scheme, the third one is suggested that the UE feeds back the best PMI with highest SINR and the cluster index that includes the best interfering PMI, named Best Companion Cluster (BCC). In Section 2, these three schemes and corresponding scheduling and pairing schemes will be described in more details. Section 3 provides the system simulation results and summary will be given in Section 4.

2 Feedback and Pairing Schemes

For a target user i, the received signal can be modeled as:

$$\mathbf{y}_i = \mathbf{H}_i \mathbf{F}_i x_i + \sum_{j=1, j\neq i}^{K} \mathbf{H}_i \mathbf{F}_j x_j + \mathbf{N}_i \qquad (1)$$

Where $\mathbf{H}i$ is the Nr×Nt channel gain matrix from Nt transmit antennas to Nr receive antennas, $\mathbf{F}i$ is the precoding vector for i_{th} user, x_i is the to-be-transmitted symbol of i_{th} user, and $\mathbf{N}i$ is additive white Gaussian noise (AWGN) with variance σ^2.

2.1 NFS

For NFS, the best PMI $\mathbf{F}_k$ for a user can be selected from a codebook based on the following rule of maximizing the received signal power:

$$\mathbf{F}_k = \arg\max_{i\in[1,...P]}\left(\left|\mathbf{H}_k \mathbf{F}_i\right|^2\right) \qquad (2)$$

where P is the largest PMI index of the codebook.

With this feedback, NodeB can identify the best PMI for the user but it does not know how to pair another user to make the mutual interference as less as possible. Therefore, NodeB can only make random pairing. Correspondingly the UE will have to assume the paired user to have highest interference to obtain a workable CQI (Channel Quality Information) as:

$$CQI_k = \min_{j\in[1,...,P], j\neq k} \frac{\left|\mathbf{H}_k \mathbf{F}_k\right|^2}{\sigma^2 + \left|\mathbf{H}_k \mathbf{F}_j\right|^2} \qquad (3)$$

2.2 BCP

In [3][4][5], the Best Companion Pairing (BCP) is suggested to coordinate the multiple users in both single cell scenario and multi-cell scenarios. Additional feedback information of so- called "Best Companion" indexes are provided, which is actually the Precoding Matrix Index (PMI) of to-be-paired user with least interference to the target user, written as $(\mathbf{F}_k, \mathbf{F}_l)$.

$$\mathbf{F}_k = \arg\max_{i\in[1,...P]}\left(\left|\mathbf{H}_k\mathbf{F}_i\right|^2\right)$$

$$\mathbf{F}_l = \arg\min_{i\in[1,...P]}\left(\left|\mathbf{H}_k\mathbf{F}_i\right|^2\right)$$

(4)

Equation (4) gives the example that one user feeds back one best PMI $\mathbf{F}_k$ and one best interfering PMI $\mathbf{F}_l$ to NodeB. In that case, the CQI can be calculated as:

$$CQI_k = \frac{\left|\mathbf{H}_k\mathbf{F}_k\right|^2}{\sigma^2 + \left|\mathbf{H}_k\mathbf{F}_l\right|^2}$$

(5)

With this scheme, for single cell scenario, to minimize the intra-cell mutual MU-MIMO interference, extra codebook-based information of the to-be-paired user(s) with least interference is reported back to NodeB. For multi-cell scenarios, to minimize the inter-cell interference, UE may report extra codebook-based information to its serving Node B to make the best companion pair and this information can be shared via backhaul to the strongest interfering neighbor cells for coordinated scheduling.

In scheduling, NodeB will try to find two users with feedbacks of $(\mathbf{F}_k, \mathbf{F}_l)$ for one user and $(\mathbf{F}_l, \mathbf{F}_k)$ for the other one. In that case, CQI needs not to be revised. If there is no such pair, there are two options: one is to fall back to single user mode; the other one is to randomly or with some rule choose another user. For both options, accurate CQI need to be recalculated. However, more accurate CQI generally means more overhead, which is another tradeoff to be taken and out of the discussion in this paper.

To make the scheduling more efficient and flexible, it is suggested that a set of Best Companion PMI be reported back to Node B, where the set gives the PMIs for which the intra-cell or inter-cell interference remains below a certain threshold.

However, more Best Companion PMIs means higher feedback overhead. Hence we investigate the possibility of reducing the PMI feedback without losing the interfering information, which leads to our scheme of BCC.

2.3   BCC

Considering the correlation between different PMIs, the set of PMIs can be clustered together. That is, besides the preferred PMI, UE may also need to feedback the index of clusters that has weakest interference:

$$\mathbf{F}_k = \arg\max_{i\in[1,...P]}\left(\left|\mathbf{H}_k\mathbf{F}_i\right|^2\right)$$

$$\mathbf{C}_l = \arg\min_{i\in[1,...T],l\in[1,...Q]}\left(\left|\mathbf{H}_k\mathbf{F}_i\right|^2\right)$$

(6)

where $\mathbf{C}_l$ is the best interfering cluster and satisfies $\mathbf{F}_l \in \mathbf{C}_l$, Q is the number of clusters of the codebook and T is the number of PMI within a cluster. Note that T may be different for different cluster.

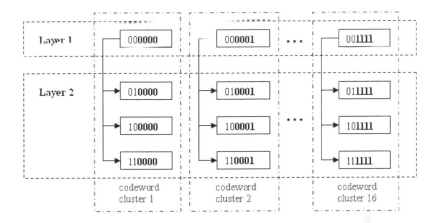

Fig. 1. Cluster Construction

Following the definition style in [3][4], this scheme can be named best companion cluster (BCC). To elaborate the issue more clearly, we can take a nesty structure codebook as an example, where the clusters can be constructed as shown in Fig.1 assuming 6bit PMI. In this scheme, all these 64 PMIs are separated into 16 clusters and each cluster has 4 PMI (Q=16, T=4). If one UE selects its preferred PMI from one cluster with 6 bits, it need only feedback the additional interfering cluster index of its best companion pairing PMI with weakest interference with only 4 bits. That is, the total feedback overhead of $\mathbf{F}_k$ and $\mathbf{C}_l$ is 10 bits. In multi-cell scenario, this cluster index will be also shared via backhaul. If this UE is scheduled, NodeB can pair another user with any PMI within the interfering cluster feedback by this UE.

Owing to the pairing PMI uncertainty within the cluster, the CQI calculation will have some ambiguity:

$$CQI_k = \min_{j \in [1,...,T]} \frac{\left| \mathbf{H}_k \mathbf{F}_k \right|^2}{\sigma^2 + \left| \mathbf{H}_k \mathbf{F}_j \right|^2} \tag{7}$$

Clearly, $\mathbf{F}_k$ and any $\mathbf{F}_j$ belong to different clusters and this ambiguity is in generally less than the calculation shown in (3), i.e., the CQI in (3) provides an upper bound for the one in (7). To improve the CQI, we can also take the average CQI from all PMIs in the interfering cluster:

$$CQI_k = \frac{1}{T} \sum_{j=1}^{T} \frac{\left| \mathbf{H}_k \mathbf{F}_k \right|^2}{\sigma^2 + \left| \mathbf{H}_k \mathbf{F}_j \right|^2} \tag{8}$$

2.4 Scheduling

The scheduling procedure to pair two UE in NodeB can be described as below:

1. Classification: Users which indicate the same preferred cluster C_k and the same interference cluster C_l ($F_k \in C_k$, $F_l \in C_l$)are classified into one class, denoted by (C_k, C_l), where C_k and C_l represent the cluster index. Class (C_k, C_l) and Class (C_l, C_k) are taken as one class pair, which exhibits good property of mutual interference;

2. Selection: Search out one UE in Class (C_k, C_l) and another one UE in Class (C_l, C_k) to combine the companion pair to meet the proportional fairness rule (or with other selection rule) with reported CQI, QoS requirement, etc;

3. Scheduling and Allocation: Schedule the UE pair found in Step 2 for transmission and allocate corresponding resource, modulation and coding scheme, etc.

3 Simulation

The system level simulation parameter configuration can be referred in Table A.1 in the appendix and the throughput is evaluated and compared. Each UE is assumed to be allocated only one stream and two UE will be paired to make the MU MIMO transmission. Consequently, for the given LTE 4Tx codebook[8] shown in Table A.2 in the appendix, we separated 16 PMI into 4 clusters, each with $T=4$ and $Q=4$: Cluster 0 with PMI index: {0,4,8,12}, Cluster 1: {1,5,9,13}, Cluster 2: {2,6,10,14} and Cluster 3: {3,7,11,15}. It can be found that one PMI is orthogonal to any PMI in any other cluster but the PMIs within same cluster are not orthogonal to each other, which to some degree explains the clustering principle shown in Fig.1.

The throughput is compared in Fig.2 in Mbps for 10 uers and 30 users separately while the relative gain is given in Table 1. With the results, the BCP (Best Companion PMI) scheme with 8 bits feedback can provide 7.17% and 14.16% system throughput gain over the Normal Feedback Scheme with 4 bits feedback corresponding 10 users and 30 users ineach cell respectively. While Best Companion Cluster scheme with 6 bits feedback provides 5.53% and 7.97% gain over Normal Feedback Scheme, corresponding 10 users and 30 users in each cell respectively. With less users, the gap between BCP and BCC is smaller. BCC is more robust to the number of users, i.e., system load. The reason is that BCP feeds back the accurate pairing PMI whileany PMI within the interfering cluster can be paired in BCC, which makes the pairing probability for BCP more sensitive to the number of users than BCC. That is why more PMIs are suggested to feedback in [3][4]. It seems that Best Companion Cluster can make relative reasonable trade-off among feedback overhead and throughput, especially in light system load.

Actually, we have also made the simulation to compare the throughput performance of 4bit and 6bit DFT codebook for NFS scheme, but unfortunately we have not seen much difference for such DFT codebooks. With two more bits overhead, the throughput for 6bit DFT codebook only provides throughput gain of less than 1%. The reason lies in the fact that the increase of the codebook size from 16 (4bits) to 64 (6bits) leads to better granularity on one hand while more sensitivity to the channel mismatch on the other hand, which makes it not much helpful to improve the system throughput. Consequently, we have not shown the 6bit NFS results here.

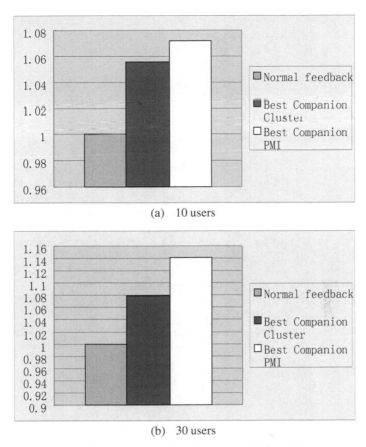

(a)   10 users

(b)   30 users

Fig. 2. Relative gain in total average cell throughput

Table 1. Relative throughput gain over Normal Feedback Scheme in total average cell throughput

Scenario	Feedback scheme	No. of Feedback bits	Relative gain
10 users	Normal Feedback Scheme	4	-
	Best Companion PMI	8	7.17%
	Best Companion Cluster	6	5.53%
30 users	Normal Feedback Scheme	4	-
	Best Companion PMI	8	14.16%
	Best Companion Cluster	6	7.97%

4   Conclusions

Different PMI feedback schemes for MU MIMO companion are evaluated in this contribution. The Normal Feedback scheme has least feedback bits but with least throughput. The Best Companion PMI scheme provides the highest throughput but with highest feedback. The Best Companion Cluster scheme gives a reasonable compromise between the feedback overhead and throughput. It should be further investigated on how to make better compromise. The CQI estimation can also be further improved.

References

1. Hottinen, A., Viterbo, E.: Optimal user pairing in downlink MU-MIMO with transmit precoding. In: 6th International Symposium on Modeling and Optimization in Mobile, Ad Hoc, and Wireless Networks and Workshops, 2008. WiOPT 2008, April 1-3, pp. 97–99 (2008)
2. Chua, W.S., Yuen, C., Guan, Y.L.: Limited feedback for multi-antenna multi-user communications with Generalized Multi-Unitary Decomposition. In: IEEE 19th International Symposium on Personal, Indoor and Mobile Radio Communications, 2008. PIMRC 2008, September 15-18, pp. 1–5 (2008)
3. Alcatel-Lucent: UE PMI feedback signalling for user pairing/ coordination, R1-090777, 3GPP TSG RAN WG1 #56, Athens, Greece, February 9-13 (2009)
4. Alcatel-Lucent: Best Companion reporting for improved single-cell MU-MIMO pairing, R1-090926,TSG RAN WG1 #56, Athens, Greece (February 2009)
5. Fujitsu: Proposal for user grouping scheme for MU-MIMO, IEEE 802.16m-08_392, IEEE 802.16 #55 Meeting, Macau, May 5-8 (2008)
6. LG Electronics, Huawei, Fujitsu, ETRI, MediaTek Inc., ITRI, Proposed harmonized text for DL MIMO SDD text : PMI for interfering cell, IEEE C80216m-08_859r1, IEEE 802.16 #56 Meeting, Denver, USA, July 14-17 (2008)
7. Koivisto, T.: LTE-Advanced research in 3GPP, 2008 Nokia GIGA seminar 2008 - LTE-Advanced (2008)
8. 3GPP TS 36.211: Evolved Universal Terrestrial Radio Access (E-UTRA); Physical channels and modulation

Appendix: Simulation Assumptions and Codebooks

Table A.1. Simulation assumptions

Parameter	Assumption
Cellular Layout	Hexagonal grid, 19 sites, 3 sectors per site
Inter-site distance	500m
Load	Average 10/30 UE per sector
Bandwidth	10MHz
Total BS TX power (Ptotal)	46dBm
Noise figure at UE	9dB
Lognormal Shadowing with shadowing standard deviation	8 dB
Channel model	Spatial Channel Model (SCM)
UE speeds of interest	3Km/h
Number of antenna elements (BS, UE)	(4, 2)
Antenna separation (BS, UE) [times of wavelength]	(10, 0.5)
Antenna type	Polarized
Traffic model	Full buffer
Link to system interface	Mutual information
CQI / ACK/NAK feedback delay	4 ms
Scheduler	Proportional Fair
HARQ	HARQ-CC (Chase Combing); 8 processes Maximum 3 transmission times
Receiver algorithm	MMSE

Table A.2. LTE 4Tx Rank 1 Codebook

PMI	u_n	Rank:1
0	$u_0 = \begin{bmatrix} 1 & -1 & -1 & -1 \end{bmatrix}^T$	$W_0^{\{1\}}$
1	$u_1 = \begin{bmatrix} 1 & -j & 1 & j \end{bmatrix}^T$	$W_1^{\{1\}}$
2	$u_2 = \begin{bmatrix} 1 & 1 & -1 & 1 \end{bmatrix}^T$	$W_2^{\{1\}}$
3	$u_3 = \begin{bmatrix} 1 & j & 1 & -j \end{bmatrix}^T$	$W_3^{\{1\}}$
4	$u_4 = \begin{bmatrix} 1 & (-1-j)/\sqrt{2} & -j & (1-j)/\sqrt{2} \end{bmatrix}^T$	$W_4^{\{1\}}$
5	$u_5 = \begin{bmatrix} 1 & (1-j)/\sqrt{2} & j & (-1-j)/\sqrt{2} \end{bmatrix}^T$	$W_5^{\{1\}}$
6	$u_6 = \begin{bmatrix} 1 & (1+j)/\sqrt{2} & -j & (-1+j)/\sqrt{2} \end{bmatrix}^T$	$W_6^{\{1\}}$
7	$u_7 = \begin{bmatrix} 1 & (-1+j)/\sqrt{2} & j & (1+j)/\sqrt{2} \end{bmatrix}^T$	$W_7^{\{1\}}$
8	$u_8 = \begin{bmatrix} 1 & -1 & 1 & 1 \end{bmatrix}^T$	$W_8^{\{1\}}$
9	$u_9 = \begin{bmatrix} 1 & -j & -1 & -j \end{bmatrix}^T$	$W_9^{\{1\}}$
10	$u_{10} = \begin{bmatrix} 1 & 1 & 1 & -1 \end{bmatrix}^T$	$W_{10}^{\{1\}}$
11	$u_{11} = \begin{bmatrix} 1 & j & -1 & j \end{bmatrix}^T$	$W_{11}^{\{1\}}$
12	$u_{12} = \begin{bmatrix} 1 & -1 & -1 & 1 \end{bmatrix}^T$	$W_{12}^{\{1\}}$
13	$u_{13} = \begin{bmatrix} 1 & -1 & 1 & -1 \end{bmatrix}^T$	$W_{13}^{\{1\}}$
14	$u_{14} = \begin{bmatrix} 1 & 1 & -1 & -1 \end{bmatrix}^T$	$W_{14}^{\{1\}}$
15	$u_{15} = \begin{bmatrix} 1 & 1 & 1 & 1 \end{bmatrix}^T$	$W_{15}^{\{1\}}$

On Mitigating Packet Reordering in FiWi Networks

Shiliang Li[1,3], Jianping Wang[1], Chunming Qiao[2], and Bei Hua[3]

[1] Department of Computer Science, City University of Hong Kong, Hong Kong
{lshiliang2,jianwang}@cityu.edu.hk
[2] Department of Computer Science and Engineering, SUNY at Buffalo, NY
qiao@computer.org
[3] Department of Computer Science, University of Science and Technology of China
bhua@ustc.edu.cn

Abstract. In an integrated fiber and wireless (FiWi) access network, multi-path routing may be applied in the wireless subnetwork to improve throughput. Due to different delays along multiple paths, packets may arrive out of order, which may cause TCP performance degradation. Although the effect of packet reordering due to multi-path routing has been well studied, remedy solutions are either to schedule packets at the source node to proactively reduce the chance of packet reordering, or to modify TCP protocol. Resequencing packets arrived out-of-order has only been considered at the end systems which can cause long delay as packets must be buffered until there is no sequence gap. As all traffic in a FiWi network is sent to the Optical Line Terminal (OLT), the OLT serves as a convergence node which naturally makes it possible to resequence packets at the OLT before they are sent to the Internet. However, the challenge is that OLT must re-sequence packets effectively with a very small delay to avoid a performance hit. In this paper, we propose a scheduling algorithm at the OLT to resequence packets while providing fairness. Simulation results validate that our packet scheduling algorithm is effective in improving the performance of TCP flows. Since resequencing is conducted in the access network which has a much fewer number of flows compared with those at routers, our proposed work provides a scalable solution to mitigate the side-effect of packet reordering caused by multi-path routing.

Keywords: FiWi, PON, WMN, Packet Reordering, Multi-path Routing, Resequence.

1 Introduction

Recently, the hybrid fiber-wireless (FiWi) [1] access network integrating the passive optical networks (PONs) and wireless mesh networks (WMNs) has been proposed to provide cost efficient, high bandwidth and ubiquitous last mile Internet access. A FiWi network consists of a PON subnetwork and a wireless subnetwork as shown in Fig. 1. In the PON subnetwork of a FiWi network, Optical Line Terminal (OLT) resides in a Central Office (CO) and feeds multiple

X. Jun Hei and L. Cheung (Eds.): AccessNets 2009, LNICST 37, pp. 89–102, 2010.

Optical Network Units (ONU). In the wireless subnetwork of a FiWi network, WMN is deployed for ubiquitous communications at users' premises. Typically, the WMN consists of multiple gateways for the Internet access where one or more gateways can be connected to an ONU through wired line, a group of wireless mesh routers that provide multi-hop wireless communications and a group of wireless mesh clients.

Multi-path routing has been widely considered in the wireless/wired networks as an approach to achieve load balancing, fault tolerance, and a higher network throughput [2–5]. In a FiWi network, packets of a flow can be sent through multiple paths in the wireless subnetwork to the OLT so that network congestion is alleviated and throughput can be improved. These packets, however, may be reordered when they arrive at the OLT due to delay variance along different paths. As a result, the increase of throughput by exploiting multi-path routing may be affected by packet reordering [6, 7].

In the literature, many efforts have been made to mitigate the effects of packet reordering caused by multi-path routing. The work can be classified into three main categories: (1) to determine which path each packet should be sent to so that packet reordering can be proactively avoided. FLARE is introduced as a traffic splitting algorithm in [10] where it is shown that it is possible to systematically slice a TCP flow across multiple paths without causing packet reordering. The work in [8] studied how to route packets efficiently at the sender side. Two traffic congestion control techniques, namely, flow assignment and packet scheduling, have been investigated in [8]. (2) to modify the TCP protocol to improve TCP performance. The work in this category needs to be implemented at TCP clients to generate congestion responses when packet reordering occurs, and/or at participating routers to report packet dropping information to TCP clients. Most reordering-tolerant approaches are sender-side solutions which increase the threshold of fast retransmission. RR-TCP [11] uses the false fast retransmission avoidance ratio (FA ratio) to adjust *dupthresh*. The work in [12] provides receiver-side solutions which delay ACKs for out-of-order segments and immediately sends ACKs for retransmitted segments. A more comprehensive survey of reordering-tolerant algorithms can be found in [14]. (3) to resequence packets at the end systems. Resequencing packets to deliver the arrived packets to the application in sequence has been well studied in the literature [15, 16] where resequencing is conducted at the end application. In such work, packets stay in the resequencing buffer until there is no sequencing gap in the accepted packets.

All above mentioned works resolve the effects of packet reordering at either the source node or the destination node. One question arose is whether some work can be done at the intermediate "nodes" to resequence out-of-order packets. Resequencing is seldom considered at the routers since a router may forward packets for many flows. Obviously, if an "intermediate" node which can resequence packets is at the access network where there are relatively fewer number of flows than routers, resequencing can be considered as one of the effective approaches to avoid packet reordering at the core network. In a FiWi network, the OLT serves as the gateway to the core network. Since there is only a single path from the OLT to the destination in the core network for each connection, it can be expected that packets from each flow will arrive at their destination in almost the same order as they are sent from the OLT. In other words, if the OLT can resequence the packets, it can mitigate the effects of packet reordering caused by multi-path routing in the wireless subnetwork. Thus, throughput can be improved. Compared with resequencing at the end system, resequencing at the OLT requires negligible resequencing delay as packets may experience un-predictable delay at the core network and we can not afford long resequencing delay at the access network. The tight resequencing delay implies that 100% in-order resequencing is impossible to achieve when resequencing is conducted at the intermediate node. Thus, a fast resequencing algorithm which can reduce the out-of-order probability of packets departing from the OLT is desired.

In this paper, given the out-of-order (OOD) packet arrivals at the OLT from different flows, we propose a packet scheduling algorithm at the OLT which aims to resequence the packets of each flow to assure possible in-order arrivals at the destinations. The work proposed in this paper requires that the OLT is capable of maintaining some information for each flow (as to be introduced shortly, minimum amount of information for each flow is maintained at the OLT to provide scalabil-ity). We would like to note that some scheduling algorithms at the E-PON OLT [17] has been proposed to provide per-flow and per-class forwarding discipline to satisfy various types of QoS constraints for downstream traffic.

The rest of the paper is organized as follows. In Section 2, we give an example to demonstrate how resequencing may be able to mitigate the effect of packet reordering. The problem description is given in Section 3. Section 4 presents the scheduling algorithm. Section 5 evaluates the proposed algorithm through simulations, and Section 6 concludes the paper.

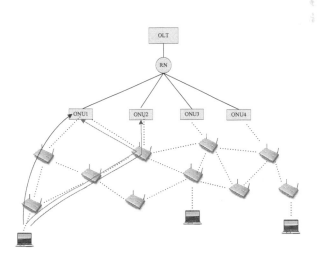

Fig. 1. A conceptual architecture of FiWi Networks

2   Motivation Example

As mentioned earlier, the OLT serves as a *convergence* node in the FiWi network. For the upstream traffic, the OLT needs to send packets from different flows to their destinations where the sending sequence at the OLT will be the last chance in a FiWi network to ensure in-order packet delivery in the core network. In this section, we give one motivation example to demonstrate how packet scheduling algorithm can resequence packets and mitigate the effect of packet reordering.

Suppose that there are two flows sending packets through the OLT to different destinations as shown in Fig. 2 (a). Seven packets are now in the OLT's buffer, and two packets will arrive at the end of time slots 4 and 5 respectively. We denote $P_{i,j}$ as the j-th packet of flow i, and $A_{i,j}$ as the acknowledgment of $P_{i,j-1}$. The service rate of the OLT's outgoing link is one packet per time slot.

Suppose that Round Robin (RR) scheduling mechanism is applied at the OLT. Then these packets will arrive at destinations in the order of $\{P_{1,1}, P_{1,3}, P_{1,4}, P_{1,5}, P_{1,2}\}$ and $\{P_{2,1}, P_{2,2}, P_{2,4}, P_{2,3}\}$, respectively (Fig. 2 (b)). Suppose that packets from a flow will arrive at their destination following the same order as they depart from the OLT, then we will get the following ACK sequences: $\{A_{1,2}, A_{1,2}, A_{1,2}, A_{1,2}, A_{1,6}\}$ and $\{A_{2,2}, A_{2,3}, A_{2,3}, A_{2,5}\}$ from the perspective of the OLT. Thus, it is very likely that the TCP sender of flow 1 will receive three duplicate ACKs ($A_{1,2}$), and then will perform fast retransmission and fast recovery. This will cause multiplicative decrease (and additive increase) in TCP's congestion window size. However, this is a spurious segment retransmission and keeping congestion window small is unnecessary. In fact, the network has not been in congestion condition yet. Therefore, RR scheduling at the OLT can not utilize bandwidth efficiently and may reduce throughput significantly.

We observe that if the OLT can estimate the number of duplicate ACKs (denote by $dack'$) which may be caused by scheduling the head-of-line (HOL) packet of each flow and schedule the HOL packet of the flow with the lowest $dack'$, it increases the chance for the OLT to resequence packets for flows with higher $dack'$. Using such an observation, for the example given in Fig. 2, the OLT will postpone the departure of packet $P_{1,3}$ and sends $P_{2,2}$ instead since flow 2's $dack'$ (0) is lower than flow 1's $dack'(1)$, as shown in Fig. 2 (c). After sending 4 packets, packet $P_{1,2}$ has already arrived at the OLT's buffer (Fig. 2 (d)). Thus, we transmit $P_{1,2}$ immediately since flow 1's $dack'$ (0) is lower than flow 2's $dack'$ (1)(Fig. 2 (e)). After sending all packets according to the order given in Fig. 2 (f)), we expect to receive the following ACK sequences $\{A_{1,2}, A_{1,2}, A_{1,4}, A_{1,5}, A_{1,6}\}$ for flow 1 and $\{A_{2,2}, A_{2,3}, A_{2,4}, A_{2,5}\}$ for flow 2. All packets are sent out within 9 time slots with only one duplicate ACK ($A_{1,2}$). It is inadequate to trigger fast retransmission and fast recovery. This motivation example shows that a good packet scheduling algorithm at the OLT can resequence packets to reduce the effect of packet reordering caused by the multi-path routing in wireless subnetwork and assure possible in-order arrivals at destinations. This paper focuses on designing such a packet scheduling algorithm at the OLT.

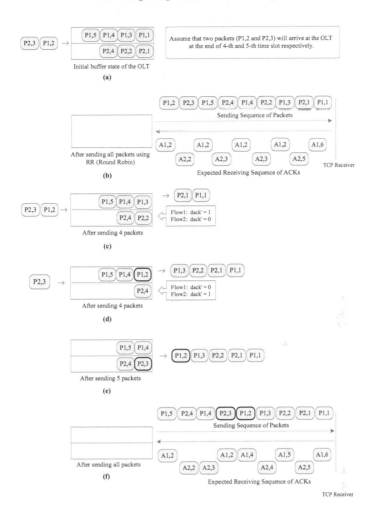

Fig. 2. An illustration of packet scheduling at the OLT and it's impact on TCP performance

3 Problem Description

Suppose that a pool of packets arrive dynamically from F different flows with packet reordering at the OLT where the OLT maintains a queue for each flow. Suppose that the time is partitioned into equal time slots where in each time slot at most one packet can be sent out from the OLT to the Internet. At each time slot, the OLT needs to determine which flow (queue)'s packet should be sent and which packet from that selected flow (queue) should be sent. As duplicate ACKs (three dupacks) may trigger the fast retransmission and fast recovery, which will cause multiplicative decrease (and additive increase) in TCP's congestion window size (*cwnd*), it is important to avoid triggering three dupacks when we schedule packets. To achieve such a goal, at each time slot, a flow should be selected for transmission if it will most unlikely reduce the sender's *cwnd* and when a flow is selected for transmission, the packet with the smallest sequence number in the queue should be scheduled. In other words, we can implement a min-heap queue for each flow and assure that the HOL packet of each flow has the smallest sequence number. On the other hand, fairness among flows shall also been considered when we schedule packets.

In this section, we first analyze the potential change of the sender's *cwnd* if a flow's HOL packet is scheduled for transmission. Suppose that $P_{i,j}$ is the head packet of queue i at time t. Let $dack_i'(t)$ denote the total number of dupacks which may be caused by sending $P_{i,j}$. The impact of $dack_i'(t)$ on the change of the sender's *cwnd* can be summarized as follows:

– In-order delivery,
  • case 1: $dack_i'(t) = 0$ where $P_{i,j}$ is the expected packet. To transmit $P_{i,j}$ will increase the sender's *cwnd* and allow the receiver to generate cumulative ACKs.
– Out-of-order delivery,
  • case 2: $dack_i'(t) = 1$. To transmit $P_{i,j}$ will cause one dupack to be sent to the sender, which, however, will not cause any change on the sender's *cwnd*,
  • case 3: $dack_i'(t) = 2$, Same to case 2.
  • case 4: $dack_i'(t) = 3$. To transmit $P_{i,j}$ will cause one dupack to be sent to the sender, which will consequently trigger the fast retransmission and cause the reduction on the sender's *cwnd*;
  • case 5: $dack_i'(t) > 3$, TCP sender is now at the stage of fast recovery. To send $P_{i,j}$ will cause one dupack to be sent to the sender and increase the sender's *cwnd*.

As the sender's *cwnd* in both case 1 and case 5 will be increased, such a flow i should have the highest priority to be scheduled for transmission at time slot t. Case 4 will cause the reduction on the sender's *cwnd*, thus, such a flow should be scheduled later with the hope that the expected packet will arrive at the queue. Case 2 and case 3 will not cause the immediate change of the sender's *cwnd* and can be assigned with the priority between the highest priority and the lowest priority.

Let $p_i(t)$ be the priority of sending $P_{i,j}$, which is defined as follows:

$$p_i(t) = \begin{cases} 2 & \text{if } dack_i'(t) = 0 \text{ or } dack_i'(t) > 3 \\ 1 & \text{if } dack_i'(t) = 1 \text{ or } dack_i'(t) = 2 \\ 0 & \text{if } dack_i'(t) = 3 \end{cases} \tag{1}$$

In order to mitigate the effect of packet reordering, the HOL packet of queue i^* with the maximum $p_{i^*}(t)$ will be scheduled, which enhances the chance of other queues with lower priority value to be resequenced.

Apart from dupack, we also need to consider fairness among flows. Let $swait_i(t)$ be the time elapsed since last time when queue i is scheduled for transmission. If queue i not backlogged, we set $swait_i(t) = 0$. Thus, for the sake of fairness, the queue with highest $swait_i(t)$ should be scheduled.

Let $f_i(t)$ be the scheduling weight of flow i at time slot t. Considering both priority from the perspective of potential change on the sender's $cwnd$ and fairness, we define the following total order among flows: $f_i(t) \succ f_j(t)$ iff $p_i(t) > p_j(t)$ or $p_i(t) = p_j(t)$ and $swait_i(t) > swait_j(t)$.

At the beginning of scheduling, $p_i(0) = 2$ and $swait_i(0) = 0$ for $i \in F$ (F is the set of active flows at the OLT), indicating that no dupack is produced and the OLT doesn't have any packet waiting for transmission initially. Every time when a packet is to be transmitted, the scheduler schedules the head packet of the backlogged flow i^* with the maximum lexicographical order of $f_{i^*}(t)$, i.e.,

$$i^* = argmax_{i \in F} f_i(t) \qquad (2)$$

Suppose that flow i^* is scheduled for tranmission at time slot t, if $p_{i^*}(t) = 0$, to send the HOL packet of flow i^* may trigger three dupacks, thus the sender's $cwnd$ will be reduced. In such a case, we may prefer to delay the transmission at current time slot and wait for the expected packet. Note that in the next time slot, with the new arrival packets to each flow, a new flow may be selected for transmission or the current flow will be selected for transmission again. On the other hand, if the expected packet is lost, a TCP timeout will eventually be triggered. In such a case, it is more desirable that we send the packet immediately to trigger fast retransmission. To resolve such a dilemma, the OLT needs to have an estimation on whether the expected packet of flow i^* is lost or not. If enough time (more than a predefined threshold) has elapsed since flow i^* is scheduled for transmission last time, the OLT can regard the expected packet as lost packet and send the current HOL packet immediately. Such a threshold is denoted as max_hold_i for each flow i where max_hold_i can be determined by the delay difference of multiple paths in the wireless subnetwork.

4   Data Structure and Packet Scheduling Algorithm

The most challenging part of making the scheduling decision is to maintain the number of dupacks for each queue. In this section, we first use some examples to illustrate what information must be maintained for each queue in order to derive the number of dupacks. We then use a Finite State Machine (FSM) to formally describe the state change at each queue. We finally present our scheduling algorithm.

Assume that queue i has sent out $P_{i,1}$ and $dack_i(t) = 0$. The OLT is now expecting $P_{i,2}$. When packet $P_{i,3}$ becomes the HOL packet, suppose queue i is scheduled for transmission and packet $P_{i,3}$ is sent out, $dack_i(t)$ becomes 1. In the next time slot, suppose that packet $P_{i,5}$ becomes the head of queue i. In this case, the current packet's $seqno$ is even higher than the highest $seqno$ sent so far for this queue (3 in this case). Suppose that this packet is sent out immediately, $dack_i(t)$ becomes 2. In the next time slot, if the expected packet $P_{i,2}$ arrives at the OLT and is sent out immediately. The expected $seqno$ will be 4 as packet

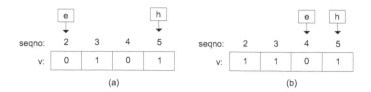

Fig. 3. A bit_vector for recording the OOD packet delivering

$P_{i,3}$ has been sent out from the OLT. This situation indicates that in order to update the expected *seqno*, we have to record which packets have been sent among the packets with *seqno* between current expected *seqno* and the highest *seqno*. We use a bit_vector v to record which packets between the expected one and the highest *seqno* have been sent out (Fig 3) where $v[i] = 0$ indicates that the corresponding packet has not been sent out from the OLT, and vice versa. As shown in (Fig 3 (a)), the expected packet's *seqno* is 2, the highest packet's *seqno* sent so far is 5, packet 3 has been sent out. Thus, when the expected packet $P_{i,2}$ arrives, we can immediately obtain that the next expected *seqno* is 4 (Fig 3 (b)).

This shows that, in order to maintain the number of dupacks, we need the information of the expected *seqno*, the highest *seqno* sent so far, and a vector for recording information about out-of-order packet delivering.

The above example only shows how to update the number of dupacks after the HOL packet of a queue is committed for transmission. However, in order to decide which queue's HOL packet should be transmitted at a time slot, we need to compute the number of dupacks *if* the HOL packet of a queue is scheduled for transmission. In other words, besides maintaining the number of *committed* dupacks from the perspective of sent packets, we also need to estimate the consequence if the current HOL packet is scheduled for transmission, which is the number of *potential* dupacks. For instance, as shown in Fig. 2 (c), after $P_{1,1}$ and $P_{2,1}$ were sent out, the number of *committed* dupacks for both queues is 0. Now, $P_{1,3}$ and $P_{2,2}$ become the head packet of each queue. If $P_{1,3}$ or $P_{2,2}$ is scheduled for transmission, the number of *potential* dupacks for each queue is 1 and 0, respectively.

We now formally present how to maintain *the expected seqno, the highest seqno, the number of committed dupacks,* and *the number of potential dupacks* for each queue. The OLT maintains a quadruplet $\{e, dack, dack', h\}$ and a variable $(swait)$ for each flow i, where e denotes the expected *seqno*, h denotes the highest *seqno* of packet which has been sent, $dack$ denotes the number of committed dupacks, $dack'$ denotes the number of potential dupacks, and $swait$ denotes the time elapsed since flow i is scheduled for transmission last time. Each queue is maintained as a min-heap queue where the HOL packet has the minimum *seqno*.

Initially, $\{e = 0, dack = 0, dack' = 0, h = -1\}$ and $swait = 0$ for each queue, which indicates that no packet has been sent for this flow and the packet with $seqno = 0$ is expected to be sent next. Whenever a packet enters a queue, min-heap insertion operation will be conducted at the queue. If the HOL packet of

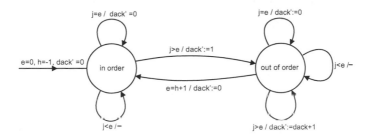

Fig. 4. State change of *dack'* at each queue

the queue remains to be the same, no update is necessary. Suppose that the current packet becomes the HOL packet and its *seqno* is j. We need to see how *dack'* will be changed if the HOL packet of this queue is scheduled next. We have the following cases:

– If there is in-order transmission which means $e = h + 1$,
  • if $j = e$ (or equivalently $j = h + 1$), this is still an in-order packet transmission, set $dack' = 0$;
  • if $j > e$, set $dack' = 1$, and bit_vector v is initialized for recording the sending information of OOD packets;
  • if $j < e$, it is a retransmitted packet and no update is necessary.
– If there is out-of-order transmission which means $e \leq h$,
  • if $j = e$, this is an in-order packet transmission, set $dack' = 0$;
  • if $j > e$, we need to update $dack'$ by $dack' = dack + 1$;
  • if $j < e$, it is a retransmitted packet and no update is necessary.

Such state change can be described using a Finite State Machine (FSM) as shown in Fig. 4. When a new packet enters a queue and becomes the HOL packet, state maintenance process will be triggered. When a packet from a queue with maximum $f_i(t)$ is scheduled for departure, we first make necessary update on e, v, $dack$ and h, then trigger the state maintenance for this queue since a new packet will become the head of the queue. The algorithm schedules packets so that the precedence constraint among packets are followed as much as possible. Such an algorithm is referred to as soft precedence constraint scheduling (*SPCS*) algorithm.

5 Performance Evaluation

In this section, we present our simulation results and compare our algorithm with other scheduling algorithms. Section 5.1 discusses the experimental setup for our simulation study. Simulation results are presented in Section 5.2.

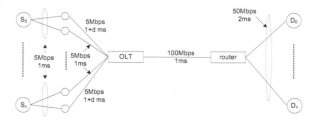

Fig. 5. Simulation Network Topology

5.1 Experimental Setup

We evaluate the performance of our algorithm using ns-2 (version 2.34) [18] running under ubuntu linux 9.04. Figure 5 shows the simulation topology. There are 10 wireless clients, each sending packets to the OLT through 2 paths in a round-robin fashion. Each path from the source to the OLT can provide 5 Mbps link capacity. The OLT is connected to the Internet through an Ethernet. As mentioned early, packets of a flow may arrive at the OLT through different paths. Due to different paths' delay, OOD packet arrivals will be produced. In order to simulate the delay difference between paths, for the two paths from each source to the OLT, one's delay is 1ms and the other is $1 + d$ ms where d varies from 0 to 100 ms. A larger d will introduce more variation in the path delay, thus increasing the degree of packet reordering.

We use TCP/Reno as the agent for TCP connections. TCP/Reno is chosen for its implementation of fast retransmission and fast recovery. The TCP window is set to be 50 segments and packet size is fixed to be 1000 bytes. A FTP application is started at $t = 0.05i$ s and is stopped at $t = 10 + 0.05i$ s at each wireless client s_i. In the simulation, max_hold is set to d.

5.2 Simulation Results

In this section, we compare the performance of our proposed *SPCS* algorithm with classical scheduling algorithms such as FIFO and DRR, and HPCS [19].

We use *goodput*, which is defined as the number of packets successfully received and acknowledged by the receiver, excluding retransmissions, as a performance metric to compare our proposed packet scheduling algorithm with other packet scheduling algorithms.

Firstly, the buffer size at the OLT is set to be large enough to ensure that no packet drops at the OLT. Fig. 6 shows the average goodput of all flows when d varies between 0 ms and 100 ms at intervals of 10 ms. From Fig. 6, we can see that a larger d does lead to lower goodput. We can also see that both our SPCS and HPCS outperform the other two classical scheduling algorithms.

Though the goodput metric of HPCS is similar to SPCS, Figure 7 shows that packets experience much longer queuing delay at the OLT in HPCS than other schedulers, which is not practical to be used as a resequencing algorithm at the

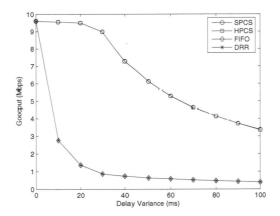

Fig. 6. Goodput vs. delay variance

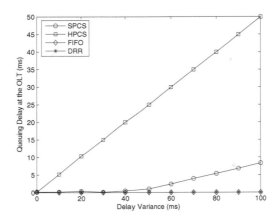

Fig. 7. Queueing delay at the OLT vs. delay variance

intermediate nodes. Our proposed SPCS scheduling algorithm will experience much less queuing delay at the OLT when the delay difference among multiple paths are moderate.

To verify fair bandwidth sharing, we use *min-max* ratio, $r_{min-max}$, as our fairness index, which is defined as follows: given a set of goodput $(x_1, x_2, ..., x_n)$, the following function assigns a fairness index to the set:

$$r_{min-max} = \frac{min_j\{x_i\}}{max_j\{x_i\}} = min_{i,j}\{\frac{x_i}{x_j}\} \tag{3}$$

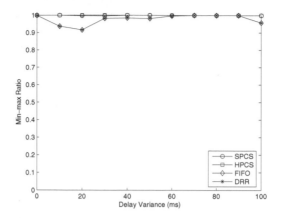

Fig. 8. Min-max ratio vs. delay variance

Fig. 8 shows the achieved min-max ratio of those scheduling algorithms when d changes from 0 ms to 100 ms. The results show that all compared algorithms can achieve the goal of providing fair bandwidth sharing. This validate the effectiveness of our fairness design criterion.

At last, we show the required buffer size at the OLT for each scheduler. We set d to 50 ms and simulate the goodput when the buffer size varies from 12.5 Kbytes to 250 Kbytes. Here, we adopt the shared buffer scheme, i.e., all flows share a common buffer pool in the OLT. When overflow happens, we use a pointer to drop the tail of each queue periodically. With the increase in buffer size, fewer packets are dropped. Hence, the goodput for upstream TCP traffic also increases. From Fig. 9, we can see that the goodputs of both SPCS and HPCS indeed increase with the buffer size while there is no change in FIFO and

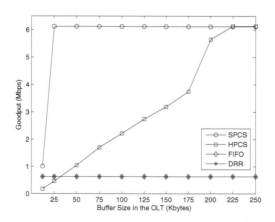

Fig. 9. Goodput vs. buffer size in the OLT

DRR. Fig. 9 also shows that SPCS only needs 25 Kbytes to behave well while HPCS requires as much as 225 Kbytes.

6 Conclusion

The integration of a PON and a WMN makes the OLT as a convergence node, which naturally makes it possible to resequence packets at the OLT before they are sent to the Internet. In this paper, we propose a scheduling algorithm at the OLT to resequence packets while providing fairness. Simulation results show that the proposed packet scheduling algorithm is efficient in reducing the effect of packet reordering, assuring fairness among different flows and reducing the required buffer size in the OLT. Compared with other reordering-tolerant algorithms which need to modify TCP protocol at clients, our proposed work provides a scalable solution since resequencing is conducted in the access network at the sender's side. The proposed resequence scheduling can be used not only at the OLT, but also at edge routers where per-flow packet scheduling is possible.

References

1. Sarkar, S., Dixit, S., Mukherjee, B.: Hybrid Wireless-Optical Broadband-Access Network (WOBAN): A Review of Relevant Challenges. Journal of Lightwave Technology 25(11), 3329–3340 (2007)
2. Mueller, S., Tsang, R., Ghosal, D.: Multipath Routing in Mobile Ad Hoc Networks: Issues and Challenges. In: Calzarossa, M.C.i., Gelenbe, E. (eds.). LNCS. Springer, Heidelberg (2004)
3. Liu, J.: On a Self-Organizing Multipath Routing Protocol in Mobile Wireless Networks. Journal of Network and Systems Management 14(1), 103–126 (2006)
4. Maxemchuk, N.F.: Dispersity routing in high-speed networks. Computer Networks and ISDN Systems 25(6), 645–661 (1993)
5. Pham, P.P., Perreau, S.: Performance analysis of reactive shortest path and multipath routing mechanism with load balance. In: IEEE INFOCOM 2003, vol. 1, pp. 251–259 (2003)
6. Lee, Y., Park, I., Choi, Y.: Improving TCP Performance in Multipath Packet Forwarding Networks. Journal of Communications and Networks 4(2) (2002)
7. Floyd, S.: A report on recent developments in TCP congestion control. IEEE Communications Magazine 39(4), 84–90 (2001)
8. Leung, K.-C., Li, V.O.K.: Flow Assignment and Packet Scheduling for Multipath Routing. Journal of Communications and Networks 5(3) (2003)
9. Rao, N.S.V., Batsell, S.G.: QoS routing via multiple paths using bandwidth reservation. In: IEEE INFOCOM 1998, pp. 11–18 (1998)
10. Kandula, S., Katabi, D., Sinha, S., Berger, A.: Dynamic Load Balancing Without Packet Reordering. ACM SIGCOMM Computer Comm. Rev. 37(2) (2007)
11. Zhang, M., Karp, B., Floyd, S., Peterson, L.: RR-TCP: A Reordering-Robust TCP with DSACK. In: Proc. IEEE ICNP 2003 (2003)
12. Lee, Y., Park, I., Choi, Y.: Improving TCP performance in multipath packet forwarding networks. J. Comm. and Networks 4(2), 148–157 (2002)

13. Sathiaseelan, A., Radzik, T.: Improving the Performance of TCP in the Case of Packet Reordering. In: Mammeri, Z., Lorenz, P. (eds.) HSNMC 2004. LNCS, vol. 3079, pp. 63–73. Springer, Heidelberg (2004)
14. Leung, K.-C., Li, V.O.K., Yang, D.: An Overview of Packet Reordering in Transmission Control Protocol (TCP): Problems, Solutions, and Challenges. IEEE Transactions on Parallel and Distributed Systems 18(4) (2007)
15. Xia, Y., Tse, D.: Analysis on packet resequencing for reliable network protocols. In: Proceedings of INFOCOM (2003)
16. Baccelli, F., Gelenbe, E., Plateau, B.: An end-to-end approach to the resequencing problem. Journal of ACM 31(3), 474–485 (1984)
17. Kim, M., Park, H.: Superposed Multiple QoS Guarantee in Optical Access Networks. In: Chung, C.-W., Kim, C.-k., Kim, W., Ling, T.-W., Song, K.-H. (eds.) HSI 2003. LNCS, vol. 2713, pp. 619–625. Springer, Heidelberg (2003)
18. http://www.isi.edu/nsnam/ns
19. Lane, J.R., Nakao, A.: Best-Effort Network Layer Packet Reordering in Support of Multipath Overlay Packet Dispersion. In: IEEE GLOBECOM 2008 (2008)

Adaptive BU Association and Resource Allocation in Integrated PON-WiMAX Networks

Ming Gong[1], Bin Lin[1,2], Pin Han Ho[1], and Patrick Hung[3]

[1] Electrical and Computer Engineering Department,
University of Waterloo, Waterloo, Ontario, Canada
{mgong,b2lin,p4ho}@uwaterloo.ca

[2] Department of Information Technology,
Dalian Maritime University, Dalian, China

[3] Faculty of Business and Information Technology,
University of Ontario Institute of Technology, Oshawa, Ontario, Canada
Patrick.Hung@uoit.ca

Abstract. This paper addresses the issue of base station user association and resources allocation (BUA-RA) in OFDM-TDMA-based broadband wireless access (BWA) networks under PON-WiMAX integration. With the powerful coordination capability at the optical line terminal (OLT), a key technology of inter-cell collaborative transmission (CT) is incorporated in the integrated network architecture, which is so called cooperative PON-WiMAX network (CPWN). To achieve an efficient integration and inter-cell CT in the CPWNs, BUA-RA is critical to the Quality of Service (QoS) provisioning for each user. In order to minimize the network resource usage, we provide three new BUA-RA schemes, which can be adaptively applied according to the network loads and wireless users' moving speeds. Simulations are conducted to verify the proposed BUA-RA schemes by comparing with those without CT technology and to demonstrate the efficiency of the proposed mathematical formulations and linearization approach.

Keywords: adaptive control, resource assignment, cooperative transmission.

1   Introduction

The next-generation broadband wireless access (NG-BWA) network, such as 3GPP LTE [1], IMT-Advanced [2], or IEEE 802.16m [3], is defined as a high data rate, low delay, and high speed mobility IP based mobile telecommunication system. A novel research paradigm for broadband Fixed/Mobile Convergence (FMC) is initiated by integrating WiMAX and Passive Optical Networks (PONs) at both industry and academia [4] to build such an NG-BWA network. By virtue of the tree topology and point-to-multipoint (P2MP) architecture of the PONs, the deployment and maintenance cost of fibers can be reduced significantly compared with that of traditional point-to-point networks without sacrificing the transmission bandwidth. The cost and performance advantages of a PON make it desirable to serve as the network backhaul

X. Jun Hei and L. Cheung (Eds.): AccessNets 2009, LNICST 37, pp. 103–120, 2010.
© Institute for Computer Sciences, Social-Informatics and Telecommunications Engineering 2010

for connecting multiple Optical Network Units (ONUs). The WiMAX is concatenated with the PON by integrating a Base Station (BS) with an ONU such that service coverage extension and superb support of user mobility can be achieved with fast, easy and cost-effective deployment. In the integrated Fiber and Wireless (FiWi) network architecture; we study the issues of BS-user association and resource allocation (BUA-RA) to achieve the following three basic targets of the NG-BWA network: 1) wireless spectrum utilization increase; 2) mobile coverage extension and data rate improvement, especially the users at the edge of a cell; 3) transmission delay decrease.

Orthogonal frequency division multiplexing (OFDM) is a frequency division multiplexing (FDM) scheme utilized as a digital multi-carrier modulation technique. The data is divided into several parallel data streams or channels, one for each sub-carrier. The primary advantages of OFDM are efficient wireless frequency usage, eliminating inter-symbol interference (ISI), low complexity of implement and multiple-input and multiple-output (MIMO)-applicableness. Combining OFDM with time division multiple access (TDMA) or frequency division multiple access (FDMA), two basic multiple access techniques, OFDM-TDMA and OFDMA, are adopted by the IEEE 802.16e standard [5] as two options.

Cooperative transmission (CT) technology is taken as a popular approach for coverage extension and throughput enhancement in wireless networks [6]. The collaboration among distributed BSs is supported by the centralized coordination at the optical line terminal (OLT) by using the space-time coding technique. The integrated PON and WiMAX network that incorporates inter-cell CT technology is called *Cooperative PON-WiMAX network* (*CPWN*) in this paper. With inter-cell CT, the data segments are coded with different space-time codes in the associated BSs. These orthogonal space-time codes are then transmitted to the receiver where the same copy or a portion of the data can be aggregated and jointly decoded. In this way, the end-users' signal to interference plus noise ratio (SINR) can be improved significantly. We aim to exploit the significant performance benefits due to inter-cell CT to achieve the aforementioned targets of the NG-BWA network.

With the powerful computation and control capabilities at the OLT and the high speed optical connection between BSs and OLTs, the whole CPWN network status, such as channel status information (CSI), the bandwidth utilization of each BS, the rate requirement of each end-user, can be updated dynamically. The issues of BUA-RA are critical to the Quality of Service (QoS) provisioning for each user as well as the integrated network performance in terms of capacity. In CPWN, the OLT can execute adaptive resource allocation which also takes into account interference cancellation and optimal connection admission control, etc.

In this research, we propose three new BUA-RA schemes to minimize the network resource usage. These three different BUA-RA schemes are designed for three kinds of users respectively with different moving speed in the CPWN. They are static subscriber (SS), portable subscriber (PS) with walking speed and mobile subscriber (MS) with driving speed. Adaptively choosing one of the three CT BUA-RA schemes based on different moving speeds of users and network loads can achieve a near-optimal BU association and resources allocation solution. We first provide an optimal BUA-RA scheme (CT_LP) with CT technology. In the scheme, a multi-user nonlinear optimal model is provided with the objective of minimizing time slots usage, and then it is linearized to a linear programming (LP) model which can be solved by LP solver. Then, we introduce two new fast single user BUA-RA schemes, i.e. H_CT_LP and H_CT schemes, which are suitable for real-time operations.

The remainder of the paper is organized as follows. Section 2 gives an overview of the related work about fiber-wireless access network and OFDM wireless network management. Section 3 describes the system model of a CPWN. The proposed BUA-RA schemes are provided in section 4. Simulation results and analyses of the BUA-RA schemes are in section 5. Conclusion is given in section 6.

2   Related Works

Research on either optical or broadband wireless access network has been extensively reported in the past. A few research efforts have been reported on the integration of the two networks [4], [7-12]. In [4], the wireless-optical broadband-access network (WOBAN) was described as a promising architecture for next-generation mobile access networks. The authors reviewed some hot optical and wireless access technologies, such as EPON, GPON, Wi-Fi and WiMAX. A novel hybrid WOBAN architecture was presented in their paper; based on it, they compared some BSs placement and routing algorithms. In [7], a framework on integration of EPON and WiMAX for broadband FMC access was proposed, in which the research issues on the MAC layer and integrated control plane were elaborated. An optimal BS placement model in integrated EPON-WiMAX networks was developed in [8], where CT was also incorporated, and bandwidth and power breakdown assignment were jointly considered in the initial long-term network planning and dimensioning phase. In [9], two BU association schemes were put forward for two cases: 1) BS allocates the same time to its users and 2) BS allocates the same throughput to its users. The results showed that the first case was better than the second in terms of fairness and efficiency. In [10], two BS selection algorithms were presented in cooperative cellular network, namely, a genetic-based approach and a sphere decoder inspired approach. Nevertheless, few researches of BU association algorithms have jointly taken resource allocation into account.

In the past ten years, a plethora of resource management schemes have been proposed for various OFDM systems. In [11], an adaptive subcarrier-bit-and-power allocation algorithm was proposed to achieve a dramatic gain in power efficiency. A Lagrangian method of optimization was used to minimize the total transmit power under the constraints of the users' QoS requirements. However, the prohibitively high computational complexity renders it impractical. After that, many other adaptive allocation algorithms with multifarious objectives have been proposed to reduce the complexity of resource allocation algorithm [12-14]. [15] gave an overview of adaptive multi-user resource allocation methodologies. Adaptive modulation, adaptive multiple-access control and adaptive cell selection for SISO- and MIMO- OFDM were introduced. [16] provided two multi-cell resource management strategies for OFDMA-based cellular systems. The authors developed inter-cell interference (ICI), spectral efficiency and the service outage probability models in the research. [17] developed a distributed game theory approach to adaptively allocate the sub-channels, rates, and power for multi-cell OFDMA networks. To regulate the competition for the resource usage, the authors employed a virtual referee scheme which made their algorithm outperforms the iterative water-filling method in terms of both transmission power consumption and throughput. However, to the best of our survey, few studies have jointly considered BUA-RA scheme in the multi-user multi-cell network scenarios with CT technology. Because of lack of a central controller structure, the researches of cooperative resource allocation schemes mainly focus on using relay nodes or other wireless users to achieve the cooperative communication [18][19]. In our previous research [20] and [21], we provided a serial of BUA-RA schemes for PON+OFDMA and PON+OFDM-TDMA systems respectively. In [20], four LP models were designed to solve four different BUA-RA optimal objectives in the CPWN. [21] provided three BUA-RA schemes to maximize the network throughput.

3   System Model

A general system model for a CPWN is shown in Fig. 1, which is composed of a PON and multiple WiMAX cells as backhaul and front-end wireless access networks, respectively. The major entities in the network model include an OLT, a splitter, a number of fibers and *multiple* ONU-BSs. An OLT functions as a root node in the tree structure. With powerful computing capability and intelligence, the OLT can process the incoming jobs in a parallel fashion. The OLTs can connect to a metropolitan optical network such as a synchronous digital hierarchy (SDH) ring.

To extend from the OLT with fibers, a passive optical splitter fans out to multiple optical fibers connected to a number of ONU-BSs. An ONU-BS is a single device box integrating a PON ONU and a WiMAX BS [7]. In addition to the savings on hardware cost, such integration achieves a flat control plane and seamless integration between the PON and WiMAX, where signaling and control messages can be exchanged directly between the OLT and the end users (fixed or mobile stations). The ONU-BS functions as border devices to interconnect the PON and WiMAX network. The resource management functions are located at the OLT, which can collectively control the BUA-RA of all wireless users within the coverage areas. OFDM-TDMA is used as the multi-access technology by the CPWN.

All network status data, such as time slot usage of each BS, wireless channels status information, data rate requirement of each user, users' moving speed are stored and dynamically updated at OLT. Based on these data, while a new user arrives, OLT can compute the resource and associating BS(s) for the user to satisfy its data rate requirement base on the BUA-RA schemes. According to the moving speed of the user and current network load, OLT can adaptively choose one BUA-RA scheme. In our model, Shannon's channel capacity function is used to estimate the data rate of the user n. The notions are listed in Table 1.

$$R_n = B \times Tp_n \times \log\left(1 + \text{SINR}_n\right) \tag{1}$$

$$\text{SINR}_n = \frac{P_n^R}{N_0 + P_n^I} \tag{2}$$

In the CPWN, one or more BSs can cooperatively transmit to a user with CT, so P^R_n and P^I_n are calculated as follows.

$$P^R_n = \sum_{m=1}^{M} A_{mn} P^r_{mn} \tag{3}$$

$$P^I_n = \sum_{m=1}^{M} (1 - A_{mn}) P^r_{mn} \tag{4}$$

where

$$A_{mn} = \begin{cases} 1 & \text{BS } m \text{ associates user } n \\ 0 & \text{otherwise} \end{cases} \tag{5}$$

For simplicity, we use the path loss model [22] to estimate the signal power of user n from BS m. In the real network, the receive power can be obtained by the user, and then feedback to the OLT.

$$P^r_{mn} = P^t_m \times \left(\frac{d_0}{d_{mn}} \right)^\alpha \tag{6}$$

4   BUA-RA Schemes

In this section, we will introduce three BUA-RA schemes in the CPWN. The BU association concerns which BS(s) should be associated with a specific user; and resource allocation is to determine how many time slots should be allocated to a specific user from the associated BS(s) within a CPWN.

The subscribers are classified into three categories in the CPWN, i.e., 1) static subscriber (SS), 2) portable subscriber (PS), and 3) mobile subscriber (MS).

1) As the SS is fixed in the network, the CSI of the SS is relatively stable; and after the network initialization, the SSs' resource allocation rarely refresh. So, the SSs can tolerant a time consuming resource allocation method to obtain an optimal solution. In this paper, we formulate the BUA-RA as an LP, in which all SSs' requirements are considered at the same time (so-called multi-user LP scheme).

For the mobile subscriber, i.e. PS and MS, the BUA-RA should be more efficient than the SS, since their CSI changes more frequently. The RA should be refreshed after user's CSI changed.

2) The PS moves slowly, typically a subscriber using a notebook, a netbook, or a cell phone with a walking speed. The CSI of the PS changes slowly, so we don't need a very fast BUA-RA scheme. If normally a solution can be obtained in 1.5 second, the scheme is acceptable. The second scheme allocates resource to each PS one by one by an LP model (so-called single-user LP scheme).

3) The MS moves fast in the network, such as a computer in the vehicle. The CSI of the MS changes continually, so RA should be refreshed very fast. We provide a fast heuristic RA scheme (so-called single-user heuristic scheme) for the MS, which can obtain the solution in 10ms.

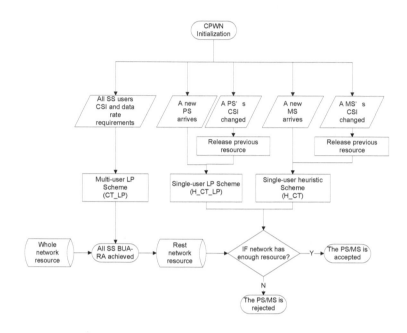

Fig. 2 Flowchart of BUA-RA

The BUA-RA procedure in the CPWN is shown in Fig. 2. When a network initiated, the first optimal scheme is solved by using some LP tools to assign BSs and allocate resources for all the SSs. Then for the PSs and MSs, the second BUA-RA scheme or the third one can be chosen based on their moving speeds. If there is no enough resource remaining in the network, the user will be blocked. If a user moves out of the CPWN, the original allocated resource will be released and re-allocated. For the sake of fair resource allocation, we assume all the users have the same priority to be admitted.

The notations adopted in the problem formulation are introduced as follows. The decision variable Tp_{mn} denotes the time slots allocated to user n from BS m. Tp_{mn} is normalized to percentage of the total time slots of a BS. If Tp_{mn} is larger than 0, it means that BS m is associated with user n; otherwise it does not associate with the user. Table 1 lists all the notations.

4.1　Multi-user LP Scheme (CT_LP)

In the optimal scheme, the BUA-RA problem is formulated as a multi-user optimization model to minimize the total time slots consumption of the BSs in a CPWN, where the CT technology is employed. The objective is to:

Table 1. Notations

Symbol	Notation
R_n	The data rate of user n
α	The path-loss exponent
d_0	The reference distance to BS antenna
N_0	The noise power
d_{mn}	The distance between user n and BS m
P^R_n	The signal power received by user n
P^I_n	The interference signal power received by user n
P^r_{mn}	The transmission power received by user n from BS m
P^t_m	The transmission power of BS m
N	The number of total users
M	The number of total BSs
B	The total wireless bandwidth
R^{Req}_n	The data rate required by user n
A_{mn}	The associating indicator of user n and BS m
Tp_{mn}	The normalized time slots allocated to user n from BS m
x_{jn}	The associating indicator of user n and AM j
Tp_{jn}	The normalized time slots allocated to user n by AM j
Tp_n	The normalized time slots allocated to user n

AM: associating mode

$$\text{minimize} \sum_{m=1}^{M} \sum_{n=1}^{N} Tp_{mn} A_{mn} \tag{7}$$

which is subject to the following constraints:
1) Total time slot constraint

$$\sum_{n=1}^{N} Tp_{mn} A_{mn} \leq 1, \forall m = 1...M \tag{8}$$

2) Data rate requirement of each user

$$R_n = B \times Tp_{mn} \times \log\left(1 + \frac{\sum_{m=1}^{M} A_{mn} P^r_{mn}}{N_0 + \sum_{m=1}^{M} (1 - A_{mn}) P^r_{mn}}\right) \geq R^{Req}_n, \forall n = 1...N \tag{9}$$

Because constraints (8) and (9) are non-linear, we apply the following approach to linearize them. Because of using CT technology, a user can be associated with one or more BSs. The number of associating BS(s) of a user can be from 1 to M. So, we define $J (= 2^M - 1)$ as associating mode which indicates the number of BSs to be potentially chosen to associate a user in the CPWN. Describing the jth association mode with binary number, we will have following table:

Table 2. Bit (b_{jm}) Map of association mode

j	b_{jM}	...	b_{jm}	...	b_{j2}	b_{j1}
1	0	...	0	...	0	1
2	0	...	0	...	1	0
:	:	:	:	:	:	:
J	1	1	1	1	1	1

The mth bit (b_{jm}) of the integer number j indicates whether BS m associates a user or not, in the jth association mode.

$$b_{jm} = \begin{cases} 1 & \text{BS } m \text{ associates a user in } j\text{th association mode} \\ 0 & \text{otherwise} \end{cases} \tag{10}$$

Then we have:

$$LOG\_SINR_{jn} = \log\left(1 + \frac{\sum_{m=1}^{M} b_{jm} P_{mn}^{r}}{N_0 + \sum_{m=1}^{M}(1 - b_{jm}) P_{mn}^{r}}\right) \tag{11}$$

The LP model of this BUA-RA scheme (CT_LP) can be expressed as follows:
Objective:

$$\text{minimize} \sum_{m=1}^{M} \sum_{n=1}^{N} \sum_{j=1}^{J} \left(b_{jm} \times Tp_{jn}\right) \tag{12}$$

Constraints:
1) Total time slots constraint of each BS

$$\sum_{n=1}^{N} \sum_{j=1}^{J} \left(b_{jm} \times Tp_{jn}\right) \leq 1, \forall m = 1...M \tag{13}$$

2) Data rate requirement of each user

$$R_n = \sum_{j=1}^{J} \left(Tp_{jn} \times (B \times LOG\_SINR_{jn})\right) \geq R_n^{\text{Req}} \tag{14}$$

$$\forall n = 1...N$$

3) A user can only use one associating mode

$$\sum_{j=1}^{J} x_{jn} = 1 \tag{15}$$

$$x_{jn} - Tp_{jn} \geq 0, \forall j = 1...J, \forall n = 1...N \tag{16}$$

4) Variables

$$Tp_{jn} \in [0, 1] \tag{17}$$

$$x_{jn} \in \{0, 1\} \tag{18}$$

$$x_{jn} = \begin{cases} 1 & j\text{th association mode is used to associate user } n \\ 0 & \text{otherwise} \end{cases}$$

Constraint (13) ensures that the total allocated time slots to each user are no more than the total time slots of one BS. Constraint (14) makes sure that the data rate requirement of each user must be satisfied. Constraints (15) and (16) stipulate that one user can only use one associating mode. Equations (17) and (18) state the boundaries of the decision variables.

In practice, the SSs mainly refer to as the residential and business users which have certain unchanged rate requirements when being subscribed. And the optimal BUA-RA for each SS can be obtained *off-line* by solving the above LP model. However, the BUA-RA for mobile users are required to be *on-line*, namely, quick response to the instantaneous connection requests of mobile users requires fast BUA-RA schemes.

In the following two sections, we present two schemes for PS and MS, respectively. Heuristic BUA-RA schemes are used for these mobile users, which assign BS and allocates resource to each new user one by one, based on user's requirement and current network status. Let TS_m (=1) to be the normalized total time slots of BS m, F_m to be the free time slots of BS m, W_m is the total reserved working time slots of BS m ($TS_m = W_m + F_m$).

4.2   Single-User LP Scheme (H_CT_LP)

In the second BUA-RA scheme, we use the similar LP model and the same notations as above optimal scheme to minimize the time slot usage to satisfy the data rate requirement of a new user. The single user LP model is expressed as follows:
    Objective:

$$\text{minimize} \sum_{m=1}^{M} \sum_{j=1}^{J} \left(b_{jm} \times Tp_{jn} \right) \tag{19}$$

Constraints:
1) All the associating BS(s) should have enough free time slot

$$\sum_{j=1}^{J} \left(b_{jm} \times Tp_{jn} \right) \leq F_m \tag{20}$$

2) Data rate requirement of the new user

$$R_n = \sum_{j=1}^{J} \left(Tp_{jn} \times (B \times LOG\_SINR_{jn}) \right) \geq R_n^{Req} \tag{21}$$

3) The new user can only use one association mode

$$\sum_{j=1}^{J} x_{jn} = 1 \tag{22}$$

$$x_{jn} - Tp_{jn} \geq 0 \tag{23}$$

4) Variables

$$Tp_{jn} \in [0,\ 1] \tag{24}$$

$$x_{jn} \in \{0,\ 1\} \tag{25}$$

If the LP has no solution, the user's requirement will be rejected.

4.3   Single-User Heuristic Scheme (H_CT)

This fast heuristic scheme (H_CT) is designed for the MS. This scheme tries to associate a new user via following five steps:

Step 1: Find the closest BS m to the new user n, denote the minimum distance as $d_{min} = d_m$, BS m will associate the user.

Step 2: Find the next closest BS l which has distance d_l to the user n.

Step 3: If $d_l - d_{min} < \Delta d\_ct$, then the user l will also associate the user n, go back *Step 2*; otherwise go to Step 4.

Step 4: Calculate the amount of time slots (Tp_n) to be allocated to the user by following formulas

$$Tp_n = R_n / (B \times SINR\_CT_n) \tag{26}$$

$$SINR\_CT_n = \log\left(1 + \frac{\sum_{m=1}^{M} A_{mn} P_{mn}^r}{N_0 + \sum_{m=1}^{M} (1 - A_{mn}) P_{mn}^r} \right) \tag{27}$$

Step 5: Check if all the associating BS(s) have enough time slots. If YES, then the user will be associated by the BS(s), update time slots usage info of all association BS(s) at OLT by (28) and (29); if NO, the user will be rejected.

$$TS_m = W_m + Tp_n \tag{28}$$

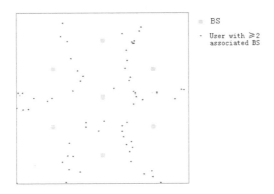

Fig. 3. Users with two or more associating BSs

$$F_m = F_m - Tp_n \qquad (29)$$

d_m is the distance from the BS m to the new user n. Δd_ct is the maximum acceptable difference between the distance of the cooperative BSs to the user and the d_{min}. If distance difference is greater than Δd_ct, the BS will not be selected as a cooperative associating BS. The small points in Fig. 3 show the positions of the users who have two or more associating BSs (shown as big light-blue points). This figure is obtained by the simulation of the CT_LP scheme. From this figure, we can find that the users with CT are always distributed in the middle area of two or three BSs. So, we can conclude that a user is suitable to use CT when it is at the edge area of the cells. We use Δd_ct to control the scope of this area. By observing the CT_LP scheme simulation results such as Fig. 3, we can estimate the suitable value of the Δd_ct.

5   Simulation Results

In this section, the performances of the proposed BUA-RA schemes are evaluated; and we also compare against the conventional resource allocation schemes without using CT technology; more specifically, three non-CT BUA-RA schemes (NCT_LP, H_NCT_LP, and H_NCT) corresponded to the proposed schemes are used as the benchmarks. The simulation program is coded by C#, and the LP models are solved by the CPLEX version 11.0 [23]. All the simulations are conducted on a computer with Intel Pentium D-805 CPU and 1G memory. We are interested in testing the time slots usage performance, the network capacity (the total data rate of associated users in the network), and the computation complexity of these schemes.

Fig. 4 illustrates the simulated network which is similar to conventional cellular networks in. In the simulated network, seven BSs, represented as the big point in Fig. 4, are located in a $1500 \times 1500 m^2$ area. The setting of simulation parameters is shown in Table 3. We examine 63 scenarios, where a different numbers of mobile

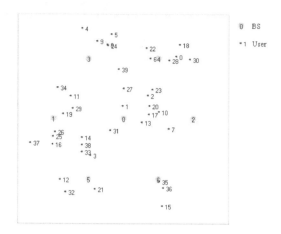

Fig. 4. A snapshot on the mobile user distribution in the AOI. The 7 BSs are fixed.

users are launched and randomly moving in the area of interest (AOI). Table 4 shows the data rates of a user for all 63 scenarios. After running a BUA-RA scheme in each scenario, the expected output is the total time slots usage in percentage, total unassociated users in percentage, and the computation time for each user.

Table 3. Simulation parameters setting

Parameters	B(MHz)	$P_m(w)$	$N_0^*(w)$	$d_0(m)$	α	Δd_ct
Value	20	20	1×10^{-6}	1	2.5	100

* The thermal noise power (N_0) is assumed equivalent at any point in the network.

Table 4. Data rate of a user in each scenario (*Mbps*)

Number of Users	Total Data Rate Requirement (Mbps)								
	20	40	80	120	160	200	250	320	400
20	1	2	4	6	8	10	12.5	16	20
40	0.5	1	2	3	4	5	6.25	8	10
80	0.25	0.5	1	1.5	2	2.5	3.125	4	5
100	0.2	0.4	0.8	1.2	1.6	2	2.5	3.2	4
160	0.125	0.25	0.5	0.75	1	1.25	1.5625	2	2.5
250	0.08	0.16	0.32	0.48	0.64	0.8	1	1.28	1.6
400	0.05	0.1	0.2	0.3	0.4	0.5	0.625	0.8	1

To generalize the randomness due to the user mobility, each data in the simulation is the average result by run a BUA-RA scheme on 50 different user distributions in each scenario. We show the criteria in two dimensions, 1) under same number of users, the results are shown as a function of the total data rate requirements; 2) under same total data rate requirement, the results are shown as a function of the number of users. Before showing the three performance results, we will introduce a criterion for the multi-user LP scheme in following sub-section.

5.1   How Many Times the LP Models Cannot Be Solved

The multi-user LP schemes try to accept all the SSs in the network and satisfy their data rate requirements. If the LP model cannot be solved, it means that some users' requirements cannot to be satisfied and these users cannot be accepted in the network. Obviously, if the total data rate requirement is higher than the capacity of the network, the LP model will fail to find a solution.

A. Under same number of users and different total data rates
Fig. 5 shows that there are more no solution times of the NCT_LP scheme than the CT_LP scheme, when the total data rate requirement reaches 80 Mbps or higher. Because of CT_LP using CT technology, we know that the network capacity is increased by using CT. All the results show the same situation; we only choose some figures of them to show in Fig. 5.

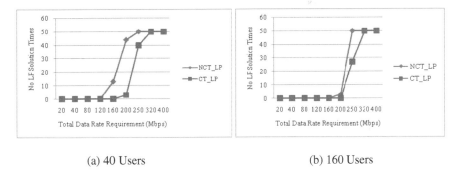

(a) 40 Users   (b) 160 Users

Fig. 5. No LP Solutions Times

B. Under same total data rates and different number of users
Fig. 6 shows: when the total data rate requirements are the same, the more users in the network, the less no LP solution times will happen. In other words, when the number of user in the network increases, the resource of the network can be used more efficient and the capacity of the network will increase. Moreover, it is observed that the CT_LP scheme outperforms NCT_LP in terms of network capacity.

5.2   Total Time Slots Usage

We take the summation of time slots (normalized to percentage) allocated to each user as measure on how much system resource is spent on satisfying the given traffic load

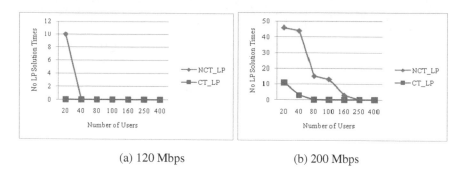

(a) 120 Mbps   (b) 200 Mbps

Fig. 6. No LP Solutions Times

demand. Obviously, a specific BUA-RA scheme achieves better performance if less total time slot is consumed in a wireless network to satisfy a given pattern of traffic load demand.

A. Under same number of users and different total data rates
From Fig. 7, we can only conclude that when the total data rate requirement increases, the time slots usage also increases. However, it is difficult to figure out which method of the six has the best time slots usage performance. We will find out the result in next sub-section.

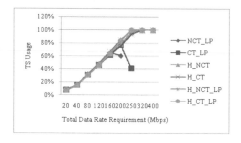

Fig. 7. Total Time Slot Usage (100 Users)

B. Under same total data rates and different number of users
Fig. 8 shows that at low and mid network load (total data rate requirement < 160Mbps), the CT_LP and H_CT_LP schemes outperform H_CT in terms of time slot usage performance. H_CT costs a little more time slots than these two schemes; however it can save more resource (about 2%) than the other three NCT schemes.

Fig. 9 shows that when the network load becomes high (total data rate requirement ≥ 200 Mbps), the performance of H_CT_LP becomes worse. This is because when a new user arrives, the H_CT_LP scheme always tries to accept its requirement sometime the channel status of the new user is very poor, it will cost too many

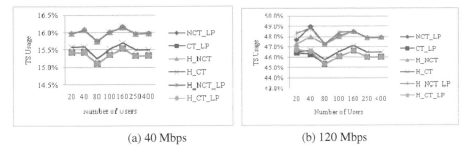

(a) 40 Mbps   (b) 120 Mbps

Fig. 8. Total Time Slot Usage

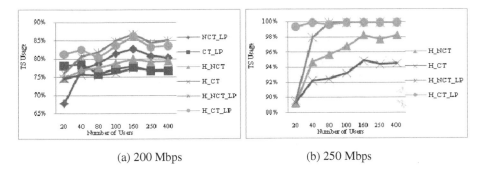

(a) 200 Mbps   (b) 250 Mbps

Fig. 9. Total Time Slot Usage

resources (time slots) to satisfy the user's data rate; then, the resource will be exhausted fast. However, under this situation the H_CT scheme will reject the new user whose channel status is not good, because it will cost too many resources to accept such a user; and then it can save some resource to accept more future users with good channel condition. At high network load, the H_CT scheme can save 5-10% time slots than the other schemes.

When the total data requirement is higher than 300Mbps, the network is overload, and then the time slot usage reaches 100%.

5.3   Percentage of Unassociated Users

A network capacity efficient BUA-RA scheme should be able to accept as more users as possible; in the other words, the network capacity, i.e. total accepted data rate, is higher. We use the total number of unassociated users (normalized to percentage) as the criterion of the network capacity efficiency.

A. Under same number of users and different total data rates
For the multi-user LP scheme, when some user is unacceptable by the network, the LP problem will not be solved, which is shown in the first sub-section (5.1). However, for the heuristic scheme, when a new arrival user's requirement cannot be

accepted, the user will be rejected by the network, and then the user will be recorded as an unassociated user by our simulation program. Fig. 10 shows that when the total data rate requirement increases, the percentage of unassociated users increase too. By comparing the performances of the six schemes, we can find that at low network load (total data requirement ≤ 80 Mbps), there is no unassociated user by using any scheme; at mid load (120-160 Mbps), CT_LP can accept all users, when other schemes begin to reject some users; at high load (total data rate requirement 200-250 Mbps) the CT_LP scheme cannot get solution, at this time H_CT_LP plays the best, and H_CT is a little worse, but better than the NCT schemes; when the network is overload (total data rate requirement > 250 Mbps), H_CT outperforms of all the other schemes in the terms of unassociated users performance, however H_CT_LP plays worse, this result well matches what is observed in the previous sub-section (5.2-B). Over all, the CT schemes perform better than the NCT ones.

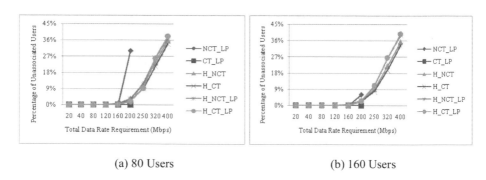

(a) 80 Users   (b) 160 Users

Fig. 10. Percentage of Unassociated Users

B. Under same total data rates and different number of users
When the network load is low (total data rate requirement ≤ 80 Mbps), the number of unassociated user is zero, so we don't show the figures here. By observing Fig. 11, we can easily obtain same conclusions as previous sub-section (5.3-A). On the other hand, the similar character as the sub-section (5.1-B) can also be found here; that is when the number of users increases, the percentage of unassociated users decreases.

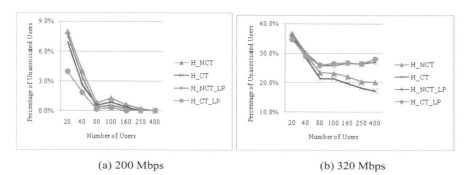

(a) 200 Mbps   (b) 320 Mbps

Fig. 11. Percentage of Unassociated Users

5.4   Computation Time

All results of the different number of users and different total data rate requirements show the similar situation, thus we only choose 100 users and 160 Mbps results to show in Table 5 and Table 6.

By observing the result tables, we know that the CT_LP scheme takes the longest time to obtain a solution, especially when the network is close to the full load. The single user LP scheme costs much less time than the optimal one; however for the H_CT_LP scheme, the 1.33 second computation time is good enough for the low speed PSs. Just as well, H_CT works so efficient that it only costs around 10 msec to calculate the association BS and the time slot for a high speed MS user.

Table 5. Computation Time (sec) (100 Users)

BUA-RA schemes	Total Data Rate Requirement (Mbps)					
	20	80	160	200	250	320
CT_LP	9.90	10.10	49.18	120.53	1595.78	10.05
H_CT_LP	1.33	1.33	1.33	1.34	1.35	1.31
H_CT	0.0090	0.0089	0.0092	0.0091	0.0090	0.0090

Table 6. Computation Time (sec) (160 Mbps)

BUA-RA schemes	Number of Users in the Network					
	20	40	80	100	160	250
CT_LP	23.54	25.23	60.63	49.18	30.55	61.84
H_CT_LP	1.31	1.33	1.34	1.33	1.33	1.33
H_CT	0.0091	0.0089	0.0095	0.0092	0.0102	0.0118

6   Conclusion

This paper has proposed three BU association and resource allocation (BUA-RA) schemes for the integrated PON-WiMAX networks where OFDM-TDMA and inter-cell CT technology are employed, we have integrated evaluated these three schemes and further compared against the conventional BUA-RA schemes which do not have the CT technology. The simulation results show the network capacity and resource usage efficiency can be increased by using the CT technology.

The multi-user LP scheme, CT_LP, can obtain the optimal BUA-RA for the SSs. For the PSs, when the network load is not high, the H_CT_LP scheme is suitable, since it can obtain a better solution than the H_CT scheme in a relative short time (less than 1.5 second); however, when the network load become high, the H_CT scheme should be used. For the high speed MSs whose wireless channel statuses are changed fast, the H_CT scheme is a good choice, since it can calculate the BUA-RA result within 10ms.

References

1. 3rd Generation Partnership Project (3GPP),
   `http://www.3gpp.org/Highlights/LTE/lte.htm`
2. ITU-R, `http://www.itu.int/ITU-R/`
   `index.asp?category=study-groups&rlink=rsg5-imt-dvanced`
3. IEEE 802.16m Task Group m, `http://wirelessman.org/tgm/`
4. Sarkar, S., Dixit, S., Mukherjee, B.: Hybrid Wireless-Optical Broadband-Access Network (WOBAN): A Review of Relevant Challenges. J. Lightwave Technology 25(11), 3329–3340 (2007)
5. IEEE 802.16e Task Group, `http://wirelessman.org/tge/`
6. Xie, L.-L., Kumar, P.R.: Multisource, Multidestination, Multirelay Wireless Networks. IEEE Trans. Information Theory 53(10), 3586–3595 (2007)
7. Shen, G., Tucker, R.S., Chae, C.-J.: Fixed Mobile Convergence Architectures for Broadband Access: Integration of EPON and WiMAX. IEEE Communications Magn. 45(8), 44–50 (2007)
8. Lin, B., Ho, P.-H., Shen, X.: Network Planning for Next-Generation Metropolitan-Area Broadband Access under EPON-WiMAX Integration. IEEE Globecom, 1–5 (2008)
9. Jiang, L., Parekh, S., Walrand, J.: Base Station Association Game in Multi-Cell Wireless Networks (Special Paper). IEEE WCNC, 1616–1621 (2008)
10. Kamoun, M., Mazet, L.: Base-station selection in cooperative single frequency cellular network. IEEE SPAWC, 1–5 (2007)
11. Wong, C.Y., Cheng, R.S., Lataief, K.B., Murch, R.D.: Multiuser OFDM with adaptive subcarrier, bit, and power allocation. IEEE JSAC 17(10), 1747–1758 (1999)
12. Shen, Z., Andrews, J.G., Evans, B.L.: Optimal power allocation in multiuser OFDM systems. IEEE Globecom 1, 337–341 (2003)
13. Kim, I., Park, I.-S., Lee, Y.H.: Use of linear programming for dynamic subcarrier and bit allocation in multiuser OFDM. IEEE Trans. Vehicular Technology 55(4), 1195–1207 (2006)
14. Xu, H., Tian, H., Feng, Y., Gao, Y., Zhang, P.: An Efficient Resource Management Scheme with Guaranteed QoS of Heterogeneous Services in MIMO-OFDM System. IEEE WCNC, 1838–1843 (2008)
15. Letaief, K.B., Zhang, Y.J.: Dynamic Multiuser Resource Allocation and Adaptation for Wireless Systems. IEEE Wireless Communications 13(4), 38–47 (2006)
16. Kim, K.T., Kwon, K.B., Oh, S.K.: Performance Analysis of OFDMA Cellular Systems Using a Multi-Cell Resource Management Scheme. In: APCC, pp. 1–6 (2006)
17. Zhu, H., Zhu, J., Liu, K.J.R.: Non-Cooperative Resource Competition Game by Virtual Referee in Multi-Cell OFDMA Networks. IEEE J. on Areas in Commun. 25(6), 1079–1090 (2007)
18. Can, B., Yanikomeroglu, H., Onat, F.A., Carvalho, E., Yomo, D.H.: Efficient Cooperative Diversity Schemes and Radio Resource Allocation for IEEE 802.16j. In: IEEE WCNC, pp. 36–41 (2008)
19. Bo, G., Cimini, L.J.: Resource Allocation Algorithms for Multiuser Cooperative OFDMA Systems with Subchannel Permutation. In: CISS, pp. 692–697 (2008)
20. Gong, M., Lin, B., Ho, P.-H., Hung, P.: Adaptive Control and Resource Assignment in Cooperative PON-WiMAX Networks. Accepted by AICT (2009)
21. Gong, M., Lin, B., Ho, P.-H., Hung, P.: BU Association and Resource Allocation in Integrated PON-WiMAX under Inter-cell Cooperative Transmission. Submitted to GlobeCom (2009)
22. Rappaport, T.S.: Wireless Communications Principles and Practice, 2nd edn. Prentice Hall, Englewood Cliffs (2002)
23. ILOG CPLEX 11.0, CPLEX Optimization Inc. (2006)

A Future Access Network Architecture for Providing Personalized Context-Aware Services with Sensors

Masugi Inoue[1], Masaaki Ohnishi[1], Hiroaki Morino[2,1], and Tohru Sanefuji[3]

[1] National Institute of Information and Communications Technology,
4-2-1 Nukui-Kitamachi, Koganei, Tokyo 184-8795 Japan
{inoue,ohnishim}@nict.go.jp, morino@shibaura-it.ac.jp
[2] Shibaura Institute of Technology, 3-7-5 Toyosu, Koto-ku, Tokyo 135-8548 Japan
[3] Nassua Solutions Corp., LAND DEN Bld. BF1, 1-17-1 Shinjuku Shinjuku-ku,
Tokyo 160-0002 Japan
sanefuji@nassua.co.jp

Abstract. We propose a future access network architecture that can provide advanced context-aware services by securely delivering diverse kinds of dynamically changing sensor information about specific localities or private individuals. The architecture features individual and group management of peer-to-peer-based secure connections established between terminals and servers. It implements multi-access functions that enable terminals to deliver sensor information to multiple different application servers and multi-service functions that enable the terminals to receive information-provision services from those servers.

Keywords: Internet of things, wireless mesh network, sensor networks, context-awareness, platform.

1 Introduction

AS part of our research related to a New Generation Network [1], we have been conducting research on access networks. In this research, we are focusing on the future access networks based on the clean slate design approach that is not limited by the constraints of conventional networks.

It is generally believed that new sensor devices will be connected to the network in addition to PCs or mobile phones. However, considerable discussion is still required regarding the kinds of access networks to which the sensor devices will be connected, the manner in which those devices will be connected, the locations to which the sensor information will be transferred, the manners in which those transfers will be carried out, and so on. If we turn our attention to the "local region" that an access network will directly cover, the "individuals" who live in that local region, the various "communities" that are formed by that local region and those individuals, and the communications that they desire, it is apparent that new features will be needed which are not provided by existing networks.

X. Jun Hei and L. Cheung (Eds.): AccessNets 2009, LNICST 37, pp. 121–132, 2010.

From this perspective, we presented requirements for a community communications service platform and proposed a managed wireless mesh technology as the means of implementing it [2, 3]. Then, based on the concept that a platform is required to implement diverse sensor application services which make practical use of information from sensors, a sensor application platform and sensor application operation model based on the same technology were shown [4].

In this paper, we will discuss future access networks viewed from the perspective of sensors that are connected to the network to serve a local region, individuals, and communities.

2 From Access Network to Regional Network

2.1 Existing Access Networks

As its name implies, an access network in an existing network mainly provides a means of "access" to the networking facility. In other words, it functions as a relay medium for connecting a terminal located at an edge of the network to a central facility on the network such as the Internet. This is not just because the terminal communicates with other terminals located at remote locations through the central network. It is also because the central network is a place where various kinds of information provided to the terminal by the client-server model is collected, summarized, accumulated, processed, and provided. This kind of central network-based information processing and information exchange model had been developed because it had been extremely efficient both technologically and from a business standpoint to gather, process, and provide information that was commonly required by many users in a central and collective manner.

2.1 Future Regional Networks

The first kinds of information that will be detected by sensors includes information related to the environment such as traffic or weather conditions of a certain locality and information related to a specific individual or group of individuals. It must be handled appropriately with regard to ensuring public and private safety and security. Another important point to note is that the primary users of these kinds of information are the local region and its citizens and communities.

From this perspective, central network-based sensor information processing model, on which sensor information for a certain local region is transported, accumulated, processed, and provided to other places through the global Internet, would need to be investigated carefully in terms of safety, security and efficiency although this can certainly provide benefits.

In light of this, we believe that the information that will be detected by various types of sensors will be so-called "local-oriented fresh information" (time-sensitive information about a specific locality that may quickly become inaccurate or irrelevant) of that local region. The information should be used efficiently and safely for services targeting the relevant local region and its citizens. To achieve this, a network is required for appropriately circulating those kinds of information within the local region. That will be the access network of the future, whose concept is illustrated in Fig. 1. It will not only provide a terminal with a means of accessing a central network (core network) such as the Internet, but it will also include information processing and exchange functions, which have conventionally been provided by the central network. To avoid implying that it just has network access functions, we will refer to the future access network here as a regional network.

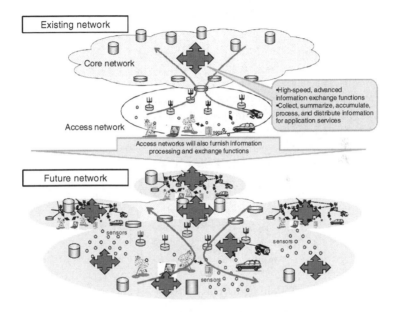

Fig. 1. Future access network will be a regional network that includes information processing and exchange functions

When viewed from the perspective of the characteristics of the information, the central network is good at accumulating a massive amount of information that is used "in common" or information that is relatively "static". On the other hand, a regional network is good at collecting, accumulating, and processing information that is related to real space or people and will be used mainly in that local region because the information is "dynamically changing" and carries a sense of "locality" or "privacy".

However, local-oriented sensor information is not information that should only be used within that local region. It also includes information that is required by users in other regions. Therefore, it is important for a regional network to be able to circulate sensor information, when necessary, between itself and another regional network or external wide-area network such as the Internet. This circulation of information will facilitate business development and service cooperation that is beneficial to both network parties.

By safely gathering and accumulating local-oriented fresh information and providing various application services, the regional network can contribute not only to the enrichment of that local region and the lives of its citizens but also to the renewal or growth of the local region by creating new industries and employment.

2.3   Requirements of a Regional Network

Generally, the existing local information services that are distributed from a service provider include newspaper insert advertisements, fliers distribution in front of stations, and electronic billboards. The existing distribution of local information had relied on physical media such as paper or objects in this way. There have been cases in which an application service provider (ASP) that uses a wide-area network such as the Internet to provide application services also provides local information services. However, when a wide-area network is used in this way, it is basically limited to information distribution to individuals through email. Problems that tend to occur with this method are that personal information must be registered first, email is distributed to individuals regardless of their own situation, and sometimes it is delivered with high frequency, making the recipients annoyed. Some ASPs have attempted to deal with these problems by emailing information according to position information gathered by using the GPS function installed in mobile phones. However, since the number of users is limited, business development is difficult for the conventional ASPs because the cost benefit ratio is low when they use systems or operating technologies designed on the assumption that a wide-area network infrastructure would be used. Also, it will be difficult to apply their service model in which an ASP charges a fee for each information service to the citizens who will be regularly receiving various types of information services.

Based on the considerations mentioned above, we believe that a new business model that has not previously been used is required to enable a service for providing local-oriented fresh information to be successful in the future as a business. Also, if a new service model is assumed in which, for example, the position information of an individual or the environmental information in the vicinity of an individual is collected in real-time to provide beneficial services to the individual, the terminal system itself must be newly designed in addition to the means of constructing and operating the network and providing services.

Specifically, let's consider some scenarios for using future sensor networks. A situation is being considered in which the mobile terminals that individuals will carry in the future will themselves fulfill the roles of sensors [5]. Also, a model has been considered in which various sensors that have been installed surrounding an individual's body form a body area network (BAN), and sensor information that is detected by those sensors is delivered to the network through a mobile terminal [6, 7]. In both of these cases, various types of sensor information continue to be accumulated in servers on the network. The application server classifies and analyzes that information and processes it so that it becomes appropriate service for each individual. To link the collection of information and the provision of service as replies, the terminal must be provided with "multi-access" functions, which enable the terminal to simultaneously access multiple application servers, and "multi-service" functions, which enable services to be offered to the terminal by each application server. Figure 2 illustrates this concept.

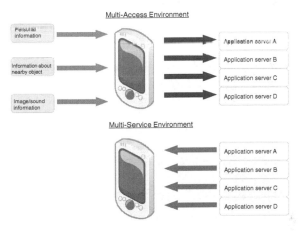

Fig. 2. Multi-access and multi-service environments

Also, a regional network must not operate independently, but must also be interconnected with other regional networks to form a regional information infrastructure so that the service provision area can be selected according to the service content or objective. The regional information infrastructure should be a platform that is operated as a network system that can collect various information in real-time from sensors that are deployed throughout each regional network and after classifying and analyzing it by application use, processes and generates it as value-added information that can be distributed to terminals. Because of the regional information infrastructure, an independent system will no longer have to be constructed for each domain (communications provider or service provider) as in the past. Instead, system resources such as sensors or terminals that were installed by separate service providers can operate while being shared by various separate service domains. Sharing system resources in this way not only provides cost and operational benefits to service providers on the regional information infrastructure but also enables higher value-added information to be provided to users since one piece of sensor information can be used and applied by various applications.

Figure 3 shows the layer configuration of the platform. The platform provides networking functions and sensor management functions. It also provides the sensor connection gateway interface (SCGI) as the interface to the sensors and end devices, and the sensor network application gateway interface (SNAGI) as the interface to the applications. As for functions for sensors, the SCGI provides gateway functions for collecting data from the sensors and transferring that information to the upper layer, and the SNAGI provides functions for collecting, classifying, and accumulating information and transferring it to various applications.

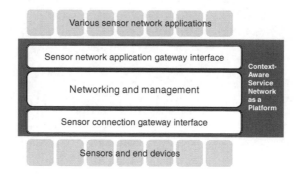

Fig. 3. Layer Configuration of the Proposed Platform

3   Regional Network Configuration

The following two kinds of connections are defined in a regional network.

1. Seamless connection to a wide-area network
2. Community domain connection within the regional network

These two types of connections are provided by a service gateway that is called a community service gateway (CSG). A CSG, which is installed at a location that provides a service, is connected to both the regional network and wide-area network. Fig. 4 shows a physical network configuration when a managed wireless mesh is used as the means of implementing the regional network [2, 3].

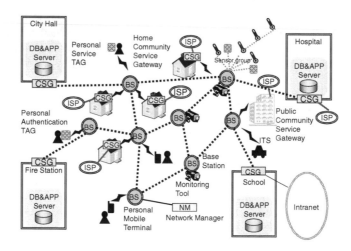

Fig. 4. Regional network configuration based on managed wireless mesh technology

The CSG governs a logical domain called a community domain, which is constructed on the regional network. A community domain is easy to understand if it is considered as a virtual network. Each CSG can accommodate various types of terminals such as mobile terminals or sensors in the community domain that it governs and can independently provide applications according to usage objectives. In addition, a CSG provides gateway functions for seamlessly connecting the group of terminals accommodated in the community domain to the wide-area network. Since the CSG itself also has terminal functions, it can also connect as a terminal to a community domain that is managed by another CSG.

Figure 5 describes an example of the relationships between a regional network and community domains. Community groups exist in various forms such as welfare centers, schools and companies. Individuals live their lives while participating in multiple community groups. Therefore, a regional network must be able to multiplex community groups. Moreover, the terminal that an individual possesses must be able to belong to multiple different community groups.

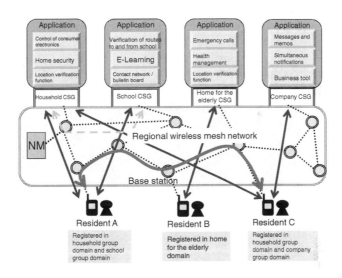

Fig. 5. Relationships among regional network, communities, and users

To accomplish this, a CSG forms and governs a community domain. Also, the terminal has functions for simultaneously belonging and connecting to different CSGs. These functions enable relationships between real world communities and individuals as well as communications based on those relationships to be implemented on the regional network.

In a normal access network that contains an existing mesh network, communications between terminals and application servers are generally first temporarily concentrated at a gateway, which is a relay point between the access network and external network, and then routed to the individual application servers that are on the external network. On the other hand, a regional network proposed here is configured in the mesh network, and the individual routes from terminals to multiple CSGs generally differ. Therefore, those routes must be managed or controlled. The device that administers this is the network manager (NM). The NM distributes IP network addresses to each base station in advance. Those addresses will be used for service domains managed by CSGs that are connected to base stations. When a CSG connects to a nearby base station, the base station assigns a service domain IP network address to the CSG. At the same time, the NM also configures data paths to reach the CSG that the group of terminals managed by the CSG take while passing through various base stations in the mesh network. The NM that manages resources of an entire mesh network in this way is established for an individual mesh network.

The applications that will be provided by CSGs will continue to become more diverse depending on uses and objectives. For example, in a household CSG, there will probably be a demand for remote monitoring and control applications that can control home electronics and provide home security or applications that can obtain the locations of family members in real-time. In schools, there will probably be a demand for applications that will distribute information verifying routes to and from school or applications that will distribute educational videos that were recorded as part of a student's home study for supplementing lessons in school.

4   Multi-service and Multi-access Implementation Methods

A characteristic of a multi-service and multi-access environment on this regional wireless mesh network is that peer-to-peer-type virtual private network (VPN) paths between CSGs and terminals can be dynamically constructed and those VPNs can be grouped together at the CSG side for each application service. A group, which is a single domain on the network, is managed by the CSG. The multi-service and multi-access functions that were described earlier are implemented when individual terminals are connected by peer-to-peer-type VPN paths to multiple different domains.

Figure 6 explains the multi-service function. The CSG provides applications 1 and 2 to terminals. For providing application-1, the CSG establishes VPN tunnels with

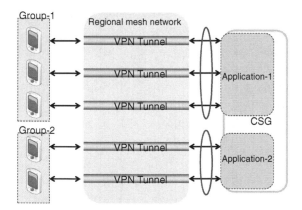

Fig. 6. Domain management and multi-service function achieved by configuring and grouping peer-to-peer-type VPNs for which the CSG, which is a server, is considered as a terminal

terminals belonging to Group-1 (a service domain) on the regional mesh network in advance. Also, for providing application-2, the CSG configures another service domain named Group-2 and sets up VPN tunnels with terminals in Group-2. The multiservice function by CSGs is provided by configuring multiple VPN tunnels between terminals and CSGs in this way. Figure 7 explains the multi-access function. The terminal starts three applications, which connects with application services provided by different CSGs. Separate VPN tunnel is used for each connection. The terminal manages the tunnels.

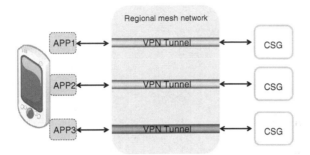

Fig. 7. Multi-access from a terminal to CSGs, which is implemented by configuring peer-to-peer-type VPNs with the CSGs that provide each application

5   Secure Communication Function

An authentication session is essential in control communications to perform peer-to-peer group communication between CSGs and terminals, and if a regional wireless mesh network provides those functions, safe regional services can be offered.

Since the existing IP network platform in the Internet uses a connectionless protocol, it is difficult to know who got access to the network, where they got access to it from, and through which path they connected. Therefore, access is generally restricted by a user authentication in which ID and password are entered. As shown at the top of Fig. 8, in a conventional network system, a firewall function or encryption-based security function such as IP-VPN or SSL-VPN must be introduced as a means of dealing with DoS attacks to a server system that has a global fixed IP address. As a result, not only do system management and operation costs and equipment costs increase, but the installation locations may also be limited from a secure maintenance and operation standpoint.

In contrast, the proposed regional wireless mesh network provides an environment in which CSGs can be deployed at various locations and facilities within the local region, and community domains are managed and operated by the CSGs. For the CSGs to provide services to terminals that are participating in community domains, the regional wireless mesh network platform must provide high-security functions. This is specifically accomplished as follows.

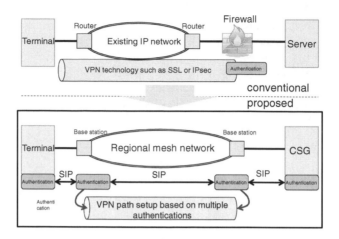

Fig. 8. Provision of security function

When a CSG and terminal perform peer-to-peer communication, each of them first performs access authentication between itself and a base station. Then, device authentication and group participation authentication are performed in both directions between the CSG and terminal, and application connections are established. If a terminal or CSG that has not been registered in advance in the regional wireless mesh network attempts to accesses the network, it will be completely denied by the base station. In addition, an access to a terminal from a CSG at which that terminal has not been registered or is not participating or an access to a CSG from a terminal that has not been registered at that CSG will be completed filtered (denied) at the communication level, and application communication within the mesh network will not be executed.

Note that since a base station completely disables resources for VPN paths that had been assigned for application communications between terminals and CSGs when they terminate the communications normally, all base stations that form the mesh network effectively work as a firewall function. As a result, robust network admission control (NAC) can be provided within the entire regional network.

6   Support for Context-Aware Services

A feature of the proposed platform is that open APIs provided by the mesh communication control module can be used to independently develop special-purpose applications for CSGs and terminals according to usage objectives. Also, intranet or LAN type community domains can be developed on the regional network to manage services independently. In addition, users can easily make practical use of regional network resources without configuring network information or managing network operation. By constructing this kind of regional network infrastructure environment, a sensor network environment that is closely tied to everyday life can be created.

Finally, we will present an example of support for context-aware services. Assume that a person is regularly using a sensor network to check his health. Figure 9 illustrates the operation of linked personal terminal and CSG applications involved in the health check. First, consider a scenario in which the person will be eating in a restaurant. The personal terminal senses store-provided menu information and sends it to the household CSG. Then, it senses the person's order information and sends that to the household CSG. The person's health application that is running at the household CSG automatically creates advice information for menu selections based on the information that was sensed and sends it to the terminal. In addition, the terminal senses information such as the menu that the person brought with him and meal status video information (including information from sensors in the environment that was received by the terminal) and sends it to the store CSG. The store CSG determines the meal time or amount of leftovers for each menu selection and calculates the total number of calories and provides this information as a customer information service. Also, the store CSG runs a menu consulting application, which helps improve store management and make it more efficient by using customer sensing information to collect and analyze the order rates of the store's menu items, the amounts of leftovers, and the status of customers' meals (such as meal times or facial expressions) in real-time. Service information that the store CSG sent to the terminal is also transferred from the terminal to the household CSG, and a household CSG application associates it with detailed meal guidance or insufficient nutrients and then analyzes the person's health status and reports it to the terminal.

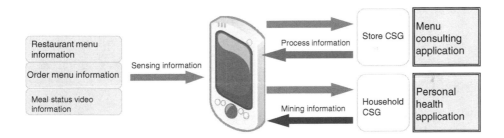

Fig. 9. Example healthcare service by linking restaurant's CSG and household CSG

7   Conclusions

As a new generation access network, we proposed a regional network for safely and efficiently providing context-aware services to a local region that is making practical use of sensors as well as to its citizens and communities. We also described requirements for this regional network, configuration methods, and implementation methods for multi-service and multi-access functions. In future work, we plan to continue to make the regional network platform more specific and extend the managed wireless mesh functions that support its implementation.

References

[1] AKARI Project, http://akari-project.nict.go.jp/

[2] Inoue, M., Nakauchi, K., Kafle, V., Morino, H., Sanefuji, T.: Community Service Platform using Wireless Logical Mesh Paths. In: WPMC (September 2008)

[3] Morino, H., Kawamura, H., Inoue, M., Sanefuji, T.: Load-balanced multipath routing for wireless mesh networks: A step by step rate control approach. In: Proc. of the 9th international Symposium on Autonomous Decentralized Systems (ISADS 2009), March 2009, pp. 281–286 (2009)

[4] Inoue, M., Kafle, V., Morino, H., Sanefuji, T.: Sensor Application Platform on a Novel Managed Wireless Mesh. In: IEEE Globecom Workshop, on Wireless Mesh and Sensor Networks (November 2008)

[5] Mastroianni, S., Lewis, J., Manes, G., Giorgetti, G., Gupta, S.: The personal sensor network: a user-centric monitoring solution. In: Bodynets 2007: Proceedings of the International Conference on body Area Networks (2007)

[6] FP6 IST e-SENSE Project, http://www.ist-e-sense.org/

[7] Zhong, L., Sinclair, M., Bittner, R.: A phone-centered body sensor network platform: cost, energy efficiency & user interface. In: BSN 2006: Proceedings of the International Workshop on Wearable and Implantable Body Sensor Networks, pp. 179–182 (2006)

How to Optimally Schedule Cooperative Spectrum Sensing in Cognitive Radio Networks

Ke Lang, Yuan Wu, and Danny H.K. Tsang

Department of Electronic and Computer Engineering
Hong Kong University of Science and Technology
langke@ust.hk, ecewuy@ust.hk, eetsang@ece.ust.hk

Abstract. In cognitive radio (CR) networks, secondary users can be coordinated to perform spectrum sensing so as to detect primary user activities more accurately. However, in a dynamic spectrum environment, more sensing cooperations may induce every secondary user to sense more channels, thus decreasing their transmission time. In this paper, we study this tradeoff by using the theory of partially observable Markov decision process (POMDP). This formulation leads to an optimal sensing scheduling policy that determines which secondary users sense which channels with what miss detection probability and false alarm probability. A myopic policy with lower complexity yet comparable performance is also proposed. Numerical and simulation results are provided to illustrate that our design can utilize the spectrum more efficiently for cognitive radio users.

Keywords: cognitive radio, cooperative sensing scheduling, partially observable Markov decision process.

1 Introduction

Cognitive radio (CR) [1] [2] is a new technology that provides a novel solution to the spectrum inefficiency problem. In CR networks, there are two types of users: primary users and secondary users. A primary user (PU) is a licensed owner of a channel, while a secondary user (SU) periodically scans the PU spectrum, identifies the idle channels and accesses the channels opportunistically without causing intolerable interference to PUs.

IEEE 802.22 wireless regional area networks (WRANs) standard [3] is aimed at using CR techniques to allow sharing of the unused spectrum. The 802.22 system uses base stations (BSs) to manage their cells and all associated SUs. In addition to the traditional role of a BS, the 802.22 BS has a new function of coordinating cooperative sensing [3] to make sensing results more accurate.

Many research works were carried out to analyze the performance of cooperative sensing [4] [5] [6]. Although cooperative sensing can improve the spectrum sensing accuracy, it also has some drawbacks, especially when the number of SUs

X. Jun Hei and L. Cheung (Eds.): AccessNets 2009, LNICST 37, pp. 133–148, 2010.

is limited and only sequential (narrowband) sensing is allowed[1]. A typical example can be given by that in cooperative sensing some SUs may be scheduled to sense several channels sequentially, which in turn will decrease their transmission time significantly. Therefore, there is a tradeoff between cooperative sensing time and transmission time. Meanwhile, the idle spectrum available for SUs to access is time-changing, and the information about the changing idle spectrum can only be partially observed by SUs (due to both the imperfect spectrum sensing and sensing scheduling policy, which we will describe in detail in sections 2 and 3). Based on these considerations, in this paper we study the dynamic scheduling for cooperative sensing under time-varying spectrum environment. Specifically, we formulate our dynamic sensing scheduling problem with the partially observable Markov decision process (POMDP), and derive an optimal sensing scheduling policy (i.e. determining which SUs to sense which set of channels with what miss detection probability and false alarm probability) via solving the formulated problem. To the best of our knowledge, our work is the first one in this direction, and shed light on how to implement cooperative spectrum sensing function proposed in 802.22 standard.

POMDP was used in [7] [8] to study the dynamic spectrum access for an Ad hoc CR networks. An incremental pruning algorithm was proposed in [10] which could solve the POMDP problem. In our paper, we adopt this algorithm to get the optimal sensing scheduling policy of a multi-user cooperative spectrum sensing problem in a centralized manner.

The rest of the paper is organized as follows. We present the network model and propose our protocol in section 2. We then formulate the problem of the tradeoff between cooperative sensing time and transmission time as a POMDP in section 3. We derive the optimal policy and myopic policy for our problem in section 4. Section 5 presents numerical and simulation results. Finally, we conclude this paper in section 6.

2   System Model

2.1   Network Model

In this work, we consider a centralized CR network with a base station (or access point), which manages the cooperative sensing scheduling as well as data transmission. All SUs in a cell need to be synchronized. In the following part, we further assume there exists a set of SUs $\mathcal{M} = \{1, 2, ..., M\}$, and a set of orthogonal frequency channels $\mathcal{N} = \{1, 2, ..., N\}$ with a BS in a cell.

Each SU is equipped with a single radio interface. In this work, we assume all SUs use energy detection mechanism for spectrum sensing and each SU can

---

[1] According to [11], the wideband spectrum sensing refers to that the sensing device can sense multiple spectrum bands over a wide frequency range at a time. Meanwhile, the sequential spectrum sensing refers to that the sensing device can only sense one spectrum band at a time, and thus different spectrum bands have to be sensed sequentially.

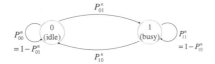

Fig. 1. DTMC model for PU channel n

only carry out the sequential spectrum sensing instead of the wideband spectrum sensing due to some PHY layer limitations.

2.2   Opportunistic Channel Availability Model

In this paper, we assume primary system operates in a time slotted manner with fixed slot length T. In the PU network, each channel's occupancy (from slot to slot) follows a two-state discrete time Markov chain (DTMC) as shown in Figure 1. Let $s_n(t)$ denote the availability state of channel n ($n \in \mathcal{N}$) in time slot t. $s_n(t) = 0$ denotes channel n is idle (available for SU to use) in slot t, while $s_n(t) = 1$ denotes channel n is busy (not available for SU to use) in slot t. Furthermore, let the $1 \times N$ vector $\mathbf{s}(t) = (s_1(t), ..., s_N(t))$ denote the channel availability state vector for all the PU channels in slot t, which has the state space $\Omega^s = \{(\omega_1, \omega_2, ..., \omega_N) | \omega_n = \{0, 1\}, \forall n \in \mathcal{N}\}$. By assuming independence across different channels, the dynamics of $\mathbf{s}(t)$ follow a DTMC with transition probability from state vector ω to state vector ω' given as:

$$P_{\omega\omega'} = \Pr(\mathbf{s}(t+1) = \omega' | \mathbf{s}(t) = \omega) = \prod_{n=1}^{N} P^n_{\omega_n \omega'_n}, \forall \omega, \omega' \in \Omega^s \qquad (1)$$

where ω_n, ω'_n denote the nth element of state vector ω and ω', respectively. $P^n_{\omega_n \omega'_n}$ has been shown in Figure 1, representing channel n's state transition probability. We consider the DTMC model as time homogeneous, i.e. $P^n_{01}, P^n_{10}, \forall n \in \mathcal{N}$, are time independent. We assume the PU channels' statistical behavior $P^n_{01}, P^n_{10}, \forall n \in \mathcal{N}$, can be obtained from a long term measurement by some channel parameter estimator [12], and this information is provided to CR BS. Note that for each channel n, the stationary probabilities of being idle and busy $\pi^n_0, \pi^n_1, \forall n \in \mathcal{N}$ can be calculated as $\pi^n_0 = \frac{P^n_{10}}{P^n_{01}+P^n_{10}}$, and $\pi^n_1 = \frac{P^n_{01}}{P^n_{01}+P^n_{10}}$. In section 5, we use different values of π^n_0 to show the impact of PUs' activities on the SUs' performance.

2.3   Spectrum Sensing Technique and Cooperative Detection

Several well-known spectrum sensing techniques have been proposed including matched filter detection, energy detection, cyclostationary feature detection and wavelet detection [1] [5]. In this paper, we adopt the energy detection method [13]. The received signal $x_R(t)$ takes the form

$$x_R(t) = \begin{cases} e(t), & H_0(t) \\ h \cdot x_T(t) + e(t), & H_1(t) \end{cases}$$

where $x_R(t)$ is the received signal at a secondary user on a channel, $x_T(t)$ is the transmitted signal of the primary user, $e(t)$ is the additive white Gaussian noise, h is the channel gain of the sensing channel between the primary user and the secondary user. Hypothesis 0 (H_0) corresponds to no signal transmitted, hypothesis 1 (H_1) corresponds to signal transmitted. Then, in a non-fading environment, the detection probability P_D and false alarm probability P_{FA} are given as follows [13],

$$P_D = \Pr(Y > \lambda | H_1) = Q_u(\sqrt{2\gamma}, \sqrt{\lambda}) \tag{2}$$

and

$$P_{FA} = \Pr(Y > \lambda | H_0) = \Gamma(u, \frac{\lambda}{2})/\Gamma(u) \tag{3}$$

where Y is the test or decision statistic, λ is the decision threshold, u is the time bandwidth product, γ is the SNR, $Q_u(\cdot, \cdot)$ is the generalized Marcum Q-function, $\Gamma(\cdot)$ and $\Gamma(\cdot, \cdot)$ are the complete and incomplete gamma functions. Then, the miss detection probability is $P_{MD} = 1 - P_D$. For a fading environment, P_{MD} and P_{FA} have more complicated expressions [5] [13].

We adopt a simple cooperative sensing scheme, which is called "OR" rule [5] in this paper. This rule works like this: every SU sends its sensing result (0 or 1) of a channel to the BS, and as long as one SU senses the channel as busy, the BS will take this channel as busy. Only if all SUs sense the channel as idle, BS will take the channel as idle. In this case, the miss-detection probability and false alarm probability of channel n are

$$P_{MD}(n) = \prod_{m \in \mathcal{M}(n)} P_{MD}(m, n)$$

$$P_{FA}(n) = 1 - \prod_{m \in \mathcal{M}(n)} (1 - P_{FA}(m, n))$$

where $P_{MD}(m, n)$ and $P_{FA}(m, n)$ are SU $m's$ miss detection probability and false alarm probability of channel n, and $\mathcal{M}(n)$ is the set of SUs sensing this channel.

If we further assume that each SU which is scheduled to sense channel n uses the same miss detection probability and false alarm probability, then we have

$$P_{MD}(m, n) = \sqrt[|\mathcal{M}(n)|]{P_{MD}(n)}$$

where $|\mathcal{M}(n)|$ denotes cardinality of set $\mathcal{M}(n)$. This means if we set $P_{MD}(n)$ as a constant target value, and we have $|\mathcal{M}(n)|$ SUs to cooperatively sense channel n instead of having only one SU to sense it, then the tolerable miss detection probability for each of the $|\mathcal{M}(n)|$ SUs $P_{MD}(m, n)$ will increase to $\sqrt[|\mathcal{M}(n)|]{P_{MD}(n)}$.

A larger $P_{MD}(m,n)$ means the decision threshold λ in (2) becomes larger[2]. Then from (3), we will have a smaller $P_{FA}(m,n)$. We can further see that as $P_{MD}(n)$ is set as a constant target value, $P_{FA}(n)$ will become smaller if $|\mathcal{M}(n)|$ SUs cooperatively sense channel n instead of no cooperation. The larger the number of cooperative SUs, the smaller $P_{FA}(n)$ we will get, this means the sensing accuracy becomes better when more SUs sense the channel [5].

2.4   Proposed Protocol

Figure 2 shows an example to illustrate the operation process of the BS and SUs in CR network using our proposed protocol. At the beginning of each slot, each channel will have a state transition according to the DTMC model described in subsection 2.2, and at the same time, the BS decides which SU senses which set of channels with what probabilities of miss detection and false alarm based on our optimal policy which will be presented later. For example, in Figure 2, BS decides SU1 to sense channels $1, 3, 4$, and SU2 to sense channels $1, 2, 5$. After receiving the decisions from the BS, SU1 and SU2 will sequentially sense the assigned channels, and the channel sensing sequence can be arbitrarily determined. Since the sensing duration for each channel is a fixed value ΔL, and we have limited number of SUs, if the BS decides some channels are sensed by more SUs in order to increase these channels' sensing accuracy, then each SU may need to sense more channels accordingly, thus causing less time for transmission (Notice that in Figure 2, the slot length is L. The time duration for BS scheduling cooperative sensing is η_1. The time duration for SUs uploading their sensing results and BS allocating channels to SUs is η_2. All these three values are constant). There is a tradeoff between cooperative sensing time and transmission time.

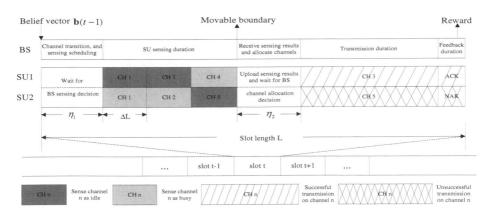

Fig. 2. An example of the operation process of our proposed protocol

---

[2] In our work both the values of receiver SNR γ in a non-fading environment or average receiver SNR in a fading environment, and time bandwidth product u are fixed.

Since we adopt in our protocol the cooperative sensing scheme using "OR" rule, although SU1 senses channel 1 as idle, and SU2 senses it as busy, BS determines channel 1 is busy and not to use it in the example of Figure 2.

In our proposed protocol, data transmission works as follows: if a channel's sensing result is idle, then although there exists the probability of miss detection, the BS will allocate this channel to one of SUs. As seen from Figure 2, channel 5 turns out to be busy when SU2 tries to use it. Our protocol requires sensing synchronization for all SUs, i.e., each SU senses the same number of channels.

At the end of a slot, the SU using the channel will send an ACK or NAK to the BS, which will be used as an important information for future decisions. In this paper, we only consider the case of downlink transmission, but our proposed protocol can also be applied to the uplink transmission.

3   Problem Formulation

At the beginning of each time slot, based on previous actions and observations, the BS could have a belief state over every channel, which is the probability of a PU channel being in that state in the previous time slot. This is different from traditional Markov decision process, because in our case, the BS may not know the exact state of a channel. For instance, if BS determines the channel as busy, it can not be sure if it is busy due to the probability of false alarm. Besides, if some channels are not sensed by any SU, the exact state of these channels will not be known either.

Before we present our complete problem formulation, we first describe our optimal cooperative sensing scheduling problem from the perspective of POMDP.

(i) Action

In our formulation, at the beginning of time slot t there are two actions, a^I and a^{II}. a^I determines which SU senses which channels. a^{II} determines how to tune the sensor operating point of each SU (i.e. miss detection probability and false alarm probability) when sensing a channel.

$$a^I(t) = \begin{bmatrix} a_{11}^1(t) & ... & a_{1N}^1(t) \\ a_{21}^1(t) & ... & a_{2N}^1(t) \\ ... & ... & ... \\ a_{M1}^1(t) & ... & a_{MN}^1(t) \end{bmatrix}$$

where $a_{mn}^1(t) \in \{0,1\}$, $a_{mn}^1(t) = 1$ denotes SU m senses channel n in time slot t, and $a_{mn}^1(t) = 0$ means the opposite. We define the set of SUs that are scheduled to sense channel n in slot t as $\mathcal{M}(n,t) = \{m|a_{mn}^1(t) = 1\}$.

$$a^{II}(t) \doteq \begin{bmatrix} a_{11}^2(t) & ... & a_{1N}^2(t) \\ a_{21}^2(t) & ... & a_{2N}^2(t) \\ ... & ... & ... \\ a_{M1}^2(t) & ... & a_{MN}^2(t) \end{bmatrix}$$

where $a_{mn}^2(t) = P_{MD}(m,n,t)$ denotes the specified miss detection probability for SU m on channel n in time slot t. Notice that by setting the value of miss detection probability $P_{MD}(m, n, t)$, we actually determine the sensor operating point for SU m on channel n in slot t, because both the sensing decision threshold λ and the false alarm probability $P_{FA}(m, n, t)$ for SU m on channel n in slot t can be calculated via (2) and (3), respectively. Specifically, in this work we choose the value of miss detection probability $P_{MD}(m, n, t)$ from a set of discrete values, which is practical for most spectrum sensing modules' operation because the sensing operation point cannot be tuned continuously.

We define $\mathbf{a}(t) = [a^{I}(t), a^{II}(t)]$.

(ii) Observation

Let $\theta_n(t)$ denote the observation result of channel n in time slot t. Then $\theta_n(t)$ could have the following 4 possible observations,

- BS determines the channel as idle and receives ACK after transmission; denote this as observation 0.
- BS determines the channel as idle and receives NAK after transmission due to miss detection; denote this as observation 1.
- BS determines the channel as busy, does not use the channel, and thus the BS receives no ACK or NAK; denote this as observation 2.
- BS decides not to sense the channel and thus observes nothing; denote this as observation 3.

Further, let the $1 \times N$ vector $\theta(t) = (\theta_1(t), ... \theta_N(t))$ denote the channel observation vector for all the PU channels at the end of slot t, which has the observation space $\mathbf{Z}^{\theta} = \{(z_1, z_2, ..., z_N) | z_n = \{0, 1, 2, 3\}, \forall n \in \mathcal{N}\}$.

The individual channel observation probability is defined as the probability of the observation given the action we take and the current state of channel n, $i.e.$

$$\Pr(\theta_n(t)|\mathbf{a}(t), s_n(t)) = \begin{cases} 1, & if \ \sum_{m=1}^{M} a_{mn}^{1}(t) = 0, \ \theta_n(t) = 3 \\ 1 - P_{FA}(n, t), \\ & if \ \sum_{m=1}^{M} a_{mn}^{1}(t) > 0, \ s_n(t) = 0, \ \theta_n(t) = 0 \\ P_{FA}(n, t), \\ & if \ \sum_{m=1}^{M} a_{mn}^{1}(t) > 0, \ s_n(t) = 0, \ \theta_n(t) = 2 \\ P_{MD}(n, t), \\ & if \ \sum_{m=1}^{M} a_{mn}^{1}(t) > 0, \ s_n(t) = 1, \ \theta_n(t) = 1 \\ 1 - P_{MD}(n, t), \\ & if \ \sum_{m=1}^{M} a_{mn}^{1}(t) > 0, \ s_n(t) = 1, \ \theta_n(t) = 2 \\ 0, & otherwise \end{cases}$$

where $P_{MD}(n, t)$ is the miss detection probability of channel n in time slot t. $P_{FA}(n, t)$ is the false alarm probability of channel n in time slot t. Because of the "OR" rule in cooperative sensing, we have

$$P_{MD}(n, t) = \prod_{m \in \mathcal{M}(n,t)} P_{MD}(m, n, t), \ P_{FA}(n, t) = 1 - \prod_{m \in \mathcal{M}(n,t)} (1 - P_{FA}(m, n, t))$$

In the above observation probability function, if $\sum_{m=1}^{M} a_{mn}^{1}(t) = 0$, which means SUs do not sense channel n, then no matter what the current state is, we will have observation 3 with probability 1, and we will not have any other observations.

If $\sum_{m=1}^{M} a_{mn}^1(t) > 0$, $s_n(t) = 0$, which means when SUs sense channel n and the current state is idle, we will have observation 0 when no false alarm happens, or we will have observation 2 when false alarm happens.

If $\sum_{m=1}^{M} a_{mn}^1(t) > 0$, $s_n(t) = 1$, which means when SUs sense channel n and the current state is busy, we will have observation 1 when miss detection happens, or we will have observation 2 when no miss detection happens.

Then, the observation probability is

$$\Pr(\theta(t) = \mathbf{z}|\mathbf{a}(t), \mathbf{s}(t) = \omega) = \prod_{n=1}^{N} \Pr(\theta_n(t) = z_n|\mathbf{a}(t), s_n(t) = \omega_n) \quad (4)$$

where $\mathbf{z} \in \mathbf{Z}^{\theta}$ is the observation vector, and z_n denotes the nth element of observation vector $\mathbf{z}$.

For the sake of simplicity, we assume every SU being scheduled to sense channel n should tune to the same sensor operating point (i.e. $P_{MD}(m,n,t) = \sqrt[|\mathcal{M}(n,t)|]{P_{MD}(n,t)}, \forall m \in \mathcal{M}(n,t)$).

(iii) Belief vector

Because of the partial spectrum sensing decisions and the presence of sensing errors, a BS may not observe the true system state. However, the BS can infer the system state based on all its past decisions and observations, and summarize this information into a belief vector [8], $\mathbf{b}(t) \triangleq \{b_\omega(t)\}_{\omega \in \Omega^s}$[3] where $b_\omega(t) \triangleq \Pr(\mathbf{s}(t) = \omega|\mathbf{b}(0), \{\mathbf{a}(\tau), \theta(\tau)\}_{\tau=1}^{t}) \in [0,1]$ is the conditional probability (given all past decisions and observations) that the system state is ω in the current time slot t. $b_\omega(t)$ can only be computed at the end of the current time slot t when $\theta(t)$ is known (as shown in Figure 2). The BS will make actions at slot $t+1$ based on its belief vector of the system state $\mathbf{b}(t)$.

We define the updated belief vector as follows:

$$\mathbf{b}(t) \triangleq \mathcal{T}(\mathbf{b}(t-1), \mathbf{a}(t), \theta(t)) \triangleq \{b_{\omega'}(t)\}_{\omega' \in \Omega^s} \quad (5)$$

where $\mathcal{T}(\mathbf{b}(t-1), \mathbf{a}(t), \theta(t))$ represents the updated knowledge of the network state after incorporating the action and observation obtained in slot t. Then, from Bayes rule, we have

$$
\begin{aligned}
b_{\omega'}(t) &= \Pr(\mathbf{s}(t) = \omega'|\mathbf{b}(t-1), \mathbf{a}(t), \theta(t)) \\
&= \frac{\sum\limits_{\omega \in \Omega^s} b_\omega(t-1) P_{\omega\omega'} \Pr(\theta(t)|\mathbf{a}(t), \mathbf{s}(t) = \omega')}{\sum\limits_{\omega \in \Omega^s} \sum\limits_{\omega'' \in \Omega^s} b_\omega(t-1) P_{\omega\omega''} \Pr(\theta(t)|\mathbf{a}(t), \mathbf{s}(t) = \omega'')}
\end{aligned} \quad (6)
$$

From these equations, we know that we have regained the Markov property for the belief state in that the next belief state depends only on the previous belief state, the current action and the current observation received.

---

[3] Here we abuse the notation a little since we just want to list all the elements in the set Ω^s and assign them to the vector $\mathbf{b}(t)$, and the element order is not important.

To illustrate this concept clearly, we take a simple example. Suppose we focus on one channel (e.g. channel n), according to the above equation, we have the following belief updating rule.

If we take the action of sensing channel n, we may have observation 0, 1, or 2.

When we have observation 0, the BS receives an ACK, so it knows the channel state is idle, and according to (6), $h_0(t) = 1$.

When we have observation 1, the BS receives a NAK, so it knows the channel state is busy, and according to (6), $b_0(t) = 0$.

However, for the case of observation 2, the situation becomes partially observable, because we do not know the exact channel state. When we have observation 2, due to the existence of false alarm probability, although the BS determines the channel as busy, it may be actually idle. Then according to (6), $b_0(t) = \{b_0(t-1) \cdot P_{00}^n \cdot P_{FA}(n,t) + b_1(t-1) \cdot P_{10}^n \cdot P_{FA}(n,t)\} / \{b_0(t-1) \cdot P_{00}^n \cdot P_{FA}(n,t) + b_1(t-1) \cdot P_{10}^n \cdot P_{FA}(n,t) + b_0(t-1) \cdot P_{01}^n \cdot (1 - P_{MD}(n,t)) + b_1(t-1) \cdot P_{11}^n \cdot (1 - P_{MD}(n,t))\}$. If false alarm probability becomes 0, we can see that $b_0(t)$ becomes 0.

Similarly, if we take the action of not sensing channel n, we will have observation 3, since we do nothing on the channel in this time slot, we do not know the exact channel state, its belief state just updates according to the DTMC model, and according to (6), $b_0(t) = b_0(t-1) \cdot P_{00}^n + b_1(t-1) \cdot P_{10}^n$.

Here, $b_0(t)$ is the belief of the state being idle in slot t, and the belief of the state being busy is $b_1(t) = 1 - b_0(t)$.

(iv) Reward function

There will be a reward when the channel is sensed and finally the BS receives an ACK, the immediate reward for channel n $(n \in \mathcal{N})$ is

$$R_n(\mathbf{a}(t), \theta_n(t)) = \begin{cases} \frac{L-k-\eta}{L}, & if\ \sum_{m=1}^{M} a_{mn}^1(t) > 0, \theta_n(t) = 0 \\ 0, & otherwise \end{cases} \quad (7)$$

where $k = \Delta L \cdot \sum_{n=1}^{N} a_{mn}^1(t),\ \forall m \in \mathcal{M}$, is the sensing duration (note that to keep synchronization, each SU should sense same number of channels, then $\sum_{n=1}^{N} a_{1n}^1(t) = \sum_{n=1}^{N} a_{2n}^1(t) = ... = \sum_{n=1}^{N} a_{Mn}^1(t)$), ΔL is the sensing duration for one channel, and $\eta = \eta_1 + \eta_2$ is a constant time used for BS decisions and getting sensing results from SUs. Then, the immediate reward for all the channels in time slot t is

$$R(\mathbf{a}(t), \theta(t)) = \sum_{n=1}^{N} R_n(\mathbf{a}(t), \theta_n(t)) \quad (8)$$

Finally, the expected reward for BS to make a decision at the beginning of slot t is

$$\tilde{R}(\mathbf{a}(t), \mathbf{s}(t-1) = \omega)$$
$$= \sum_{\omega' \in \Omega^s} \sum_{\mathbf{z} \in \mathbf{Z}^\theta} P_{\omega\omega'} \Pr(\theta(t) = \mathbf{z} | \mathbf{a}(t), \mathbf{s}(t) = \omega') R(\mathbf{a}(t), \theta(t) = \mathbf{z}) \quad (9)$$

(v) Complete problem formulation
We aim to develop the optimal policy that can maximize the expected total throughput of the SUs over a finite time horizon T, and at the same time it must satisfy the synchronization constraint and primary user interference constraint. The problem is formulated as follows:

$$\max \ E\{\sum_{t=1}^{T} R(\mathbf{a}(t), \theta(t))|\mathbf{b}(0) = \mathbf{b}\} \tag{10}$$

$$\text{subject to: } \sum_{n=1}^{N} a_{1n}^{1}(t) = \sum_{n=1}^{N} a_{2n}^{1}(t) = ... = \sum_{n=1}^{N} a_{Mn}^{1}(t) \tag{11}$$

$$L - \Delta L \cdot \sum_{n=1}^{N} a_{mn}^{1}(t) - \eta > 0, \ \forall m \in \mathcal{M} \tag{12}$$

$$P_c(n, t) \leq \zeta, \ \forall n \in \mathcal{N} \tag{13}$$

In the above formulation, $\mathbf{b}$ is the initial belief vector which could be set according to the channels' statistical behavior. Constraint (11) is a synchronization constraint, which guarantees that each SU senses the same number of channels. Constraint (12) guarantees the transmission time is positive. Constraint (13) is the interference constraint, which aims to satisfy primary users' interference tolerance. Here, $P_c(n, t)$ is the collision probability of channel n in slot t, if we want to guarantee this value below the prescribed primary channel collision probability ζ, it is equivalent to require the miss detection probability of channel n in slot t below this threshold ζ,

$$P_{MD}(n, t) \leq \zeta, \ \forall n \in \mathcal{N} \tag{14}$$

Then the formulation with objective (10) constrained by (11), (12), and (13) changes into the formulation with objective (10) constrained by (11), (12), and (14).

4   Optimal Policy and Myopic Policy

4.1   Optimal Policy

In order to solve the objective function (10), we could solve the following value function $V_t(\mathbf{b}(t-1))$ which denotes the maximum expected remaining reward that can be obtained from the beginning of slot t when the current belief vector is $\mathbf{b}(t-1)$. We use backward induction method to calculate the value function from two parts. One part is the expected immediate reward $\widetilde{R}(\mathbf{a}(t), \mathbf{s}(t-1) = \omega)$ in the current time slot, and the other part is the expected future reward $V_{t+1}(\mathcal{T}(\mathbf{b}(t-1), \mathbf{a}(t), \theta(t) = \mathbf{z}))$. The optimal policy finds a balance between gaining immediate reward and gaining future reward.

(i) When $t = 1, 2, ...T - 1$,

$$V_t(\mathbf{b}(t-1)) = \max_{\mathbf{a}(t)} \{ \sum_{w \in \Omega^s} b_w(t-1)[\tilde{R}(\mathbf{a}(t), \mathbf{s}(t-1) = w) +$$

$$\sum_{w' \in \Omega^u} P_{ww'} \sum_{\mathbf{z} \in \mathbf{Z}^\theta} \Pr(\theta(t) = \mathbf{z}|\mathbf{a}(t), \mathbf{s}(t) = w') V_{t+1}(\mathcal{T}(\mathbf{b}(t-1), \mathbf{a}(t), \theta(t) = \mathbf{z}))]\}$$

subject to. (11), (12), (14)

(ii) When $t = T$,

$$V_t(\mathbf{b}(t-1)) = \max_{\mathbf{a}(t)} \sum_{w \in \Omega^s} b_w(t-1)\tilde{R}(\mathbf{a}(t), \mathbf{s}(t-1) = w)$$

subject to: (11), (12), (14)

where $\tilde{R}(\mathbf{a}(t), \mathbf{s}(t-1) = w)$ is given by (9), $P_{ww'}$ is given by (1), $\Pr(\theta(t) = \mathbf{z}|\mathbf{a}(t), \mathbf{s}(t) = w')$ is given by (4), and $\mathcal{T}(\mathbf{b}(t-1), \mathbf{a}(t), \theta(t) = \mathbf{z})$ is given by (5) and (6).

Therefore, the optimal policy could be obtained as follows:
(i) When $t = 1, 2, ...T - 1$,

$$\mathbf{a}^*(t) = \arg\max_{\mathbf{a}(t)} \{ \sum_{w \in \Omega^s} b_w(t-1)[\tilde{R}(\mathbf{a}(t), \mathbf{s}(t-1) = w) +$$

$$\sum_{w' \in \Omega^s} P_{ww'} \sum_{\mathbf{z} \in \mathbf{Z}^\theta} \Pr(\theta(t) = \mathbf{z}|\mathbf{a}(t), \mathbf{s}(t) = w') V_{t+1}(\mathcal{T}(\mathbf{b}(t-1), \mathbf{a}(t), \theta(t) = \mathbf{z}))]\}$$

$$(15)$$

subject to: (11), (12), (14)

(ii) When $t = T$,

$$\mathbf{a}^*(t) = \arg\max_{\mathbf{a}(t)} b_w(t-1)\tilde{R}(\mathbf{a}(t), \mathbf{s}(t-1) = w) \qquad (16)$$

subject to: (11), (12), (14)

We use the incremental pruning algorithm to solve (15) and (16). Detailed algorithm and its complexity analysis could be referred to [10].

4.2 Myopic Policy

Although the optimal scheduling policy for cooperative spectrum sensing can be derived via (15) and (16), the required computation complexity grows tremendously with the numbers of SUs and channels, even using the incremental pruning algorithm. Moreover, the optimal scheduling policy requires maintaining a table that specifies the optimal actions in every time slot. Therefore, the table could become very large as the time horizon increases. One solution for this computational complexity problem is the divide and conquer approach. For example, we separate all SUs into two smaller SU groups and also separate all channels into two smaller channel groups. Then, we can carry out two POMDP algorithms each consisting of one group of SUs and one group of channels.

To further address the computational complexity problem, in this work we also consider a myopic scheduling policy for cooperative spectrum sensing, which can be expressed as follows:

$$\mathbf{a}^*(t) = \arg\max_{\mathbf{a}(t)} \sum_{\omega \in \Omega^s} b_\omega(t-1)\widetilde{R}(\mathbf{a}(t), \mathbf{s}(t-1) = \omega)$$

subject to: (11), (12), (14)

Essentially, in our myopic policy, SU BS aims to maximize its instantaneous expected reward in each time slot t. (Notice that SU BS also uses (5) and (6) to update its belief state $b_\omega(t)$). Our following simulation results show that the myopic scheduling policy can achieve a comparable performance as that of the optimal policy based on POMDP formulation.

5   Numerical and Simulation Results

We set the CR network with a set of SUs $\mathcal{M} = \{1, 2\}$, and a set of orthogonal frequency channels $\mathcal{N} = \{1, 2\}$. Both of the channels have the same unit bandwidth. We set $\Delta L = 0.2L$ as the sensing duration for each channel. We also set $\eta = 0.1L$ as the duration for BS's sensing decision, receiving sensing results from SUs, and channel allocation decision. We assume Rayleigh fading channels with the same average receiver SNR=10dB [5] [13] and we use the same time bandwidth product $u = 5$. In Figure 3, the time horizon is 15 slots, and in the other simulations the time horizon is 10 slots. In these simulations we set every channel as homogeneous for different SUs. In this case there may exist several optimal solutions for (15) and (16), the BS will just pick one of them randomly.

To compare with the optimal policy and myopic policy, we consider a simple random policy which randomly picks an action as long as it can satisfy all the constraints (11), (12), (14).

Figure 3 shows the throughput comparison of the theoretical results of optimal policy, the simulation results of myopic policy and random policy. We set the scenario that both channels have the same statistical behavior (i.e. $P_{00}^n = 0.8, P_{10}^n = 0.2, \ n = 1, 2$), and the same prescribed collision probability $\zeta = 0.1$. This figure shows the advantages of the optimal policy and myopic policy over the random one with time horizon increasing. It also shows the optimal policy and myopic policy have very similar throughput performance in this scenario.

In Figure 4, we also set the scenario that both channels have the same statistical behavior (i.e. $P_{00}^n = 0.8, P_{10}^n = 0.2, \ n = 1, 2$), and the same prescribed collision probability ζ from 0.05 to 0.3. This figure shows that with the increase of the prescribed collision probability ζ, SUs' throughput becomes larger because of PUs' more collision tolerance. Nevertheless, when the prescribed collision probability reaches some level, SUs' throughput will stop increasing, this is because

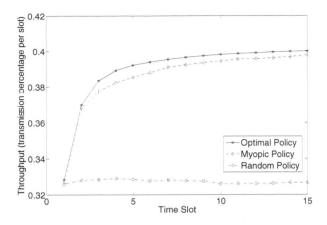

Fig. 3. SUs throughput performance comparison with $P_{00}^1 = P_{00}^2 = 0.8, P_{10}^1 = P_{10}^2 = 0.2$, and the same $\zeta = 0.1$

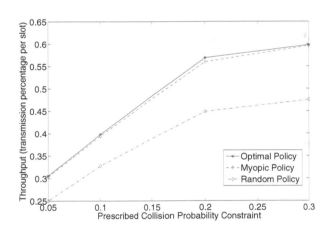

Fig. 4. SUs throughput performance comparison with $P_{00}^1 = P_{00}^2 = 0.8, P_{10}^1 = P_{10}^2 = 0.2$

it has already arrived at the maximum point of the primary channels' unutilized opportunity.

In Figure 5, we study the SUs' throughput performance under different memories of PU channel transition process. According to [9], the memory of channel n's transition process is defined as $\mu_n = 1 - P_{01}^n - P_{10}^n, \; n \in \mathcal{N}$, which is the probability of remaining in the same channel state. In this paper, we set $\mu_n > 0, \; n \in \mathcal{N}$, which means all the channels have positive transition process memories. The larger the memory, the higher tendency a channel will remain in the same state. We also consider the case of both channels having the same

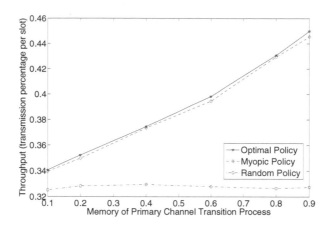

Fig. 5. SUs throughput performance comparison with $\pi_0^1 = \pi_0^2 = 0.5$, and the same $\zeta = 0.1$

statistical behavior (i.e. $P_{00}^1 = P_{00}^2, P_{10}^1 = P_{10}^2$), the same stationary idle probability (i.e. $\pi_0^n = 0.5$, $n = 1, 2$), and the same prescribed collision probability $\zeta = 0.1$. Figure 5 shows that when the channels' transition process memories grow larger, the throughput performance of optimal policy and myopic policy grow much better than the random policy. This indicates that if all the channels have positive transition process memories, then the larger the memories, the better throughput performance we can get by using our optimal and myopic policies. In fact, if some channels have negative transition process memories, then the larger the absolute value of the channel transition process memories, the better throughput performance we can get by using our optimal and myopic policies.

In Figure 6, we study the SUs' throughput performance when the two channels' statistical behaviors become different. Here, we set the prescribed collision probability ζ as 0.1 for each channel, and we set the sum of the two channels' transition process memories as a constant (i.e. $\mu_1 + \mu_2 = 1.2$). Besides, their stationary idle probabilities are the same (i.e. $\pi_0^1 = \pi_0^2 = 0.5$). This figure shows that although their stationary idle probabilities are the same and the sum of the two channels' transition process memories does not change, using the optimal policy can obtain a better throughput performance than the myopic policy when the diversity of the two channels' transition process memories (i.e. $|\mu_1 - \mu_2|$) grows larger. This is because that when the two channels' statistical behaviors are similar, the myopic policy will be similar to the optimal policy. However, when the two channels' statistical behaviors become more and more different, the myopic policy will get different decisions with the optimal policy.

Figure 7 shows the SUs' throughput performance under different stationary idle probability of PU channels. Here we set the two PU channels with the same statistical behavior (i.e. $P_{00}^1 = P_{00}^2, P_{10}^1 = P_{10}^2$) and the same prescribed collision

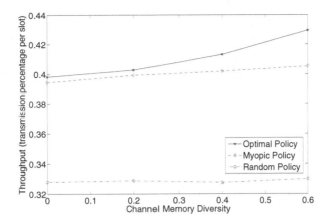

Fig. 6. SUs throughput performance comparison with $\pi_0^1 = \pi_0^2 = 0.5$, and the same $\zeta = 0.1$, and $\mu_1 + \mu_2 = 1.2$

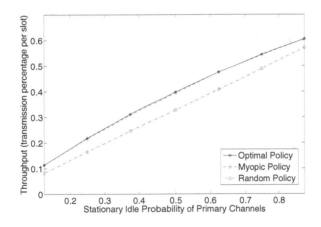

Fig. 7. SUs throughput performance comparison with the same $\zeta = 0.1$, and $\mu_1 = \mu_2 = 0.6$

probability $\zeta = 0.1$, and then we change their stationary idle probability while maintaining their channel transition process memories (*i.e.* $\mu_1 = \mu_2 = 0.6$). It is shown from the figure that when PU channels' stationary idle probability increases, SUs' throughput increases accordingly. This is because SUs will get more opportunities as the PU channels' idle probability increases.

6 Conclusion

In this paper, we study the cooperative sensing scheduling problem in cognitive radio networks. We first formulate this problem as a POMDP which aims to maximize the total CR system throughput with the guarantee of primary users' prescribed collision probability. Then, we derive the optimal policy and a myopic policy that determines which SUs sense which channels with what miss detection probability and false alarm probability. Numerical and simulation results are provided to illustrate the throughput performance of our optimal and myopic scheduling policies for cooperative spectrum sensing.

References

1. Akyildiz, I.F., Lee, W.-Y., Vuran, M.C., Mohanty, S.: Next generation/dynamic spectrum access/cognitive radio wireless networks: A survey. Comput. Netw. Int. J. Comput. Telecommun. Netw. 50(13), 2127–2159 (2006)
2. Haykin, S.: Cognitive radio: Brain-empowered wireless communications. IEEE J. Sel. Areas Commun. 23(2), 201–220 (2005)
3. Cordeiro, C., Challapali, K., Birru, D., Shankar, S.: IEEE 802. 22: The First Worldwide Wireless Standard based on Cognitive Radios. J. Commun. 1(1), 60–67 (2006)
4. Mishra, S.M., Sahai, A., Brodersen, R.W.: Cooperative Sensing among Cognitive Radios. In: Proc. IEEE Int. Conf. Commun., Turkey, vol. 4, pp. 1658–1663 (2006)
5. Letaief, K.B., Zhang, W.: Cooperative Spectrum Sensing. In: Cognitive Wireless Communication Networks, pp. 115–138. Springer, Heidelberg (2007)
6. Zhang, W., Letaief, K.B.: Cooperative Spectrum Sensing with Transmit and Relay Diversity in Cognitive Radio Networks. IEEE Trans. Wireless Commun. 7(12), 4761–4766 (2008)
7. Zhao, Q., Tong, L., Swami, A., Chen, Y.: Decentralized Cognitive MAC for Opportunistic Spectrum Access in Ad Hoc Networks: A POMDP Framework. IEEE J. Sel. Areas Commun. 25(3) (2007)
8. Chen, Y., Zhao, Q., Swami, A.: Joint design and separation principle for opportunistic spectrum access in the presence of sensing errors. IEEE Trans. Inf. Theory. 54(5), 2053–2071 (2008)
9. Hoang, A.T., Liang, Y.C., Wong, D.T.C., Zeng, Y.H., Zhang, R.: Opportunistic Spectrum Access for Energy-Constrained Cognitive Radios. IEEE Trans. Wireless Commun. 8(3) (2009)
10. Cassandra, A., Littman, M.L., Zhang, N.L.: Incremental Pruning: A simple, Fast, Exact Method for Partially Observable Markov Decision Processes. In: Proc. 13th Conf. Uncertainty in Artificial Intelligence (UAI), Providence RI, pp. 54–61 (1997)
11. Lee, W.-Y., Akyildiz, I.F.: Optimal Spectrum Sensing Framework for Cognitive Radio Networks. IEEE Trans. Wireless Commun. 7(10) (2008)
12. Kim, H., Shin, K.G.: Efficient Discovery of Spectrum Opportunities with MAC-Layer Sensing in Cognitive Radio Networks. IEEE, Trans. Mobile Computing 7(5) (2008)
13. Digham, F.F., Alouini, M.-S., Simon, M.K.: On the Energy Detection of Unknown Signals over Fading Channels. In: Proc. IEEE ICC 2003, vol. 5, pp. 3575–3579 (2003)

Efficient Spectrum Sharing in Cognitive Radio Networks with Implicit Power Control

Miao Ma and Danny H.K. Tsang

Department of Electronic and Computer Engineering
The Hong Kong University of Science and Technology
Clear Water Bay, Kowloon, Hong Kong
eemma@ust.hk, eetsang@ust.hk

Abstract. Cognitive radio technology solves the spectrum under-utilization problem by enabling the secondary users access the spectrum holes opportunistically. How to efficiently share the spectrum holes among the secondary users, therefore, is of interest. Previous studies on spectrum sharing either do not consider interference constraints or assume the links being unidirectional. For simplicity the power control is usually not jointly considered when modeling the spectrum sharing in most of the previous studies. In this paper, we present a cross-layer design by modeling the spectrum sharing and power control with the interference constraints. A binary integer linear programming (BILP) problem is formulated to determine which link will be established, which channel will be assigned to each established link and which power level each established link will use for transmission. Different from the previous work, we assume links being bidirectional because we believe the link level acknowledgements in an ad-hoc network are a must. Moreover, we propose an implicit power control approach, where the power level for each link is predefined and implicitly embedded in the formulation, which makes the problem formulation very simple. Numerical results show that the power control helps to reduce the interference and therefore significantly (up to 56.3% in the simulated scenario) improves the total spectrum utilization.

Keywords: Cognitive radio, cross-layer design, spectrum sharing, power control, interference constraints.

1 Introduction

Cognitive radio technology [1] [2] [3] provides a novel way to solve the spectrum under-utilization problem. In cognitive radio (CR) networks there are two types of users: primary users and secondary users. A primary user is the rightful owner of a channel[1], while a secondary user periodically scans the channels, identifies the currently unused channels and accesses the channels opportunistically. The secondary users organize among themselves an ad-hoc network, and communicate with each other using these identified available channels. Different from the

---

[1] We use the term channel and spectrum interchangeably in this paper.

X. Jun Hei and L. Cheung (Eds.): AccessNets 2009, LNICST 37, pp. 149–163, 2010.

existing multi-channel multi-radio (MCMR) networks where the set of available channels at each node is identical, in CR networks the set of available channels is different from node to node.

In this paper, we are interested in the cross-layer design which takes into account the interference constraints, spectrum sharing and power control. The main issues we are going to address include:

(1) How does a node determine which neighbor it will communicate with?

(2) How does a node decide which channel on which this communication will take place?

(3) How does a node decide which power level it will use for each link?

There has been some research work on spectrum sharing in CR networks. Wang et al. [4] formulated the channel allocation problem among secondary users as a list-coloring problem with the objective of maximizing the total spectrum utilization. Zheng et al. [5] developed a graph-theoretical model to characterize the spectrum access problem under a number of different optimization functions. Thoppian et al. [6] presented a formulation of MAC-layer scheduling in CR network. All the formulations in [4], [5] and [6] do not consider interference constraints. Hou et al. [7] modeled the spectrum sharing and sub-band division, scheduling and interference constraints, and flow routing; but they assume unidirectional links, which is not a very realistic assumption. The impact of power control is not considered in all the above work [4], [5], [6], [7].

Shi et al. [8] developed a formal mathematical model for scheduling feasibility under the influence of power control; the formulation is a cross-layer design optimization problem encompassing power control, scheduling and flow routing. However, the authors also consider unidirectional links; and particularly, the problem formulation becomes substantially larger and complicated since the authors regard the power level at each node as a decision variable.

In this paper, we propose a cross-layer optimization framework to jointly design the spectrum sharing and power control with the interference constraints. We do not include the flow routing in our formulation since we assume that the traffic demands are unknown. Different from the work in [7] and [8], we consider bidirectional links and adopt an 802.11-style protocol interference model, because we believe the link level acknowledgements in an ad-hoc network are a must [10]. Most importantly, we propose an implicit power control approach, where the links are classified into different classes and where a class determines the power level being chosen by this link, rather than explicitly regarding the power level at each node as a decision variable. As a result, the power level for each link is implicitly embedded in the formulation, which makes the formulation much simpler than that in [8]. To evaluate the performance, we study two types of scenarios: one is homogeneous node location and the other is heterogeneous node location. Numerical results show that for both scenarios the power control can significantly improve the total spectrum utilization.

The rest of this paper is organized as follows. In Section 2, we describe the assumptions and system model. The modeling of interference constraints and spectrum sharing is presented and a binary integer linear programming (BILP) formulation is proposed in Section 3. Section 4 studies the impact of power control. Section 5 presents numerical results. Finally, Section 6 concludes the paper.

2   Assumptions and System Model

We consider a cognitive radio (CR) network with n secondary users. There are M orthogonal channels in the network, denoted by the set C and the cardinality $|C| = M$. Each secondary user individually detects the available channels, and the set of available channels that can be used for communication is different from node to node. Let C_i and m_i denote the set and the number of available channels observed by node i, respectively. We have $C_i \subseteq C$ and the cardinality $|C_i| = m_i \leq M$.

Each secondary user i (where $1 \leq i \leq n$) has a programmable number of radio interfaces, denoted by γ_i. We assume that the radio interface is able to tune in a wide range of channels, but at a specific time each radio interface can only operate on one channel [9].

2.1   Bidirectional Links

We represent the CR network with an undirected graph $G = (N, E)$, where N is the set of secondary users denoted by the vertices of the graph, and E is the set of edges between two vertices (i.e., secondary users). As long as a pair of secondary users are within the maximum transmission range, we draw an edge between them. As a result, E includes all the possible links. The secondary users form among themselves an ad-hoc network. We consider bidirectional links, rather than unidirectional links, due to two reasons [10]:

(1) Wireless channels is lossy. We can not assume a packet can be successfully received by a neighbor unless the neighbor acknowledges it. In an ad-hoc network, the link level acknowledgements are necessary.

(2) Medium access controls such as IEEE 802.11 implicitly rely on bi-directionality assumptions. For example, a RTS-CTS exchange is usually used to perform virtual carrier sensing.

Thus if node i can transmit data to node j and vice versa, then we represent this by a link, denoted by $e : i \leftrightarrow j$, between node i and node j. Moreover, we let C_e and δ_e denote the set and the number of available channels for the link e, respectively. We have $C_e = C_i \cap C_j$, and the cardinality $|C_e| = \delta_e$.

2.2   Power Control and Bi-directionality

We assume each secondary user is equipped with an omnidirectional antenna and each node's transmitter has power control capability. By adjusting the transmission power level, the sender can reach destination nodes located at different distances. Therefore, for any pair of sender i and receiver j there exist a transmission range r_{ij} and an interference range R_{ij}. We have $R_{ij} = (1 + \Delta)r_{ij}$, where Δ is the guard zone to prevent a neighboring node from being assigned a same channel [11].

To ensure the bi-directionality, we assume that for each bidirectional link, say $e : i \leftrightarrow j$, both nodes i and j transmit at the same power. This is because all physical paths taken by radio waves from node i to node j can be reversed, it follows that if two nodes i and j transmit at the same power, then if j can hear i, i can also hear j [10]. Therefore, for each link $e : i \leftrightarrow j$ we have $r_{ij} = r_{ji}$ and the power control is on each link individually.

2.3   Static Node Location with a Centralized Server

In this paper, we focus on a model with static node location. We also assume the set of available channel at each secondary user is static. This corresponds to the applications with a slow varying spectrum environment (e.g., TV broadcast bands).

We assume that there exists a centralized server in the CR network. Each secondary user reports its location and the set of available channels to the spectrum server. The spectrum management and power control, therefore, is simple and coordinated.

Table 1 lists the notations used in this paper.

Table 1. Notations

Symbol	Meaning
N	set of secondary users
E	set of possible links
G	network graph
C	set of available channels
C_i	set of available channels at node i
C_e	set of available channels at link e
n	number of secondary users $|N|$
M	number of available channels $|C|$
m_i	number of available channels at node i, i.e., $|C_i|$
γ_i	number of radio interfaces at node i
δ_e	number of available channels at link e, i.e., $|C_e|$
β_e	max number of channels can be assigned to link e
t_i	min number of active links at node i
E_i	the set of links incident on node i
I_e	the set of links that interfere with link e
P_{ij}	transmission power at node i to node j
r_{ij}	transmission range at node i to node j
R_{ij}	interference range at node i to node j
K	number of discrete levels of transmission range
Δ	guard zone
d_{ij}	distance between i and j
α	path loss exponent
η	detection power threshold at the receiver
F	the set of clusters
A_i	the set of nodes belonging to the i-th cluster
B_{jk}	the set of inter-cluster links between j-th and k-th clusters

3   Modeling of Spectrum Sharing

In this section, we model the interference constraints and spectrum sharing and present a binary integer linear programming (BILP) formulation. Spectrum sharing can be done either in time domain or frequency domain. In this paper, we consider frequency domain channel assignment. Spectrum sharing is to determine which link is going to be active and which channel will be assigned to each active link. Our target is to *activate as many links as possible* to increase *channel reuse*.

3.1   Link Assignment

For direct communication, two secondary users need to be within transmission range of each other, and each will tune one of its radio interface to a common channel. We say link e is active only if some channel m has been assigned to link e. We define a 0-1 binary variable x_e^m as follows:

$$x_e^m = \begin{cases} 1 & \text{if link } e \text{ is active on channel } m, \\ 0 & \text{otherwise.} \end{cases} \tag{1}$$

3.2   Interference Model

Protocol Interference Model. Protocol interference model [11] considers the links being unidirectional, and only receiver is required to be free of interference for successful transmission.

Suppose that node i transmits data to node j. Let d_{ij} denote the distance between node i and node j. This transmission from node i to node j is successful if and only if

(i) The distance between node i and node j is no more than the transmission range, i.e., $d_{ij} \leq r_{ij}$.

(ii) For any node k to node h being assigned a same channel, the receiving node j must be out of the interference range, i.e., $d_{kj} > R_{kh}$.

802.11-Style Protocol Interference Model. Different from protocol interference model, an 802.11-style protocol interference model considers the links being bidirectional, and both the sender and the receiver are required to be free of interference for successful transmission.

Let e denote a link between nodes i and j, and e' denote another link between nodes k and h. The transmission on link e is successful if and only if

(i) The distance between nodes i and j is no more than the transmission range, i.e., $d_{ab} \leq r_{ab}$ for $ab = ij, ji$.

(ii) For any link $e' : k \leftrightarrow h$ being assigned a same channel, the receiving nodes i and j must be out of the interference range, i.e., $d_{ab} > R_{kh}$ for $ab = ki, kj$ and $d_{ab} > R_{hk}$ for $ab = hi, hj$.

Note that the second requirement implicitly includes the cases where link e and link e' have a node in common (i.e., $i = k$ or $i = h$ or $j = k$ or $j = h$).

For ease of presentation, we define two *link sets* as follows: we let E_i denote the set of links incident on node i, and I_e denote the set of links which interfere with link e. We have

$$E_i = \{i \leftrightarrow j : d_{ij} \leq r_{ij}\} \cap \{i \leftrightarrow j : d_{ij} \leq r_{ji}\},$$
$$I_e = \{e' : d_{ki} \leq R_{kh}\} \cup \{e' : d_{kj} \leq R_{kh}\} \cup$$
$$\{e' : d_{hi} \leq R_{hk}\} \cup \{e' : d_{hj} \leq R_{hk}\}.$$

Note also that in our model we have $r_{ij} = r_{ji}$ and $R_{kh} = R_{hk}$ (i.e., for any pair of sender and receiver, the sender and receiver transmit at the same power) to ensure bi-directionality.

Comparison. Compared with the protocol interference model, the 802.11-style protocol interference model is a more realistic model, which well reflects the fact that 802.11 may usually use a RTS-CTS exchange to perform virtual carrier sensing.

In this paper, we consider bidirectional links and adopt 802.11-style protocol interference model.

3.3   Constraints

Interference Constraint. *Interference* only occurs among the links sharing *the same channel.* According to the 802.11-style protocol interference model, if link e is active on channel m, then channel m cannot be assigned to any link e' as long as $e' \in I_e$. Hence, we have

$$x_e^m + x_{e'}^m \leq 1 \ (m \in C_e \cap C_{e'}, e' \in I_e, e \in E). \tag{2}$$

Link-Channel Constraint. It is possible to have multiple links between the same pair of nodes (provided that the number of radio interface can support this), because a pair of nodes may share two or more channels. But we can restrict each link to be assigned no more than β_e channels (where $\beta_e \leq \delta_e$). This leads to the following constraint:

$$\sum_{m \in C_e} x_e^m \leq \beta_e \ (e \in E). \tag{3}$$

Node-Radio Constraint. A node can establish multiple links with its neighboring nodes if it can tune each of its radio interface to a different channel. But the number of established links at each node is constrained by the number of its radio interfaces. This leads to the following constraint:

$$\sum_{e \in E_i} \sum_{m \in C_e} x_e^m \leq \gamma_i \ (i \in N). \tag{4}$$

Additional Constraint. In addition, we can add a *node-connectivity* constraint to make sure that each node has established at least t_i (where $t_i \geq 1$) links. This leads to the following constraint:

$$\sum_{e \in E_i} \sum_{m \in C_e} x_e^m \geq t_i \ (i \in N). \tag{5}$$

In fact, any linear constraint can be added to the formulation whenever necessary. In Section V we will show that for the heterogeneous node location scenario we can add some *inter-cluster connectivity constraints* to guarantee the connectivity between the clusters.

3.4   Problem Formulation

The objective of spectrum sharing is to maximize the total spectrum utilization. In this paper we are interested in studying the impact of the power control on the *channel reuse* in different scenarios, and therefore we choose the objective function as the total number of active links[2]. This problem can be formulated as:

$$\max \sum_{e \in E} \sum_{m \in C_e} x_e^m \tag{6}$$

Subject to:

$$x_e^m = 0, 1 \qquad (m \in C_e, e \in E), \tag{7}$$

$$x_e^m + x_{e'}^m \leq 1 \ (m \in C_e \cap C_{e'}, e' \in I_e, e \in E), \tag{8}$$

$$\sum_{m \in C_e} x_e^m \leq \beta_e \qquad (e \in E), \tag{9}$$

$$\sum_{e \in E_i} \sum_{m \in C_e} x_e^m \leq \gamma_i \qquad (i \in N), \tag{10}$$

$$\sum_{e \in E_i} \sum_{m \in C_e} x_e^m \geq t_i \qquad (i \in N), \tag{11}$$

where β_e, γ_i and t_i are constants. x_e^m (binary integer) are optimization variables. The objective function is a linear function and all the constraints are linear. The optimization problem is in the form of *binary integer linear programming* (BILP) and can be solved by LINGO [12].

---

[2] The objective function, however, can certainly be chosen as $\left(\max \sum_{e \in E} \sum_{m \in C_e} x_e^m \cdot B_e^m \right)$, where B_e^m denotes the bandwidth for the channel m at link e. Note that B_e^m can be homogeneous or heterogeneous (where heterogeneous means the bandwidth is link-dependent and/or channel-dependent), and either case can be easily extended without much technical difficulty.

4   Impact of Power Control

In this section, we investigate the impact of power control on spectrum sharing. Power control is to decide which power level a node is going to use for each link individually.

4.1   Transmission Range and Interference Range

Recall that we assume all transmitters have power control capabilities, and the sender can reach destination nodes located at different distances by adjusting the transmission power level. We also assume all receivers have the same signal detection power threshold, denoted by η. A data transmission is successful only if the receiving power exceeds the detection power threshold.

For data transmission between node i to node j, a widely used model for power propagation gain G_{ij} is

$$G_{ij} = \frac{1}{d_{ij}^{\alpha}}, \tag{12}$$

where α denotes the path loss exponent. The typical value of α is between 2 and 4, depending on the characteristics of the communication medium.

Suppose that node i transmits data with the power P_{ij} to node j, then based on $P_{ij} \cdot G_{ij} \geq \eta$, we obtain the transmission range $r_{ij} = \left(\frac{P_{ij}}{\eta}\right)^{1/\alpha}$ and interference range $R_{ij} = (1 + \Delta) \cdot \left(\frac{P_{ij}}{\eta}\right)^{1/\alpha}$. In case that the expected transmission range r_{ij} is known, we obtain the transmission power P_{ij} as follows,

$$P_{ij} = \eta \cdot r_{ij}^{\alpha}. \tag{13}$$

4.2   Discrete Power Level

In reality, the transmission power can not be continuously adjusted. Under a quantization approach, the transmission power adjustment is only allowed for a series of discrete levels, which gives rise to that the transmission range also has a series of discrete levels.

Without loss of generality, we assume the transmission range is evenly divided and consists of at most K discrete levels r_y $(1 \leq y \leq K)$ which corresponds to the transmission power P_y, where r_K and P_K are the maximum transmission range and transmission power, respectively. We have,

$$r_y = y \cdot \frac{r_K}{K}, \quad y = 1, 2, ..., K, \tag{14}$$

$$P_y = \eta \cdot y^{\alpha} \cdot \left(\frac{r_K}{K}\right)^{\alpha}, \quad y = 1, 2, ..., K. \tag{15}$$

4.3   Implicit Power Control

As we stated earlier, E includes all the possible links between the secondary users. That is, as long as a pair of secondary users are within the maximum transmission range r_K, there exists an edge between them. Then according to a link's length we classify the links in E into K classes. More specifically, we classify a link $e : i \leftrightarrow j$ as a y-class link if $r_{y-1} < d_{ij} \le r_y$. Furthermore, the two nodes i and j separated by the distance d_{ij} use the same transmission power P_{ij} $(P_{ij} = P_{ji})$ and the same range r_{ij} $(r_{ij} = r_{ji})$ to communicate with each other, and we have $P_{ij} = P_y$ and $r_{ij} = r_y$.

In the BILP formulation, the power level for each link (i.e., y) is not a decision variable. Instead, it is predefined and implicitly embedded in the formulation (i.e., r_y and R_y for a y-class link). Since we classify the links in E into different classes and the class determines the power level being chosen by each link, we can easily obtain E_i for each node i and I_e for each link e. Then by using LINGO to solve the BILP problem, the optimal solution will show which link is active and which channel is assigned to each active link, and in particular, the (predefined) power level for each active link is automatically known according to the link's class. The implicit power control approach, therefore, significantly reduces the complexity of the problem formulation.

Note that without power control, all nodes use the maximum transmission power P_K for their transmissions, and the transmission range and the interference range for all links are r_K and R_K, respectively.

5   Numerical Results

In this section, we present numerical results for the BILP formulation and evaluate the impact of power control on spectrum sharing. We consider a 15-node ad hoc network in a 60×60 area, and study two types of scenarios: one is homogeneous node location and the other is heterogeneous node location, shown in Fig. 1(a) and Fig. 1(b), respectively. We make no claims that these two topologies are representative of typical cognitive radio networks. We have chosen these two simple topologies is to facilitate detailed discussion of the results and for the illustration purpose.

We assume there are 12 channels in the entire network. We also assume the maximum transmission range of each node is the same and $r_K = 30$. Each node has 6 discrete levels of transmission range, corresponding to 5, 10, 15, 20, 25 and 30, respectively. Table 2 summarizes the notations of the symbols and the parameter settings for both homogeneous and heterogeneous scenarios.

5.1   Scenario I: Homogeneous Node Location

First, we consider the case where the nodes are homogeneously distributed across the entire area and the topology is shown in Fig. 1(a). The set of available channels at each node is randomly generated, see Table 3. Note that the set of available channels is different from node to node.

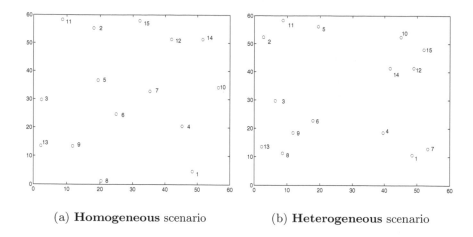

(a) **Homogeneous** scenario   (b) **Heterogeneous** scenario

Fig. 1. A 15-node ad hoc network

Table 2. Notations and parameter settings

Symbol	Meaning	Values
A^2	deployment area	$(60m)^2$
M	no. of channels in the network	12
n	no. of secondary users	15
β_e	max no. of channels assigned to link e	1
γ_i	no. of radio interfaces at node i	4
t_i	min no. of active links at node i	2
K	no. of discrete levels of transmission range	6
r_K	maximum transmission range	30
R_K	maximum interference range	45
Δ	guard zone	0.5

We use LINGO to solve the BILP problem. Fig. 3(a) shows the optimal spectrum sharing and Table 4 lists the power level that each active link will use. Fig. 3(a) shows that with power control a total number of 18 active links can be established, and the number in the figure shows which channel is assigned to each active link. It is noticed that, the channels 4, 7, 8, 10, 11 and 12 are reused.

Note that without power control, there are only 14 active links can be established and the power level of all the links is 6. But with power control, as shown in Table 4, 3, 4, 7, 2 and 2 links use power level of 2, 3, 4, 5 and 6, respectively. We comment that with power control each link properly uses its power level, which helps to reduce the interference, and therefore increases the spectrum reuse efficiency. In this example, the power control improves the total spectrum utilization by 28.6%.

Table 3. Set of available channels at each node (i.e., C_i) for **homogeneous** scenario

Node index	Location	Available channels
1	(48.5, 4.6)	1, 3, 4, 6, 8
2	(18.1, 55.3)	4, 7, 11
3	(2.5, 29.7)	1, 2, 5, 6, 12
4	(45.3, 20.5)	1, 4, 5, 8, 10
5	(19.4, 36.7)	3, 5, 8, 9, 10, 11
6	(24.9, 24.7)	2, 3, 5, 7, 9, 10
7	(35.3, 32.8)	1, 2, 6, 7, 9, 12
8	(20.3, 1.2)	2, 4, 6, 11, 12
9	(11.8, 13.4)	2, 4, 5, 6, 7, 11
10	(56.5, 34.2)	3, 6, 9, 11
11	(8.7, 58.3)	1, 5, 7 ,8
12	(42.0, 51.3)	2, 4, 8, 10, 12
13	(2.3, 13.5)	2, 3, 6, 8, 12
14	(51.7, 51.3)	1, 7, 9, 10, 11
15	(32.1, 57.9)	4, 5, 8

5.2   Scenario II: Heterogeneous Node Location

Next, we consider the case where the nodes are heterogeneously dispersed across the entire area and the topology is shown in Fig. 1(b). The set of available channels at each node is also randomly generated, see Table 5.

Different from the homogeneous scenario, the heterogeneous scenario is suitable for *clustering*. That is, we group the nodes into clusters and the hierarchy of clustering could be as deep as the number of power levels. In this example, we can simply group the nodes into four $20m$ clusters. Fig. 2(a) and Fig. 2(b) show the intra-cluster links (i.e., the link's length is less than or equal to 20) and inter-cluster links (i.e., the link's length is more than 20 but less than 30), respectively. If we let F denote the set of clusters, A_i denote the set of nodes belonging to the i-th cluster and B_{jk} denote the inter-cluster links between the j-th and k-th clusters ($B_{jk} = B_{kj}$), we have $F = \{1, 2, 3, 4\}$, and $A_1 = \{2, 5, 11\}$, $A_2 = \{3, 6, 8, 9, 13\}$, $A_3 = \{1, 4, 7\}$, $A_4 = \{10, 12, 14, 15\}$. In addition, $B_{12} = \{3 \leftrightarrow 2, 3 \leftrightarrow 11, 3 \leftrightarrow 5\}$, $B_{14} = \{5 \leftrightarrow 10, 5 \leftrightarrow 14\}$, $B_{23} = \{4 \leftrightarrow 6, 4 \leftrightarrow 9\}$ and $B_{34} = \{4 \leftrightarrow 12, 4 \leftrightarrow 14, 7 \leftrightarrow 12\}$.

Note that in the BILP formulation, the objective function is to establish as many links as possible to increase channel reuse. As long as a channel is assigned to a link, the objective function is increased by one. With power control, a short link uses a small power level and therefore incurs a shorter interference range, as compared with a long link. As a result, a short link will have more chances to be assigned a channel. But in the heterogeneous scenario, establishing an inter-cluster link is a must to guarantee the connectivity between the clusters. This reminds us to add the following *inter-cluster connectivity constraints* into BILP formulation:

Table 4. Power level of each active link

Homogeneous scenario		Heterogeneous scenario	
Active link	Power level	Active link	Power level
2 ↔ 11	2	1 ↔ 7	2
9 ↔ 13	2	2 ↔ 11	2
12 ↔ 14	2	6 ↔ 9	2
5 ↔ 6	3	8 ↔ 9	2
6 ↔ 7	3	8 ↔ 13	2
8 ↔ 9	3	10 ↔ 15	2
12 ↔ 15	3	12 ↔ 14	2
1 ↔ 4	4	12 ↔ 15	2
2 ↔ 5	4	1 ↔ 4	3
3 ↔ 9	4	3 ↔ 6	3
3 ↔ 13	4	3 ↔ 9	3
4 ↔ 7	4	4 ↔ 7	3
7 ↔ 12	4	5 ↔ 11	3
10 ↔ 14	4	6 ↔ 8	3
7 ↔ 10	5	9 ↔ 13	3
11 ↔ 15	5	10 ↔ 12	3
1 ↔ 8	6	10 ↔ 14	3
6 ↔ 13	6	14 ↔ 15	3
		2 ↔ 5	4
		3 ↔ 13	4
		2 ↔ 3	5
		4 ↔ 6	5
		5 ↔ 10	6
		5 ↔ 14	6
		7 ↔ 12	6

Table 5. Set of available channels at each node (i.e., C_i) for **heterogeneous** scenario

Node index	Location	Available channels
1	(48.5, 10.6)	1, 3, 4, 6, 8, 10, 11
2	(2.8, 52.3)	2, 3, 4, 7, 8, 9, 11
3	(6.4, 29.7)	1, 2, 5, 6, 9, 11, 12
4	(39.6, 18.5)	1, 3, 4, 5, 7, 8, 10, 12
5	(19.4, 56.1)	1, 3, 5, 6, 7, 8, 10, 11
6	(17.8, 22.7)	2, 3, 4, 5, 7, 8, 9, 10
7	(53.3, 12.8)	1, 2, 6, 7, 8, 9, 12
8	(8.6, 11.2)	1, 2, 4, 6, 9, 11, 12
9	(11.8, 18.4)	1, 2, 3, 4, 6, 8, 9, 11
10	(45.1, 52.4)	1, 3, 4, 6, 9, 10, 11
11	(8.7, 58.3)	1, 2, 5, 7, 8, 9, 12
12	(49.0, 41.3)	2, 3, 4, 6, 8, 10, .12
13	(2.3, 13.5)	2, 3, 5, 6, 8, 9, 12
14	(41.7, 41.3)	1, 3, 4, 5, 7, 9, 10, 11
15	(52.1, 47.9)	1, 3, 4, 5, 8, 9, 12

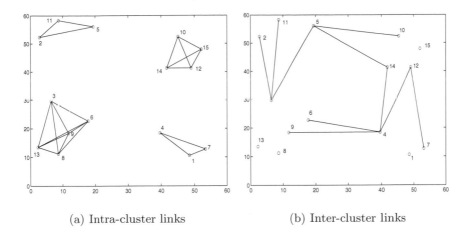

(a) Intra-cluster links   (b) Inter-cluster links

Fig. 2. Possible links for **heterogeneous** scenario

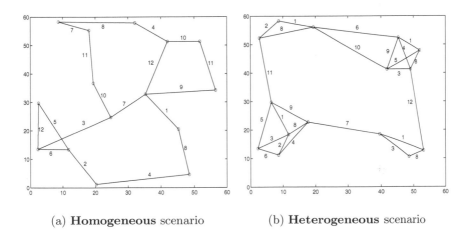

(a) **Homogeneous** scenario   (b) **Heterogeneous** scenario

Fig. 3. Optimal spectrum sharing with power control

$$\sum_{e \in B_{jk}} \sum_{m \in C_e} x_e^m \ge 1 \ (B_{jk} \ne \emptyset, k > j, k \in F, j \in F). \tag{16}$$

The purpose of the joint power control and clustering is to assign the channels properly, so that most of the intra-cluster communication is at a lower power level, and a higher power level is used for an inter-cluster link.

Fig. 3(b) shows the optimal spectrum sharing and again the channel is given next to the link in the figure. Table 4 describes the power level that each active link will use. It is observed that, there are 25 active links can be established.

Moreover, among these 25 active links there are 8, 10, 2, 2 and 3 links whose power levels are 2, 3, 4, 5 and 6, respectively.

Note that without power control, there are only 16 active links established and the power level of all links is 6. But with power control, power level 2 is chosen whenever a link's length is within $(5, 10]$, and power level 3 is selected whenever a link's length is within $(10, 15]$, etc. Therefore, as Table 4 illustrates, 8 links use power level 2 and 10 links use power level 3. Since there are many short links in heterogenous scenario due to the clustering structure, the power control significantly improves the spectrum sharing efficiency. In this example, the power control improves the spectrum utilization by 56.3%.

6   Conclusion

In this paper, we present a cross-layer design by modeling the spectrum sharing and power control with the interference constraints in cognitive radio networks. We formulate an optimization problem in the form of binary integer linear programming (BILP). The model is general and any linear constraint can be added to the formulation whenever necessary. Different from the previous work, we consider bidirectional links and adopt an 802.11-style protocol interference model. Particularly, we present an implicit power control approach, where the power level for each link is predefined and implicitly embedded in the formulation, which makes the problem formulation very simple. Numerical results show that the power control significantly improves the total spectrum utilization. For the heterogeneous node location the joint design of power control and clustering helps to assign the channels properly. For our future work, we are continuing to study the spectrum sharing problem in CR networks and our next step is to consider how to jointly design the spectrum sharing, power control and flow routing.

References

1. Mitola, J., Maguire, G.Q.: Cognitive radio: making software radios more personal. IEEE Personal Communications 6(4), 13–18 (1999)
2. Haykin, S.: Cognitive radio: brain-empowered wireless communications. IEEE Journal on Selected Areas in Communicaitons 23(2) (February 2005)
3. Akyildiz, I.F., Lee, W., Vuran, M.C., Mohanty, S.: NeXt generation/dynamic spectrum access/cognitive radio wireless networks: a survey. In: Computer Networks, May 2006. Elsevier, Amsterdam (2006)
4. Wang, W., Liu, X.: List-coloring based channel allocation for open-spectrum wireless networks. In: Proceedings of VTC (2005)
5. Zheng, H., Peng, C.: Collaboration and fairness in opportunistic spectrum access. In: Proceedings of ICC (2005)
6. Thoppian, M., Venkatesan, S., Prakash, R., Chandrasekaran, R.: MAC-layer scheudling in cognitive radio based multi-hop wireless networks. In: Proceedings of the 2006 International Symposium on a World of Wireless, Mobile and Multimedia Networks, WoWMoM (2006)

7. Hou, Y.T., Shi, Y., Sherali, H.D.: Optimal spectrum sharing for multi-hop software defined radio networks. IEEE INFOCOM (2007)
8. Shi, Y., Hou, Y.T.: Optimal power control for multi-hop software defined radio networks. IEEE INFOCOM (2007)
9. Xin, C., Xie, B., Shen, C.: A novel layered graph model for topology formation and routing in dynamic spectrum access networks. In: DysPAN (2005)
10. Narayanaswamy, S., Kawadia, V., Sreenivas, R.S., Kumar, P.R.: Power control in ad-hoc networks: theory, architecture, algorithm and implementation of the COMPOW protocol. In: Proceedings of European Wireless (2002)
11. Gupta, P., Kumar, P.R.: The capacity of wireless networks. IEEE Transacations on Information Theory 46(2) (March 2000)
12. LINGO: User's guide, LINDO Systems Inc. (2006)

Dynamic Spectrum Sharing
in Cognitive Radio Femtocell Networks
(Invited Paper)

Jie Xiang[1], Yan Zhang[1], and Tor Skeie[1,2]

[1] Simula Research Laboratory, Norway
{jxiang,yanzhang,tskeie}@simula.no
[2] Department of Informatics, University of Oslo, Norway

Abstract. Femtocell is envisioned as a highly promising solution to tackle the communications in the indoor environments, which has been a very challenging problem for mobile network operators. Currently, the spectrum allocated to femtocells is from the same licensed spectrum of macrocells, and the same mobile network operator. In this case, the capacity of femtocell networks may be largely limited due to the finite number of licensed spectrum bands and also the interference with other femtocells and macrocells. In this paper, we propose a radically new communications paradigm by incorporating cognitive radio in femtocell networks (COGFEM). In COGFEM, the cognitive radio enabled femtocells are able to access licensed spectrum bands not only from macrocells but also from other licensed systems (e.g. TV systems). Thus, the co-channel interference in femtocells can be greatly reduced and the network capacity can be significantly improved. We formulate a joint channel allocation and power control problem in COGFEM, and present two intelligent algorithms for efficient spectrum sharing in COGFEM. Results indicate that COGFEM is able to achieve much higher capacity than the femtocell networks which does not employ agile spectrum access.

Keywords: femtocell, cognitive radio, spectrum sharing, power control.

1   Introduction

The demand for higher data rates and lower power consumptions in mobile wireless networks is continuously increasing, while the capacity provided by the existing macrocell networks is limited. Studies on wireless usage have shown that more than 50% voice calls and 70% data traffic originate indoors [1]. This phenomenon motivates the reserach and development of femtocell networks, which just require that each customer installs a short-range low-cost low-power home base station. These femtocell base stations (FBSs) can communicate with macrocell networks by a broadband connection such as digital subscriber line (DSL), cable modem, or a separate wireless backhaul channel [2]. Femtocells can provide high data rates and Quality of Service (QoS) with low transmission power for consumers. For example, [2] demonstrates that the transmission power can be

X. Jun Hei and L. Cheung (Eds.): AccessNets 2009, LNICST 37, pp. 164–178, 2010.

saved about 34dB and 77dB in different fading environments. As a result, network operators may experience less traffic on their expensive macrocell networks, and can focus their resources on the truly mobile users [2][3].

The problem of spectrum sharing emerges when deploying femtocell networks. Traditional spectrum allocation in neighboring cellular networks is based on a coloring method that no neighboring cells can use the same spectrum at the same time, e.g., [4]. Since the number of femtocells could be much higher than the number of macrocells in a certain area, this kind of spectrum allocation requires more spectrum bands and will lead to inefficient and unfair spectrum utilization. This motivates our research in this paper to improve the spectrum utilization and cell capacity.

It has been shown that spectrum is not efficiently used by licensed (primary) users/systems according to the fixed spectrum allocation regulation. Recent years, cognitive radio (CR) technology has been developed to allow unlicensed users to exploit the spectrum opportunity from primary systems [5]. Thus the spectrum utilization would be improved significantly. In this paper, we incorporate the CR technology into femtocell networks, where the CR-enabled femtocell users and FBSs can identify and utilize the spectrum opportunities from the licensed systems such as macrocell networks and TV broadcast systems as shown in Fig.1. In the following of this paper, we call this kind of cognitive radio femtocell networks COGFEM. Besides the spectrum agility ability, COGFEM has the following features: (a), the number of users in each femtocell is small, e.g., 2, 4. (b), the size of the cell coverage is about the house or apartment range, e.g., $100 \ m^2$. (c), the availability of licensed channels is similar in neighboring cells, this is the major difference than cognitive radio macrocell networks, where the channel availability may vary a lot between neighbor cells.

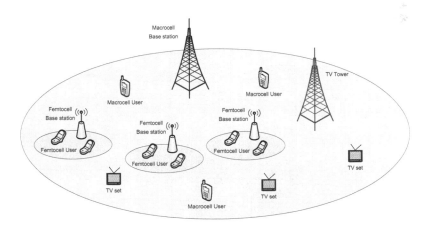

Fig. 1. An illustration of the coexistence between cognitive radio femtocells and primary systems such as macrocells and TV systems

Nevertheless, to improve spectrum utilization and cell capacity in COGFEM, spectrum sharing schemes should be present. Basically, there are two spectrum sharing modes in CR networks. One is called underlay mode, wherein the femtocell users and FBSs can use the spectrum as long as the interference to the licensed system is under a predefined threshold. The other one is called overlay mode, wherein the femtocell users and FBSs can use the spectrum only if the spectrum is not occupied by the nearby primary systems. In this paper, we focus on the overlay mode.

In literature, there are few attempts on femtocell networks. In [6], the authors applied a finite-difference time-domain (FDTD) method to predict the coverage of WiMAX femtocells. In [7], the authors used a centralized method of dynamic frequency planning (DFP) to minimize the overall femtocell network interference to allocate the spectrum to femtocells. In [8], the authors studied the resource management problem in Orthogonal Frequency-Division Multiple Access (OFMDA) femtocells and proposed a location-based allocation scheme between macro and femto cells to adapt the varying user population.

There are also attempts on the spectrum sharing in CR cellular networks. In [9], the authors studied the uplink admission and power control problem while sharing the same spectrum in one CR cellular network. In [10], the authors studied the uplink channel allocation and power control problem in one CR cellular network with multiple available channels. In [11], the authors proposed a joint spectrum and power allocation framework for inter-cell spectrum sharing in cognitive radio networks. In [12], the authors studied the downlink channel assignment and power control for several cognitive radio cellular networks with the objective to maximize the number of admitted users amongst all the cells.

In this paper address the spectrum sharing problem in COGFEM to maximize the capacity of femtocell networks. In particular, our contributions include:

- we first incorporate CR into femtocells, and analyze the interference amongst femtocell networks in overlay spectrum sharing mode.
- we propose two joint spectrum sharing and power control schemes for the downlink transmission in COGFEM networks, and present numerical results to evaluate the performance.

The rest of the paper is organized as follows. In section 2, we introduce the system model and assumptions, and formulate the downlink spectrum sharing problem in COGFEM. Then, we relax this problem and find out a solution by Lagrangian method, and propose two joint channel allocation and power control schemes in section 3. In section 4, we evaluate the performance of our proposed schemes for normal femtocells and COGFEM, respectively. Finally, we draw conclusions in section 5.

2   System Model and Problem Formulation

In this section, we will introduce the system model and assumptions of COGFEM, and formulate the downlink spectrum sharing problem.

2.1 System Model and Assumptions

Suppose that there are a set of $\mathcal{N}^B$ femtocells in a macrocell coverage. For any FBS $i \in \mathcal{N}^B$, there are a set of $\mathcal{N}_i^U$ femtocell users. Normally the number of femtocell users is between 2 and 4 as indicated in [2]. In this paper, we also use i as the ID of the femtocell where FBS i is located. Each femtocell i has a coverage of radium d_i. There are a set of $\mathcal{N}^C$ licensed channels can be used for femtocells. $\mathcal{N}^C$ may change timely depends on the activities of nearby primary systems. These channels are not only from macro cells but also from other licensed systems. In this paper, we consider OFDMA scheme, wherein the channels are narrowband subchannels containing several subcarriers typically 100KHz similar in IEEE 802.22 draft standard [13].

Each FBS is responsible to allocate spectrum to its users, and decides channel switching when any primary user returns.Synchronization between different FBSs is not obligatory, but it is an optional if any FBS wants to synchronize with its neighbors. The synchronization can be implemented by listening to neighboring FBS information to obtain the frame length and structure.

In our COGFEM architecture, each femtocell user and FBS are equipped with one cognitive radio with the ability of spectrum sensing and switching on different spectrum. The available spectrum list can be stored into a local database at FBS or a database in the Internet for future use. FBSs can do spectrum sensing cooperatively by obtaining the results from other femtocells. There are two kinds of control channels. One is called *inter-femtocell* control channel, whereby each FBS can communicate with each other to exchange spectrum sensing result, etc. The other one is called *intra-femtocell* control channel, whereby each user in a femtocell can communicate with its FBS to obtain the working channel and transmission power. These control channels could be dedicated control channels or rendezvous channels which are selected from the available spectrum according to some metrics such as channel availability.

2.2 Downlink Spectrum Sharing in Overlay Mode

In this paper, we consider the downlink spectrum sharing problem in overlay mode, where femtocells use the licensed channels when they are not occupied by primary systems. Thus, there is no co-channel interference between primary systems and femtocells. The only interference should be managed is amongst femtocells. Suppose each femtocell user in a femtocell i requires one subchannel with an equal bandwidth B. We consider the worst case when all neighboring femtocells are in downlink transmission. In the following, we will analyze the downlink capacity and then formulate the spectrum sharing problem.

Downlink capacity. Any femtocell user will receive interference from neighboring femtocells using the same channel. Consider an Additive White Gaussian Noise (AWGN) channel, the Signal to Interference-plus-Noise Ratio (SINR) of the received signal from FBS i at femtocell user j can be denoted as

$$\xi^d(i,j,c) = \frac{H(i,j,c)P(i,c)x(i,j,c)}{N_0 + I_S(i,j,c)} \tag{1}$$

where N_0 denotes the background noise power. $I_S(i,j,c)$ represents the interference measured at user j on channel c from femtocells other than i. $H(i,j,c)$ is the channel gain from FBS i to its user j on channel c including path loss and channel fading. $P(i,c)$ is the transmission power for FBS i on channel c. $x(i,j,c)$ is a binary indicator. If $x(i,j,c,) = 1$, user j in femtocell i works on channel c, zero otherwise.

The downlink capacity of any femtocell user j in femtocell i can be calculated according to Shannon's capacity theory as follows.

$$C^d(i,j) = \sum_{c \in \mathcal{N}^C} x(i,j,c)Blog_2(1 + \xi^d(i,j,c)) \tag{2}$$

where B denotes the channel bandwidth. Then, we can calculate the downlink capacity of femtocell i which is the sum of all the capacity of its users.

$$C_i = \sum_{j \in \mathcal{N}_i^U} C^d(i,j), \quad \forall i \in \mathcal{N}^B \tag{3}$$

Spectrum sharing problem. The spectrum sharing problem in COGFEM downlink transmission is to maximize the downlink capacity of all FBSs while guarantee the channel and power constraints.

$$\max \sum_{i \in \mathcal{N}^B} C_i \tag{4}$$

s.t.

$$x(i,j,c) \in \{0,1\}, \quad \forall i \in \mathcal{N}^B, j \in \mathcal{N}_i^U, c \in \mathcal{N}^C \tag{5}$$

$$\sum_{c \in \mathcal{N}^C} x(i,j,c) = 1, \quad \forall i \in \mathcal{N}^B, j \in \mathcal{N}_i^U \tag{6}$$

$$\sum_{j \in \mathcal{N}_i^U} \sum_{c \in \mathcal{N}^C} x(i,j,c) = n_i, \quad \forall i \in \mathcal{N}^B \tag{7}$$

$$\xi^d(i,j,c) \geq \psi^d, \quad if \quad x(i,j,c) = 1, \quad \forall i \in \mathcal{N}^B, j \in \mathcal{N}_i^U, c \in \mathcal{N}^C \tag{8}$$

$$P(i,c) = 0, \quad if \quad x(i,j,c) = 0, \quad \forall i \in \mathcal{N}^B, j \in \mathcal{N}_i^U, c \in \mathcal{N}^C \tag{9}$$

$$P(i,c) \geq 0, \quad \forall i \in \mathcal{N}^B, c \in \mathcal{N}^C \tag{10}$$

$$\sum_{c \in \mathcal{N}^C} P(i,c) \leq P_{max}, \quad \forall i \in \mathcal{N}^B \tag{11}$$

where ψ^d denotes the minimum required SINR for femtocell users. Constraint (6) means every user in a COGFEM can only use one channel. Constraint (7) means the total number of channels can be used in one femtocell is equal to the number of users in that femtocell. Constraint (8) represents that if channel c is allocated to user j in femtocell i for downlink transmission, the SINR received on user j should be higher than a predefined threshold. Constraint (9) means any FBS i will not allocate any power on channel c if channel c is not allocated to i. Constraint (10) represents the transmission power of any FBS i should be no less than 0, while constraint (11) indicates the total transmission power of any FBS i on all channels can not exceed the maximum power budget P_{max}.

3   Proposed Dynamic Spectrum Sharing Schemes

The formulated spectrum sharing problem in the previous section is a mixed integer optimization problem, which is generally NP-hard. The solution of that problem includes transmission power allocation variable $P(i,c)$, and channel allocation variable $x(i,j,c)$ for both inter-cell and intra-cell spectrum sharing. In this section, we try to simplify the formulation to a robust scenario, where we consider the worst case when all users of a femtocell is at the cell boundary, and have similar channel gain information. Thus, FBS will not distinguish different users in its service range. In this situation, the downlink SINR of channel c at femtocell i can be represented as

$$\xi^d(i,c) = \frac{H(d_i,c)P(i,c)}{N_0 + I_S(i,c)} \tag{12}$$

where $H(d_i,c)$ denotes the gain on channel c in femtocell i through distance d_i. $I_S(i,c)$ represents an approximate interference on channel c to all users in femtocell i. In practice, $I_S(i,c)$ can be estimated by femtocell users and FBS. Substituting (1) to (2) and (3), we can obtain

$$C_i = n_i B \sum_{c \in \mathcal{N}^C} x_B(i,c) log_2(1 + \xi^d(i,c)) \tag{13}$$

where $x_B(i,c)$ is a binary variable, whereby $x_B(i,c) = 1$ represents that channel c is allocated to femtocell i, zero otherwise. To reduce the complexity of mixed integer optimization problem, we relax the binary variable $x_B(i,c)$ into a continuous variable in a range of $[0,1]$. Thus, the inter-cell spectrum sharing problem can be formulated as follows.

$$\max_{x_B(i,c) \in [0,1], P(i,c) \geq 0} \sum_{i \in \mathcal{N}^B} C_i \tag{14}$$

s.t.

$$\sum_{c \in \mathcal{N}^C} x_B(i,c) = n_i, \quad \forall i \in \mathcal{N}^B \tag{15}$$

$$\xi^d(i,c) \geq x_B(i,c)\psi^d, \quad \forall i \in \mathcal{N}^B \tag{16}$$

$$\sum_{c \in \mathcal{N}^C} P(i,c) \leq P_{max}, \quad \forall i \in \mathcal{N}^B \tag{17}$$

By using Lagrangian $L(P(i,c), x_B(i,c), \lambda_i, \lambda_{i,c}, \mu_i)$, where λ_i, $\lambda_{i,c}$, and μ_i are Lagrange multipliers, we have

$$
\begin{aligned}
&L(P(i,c), x_B(i,c), \lambda_i, \lambda_{i,c}, \mu_i) \\
&= \sum_{i \in \mathcal{N}^B} C_i + \sum_{i \in \mathcal{N}^B} \lambda_i \left(\sum_{c \in \mathcal{N}^C} x_B(i,c) - n_i \right) + \\
&\quad \sum_{i \in \mathcal{N}^B} \sum_{c \in \mathcal{N}^C} \lambda_{i,c} \left(\xi^d(i,c) - x_B(i,c)\psi^d \right) + \sum_{i \in \mathcal{N}^B} \mu_i \left(P_{max} - \sum_{c \in \mathcal{N}^C} P(i,c) \right)
\end{aligned}
\tag{18}
$$

Suppose $P^*(i,c)$ and $x_B^*(i,c)$ are the optimal power and channel allocation, respectively, according to Karush-Kuhn-Tucker (KKT) condition [14], we have the following equations.

$$\left. \frac{\partial L(P(i,c), x_B(i,c), \lambda_i, \mu_i, \mu_i')}{\partial P(i,c)} \right|_{P(i,c)=P^*(i,c)} = 0; \tag{19}$$

$$\sum_{c \in \mathcal{N}^C} x_B(i,c) - n_i = 0, \quad \forall i \in \mathcal{N}^B; \tag{20}$$

$$\lambda_{i,c} \left(\xi^d(i,c) - x_B(i,c)\psi^d \right)\big|_{P(i,c)=P^*(i,c)} = 0, \quad \forall i \in \mathcal{N}^B, c \in \mathcal{N}^C; \tag{21}$$

$$\mu_i \left(P_{max} - \sum_{c \in \mathcal{N}^C} P(i,c) \right)\Bigg|_{P(i,c)=P^*(i,c)} = 0, \quad \forall i \in \mathcal{N}^B; \tag{22}$$

and

$$\mu_i \geq 0, \quad \lambda_{i,c} \geq 0, \quad \forall i \in \mathcal{N}^B, c \in \mathcal{N}^C. \tag{23}$$

According to (19), we can obtain

$$\frac{n_i B x_B(i,c)}{\left(\frac{N_0 + I_S(i,c)}{H(d_i,c)} + P^*(i,c) \right) ln2} + \mu_i \frac{H(d_i,c)}{N_0 + I_S(i,c)} - \mu_i' = 0 \tag{24}$$

where $I_S(i,c)$ can be estimated by each FBS in practice. Thus

$$P^*(i,c) = \left(\frac{n_i B x_B(i,c)}{\lambda_i' ln2} - \frac{N_0 + I_S(i,c)}{H(d_i,c)} \right)^+$$

$$= \begin{cases} \frac{n_i}{\lambda_i'} - \frac{N_0 + I_S(i,c)}{H(d_i,c)}, & 0 < \lambda_i' < \frac{n_i B H(d_i,c)}{(N_0 + I_S(i,c))ln2}, x_B(i,c) = 1 \\ 0, & otherwise \end{cases} \qquad (25)$$

where

$$\lambda_i' = \frac{ln2}{B} \left(\mu_i - \lambda_{i,c} \left(\frac{H(d_i,c)}{N_0 + I_S(i,c)} \right) \right) \qquad (26)$$

According to (16), we can obtain

$$P^*(i,c) \geq \frac{\psi^d(N_0 + I_S(i,c))}{H(d_i,c)} \qquad (27)$$

Substituting (25) to (22) when $x_B(i,c) = 1$, we have

$$\lambda_i' = \frac{n_i^2}{P_{max} + \sum\limits_{c \in \mathcal{N}^{C'}} \frac{N_0 + I_S(i,c)}{H(d_i,c)}} \qquad (28)$$

where $\mathcal{N}^{C'}$ is the selected channel set for FBS i. Substituting (28) to (25) when $x_B(i,c) = 1$, we have

$$P^*(i,c) = \frac{1}{n_i} P_{max} + \frac{1}{n_i} \sum\limits_{c \in \mathcal{N}^{C'}} \frac{N_0 + I_S(i,c)}{H(d_i,c)} - \frac{N_0 + I_S(i,c)}{H(d_i,c)} \qquad (29)$$

In the following, we propose two schemes to implement the solution of the formulated problem. Specially, we are interested in distributed algorithms where each FBS can decide the preferred channel by itself and allocate power for its users.

3.1   A Scheme Based on Local Measurements of FBS

The first scheme is based only on the local measurements of FBS. Any FBS i measures each available channel from primary systems and characterizes these channels with interference levels. Channels with lower interference level are preferred. Thus, it will choose the lowest n_i channels. Then, the FBS will allocate these selected n_i channels to its users randomly. After channel allocation, according to (29) the power of FBS i on each channel is roughly by

$$P(i,c) = \frac{1}{n_i} P_{max} + \frac{1}{H(d_i,c)} \left(\frac{1}{n_i} \sum\limits_{c \in \mathcal{N}^C} I_S(i,c) - I_S(i,c) \right) \qquad (30)$$

The details of the channel allocation and power control for each FBS are shown in Algorithm 1. The complexity of this scheme for any FBS i depends on the channel selection and power allocation. It is then bounded by $O(|\mathcal{N}^C||\mathcal{N}_i^U| + |\mathcal{N}_i^U|)$, where $|.|$ denotes the cardinal of the set within. If we employ sorting algorithms such

---

Algorithm 1. Channel allocation and power control algorithm based on local measurements of FBS

Input: i, $\mathcal{N}_C$, $\mathcal{N}_i^U$.
Output: $\{x(i,j,c)\}$, $\{P(i,c)\}$.

 1: Initialization: $\mathcal{N}_i^{U'} \leftarrow \mathcal{N}_i^U$, $N^{C'} \leftarrow \mathcal{N}_C$
 2: **while** $\mathcal{N}_j^{U'} \neq \emptyset$ **do**
 3:    **if** $N^{C'} = \emptyset$ **then**
 4:       //not enough channels for femtocell i.
 5:       Break;
 6:    **else**
 7:       $c^* = \arg \max\limits_{c \in \mathcal{N}^{C'}} I_S(i,c)$
 8:       Randomly choose a user j^* for channel c^*
 9:       $\mathcal{N}^{C'} \leftarrow \mathcal{N}^{C'} - c^*$
10:       $N_i^{U'} \leftarrow N_i^{U'} - j^*$
11:    **end if**
12: **end while**
13: **for** $j \in \mathcal{N}_i^U$ **do**
14:    Calculate $P(i,c_j)$ by (30).
15:    Calculate $\xi^d(i,j,c)$ by (1).
16:    **if** $\xi^d(i,j,c) < \psi^d$ **then**
17:       $P(i,c_j) \leftarrow 0$
18:       //power allocation for user j is failed.
19:    **else**
20:       $x(i,j,c) \leftarrow 1$
21:    **end if**
22: **end for**

---

as quicksort in channel selection, the complexity can be reduced to $O(|\mathcal{N}^C|^2 + |\mathcal{N}_i^U|)$ for the worst case. Whenever a FBS detects a return of primary users on the licensed channel, it will inform its users to switch to another channel with the least interference on the available channel list, decide a transmission power according to (30), and update the transmission power on other active channels.

3.2   A Scheme Based on Measurements of FBS and Its Users

In the second scheme, each FBS will make the decision of channel selection and power allocation according to the measurements not only on FBS but also on its users. In practice, each femtocell user is required to negotiate a control channel with its FBS, and reports its measurements to the FBS through this channel. Based on these information, FBS then characterizes the channels with the accurate interference levels for each user, and chooses n_i channels with lowest interference levels.

The channel allocation is based on the following metric.

$$g(i,j,c) = \frac{H(d_i,c)}{N_0 + I_S(i,j,c)}, \quad \forall i \in \mathcal{N}^B, j \in \mathcal{N}_i^U, c \in \mathcal{N}^C. \tag{31}$$

Channel c^* is allocated to user j^*, if $g(i, j^*, c^*)$ has the maximum value in the available channels and users. Then the allocated channel and user will be removed from the sets of channels and users. Repeat the channel and user selection until there is no user or channel left. After channel allocation, the power for each user j in femtocell i can be calculated according to (29) as follows

$$P_j(i, c_j) = \frac{1}{n_i} P_{max} + \frac{1}{n_i} \sum_{k \in \mathcal{N}_i^U} \frac{N_0 + I_S(i, k, c_k)}{H_k(d_i, c_k)} \quad \frac{N_0 + I_S(i, j, c_j)}{H_j(d_i, c_j)} \quad (32)$$

where $H_j(d_i, c_j)$ is the channel gain of user j on channel c_j. $I_S(i, j, c_j)$ is the interference on channel c_j reported by user j.

Algorithm 2. Channel allocation and power control algorithm based on measurements of FBS and its users

Input: $i, \mathcal{N}_C, \mathcal{N}_i^U$.
Output: $\{x(i, j, c)\}, \{P(i, c)\}$.

1: Initialization: $\mathcal{N}_i^{U'} \leftarrow \mathcal{N}_i^U, \mathcal{N}^{C'} \leftarrow \mathcal{N}^C$.
2: **while** $\mathcal{N}_j^{U'} \neq \emptyset$ **do**
3: **if** $N^{C'} = \emptyset$ **then**
4:    //not enough channels for femtocell i.
5:    Break;
6: **else**
7:    $\{j^*, c_{j^*}\} \leftarrow \arg \max_{j \in \mathcal{N}_i^{U'}, c \in \mathcal{N}^{C'}} g(i, j, c)$
8:    $\mathcal{N}^{C'} \leftarrow \mathcal{N}^{C'} - c_{j^*}$
9:    $N_i^{U'} \leftarrow N_i^{U'} - j^*$
10: **end if**
11: **end while**
12: **for** $j \in \mathcal{N}_i^U$ **do**
13: Calculate $P_j(i, c_j)$ by (32).
14: Calculate $\xi^d(i, j, c)$ by (1).
15: **if** $\xi^d(i, j, c) < \psi^d$ **then**
16:    $P_j(i, c_j) \leftarrow 0$
17:    //power allocation for user j in cell i is failed.
18: **else**
19:    $x(i, j, c) \leftarrow 1$
20: **end if**
21: **end for**

The details of the channel allocation and power control for each FBS are shown in Algorithm 2. The complexity of this scheme depends on the channel selection and power allocation. For any FBS i, it is bounded by $O((|\mathcal{N}^C| \times |\mathcal{N}_i^U|)^2)$ by employing quicksort in channel and user selection. Similar as the first scheme, in this scheme, whenever a FBS detects a return of primary users on the licensed channel, it will perform the following procedures sequentially, i.e., inform its user to switch to another channel with the least interference on the available channel list, decide a transmission power according to (32), and update the transmission power on other active channels.

4   Numerical Results

In this section, we will evaluate our proposed spectrum sharing schemes by numerical results.

We have implemented a COGFEM simulator in MATLAB, where we create an urban apartment topology as shown in Fig. 2. There are n_r rows of apartment buildings. Each row has n_b buildings, while each building has n_f floors. The length, width, height of an apartment are l, w, and h, respectively. We call the gap between neighboring buildings in a row *side gap*, and denote it as g_s , while we call the gap between neighboring rows *row gap*, and denote it as g_r. In our simulations, we choose these parameters as shown in Table 1. Each apartment has a FBS, and has n_u users in a range of 2 to 4 suggested in [3]. These users sit randomly in each apartment. For simplicity, each FBS is located at the middle of the apartment. The maximum transmission power for FBS is 10dBmW [15]. The number of subchannels for normal femtocells, n_c, is 10, while the number of channels for COGFEM, n'_c, changes randomly from a range of 10 to 20 during the simulation. For the estimation of channel gain in our simulation, we consider a slow fading channel, and the path loss is $\frac{1}{d^2}$, where d is the distance between a transmitter and its receiver. We run each case 10 times with different random seeds for the number of users in each femtocell and the number of available channels, and then calculate the average capacity per femtocell.

Figure 3 shows the variation of average capacity per femtocell while changing the available channels. Here, we fix the topology as 3 rows, 5 buildings per row, and 5 floors per building. It shows that the average capacity per femtocell increases while the number of available channels increases. That is because more channel candidates can reduce the interference from neighboring femtocells by allocating different channels to neighboring femtocells. Algorithm 2 achieved a bit higher capacity than algorithm 1, since it uses more accurate interference and channel gain information from the report of femtocell users.

Table 1. Simulation Parameters

Symbol	value	Symbol	value
l	10m	n_r	$[1, 10]$
w	10m	n_b	$[1, 10]$
h	3m	n_f	$[1, 10]$
g_s	1m	g_r	5m
n_c	10	n'_c	$[10, 20]$
P_{max}	10dBmW	n_u	$[2, 4]$
ψ^d	10dBm	N_0	-110dBmW
B	100KHz		

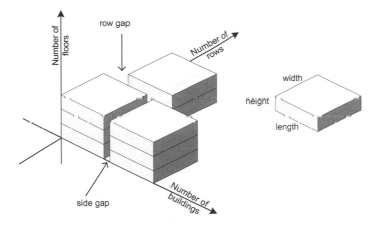

Fig. 2. An illustration of the simulation scenario

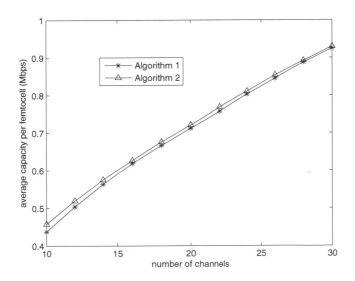

Fig. 3. Average capacity per femtocell in terms of number of channels. (3 rows, 5 buildings per row, 5 floors per building).

Figure 4, 5, and 6 show the variation of average capacity per femtocell while changing the number of floors, buildings, and rows, respectively. Specially, the average capacity per femtocell decreases while increasing the number of floors, buildings, and rows, respectively. When the number of floors, buildings, and rows increases, the number of FBSs increases. This results in more interference amongst femtocells given a limited number of available channels. In the case of normal femtocells, where the number of available channels is fixed to 10,

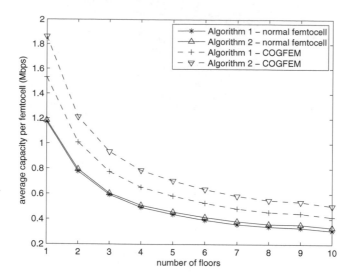

Fig. 4. Average capacity per femtocell in terms of number of floors in each building. (3 rows, and 5 buildings per row)

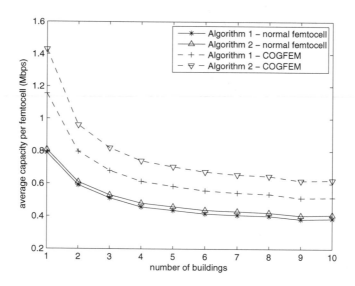

Fig. 5. Average capacity per femtocell in terms of number of buildings in each row. (3 rows, and 5 floors per building)

Algorithm 2 achieves slightly higher capacity than Algorithm 1. In the case of COGFEM, where the number of available channels is randomly changed from 10 to 20, Algorithm 2 achieves much higher capacity than Algorithm 1. From

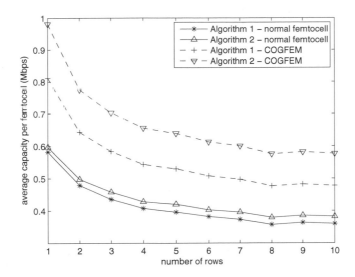

Fig. 6. Average capacity per femtocell in terms of number of rows of buildings. (5 floors per building, and 5 buildings per row)

all the results, COGFEM achieved much higher capacity than normal femtocells without CR capability by using either Algorithm 1 or 2. This is essentially due to more channel opportunities in COGFEM than normal femtocells.

5 Conclusion

In this paper, we have investigated the spectrum sharing problem in downlink transmission while applying CR technology into femtocell networks. We formulated this problem as a mixed integer problem and then relaxed it using Lagrangian method. According to the solution of the relaxed problem, we proposed two distributed schemes with low complexity to jointly select downlink channels and allocate the transmission power for each channel. Numerical results showed that COGFEM with more spectrum opportunity can achieve much higher capacity than normal femtocells by both schemes. The scheme which requires femtocell users report the channel state and interference information to their FBSs can achieve higher capacity than the scheme which only makes channel and power decision based on the local measurements on FBS.

References

1. Presentaions by ABI Research, Picochip, Airvana, IP.access, Gartner, Telefonica Espana. In: 2nd International Conference on Home Access Points and Femtocells (2007),
http://www.avrenevents.com/dallasfemto2007/purchase_presentations.htm

2. Chandrasekhar, V., Andrews, J., Gatherer, A.: Femtocell networks: a survey. IEEE Communications Magazine 46(9), 59–67 (2008)
3. Claussen, H., Ho, L.T.W., Samuel, L.G.: An overview of the femtocell concept. Bell Lab. Tech. J. 13(1), 221–245 (2008)
4. Peng, C., Zheng, H., Zhao, B.Y.: Utilization and fairness in spectrum assignment for opportunistic spectrum access. Mobile Networks and Applications 11(4), 555–576 (2006)
5. Mitola, J., Maguire, G.: Cognitive radio: making software radios more personal. Personal Communications, IEEE 6(4), 13–18 (1999)
6. Valcarce, A., Roche, G.D.L.: Applying fdtd to the coverage prediction of wimax femtocells. EURASIP Journal on Wireless Communications and Networking, 555–576 (2009)
7. Lopez-Perez, D., Roche, G.d.l., Valcarce, A., A., Juttner, J.Z.: Interference avoidance and dynamic frequency planning for wimax femtocells networks. In: Eklund, P., Haemmerlé, O. (eds.) ICCS 2008. LNCS (LNAI), vol. 5113, pp. 1579–1584. Springer, Heidelberg (2008)
8. Sundaresan, K., Rangarajan, S.: Efficient resource management in ofdma femto cells. In: MobiHoc '09: Proceedings of the tenth ACM international symposium on Mobile ad hoc networking and computing, pp. 33–42. ACM, New York (2009)
9. Xiang, J., Zhang, Y., Skeie, T., He, J.: Qos aware admission and power control for cognitive radio cellular networks. Wireless Communications and Mobile Computing (2009)
10. Digham, F.F.: Joint power and channel allocation for cognitive radios. In: IEEE Wireless Communications and Networking Conference (WCNC 2008), April 3, pp. 882–887 (2008)
11. Lee, I.F.W.-Y., Akyildiz: Joint spectrum and power allocation for inter-cell spectrum sharing in cognitive radio networks. In: 3rd IEEE Symposium on New Frontiers in Dynamic Spectrum Access Networks (DySPAN 2008), October 2008, pp. 1–12 (2008)
12. Hoang, A.T., Liang, Y.-C.: Downlink channel assignment and power control for cognitive radio networks. IEEE Transactions on Wireless Communications 7(8), 3106–3117 (2008)
13. Stevenson, C., Chouinard, G., Lei, Z., Hu, W., Shellhammer, S., Caldwell, W.: IEEE 802.22: The first cognitive radio wireless regional area network standard. IEEE Communications Magazine 47(1), 130–138 (2009)
14. Boyd, S., Vandenberghe, L.: Convex Optimization. Cambridge University Press, Cambridge (2004)
15. Lopez-Perez, D., Valcarce, A., De La Roche, G., Liu, E., Zhang, J.: Access methods to wimax femtocells: A downlink system-level case study. In: 11th IEEE Singapore International Conference on Communication Systems (ICCS 2008), November 2008, pp. 1657–1662 (2008)

Cross-Layer Routing Method for the SCTP with Multihoming MIPv6

Hongbo Shi and Tomoki Hamagami

Division of Physics, Electrical and Computer Engineering,
Graduate School of Engineering, Yokohama National University,
79-1 Tokiwadai, Hodogaya-ku, Yokohama 240-8501 Japan
shi@ynu.ac.jp, hamagami@ynu.ac.jp

Abstract. The *multihoming* is regarded as a kind of technology to provide wide-band and relaible network service. The protocol called *Stream Control Transmission Protocol (SCTP)* [1] can manage the multi-homed nodes to realize a highly-available data transfer capability in the *Transport Layer*. An *SCTP* node may keep a combination of the sets of the eligible source and destination transport addresses. The node can detect if a transport address is out of service by periodical messaging which is called *HEARTBEAT* in *SCTP*. If the *HEARTBEAT* is unacknowledged, the node will change to send data via another transport address which is with a *HEARTBEAT ACK*. The multi-homed mobility nodes, such as the cellphones implemented with both WiFi and 3G, are widely used in the world. *Mobility Support in IPv6 (Mobile IPv6, MIPv6)* [2] is a protocol to provide a mobility function in IP layer. However the *SCTP* is not a protocol designed for the moving nodes, such as the nodes using the *Mobile IP (MIP)*. Also there is an enhanced *SCTP* called *mSCTP* [3] which enables the mobility at the *Transport Layer*. But the *mSCTP* is not designed for the multihoming *Mobile IP*. In this paper, we suggest a new cross-layer routing method to use the *SCTP* with the multihoming *MIPv6*. Our proposal is mobile node can use *SCTP* to select an optimized transport peer in real time.

Keywords: multi-homed, Mobile IPv6, SCTP, Binding Update, cross-layer.

1 Introduction

Recently the multi-homed nodes is not just limited in the PCs. Even the cellphones, such as iPhone, are started to implement WiFi and 3G interfaces. Due the multi-homed mobility nodes started to be used widely in the world, the multihoming technology is required to provide a reliable wide-band ubiquitous environment. WiFi and 3G are wireless communication technologies that can keep a mobile node's connection seamlessly while it is moving in a WiFi network or a 3G network. However a mobile node will lose the network connections while switching its wireless interfaces without any upper layer support.

X. Jun Hei and L. Cheung (Eds.): AccessNets 2009, LNICST 37, pp. 179–191, 2010.
© Institute for Computer Sciences, Social-Informatics and Telecommunications Engineering 2010

Although the *Mobility Support in IPv6* can provide a mobility support in the IP layer, the management of a multi-homed mobile node (*MN*) is beyond the *MIPv6* specification. *SCTP* is a protocol in the Transport Layer that may control the multi-homed nodes. However, a multi-homed mobile node may move around different networks with different IP addresses. In the *MIPv6*, the *Routing Optimization* is used. A node can communicate with an *MN* without the forwarding service supported by the *MN*'s *Home Agent*. Though the *mSCTP* [3] provides the dynamic address reconfiguration[4], it is not designed for the multihoming *Mobile IP*. The multihoming *Mobile IP* is known that may have multiple *Home Addresses* (*HoAs*) or *Care-of Addresses* (*CoAs*).[5] The dynamic address reconfiguration *mSCTP* does not have the mechanism for dynamic updating the relationship between multiple *HoAs* and *CoAs* at the transport layer. A cross-layer routing method is required to manage the IP addresses between the *SCTP* and *MIPv6*.

In Sec.2 this paper describes the issues in the *Steam Control Transmission Protocol*. Sec.3 analyzes the current specification of the *Mobile IPv6*. Our proposal and related experiment results are introduced in Sec.4. Sec.5 shows the evaluation of our proposal and the remaining future works.

2   Stream Control Transmission Protocol: SCTP

SCTP [1] is a connection-oriented protocol in the *Transport Layer*. *SCTP* is able to control the multi-homed nodes which have multiple IP addresses. Fig.1 shows the multi-homed nodes use *SCTP* for transferring the stream.

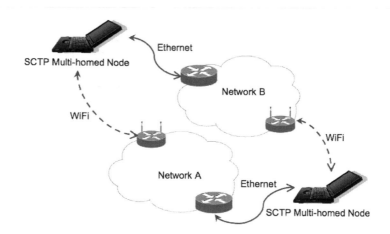

Fig. 1. Multi-homed Nodes Use SCTP

2.1 SCTP Chunks

In *SCTP*, a multi-homed node need to have a set of IP addresses used the same port number. Multiple IP addresses with an SCTP port is treated as a *list of transport addresses. SCTP* packets are delivered with a common header and several *chunks*. There are 2 types of *SCTP chunks*, one is *DATA chunk*, and the other is *control chunk. HEARTBEAT Request* and *HEARTBEAT Acknowledgement* are used as control trunks in the *SCTP* fault management. According to the *HEARTBEAT* and sharing the same *SCTP* port number as described before, multi-homed nodes can take a quick failover in *SCTP*. As start-up, *Primary Path* is set to transfer data for multi-homed nodes and an alternative path is reserved as a backup of the *Primary Path*. An *SCTP* packet consists of one or more chunks: either *data* or *control*. For the purposes of reliability and congestion control, each *data chunk* in an association is assigned a unique *Transmission Sequence Number (TSN)*. The *TSN* is similar to the sequence number used in *TCP*. Different from the *TCP*, the *SCTP* is message-oriented and chunks are atomic, *TSN* is associated only with the *data*.

As defined in the *RFC 4960* [1], the *Selective Acknowledgement (SACK)* is a chunk sent to the peer endpoint to acknowledge received *DATA* chunks as represented by their *TSNs*. The value of the *Cumulative TSN Ack* parameter is the last *TSN* received before a break in the sequence of received *TSNs* occurs. The next *TSN* value following this one has not yet been received at the endpoint sending the *SACK*.

2.2 mSCTP

Based on the *SCTP Dynamic Address Reconfiguration* [4], *Mobile SCTP for IP Handover Support (mSCTP)* [3] is suggested a mobility option in the Transport Layer. *mSCTP* uses the *SCTP* connection as a multi-homed mobile node's permanent identification while the mobile node is moving among networks. The *SCTP* connection acts a fundamental role in *mSCTP*. In short, a multi-homed mobile node cannot have the mobility option without available *SCTP* connections. It is difficult to use the *mSCTP* for the data transmission which requires a reliable mobility network service, like medical information.

2.3 CMT: Concurrent Multipath Transfer

In the original *SCTP*, the sender is not able to send new data on multiple paths simultaneously. The sender uses the *primary destination* to which all transmissions of new data are sent. *CMT-SCTP* [6] provides a reliable, multihome-aware, SACK-based SCTP. *CMT* uses *SCTP*'s multihoming feature to simultaneously transfer new data across multiple end-to-end paths to the receiver.

3 Mobility Support in IPv6: Mobile IPv6

Different from the *mSCTP*, the *Mobility Support in IPv6 (Mobile IPv6, MIPv6* [2] is a mobility support in native IP Layer. In *MIPv6*, each *Mobile Node (MN)* have 2 IP addresses. One is for the permanent use, called *Home Address* (HoA). Another one is called *Care-of Address (CoA)* for recording the current location of the mobile node. Literally, the *CoA* is changed frequently. *Home Agent (HA)* is a router for managing the location of a mobile node and routing the packets belong to the mobile node.

In *MIPv6*, a mobile node is required to send *Binding Updates* that includes the mobile node's *HoA* and *CoA* to its *HA* and the *Correspondent Node (CN)* which is communicating with the mobile node. If a *CN* has cached an entry of a *MN*'s *Binding Information*, the *MN*'s *CoA* can be used in the packet transmission between *CN* and *MN* directly. This kind of routing mechanism is called *Routing Optimization* in *MIPv6* (Fig.2). Otherwise, a *CN* without caching an *MN*'s *Binding information* is required to use *Triangular Routing* instead (Fig.3). The packet transmission between *MN* and *CN* is forwarded by the *MN*'s *HA*.

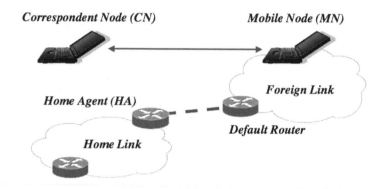

Fig. 2. Routing Optimization

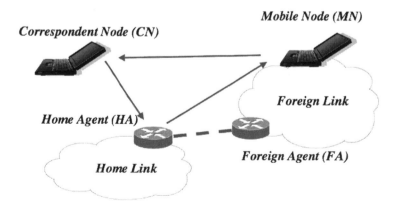

Fig. 3. Triangular Routing

3.1   Multihoming Issues in MIPv6

The management of multi-homed mobile node in *MIPv6* is discussed in the *Internet Engineering Task force (IETF)*. The investigation of the multihoming use in *MIPv6* is described in the Internet Draft document , *Analysis of Multihoming in Mobile IPv6* [5].

A *MN* has 2 IP addresses, *CoA* and *HoA*. It causes that the relation between *HoA* and it CoA is estimated to be complex in the multi homed *MN*. The mapping patterns, 1:1, 1:n, n:1 and n:n are possible in the multihoming use in *MIPv6*.

3.2   Multihoming Proposals in MIPv6

As described above, a multi-homed *MN* may have multiple *CoAs* in *MIPv6*. A new field called *Binding identification number (BID)* is added to the original *MIPv6 Binding Information* for managing the multiple *Binding Updates* sent by a multi-homed *MN* in the *IETF Internet Draft, Multiple Care-of Addresses Registration* [7]. The new field shown in Fig.4 is called *BID Mobility Option*.

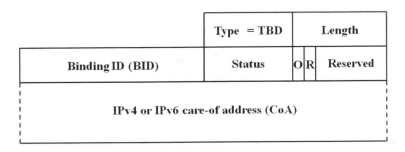

Fig. 4. BID Mobility Option

4   Cross-Layer Routing Method

This paper suggests a new routing method that enables the *SCTP* for the multi-homed *MN* in *MIPv6*. As an *MN*, it moves around different networks and changes its location frequently. An *n-CoAs-to-1-HoA* multi-homed *MIPv6* model is supposed to be used for the *SCTP* transmission.

4.1   Extension on the Binding Data Structure

The multihoming *MIPv6* network used in this paper is a *n-CoAs-to-1-HA* model. The *BID* introduced in Sec.3.2 is used to manage the multiple *Binding Information* entries sent by the different multi-homed *MN*'s *CoAs*. In this paper, the similar field is implemented in the simulation with a name, *MN's Yet another Interface (MYIF)*. However there is a lack of the consideration for the *CN*

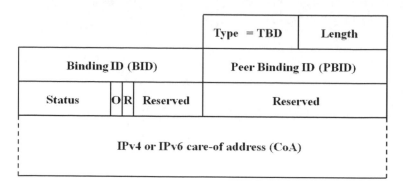

Fig. 5. New PBID tag on the BID Mobility Option

which is a *multi-homed MIPv6 MN* in the *IETF I-D, Multiple Care-of Address Registration* [7].

As shown in the Fig.5, we extended the binding data structure with a new tag, called *Peer Binding ID (PBID)*. In our simulation, the new *PBID* is implemented with a name, *PEERIF*.

4.2   Enhanced Binding Update Procedure

In order to manage the multi-homed *MN*, our proposal has modified the original *Binding Information* messages used in the *Binding Update* procedure.The multi-homed *MN* proceeds *Binding Update* procedure for each of its *interface* individually. This kind of the modification can coexist with the *Return Routerability* security function well.

Fig.6 shows 2 new functions in the *MIPv6 Binding Update Procedure*. One is a function for the *HA* and the other one is for the *CN*. When the *HA* is required to forward a packet to a multi-homed *MN*, the *HA* is designed to forward the packet to the multiple valid *CoAs* of the multi-homed *MN* in this paper. It is easy for the *HA* to distinguish multi-homed *MN* between single *MN*. A multi-homed *MN* is required to start the *Binding Update* procedures to the *CN* individually by its different network interfaces, when the *MN* finds a new *CN* which is not in the *Binding Update List* of the *MN*.

4.3   Cross-Layer Route Method in SCTP with MIPv6

Our suggestion adds a new additional function to inform the upper layer *SCTP* by the lower layer *MIPv6* while the *Binding Information* is updated. This process realizes the cross-layer sharing of the *Binding Information* of a multi-homed *MN* between *SCTP* and *MIPv6*. The original *SCTP* regards the *n-CoAs-to-1-HoA* multi-homed *MIPv6 MN* as a "single" node because there is only 1 *HoA* used in the multihoming *MIPv6*.

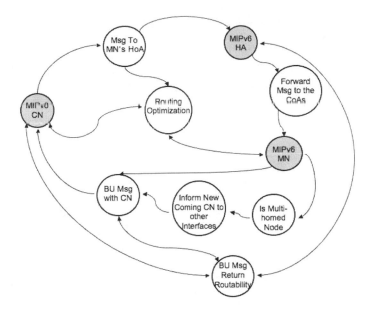

Fig. 6. Modified State Transition of MIPv6

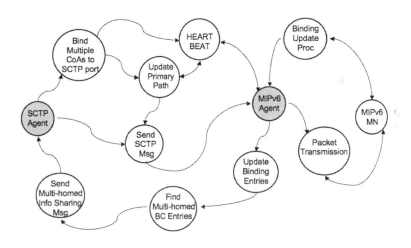

Fig. 7. Modified State Transition in an SCTP-MIPv6 node

Fig.7 shows an *SCTP and MIPv6* aware node is implemented a new function for sharing the *Binding Information* of a multi-homed *MN*. There are 2 processes in the new function. One is used to monitor the *Binding Information* of a multi-homed *MN*. Another one is for informing the upper layer, *SCTP* agent. It is an interface between *MIPv6* and *SCTP*. By using the interface, *SCTP* shares the

CoAs and *Hop Limits* information of the multi-homed *MN* cached in the *Binding Information* of the *MIPv6* .

The *Cross-layer Routing* mechanism suggested in the paper requires the *SCTP* to use the *MIPv6 Routing Optimization* for the multi-homed *MN*. The *SCTP* is modified to share the multiple IP addresses of a multi-homed *MN* from the *Binding Information* cached by itself in the lower layer, MIPv6. The sharing interface is added to both *MIPv6* and *SCTP*. Also, our proposal coexists with the original *HEARTBEAT* mechanism used in *SCTP*. The *SCTP control and data chunks* are transferred to the *multi-homed MN* by the *MIPv6 Routing Optimization*.

In our modified mechanism, the *Binding Information* sent by the multi-homed *MN* and *CN* can be cached by the *CNs* and *HAs* can be cached properly. With the enhanced cross-layer method suggested in the paper, the upper layer *SCTP* can share the *Binding Information* which are cached in the lower layer *MIPv6* and all *SCTP chunks* are able to be sent to the multi-homed *MN*'s *CoAs* directly. This paper realized an *end-to-end SCTP multihoming transmission* for the *n-CoAs-to-1-HoA MIPv6*.

4.4   Simulation

We use the simulation tool called *Network Simulation 2* (*NS*) to simulate our proposal. The *MN* and *CN* are implemented to provide the *MIPv6* functions via IEEE 802.11, the wireless bandwidth is 2Mbps. Other wired networks are connected by the 100 Mbps Ethernet. Fig. 8 shows the network topology of our simulation environment.

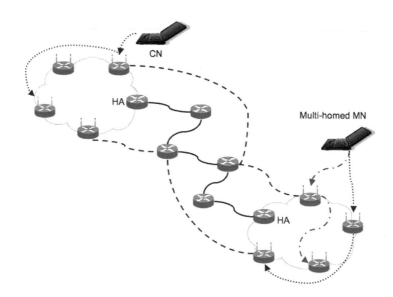

Fig. 8. Network Topology of the Simulation

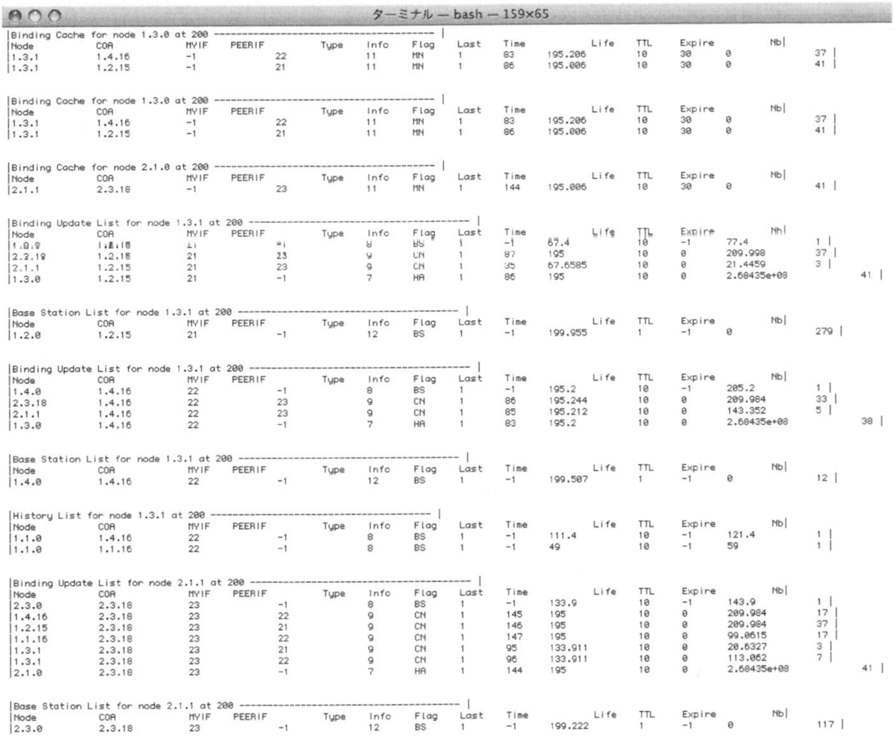

Fig. 9. Binding Information with IF Identifiers

In the simulation, both *CN* and multi-homed *MN* moves around and assigned to different networks. *MN* sends *Binding Update* with different *CoAs* which are allocated to the different interfaces to the *CN* and *HA*. *CN* is a normal *MIPv6* mobile node. It also sends *Binding Update* to the multi-homed *MN* and its *HA*. Due to the movement of the *CN* and the multi-homed *MN*, the end-to-end shortest path changes. The end-to-end distance is measured and cached during our modified *Binding Update* procedure. By using our new *Cross-layer Routing Method*, the modified *SCTP* enables to use the *MIPv6 Routing Optimization* for the multi-homed *MNs*.

As shown in Fig. 9, the multi-homed *MN* has 2 interfaces, one is the interface *21* and the other one is *22*. The Interfaces *21* and *22* are assigned to the same *HoA*, 1.3.1. Our proposal is implemented on the simulation called Network Simulation 2 (NS2). [1] In the simulation, the *CN* is an *MN* with its *HoA*, 2.1.1, and it is currently allocated with an *CoA*, 2.3.18. Fig.9 shows that the entries of the

---

[1] The IP address in the simulation NS2 is different from the real hexadecimal IPv6 address. This kind of IP address architecture does not affect the essential MIPv6 mechanism in NS2.

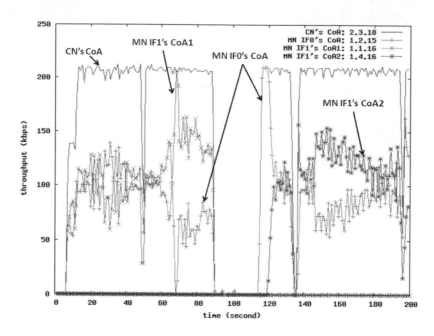

Fig. 10. Throughput of MIPv6 SCTP (CMT) + MIPv6

Binding Information from the multi-homed *MN* are cached by the *HA*, *CN* and *BS* correctly.[2]

In this simulation, *Concurrent Multipath Transfer (CMT)* [6] is in use. The line titled to "CN's CoA", shows the *SCTP* throughput of the single node, *CN*. The line with a title "MN IF0's CoA" shows the throughput of the multi-homed *MN*'s interface *IF0*. And the lines with the titles "MN IF1's CoA1" and "MN IF1's CoA2" show the throughput of the multi-homed *MN*'s interface *IF1* while the *IF1* is moving around different networks. In the simulation, *SCTP* chunks are sent by the *MIPv6 Routing Optimization*. Because of the movement of the *IF1* at the *Second 89*, *SCTP* handover and *MIPv6 overlap issues* [8] occurred. At the *Second 114*, the *SCTP Data* chunk starts to be sent by the *IF0* only. At the *Second 120*, the *IF1* is recovered. Fig.10 shows that the multi-homed *MN* increases the throughput successfully while the *MN* is changing one of its *CoAs* from *1.1.16* to *1.4.16* comparing with the single-homed *MNs*. All of the *SCTP* streams are transferred by the *MN*'s *IF0*.

The Fig. 11 shows the throughput performance was improved while the *MN* moves cross the cell coverage overlap faster, comparing the throughput with the Fig.10. The *MIPv6 overlap issue* affects the *SCTP CMT* throughput performance even in the multihoming *MIPv6*. [3]

Fig. 12 and Fig.13 show the *Windows Size (cwnd)*, *Slow-Start Threshold (ssthresh)* and the *Transmission Sequence Number (TSN)* measured at the

---

[2] The *MYIF* or *PEERIF* with a number -1 means, the node is not multi-homed.

[3] In the Fig.11 we let the *MN* moves faster at the overlapped cells.

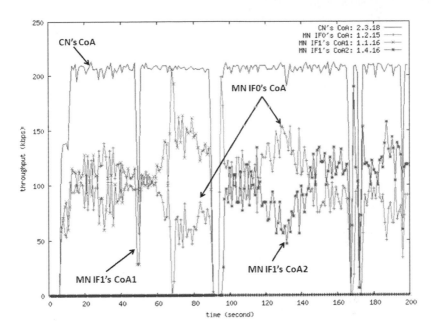

Fig. 11. Throughput of SCTP (CMT) + MIPv6: Overlap Issue

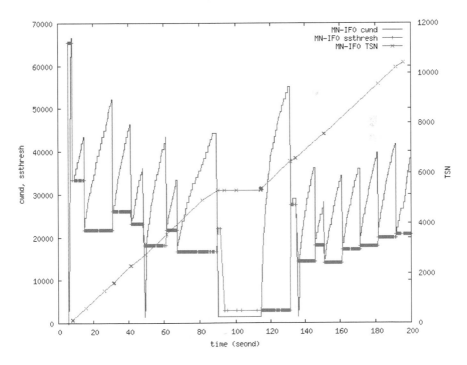

Fig. 12. Experiment of the Multi-homed MIPv6 MN, IF0

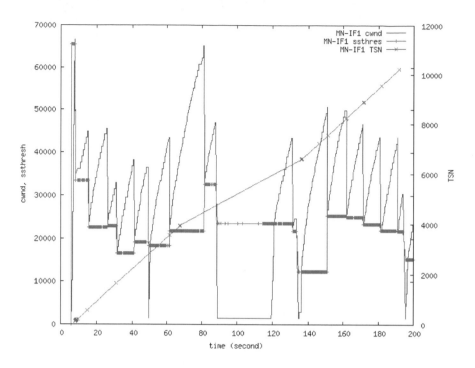

Fig. 13. Experiment of the Multi-homed MIPv6 MN, IF1

interface *IF0* an interface *IF1* of the multi-homed *MN*. Because of the movement of *IF1*, the *cwnd* is increased for the handoff recovery as shown in the Fig.12.

5   Conclusion and Future Work

This paper suggests a cross-layer routing method for using the *SCTP* via multi-homing *MIPv6*. We modified the original *Binding Update* procedure and added the interfaces between the *MIPv6* and *SCTP* for the cross-layer management. The measurement based on the modified simulation shows that our proposal let the *SCTP* work with the multihoming *MIPv6* correctly. The nodes in our simulation can use the *MIPv6 Routing Optimization* to send the *SCTP* chunks. While the handover occurs on one of the multi-homed *MN*'s interfaces, another proper interface can keep on the transmission for the end-to-end *SCTP* association.

In this paper, we suppose an n-CoAs-to-1-HoA multihoming MIPv6 model. As the future work, we need to extend this routing method to provide the remaining multihoming MIPv6 network topologies, *n-CoAs-to-n-HoAs* and *1-CoA-to-n-HoAs*.

References

1. Steward, R. (ed.): Stream Control Transmission Protocol, Internet Engineering Task Force, RFC 4960 (September 2007)
2. Johnson, D., Perkins, C., Arkko, J.: Mobility Support in IPv6, Internet Engineering Task Force, RFC 3375 (June 2004)
3. Koh, S.J., Xie, Q., Park, S.D.: Mobile SCTP (mSCTP) for IP Handover Support, Internet Engineering Task Force, draft-sjkoh-msctp (April 2006), http://tools.ietf.org/html/draft-sjkoh-msctp-01
4. Stewart, R., Xie, Q., Tuxen, M., Maruyama, S., Kozuka, M.: Stream Control Transmission Protocol (SCTP) Dynamic Address Reconfiguration, Internet Engineering Task Force, RFC 5061 (September 2007)
5. Montavont, N., Wakikawa, R., Ernst, T., Ng, C., Kuladinithi, K.: Analysis of Multihoming in Mobile IPv6, Internet Engineering Task Force, draft-ietf-monami6-mipv6-analysis (May 2008), http://tools.ietf.org/html/draft-ietf-monami6-mipv6-analysis-05
6. Iyengar, J.R., Amer, P., Stewart, R.: Concurrent multipath transfer using SCTP multihoming over independent end-to-end paths. IEEE/ACM Transactions on Networking 14(5), 951–964 (2006)
7. Wakikawa, R., Devarapalli, V., Ernst, T., Nagami, K.: Multiple Care-of Addresses Registration, draft-ietf–monami6-multiplecoa-10 (November 2008), http://tools.ietf.org/html/draft-ietf-monami6-multiplecoa-10
8. Fu, X., Karl, H., Kappler, C.: Qos-conditionalized handoff for mobile ipv6. In: Gregori, E., Conti, M., Campbell, A.T., Omidyar, G., Zukerman, M. (eds.) NETWORKING 2002. LNCS, vol. 2345, pp. 721–730. Springer, Heidelberg (2002)
9. Deering, S., Hinden, R.: Internet Protocol, Version 6 (IPv6) Specification, Internet Engineering Task Force, RFC 2460 (December 1998)
10. Shi, H., Goto, S.: Utilizing Multiple Home Links in Mobile IPv6. In: Proceedings of Wireless Communications and Networking Conference, 2004. WCNC 2004, March 2004. IEEE, Los Alamitos (2004)
11. Soliman, H., Montavont, N., Fikouras, N., Kuladinithi, K.: Flow Bindings in Mobile IPv6 and Nemo Basic Support, draft-soliman-monami6-flow-binding-05 (November 2007), http://tools.ietf.org/html/draft-soliman-monami6-flow-binding-05
12. Teraoka, F.: Cross-layer based Handover/Multi-homing Support. In: IEICE Workshop of the Technical Committee on Communication Quality (July 2008)
13. Teraoka, F., Gogo, K., Mitsuya, K., Shibui, R., Mitani, K.: Unfied Layer 2 (L2) Abstractions for Layer 3 (L3)-Driven Fast Handover, RFC 5184 (May 2008)

Challenges and Solutions in Vectored DSL

Raphael Cendrillon, Fang Liming, James Chou, Guozhu Long, and Dong Wei

Huawei Technologies Co., Ltd.
Bantian Longgang District, Shenzhen 518129, P.R. China
Raphael_2008@huawei.com

Abstract. VDSL2 is the latest generation of DSL technology, and aims to provide data-rates in excess of 100 Mbps to the home to enable next generation, high bandwidth services. Such high data-rates are achieved by transmitting at frequencies up to 30 MHz. Unfortunately transmitting at such high frequencies over twisted-pair leads to strong crosstalk between the lines. To address this issue crosstalk cancellation and precoding were developed, techniques known collectively as vectoring. The ITU is now finalizing the first version of the G.vector standard which specifies how vectoring should be implemented. This paper presents some of the more interesting problems that have been encountered in the development of this standard, and shows how creative solutions, which take advantage of the unique characteristics of the DSL environment, have helped develop vectoring from theory into a practical technology that will soon be ready for commercial deployment.

Keywords: DSL, Crosstalk Cancellation, Vectoring, DSM.

1 Introduction

VDSL is the latest generation of DSL technology, and aims to provide data-rates in excess of 100 Mbps to the home to enable next generation, high bandwidth services. Such high data-rates are achieved by transmitting at frequencies up to 30 MHz. Unfortunately transmitting at such high frequencies over twisted-pair, which was originally designed for voice-band transmission only, leads to strong crosstalk between the lines within a cable binder, an effect known as crosstalk.

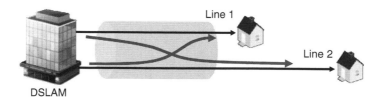

Fig. 1. The crosstalk problem

X. Jun Hei and L. Cheung (Eds.): AccessNets 2009, LNICST 37, pp. 192–203, 2010.
© Institute for Computer Sciences, Social-Informatics and Telecommunications Engineering 2010

Crosstalk is typically 20 dB larger than any other noise source in the system and leads to large reductions in data-rate and service stability as shown in Figure 2.

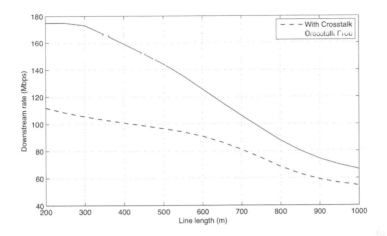

Fig. 2. Crosstalk leads to significant loss of data-rate

Crosstalk transforms the convention single-user wireline communications channel into a multi-user channel. Because of this the crosstalk problem can be solved by applying multi-user techniques like multi-user detection, power optimization and interference precoding[1][2][3][4]. These techniques exploit the fact that the central office modems from different lines are located in a common DSLAM. Since upstream receivers are co-located (a multi-access channel from the information theory perspective) joint reception is possible allowing crosstalk cancellation to be applied. In the downstream direction transmitters are co-located (a broadcast channel from the information theory perspective) allowing crosstalk precoding to be applied.

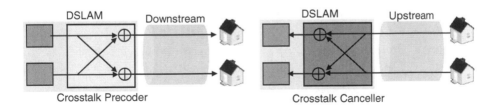

Fig. 3. Crosstalk cancellation and precoding architectures

Crosstalk cancellation and precoding are known collectively as vectoring in the DSL community. Significant work is now being done by industry on vectoring, with much of this work focused on the development of the ITU G.vector standard[5]. The goal of this standard is define the features, capabilities and protocols required to implement vectoring, and to ensure that equipment from different vendors is inter-operable.

This paper presents some of the challenges faced in the development of G.vector, with specific focus on crosstalk precoder training. It is shown how creative solutions, which take advantage of the unique characteristics of the DSL environment, have helped develop vectoring from theory into a practical technology that will soon be ready for commercial deployment.

2 Crosstalk Precoding

In the downstream direction lines are synchronized allowing transmission to be modeled independently on each tone

$$
\underbrace{\begin{bmatrix} y_k^1 \\ \vdots \\ y_k^N \end{bmatrix}}_{\mathbf{y}_k} = \underbrace{\begin{bmatrix} h_k^{1,1} & \cdots & h_k^{1,N} \\ \vdots & \ddots & \vdots \\ h_k^{N,1} & \cdots & h_k^{N,N} \end{bmatrix}}_{\mathbf{H}_k} \underbrace{\begin{bmatrix} x_k^1 \\ \vdots \\ x_k^N \end{bmatrix}}_{\mathbf{x}_k} + \underbrace{\begin{bmatrix} z_k^1 \\ \vdots \\ z_k^N \end{bmatrix}}_{\mathbf{z}_k}
\tag{1}
$$

Here u_k^n denotes the signal transmitted on tone k of line n, y_k^n denotes the signal received on tone k of line n, z_k^n denotes the noise on tone k of line n, and $h_k^{n,m}$ denotes the crosstalk channel from line m into line n on tone k.

In a vectored system the downstream signals from the different lines on tone k are precoded with a precoding matrix $\mathbf{P}_k$ prior to transmission. This precoding introduces some distortion into the transmitted signals on each line, where the distortion is selected such that it cancels with the crosstalk introduced in the channel. Denote the signal intended for line n on tone k as x_k^n. The output of the crosstalk precoder $\mathbf{u}_k$ depends on $\mathbf{x}_k$ and the crosstalk precoding matrix $\mathbf{P}_k$

$$
\mathbf{u}_k = \mathbf{P}_k \mathbf{x}_k .
\tag{2}
$$

The received signal is then

$$
\mathbf{y}_k = \mathbf{H}_k \mathbf{P}_k \mathbf{x}_k + \mathbf{z}_k .
\tag{3}
$$

Under a zero-forcing design, the precoding matrix $\mathbf{P}_k$ is chosen such that $\mathbf{H}_k \mathbf{P}_k$ is diagonal. Hence each receiver sees only its intended signal, completely free from crosstalk.

In a vectored system the downstream transmitters are co-located in the DSLAM as shown in Figure 1. Note that the crosstalk from line 1 into line 2 must propagate the full length of line 2's signal path. Similarly the crosstalk from line 2 into line 1 must propagate the full length of line 1's signal path. As a result in the downstream the crosstalk channels have a much lower magnitude than the direct channel of the corresponding victim.

$$
h_k^{n,n} \gg h_k^{n,m} .
\tag{4}
$$

In fact empirical models have been developed for the worst 1% case crosstalk channels and show that with co-located transmitters, the downstream crosstalk channels can be bounded as

$$\left|h_k^{n,m}\right| \le \alpha_k \left|h_k^{n,n}\right| , \tag{5}$$

where $\alpha_k = \sqrt{8 \times 10^{-20} \cdot (49)^{-0.6} \cdot 3.28 \cdot f_k^2 \cdot \min(l_n, l_m)}$, f_k is the frequency of sub-carrier k, and l_n is the length of line n in meters[1]. This property of the crosstalk channel causes the diagonal element of the crosstalk channel matrix to always have a larger magnitude than the other elements on its row, a characteristic referred to as row-wise diagonal dominance (RWDD). RWDD allows a simple linear crosstalk precoder, known as the diagonalizing precoder, to achieve near-optimal performance[2]. With the diagonalizing precoder

$$\mathbf{P}_k = \mathbf{H}_k^{-1} \operatorname{diag}\{\mathbf{H}_k\} , \tag{6}$$

where $\operatorname{diag}\{\mathbf{H}_k\}$ is the matrix $\mathbf{H}_k$ with the off-diagonal elements set to zero. Using (3) the received signal is then

$$\mathbf{y}_k = \operatorname{diag}\{\mathbf{H}_k\}\mathbf{x}_k + \mathbf{z}_k . \tag{7}$$

So $y_k^n = h_k^{n,n} x_k^n + z_k^n$ and each user receives their signal completely free from crosstalk. Due to the RWDD of $\mathbf{H}_k$ it can be guaranteed that application of the diagonalizing precoder causes negligible increase in the transmit power, so the spectral masks constraints and analog front end limitations will not be violated[2].

3 Precoder Training

In order to apply crosstalk precoding the coefficients $\mathbf{P}_k$ must be set to their appropriate values. This could be done by first identifying the crosstalk channel and then using a closed form design, such as the diagonalizing precoder (6). However in practice an adaptive training algorithm is preferable since it has lower complexity and allows the crosstalk precoder to track variations in the crosstalk environment as the temperature changes and lines activate and de-activate.

In the draft G.vector standard precoder training is implemented by the VDSL2 Transceiver Unit at the Operator side (VTU-O) transmitting a pilot sequence during its sync symbol. The sync symbol is a special symbol transmitted once every 257 discrete multi-tone (DMT) symbols and is traditionally used to carry a control flag between the VTU-O and VDSL2 Transceiver Unit at the Remote side (VTU-R[1]) to indicate when certain events take place, for example when a change in the bitloading table or data-rate of a line is applied.

When an initializing line first activates it transmits only during the sync symbol time slots to avoid disrupting the vectored lines in the binder that are already active and carrying data. This is shown in Figure 4. Note that the 257 symbol super-frames of all lines are synchronized, so the initializing line only creates crosstalk during the

---

[1] Note that 'VTU-R' is simply VDSL terminology for customer premises equipment (CPE).

sync symbols of the active vectored lines. The initializing line is silent during the data symbol time slots of the active vectored lines.

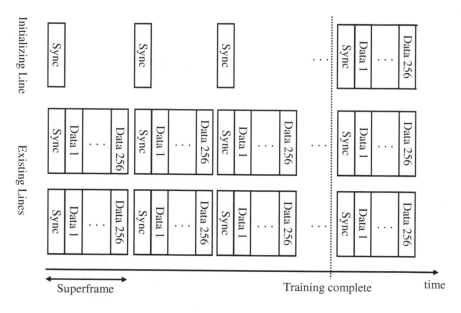

Fig. 4. Initializing lines transmit only during sync symbols to avoid disrupting active lines

The initializing line continues to transmit only during the sync symbol time slots until training of the crosstalk precoder is complete. Once the precoder coefficients for the initializing line have been determined it's crosstalk can be cancelled. At this point the initializing line may begin transmitting data during the data symbol time slots. Denote the symbol transmitted by line n on tone k during sync symbol time slot t as $d_k^n(t)$. The pilot sequence of line n on tone k can then be written as

$$\mathbf{d}_k^n = [d_k^n(1)...d_k^n(T)] , \tag{8}$$

where T denotes the periodicity of the pilot sequence and is chosen to be greater than the number of lines in the binder. In order the identify the crosstalk channels the pilot sequences on different lines are chosen to be orthogonal across time.

$$\mathbf{d}_k^n \mathbf{d}_k^{m^H} = 0, \ \forall n \neq m . \tag{9}$$

Different adaptive algorithms could be applied in order to train the crosstalk precoder. This paper will present an approach based on LMS for its simplicity and for illustration, although any other adaptive algorithm could also be used. With LMS the error at the output of the frequency-domain equalizer (FEQ) is first calculated by the VTU-R.

$$e_k^n(t) = d_k^n(t) - w_k^n y_k^n(t) . \tag{10}$$

Here w_k^n is the FEQ coefficient for line n on tone k and is ideally set to $(h_k^{n,n})^{-1}$. The pilot sequence for line n on tone k is $d_k^n(t)$ and is communicated between the vectoring control entity (VCE) and the VTU-R before training begins. The VCE is a special entity that is responsible for managing the initialization and operation of the crosstalk precoder.

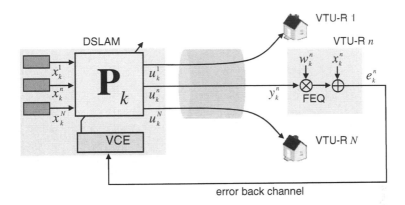

Fig. 5. Crosstalk precoder training

After the error is calculated by the VTU-R, it is encoded and sent back to the VCE through an upstream channel. The VCE then uses the error samples to update the crosstalk precoder coefficients. For example using LMS the update rule would be

$$p_k^{n,m}(t+1) = p_k^{n,m}(t) + \mu d_k^m(t)^* e_k^n(t) , \qquad (11)$$

where $p_k^{n,m}$ is the element on the nth row and mth column of the precoding matrix $\mathbf{P}_k$.

4 Challenges and Solutions

4.1 Challenge: Limited Feedback Bandwidth

Although the method for crosstalk precoder training is simple in theory it does present a number of practical challenges. To begin with, when precoder training takes place the upstream channel has not been fully initialized, and so only a very low data-rate special operations channel (SOC) is available to feed back the error samples. In its standard configuration the SOC supports only 16 bits of feedback per DMT symbol. Error samples are measured during sync symbols, which occur once every 257 DMT symbols. So per sync symbol only 257x16 or approximately 4000 bits are available for error feedback (Note that error feedback is sent continuously over the SOC in between sync symbols).

In VDSL2 there are up to 2884 downstream sub-carriers. Each sub-carrier will have its own error sample, which means that in this configuration only 1.4 bits are available to feed back each complex error sample. This corresponds to only 0.7 bits per error sample dimension.

Using such a low number of bits leads to an extremely high quantization error. This high quantization error will in turn lead to a high asymptotic error for the LMS algorithm and low data-rates at convergence. Alternatively the step size for LMS can be reduced leading to a higher data-rate, but the training time will be intolerably long as a result. Neither of these options are acceptable in practice since a subscriber must have access to high data-rates within a matter of seconds after a VDSL2 modem is switched on.

4.2 Solution: Error Subsampling

One way to reduce feedback overhead is by subsampling the error samples in frequency. Figure 6 shows a typical set of crosstalk channels taken from measurements done in the Huawei laboratory. As can be seen despite the large variations the crosstalk channels vary quite smoothly with frequency. This means that the crosstalk precoder can be accurately initialized by feeding back the error on every nth sub-carrier, running LMS on the subsampled channel, and then using interpolation to determine the crosstalk precoder coefficients for the intermediate tones[6].

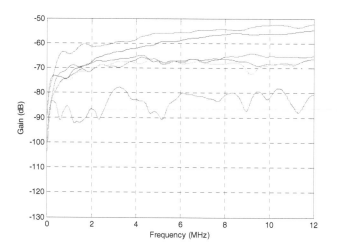

Fig. 6. Crosstalk channels vary quite smoothly with frequency

To evaluate the performance of error subsampling simulations were run in a binder consisting of 32 300m VDSL2 lines running profile 12a from Annex A. The background noise was set to -140 dBm/Hz, the coding gain was assumed to be 5 dB, and real crosstalk channel measurements were used. In all cases perfect feedback was assumed (no quantization) so that the impact of subsampling alone could be investigated.

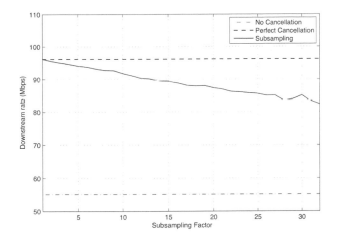

Fig. 7. Impact of error subsampling on data-rate

Figure 7 shows the average downstream data-rate as a function of the subsampling factor. As can be seen a subsampling factor of up to 8 can be used with only a minor reduction in performance.

Using a subsampling factor of 8 reduces the number of sub-carriers for feedback from 2884 to 360. This allows the number of feedback bits per error dimension to be increased from 0.7 to 5, significantly reducing the quantization error. Unfortunately though 5 bits is still not sufficient to achieve a high data-rate within a reasonable training time.

4.3 Challenge: Slow Convergence Speed

By limiting transmission of the pilot sequence to the sync symbol time slots only it is possible to ensure that initializing lines do not disrupt active vectored lines during the initialization process. The negative side to this is that since error samples are measured only during the sync symbols, which occur once every 257 DMT symbols, convergence can be extremely slow. As a result unless the LMS step size is set very high it is not possible to converge within an acceptable period of time (less than 10 seconds). Setting a high LMS step size is only possible if the quantization error of the error samples is very low.

Simulations were run to investigate the impact of the number of quantization bits per error sample dimension on the data-rate achieved at convergence of the LMS algorithm. The scenario consisted of 32 300m VDSL2 lines running profile 17a from Annex A. The background noise was set to -140 dBm/Hz, the coding gain was assumed to be 5 dB, and the beta crosstalk channel model was used[7].

Figure 8 shows the change in the achievable data-rate as the LMS algorithm converges. As can be seen converging to a high data-rate within 10 seconds requires at least 12 bits of feedback per error sample dimension. Unfortunately however only 5 bits are available with the conventional SOC, even if error subsampling is used.

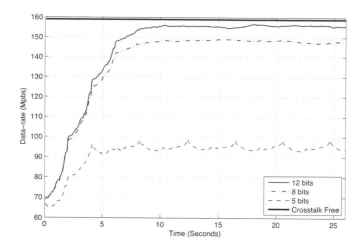

Fig. 8. Impact of number of quantization bits on data-rate at convergence

4.4 Solution: Error Scaling

The problem of high quantization error and slow training convergence can be solved by scaling the error samples prior to quantization[8].   Denote the maximum magnitude of the error samples across frequency for a particular sync symbol t and line n as

$$e_n^{max}(t) = \max_k \left| e_k^n(t) \right| . \tag{12}$$

Figure 9 shows the decay of the maximum error magnitude $e_n^{max}(t)$ as the LMS algorithm converges in a typical scenario.

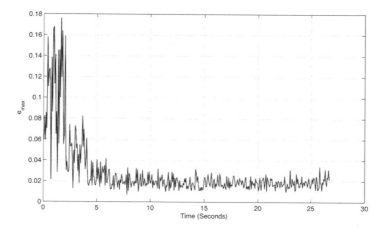

Fig. 9. The maximum error magnitude decays rapidly as LMS converges

As can be seen the error magnitude decays rapidly. This means that the quantization range can be reduced as the algorithm converges, ensuring a low quantization error even when very few feedback bits are used. In practice this is implemented with error scaling as follows. First the VTU-R determines the maximum error magnitude for the current sync symbol $e_n^{max}(t)$. The scaling factor is then set as

$$s_n(t) = 2^{\left\lceil \log_2 (e_n^{max}(t)) \right\rceil}, \tag{13}$$

where $\lceil . \rceil$ denotes the ceiling operation. The error samples on every tone are then normalized by the scaling factor $s_n(t)$.

$$\overline{e}_k^n(t) = e_k^n(t)/s_n(t) . \tag{14}$$

These scaled error samples are then quantized using the available number of bits (5 in our example) using a quantization range [-1,1]. Both the error scaling factor and the scaled, quantized error samples are then fed back to the VCE.

Using the scaling factor ensures that the scaled error samples are always in the range [-1,1] so that clipping of the error sample during quantization will never occur. In addition to this as the LMS algorithm converges the maximum error magnitude decays rapidly leading to a small value for the error scaling factor $s_n(t)$. This reduces the quantization range considerably, leading to a much lower quantization error. For example, if 5 bits are used per error sample dimension, then the maximum quantization error without error scaling is

$$e_{quant} \le 2^{-5} . \tag{15}$$

This is large enough to reduce the convergence speed to an unacceptable level. With error scaling the error magnitude will rapidly fall to a level below 2^{-7}. This will result in an error scaling factor of 2^{-7}. The 5 available quantization bits will now span a much smaller quantization range of $-2^{-7}...2^{-7}$. This reduces the quantization error to a maximum of

$$e_{quant} \le 2^{-12} . \tag{16}$$

Such a low quantization error leads to rapid convergence of the LMS algorithm, so the modem initialization time can be kept short without sacrificing data-rate. Since a common scaling factor is used for all sub-carriers it adds very little to the feedback overhead. For example, if 5 bits per error sample dimension are used, then feeding back the error samples for a single sync symbol with 360 tones requires 3600 bits. Feeding back the error scaling factor adds only 8 bits to the overall feedback requirement, or 3608 bits in total. This is an increase of only 0.2% and is negligible.

Note that the scaling factor is selected to be a power of 2 so error scaling can be implemented with a simple binary shift operation. This keeps complexity very low which is particularly important for the VTU-R (CPE).

Simulations were run to evaluate the performance of error scaling and its impact on the convergence of the LMS algorithm. The scenario consisted of 32 300m VDSL2 lines running profile 17a from Annex A. The background noise was set to -140 dBm/Hz, the coding gain was assumed to be 5 dB, and the beta crosstalk channel model was used. Performance with and without error scaling was evaluated. In both cases 5 bits of feedback per error sample dimension was used.

Figure 10 shows the change in the achievable data-rate as the LMS algorithm converges. As can be seen when error scaling is not used the high quantization error leads to a large loss in data-rate. With error scaling the data-rate is improved significantly, allowing high performance to be achieved with a convergence time of only 10 seconds.

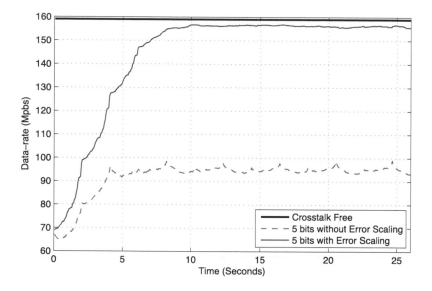

Fig. 10. Error scaling significantly improves the accuracy of crosstalk precoder training

5 Conclusions

Vectoring is an essential technology to enable next generation VDSL2 access networks to achieve their full potential and can drastically improve service data-rates, reach and reliability. Significant work is now being done by industry on vectoring, with much of this work focused on the development of the ITU G.vector standard. This paper introduced some of the challenges faced in creating this standard, and showed how creative solutions, which take advantage of the unique characteristics of the DSL environment, have helped develop vectoring from theory into a practical technology that will soon be ready for commercial deployment. The first issue of the G.vector standard is planned for completion in the October ITU meeting this year. It is believe that widespread adoption of vectoring technology in DSL networks will follow.

References

1. Ginis, G., Cioffi, J.: Vectored Transmission for Digital Subscriber Line Systems. IEEE J. Select. Areas Commun. 20(5), 1085–1104 (2002)
2. Cendrillon, R., Ginis, G., Van den Bogaert, E., Moonen, M.: A Near-optimal Linear Crosstalk Precoder for VDSL. IEEE Trans. on Communications 55(5), 860–863 (2007)
3. Cendrillon, R., Ginis, G., Van den Bogaert, E., Moonen, M.: A Near-optimal Linear Crosstalk Canceler for VDSL. IEEE Trans. on Signal Processing 54(8), 3136–3146 (2006)
4. Cendrillon, R., Yu, W., Moonen, M., Verlinden, J., Bostoen, T.: Optimal Multi-user Spectrum Balancing for Digital Subscriber Lines. IEEE Trans. on Communications 54(5), 922–933 (2006)
5. ITU-T Draft Standard G.vector: Self-FEXT Cancellation (Vectoring) for use with VDSL2 Transceivers, Temporary Document 09XC-R18R3 (2009)
6. Huawei Technologies Co., Ltd., Reducing the Back Channel Overhead of Crosstalk Channel Identification, ITU-T SG15/Q4 contribution 08CC-59 (September 2008)
7. ATIS pre-published Technical Report ATIS-PP-0600024, Multiple-Input Multiple-Output Crosstalk Channel Model (2009)
8. Huawei Technologies Co., Ltd., Speeding up the Convergence of Crosstalk Precoder Initialization with Error Scaling, ITU-T SG15/Q4 contribution 09AG-047 (February 2009)

Analysis and Suppression of MAI in WiMAX Uplink Communication System with Multiple CFOs

Xiupei Zhang and Heung-Gyoon Ryu

Department of Electronic Engineering, Chungbuk National University,
Cheongju, Chungbuk, Korea 361-763
ZhangXP.CN@gmail.com, ecomm@cbu.ac.kr

Abstract. Nowadays, OFDMA (Orthogonal Frequency Division Multiple Access) technique has been used in WiMAX communication system to achieve very high data rate as well as multi-user service. However, similar with other OFDM-based systems, OFDMA system is very sensitive to frequency synchronization errors, especially in the uplink communications where different users always have different CFOs (Carrier Frequency Offset). When multiple CFOs exist, the orthogonality which separates different subcarriers will be lost, and ICI (Inter Carrier Interference) as well as MAI (Multi-Access Interference) will be generated to disturb the received signals. Then, the system performance will be highly degraded. To overcome this problem, it is of great importance to do research on the suppression to the interferences caused by multiple CFOs. In this paper, we first analyze the interferences, including ICI and MAI, caused by multiple CFOs in the uplink communications of OFDMA system. Next, the suppression method based on block type pilots is proposed to overcome the interferences simultaneously. Compared with other interference suppression methods, the proposed method could directly get the interference components from inverse matrix, thus it doesn't need to do the CFO estimation. From the simulation results, it can be seen that the multiple CFOs will make serious degradation to the system performance. But through the proposed suppression algorithm, the system performance can be significantly improved.

Keywords: WiMAX; OFDMA; CFO; MAI; ICI; Interference Suppression.

1 Introduction

OFDM (Orthogonal Frequency division multiplexing) has been widely used in digital communication system to achieve very high data rate. In OFDM system, wide transmission bandwidth is divided into several narrow bands and data are paralleled transmitted on these narrow bands by exploiting orthogonal subcarriers. Thus, decreasing the effect of ISI (Inter Symbol Interference), good spectrum efficiency, anti frequency selective fading and many other advantages can be achieved. Combined with frequency division multiple access technique, OFDMA system is proposed to support

X. Jun Hei and L. Cheung (Eds.): AccessNets 2009, LNICST 37, pp. 204–218, 2010.
© Institute for Computer Sciences, Social-Informatics and Telecommunications Engineering 2010

multi-user service. In OFDMA system, available subcarriers are divided into several groups and these groups are assigned to different users to transmit data simultaneously. The OFDMA system inherits the advantages of OFDM and has been widely used in wireless communication system. For example, IEEE 802.16 standardization group has considered OFDMA as the broadband wireless access standard for WAN (Wide Area Network) and UMTS (Universal Mobile Telecommunications System), the European standard for the 3G cellular mobile communications, also exploits OF-DMA technique [1].

However, similar with other OFDM based systems, OFDMA system is sensitive to CFO (Carrier Frequency Offset), which is unavoidable in wireless communication system. In OFDMA uplink communications, the received signals are the combination of multiple signals coming from different users, each of which experiences a different CFO mainly due to oscillator instability and Doppler shift [2]. The multiple CFOs destroy the orthogonality among subcarriers, thus, not only ICI (Inter Carrier Interference) but also MAI (Multi-Access Interference) will be generated to disturb the received signal. Then the system performance will be seriously degraded.

Synchronization between users is difficult in OFDMA uplink communications. Conventional CFO correction methods, such as [3], which are used in the downlink communications, are designed for signal user system, and they are unable to correct the multiple CFOs in the uplink communications because one user's CFO correction will aggravate the MAI from other users. To overcome this problem, many previous works has been proposed to estimate [2, 4, 5, and 6] or suppress the multiple CFOs effects [7-13]. These synchronization methods can be classified as two groups. The first is called feedback method, which exploits a downlink control channel to transmit the estimated CFO information obtained by the base station to each user, and each user can then correct the CFO by adjusting the carrier frequency. However, this method will increase the transmission overhead and possibly cause outdated estimation in time-varying scenario. An alternative is to achieve synchronization via signal processing at the uplink receiver without the help of a control channel [7], such as [7-13]. In [8-10], SIC (Successive Interference Cancellation) as well as PIC (Parallel Interference Cancellation) methods were raised. In these methods, the received signals are classified as reliable group and unreliable group. The reliable signals are directly detected and cancelled from the received signal while the unreliable signals are detected after cancellation of the MAI effects due to reliable signals. Another kind of interference suppression methods which exploit inverse matrix, were discussed in [11-13]. However, the methods in [8-12] need perfect multiple CFOs estimation, which is impossible in practical system, and the residual CFO will also degrade system performance.

In this paper, firstly, we analyze the interferences caused by multiple CFOs in OF-DMA uplink communications. From the analysis, we can see that the received signals are seriously disturbed by multiple CFOs. Also, we express the received signal in matrix form. Then, a joint suppression method based on block type pilots is proposed.

Here we suppose different users start to communicate with the base station at different time slots. Different with other interference suppression methods, the proposed method could directly get the interference components by exploiting block type pilot, thus it don't need to do the multiple CFOs estimation. After that, the interference matrix can be reconstructed and the influence of multiple CFOs can be easily cancelled by using the inverse matrix method. Then, making suppression to the interferences caused by multiple CFOs is feasible.

This paper is organized as follows. In Section 2, we describe the system model of OFDMA uplink communications. Next, in Section 3, we analyze the effect ofmultiple CFOs, and according to the analysis, the interference suppression method is stated. Finally, the suppression method is simulated and the results are shown in Section 4. Comparing the simulation results, we can draw the following conclusion, that multiple CFOs will make great degradation to the system performance, but through the propose algorithm, the system performance can be significantly improved.

2 OFDMA Uplink System Model

Fig.1 shows the block diagram of OFDMA uplink communications.

In OFDMA uplink communications, all subcarriers are divided into several groups. Instead of being modulated on all available subcarriers, data symbols from one user are transmitted on one group of subcarriers.

Now we consider an OFDMA uplink system in which the number of total available subcarriers is N and the number of users communicating with the base station is K. According to the data transmission demand, different groups with different numbers of subcarriers are assigned to each user. Without loss of generality, we suppose each user only occupies one subcarrier group, the subcarrier group assigned to the kth user is denoted as S^k, the subcarrier number of S^k is M_k and $\mathbf{D}_k=[d^k_0, d^k_1, d^k_2..., d^k_{Mk-1}]^T$ is the transmitted data of the kth user. Then, $\bigcup_{k=1}^{K-1} S^k = \{0,1,2,...,N-1\}$ and $S^i \bigcap S^j = \phi$, for $i \neq j$.

After subcarrier mapping, the modulation symbol vector of kth user can be shown as

$$\mathbf{X^k} = \mathbf{\Theta^k} \cdot \mathbf{D_k} = [X^k_0, X^k_1, ..., X^k_{N-1}]^T, \qquad (1)$$

where $\mathbf{\Theta^k}$ is the subcarrier mapping matrix with the size of $N \times M_k$. And the components in $\mathbf{\Theta^k}$ satisfy the following demand, if the jth data in $\mathbf{D}_k$ transmitted on the ith subcarrier, $\Theta^k_{ij}=1$, otherwise $\Theta^k_{ij}=0$. Then after N-IFFT, the transmitted signal can be shown as

$$s^k(n) = \sum_{l=0}^{N-1} X^k_l \cdot e^{j2\pi nl/N} = \sum_{l=0}^{N-1} X^k_l \cdot p_{n,l} . \qquad (2)$$

A cyclic prefix is inserted in front of the transmitted signal before being sent into the communication channel, to overcome the influence of ISI.

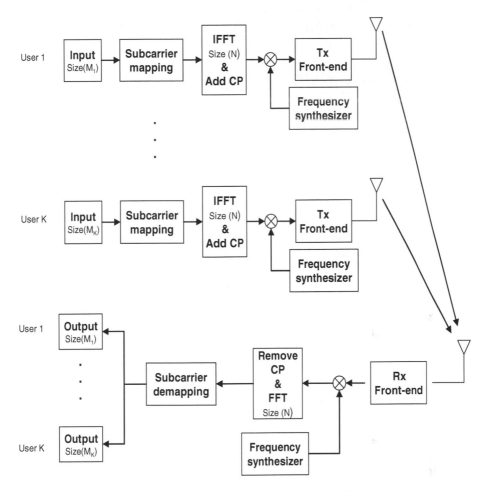

Fig. 1. This figure shows the OFDMA uplink system block diagram. The number of total available subcarriers is N and the number of users communicating with the base station is K.

Here we consider each user experiences a frequency selective channel with the impulse response $h^k(n)$, then the received signals at the base station can be written as

$$r(n) = \sum_{k=0}^{K-1} \left[s^k(n) \otimes h^k(n) + v^k(n) \right], \tag{3}$$

where $v^k(n)$ is the AWGN noise on the kth user.

All users are assumed to be synchronized in the time domain. Then after N-FFT, the output of the ith subcarrier can be written as

$$Y_i = \frac{1}{N} \sum_{n=0}^{N-1} r(n) \cdot e^{-j2\pi n i / N}. \tag{4}$$

After frequency domain equalizer and subcarrier demapping, the transmitted data of each user can be recovered.

3 Multiple CFO in OFDMA Uplink and Interference Cancellation

In this section, we will analyze ICI as well as MAI generated from the multiple CFOs in OFDMA uplink communications. Next, according to the analysis results, we describe the proposed interferences suppression algorithm.

3.1 Multiple CFO in the OFDMA Uplink

To analyze the ICI and MAI in OFDMA uplink communications, we introduce multiple CFOs into the transmitted signals. We assume the CFO of the kth user is Δf_k, then, at the receiver, after removing cyclic prefix, the received signal can be written as

$$r(n) = \sum_{k=0}^{K-1} \{ [s^k(n) \otimes h^k(n)] \cdot e^{j2\pi\Delta f_k n} + v^k(n) \} . \tag{5}$$

After N-FFT, the obtained signal on the ith subcarrier can be written as

$$
\begin{aligned}
Y_i &= \frac{1}{N} \sum_{n=0}^{N-1} r(n) \cdot e^{-j2\pi n i / N} \\
&= \frac{1}{N} \sum_{n=0}^{N-1} \sum_{k=0}^{K-1} \{ [s^k(n) \otimes h^k(n)] e^{j2\pi\Delta f_k n} \} e^{-j2\pi n i / N} + V_i \\
&= \frac{1}{N} \sum_{n=0}^{N-1} \sum_{k=0}^{K-1} \sum_{l=0}^{N-1} X_l^k H_l^k \cdot e^{j2\pi n l / N} e^{j2\pi\Delta f_k n} e^{-j2\pi n i / N} + V_i , \\
&= \frac{1}{N} \sum_{n=0}^{N-1} \sum_{k=0}^{K-1} X_i^k H_i^k \cdot e^{j2\pi\Delta f_k n} \\
&\quad + \frac{1}{N} \sum_{n=0}^{N-1} \sum_{k=0}^{K-1} \sum_{\substack{l=0, \\ l \neq i}}^{N-1} X_l^k H_l^k \cdot e^{j2\pi n(l-i)/N} \cdot e^{j2\pi\Delta f_k n} + V_i
\end{aligned} \tag{6}
$$

where H_l^k is the frequency domain channel response and V_i is the frequency domain AWGN noise.

According to the subcarrier mapping method, one subcarrier can only be assigned to one user. Thus, among the K individual X_i^k, only one X_i^k is the the transmitted data of the user who exploit the ith subcarrier, and the other X_i^k are zero. We suppose this X_i^k belongs to the k'th user. Then, Y_i can be written as

$$Y_i = \frac{1}{N}\sum_{n=0}^{N-1}\sum_{k=0}^{K-1} X_i^k H_i^k \cdot e^{j2\pi\Delta f_k n}$$

$$+\frac{1}{N}\sum_{n=0}^{N-1}\sum_{k=0}^{K-1}\sum_{\substack{l=0,\\l\neq i}}^{N-1} X_l^k H_l^k \cdot e^{j2\pi n(l-i)/N} \cdot e^{j2\pi\Delta f_k n} + V_i$$

$$=\frac{1}{N}\sum_{n=0}^{N-1} X_i^{k'} H_i^{k'} e^{\frac{j2\pi n\varepsilon_{k'}}{N}} +\frac{1}{N}\sum_{n=0}^{N-1}\sum_{\substack{l=0\\l\neq i}}^{N-1} X_l^{k'} H_l^{k'} e^{\frac{j2\pi n[(l-i)+\varepsilon_{k'}]}{N}}$$

$$+\frac{1}{N}\sum_{n=0}^{N-1}\sum_{\substack{k=0,\,l=0,\\k\neq k'\,l\neq i}}^{K-1\ N-1} X_l^k H_l^k e^{\frac{j2\pi n[(l-i)+\varepsilon_k]}{N}} + V_i$$

$$=\underbrace{X_i^{k'} H_i^{k'} \cdot I_0^{k'}}_{I} +\underbrace{\sum_{\substack{l=0,\\l\neq i}}^{N-1} X_l^{k'} H_l^{k'} \cdot I_{l-i}^{k'}}_{II}$$

$$+\underbrace{\sum_{\substack{k=0,\,l=0,\\k\neq k'\,l\neq i}}^{K-1\ N-1} X_l^k H_l^k \cdot I_{l-i}^k}_{III} +\underbrace{V_i}_{IV} \tag{7}$$

where ε_k is the normalized CFO and

$$I_L^k = \frac{1}{N}\sum_{n=0}^{N-1} e^{j2\pi n[L+\varepsilon_{k'}]/N} \tag{8}$$

is the interference coefficient.

From (7), we can see that the received signal is comprised of 4 components. Component *I* corresponds to the original data of the *kth* user transmitted on the *ith* subcarrier, component *II* corresponds to ICI caused by the other data of the *kth* user transmitted on the other subcarrier, component *III* corresponds to the MAI caused by the data of the other users, and component *IV* corresponds to the AWGN noise.

3.2 Interference Cancellation Algorithm

From the above analysis, we can see that the multiple CFOs not only generate ICI but also MAI. Thus, the received signal will be seriously disturbed and the system performance will be seriously degraded. In order to improve system performance, we have to make suppression to these interferences. In this part, we propose a suppression method which is based on block type pilots.

As described above, when multiple CFOs exist in OFDMA uplink communications, the received signal at the base station can be expressed as formula (7). Then, according to formula (7), we express the received frequency domain signal vector in matrix form as follows

$$\mathbf{Y} = \mathbf{I} \cdot \mathbf{H} \cdot \mathbf{X} + \mathbf{V} , \tag{9}$$

where $\mathbf{X} = \sum_{k=1}^{K} \mathbf{X}^k = [D_0, D_1, ..., D_{N-1}]^T$ is the modulation symbol vector transmitted on the communication band, $D_i = \sum_{k=1}^{K} d_i^k$ denotes the data transmitted on the *ith* subcarrier, $\mathbf{H} = diag(H_0^{(k)}, H_1^{(k)}, ... H_{N-1}^{(k)})$ is the frequency domain channel response, $\mathbf{V}$ is the AWGN noise vector and

$$\mathbf{I} = \begin{bmatrix} I_0^{(k)} & I_1^{(k)} & I_2^{(k)} & \cdots & I_{N-1}^{(k)} \\ I_{-1}^{(k)} & I_0^{(k)} & I_1^{(k)} & \cdots & I_{N-2}^{(k)} \\ I_{-2}^{(k)} & I_{-1}^{(k)} & I_0^{(k)} & \cdots & I_{N-3}^{(k)} \\ \cdots & \cdots & \cdots & \cdots & \cdots \\ I_1^{(k)} & I_2^{(k)} & I_3^{(k)} & \cdots & I_0^{(k)} \end{bmatrix} \tag{10}$$

is the interference matrix. The superscript of $I_L^{(k)}$ is related with the user's index. For example, if the *ith* subcarrier is assigned to the *k'th* user to transmit data, the superscripts of the components in the *ith* column of the interference matrix should be set as *k'*.

From (8), we can see that

$$I_{-L}^k = \frac{1}{N} \sum_{n=0}^{N-1} e^{j2\pi n[-L+\varepsilon_{k'}]/N}$$

$$= \frac{1}{N} \sum_{n=0}^{N-1} e^{j2\pi n[N-L+\varepsilon_{k'}]/N} . \tag{11}$$

$$= I_{N-L}^k$$

Thus the interference can be rewritten as

$$\mathbf{I} = \begin{bmatrix} I_0^{(k)} & I_1^{k()} & I_2^{(k)} & \cdots & I_{N-1}^{(k)} \\ I_{N-1}^{(k)} & I_0^{(k)} & I_1^{(k)} & \cdots & I_{N-2}^{(k)} \\ I_{N-2}^{(k)} & I_{N-1}^{(k)} & I_0^{(k)} & \cdots & I_{N-3}^{(k)} \\ \cdots & \cdots & \cdots & \cdots & \cdots \\ I_1^{(k)} & I_2^{(k)} & I_3^{(k)} & \cdots & I_0^{(k)} \end{bmatrix} . \tag{12}$$

From the above formula, we can see that the interference matrix is comprised of $K \times N$ different components. However, the rank of matrix in formula (9) is N, thus it is impossible to get these $K \times N$ components directly.

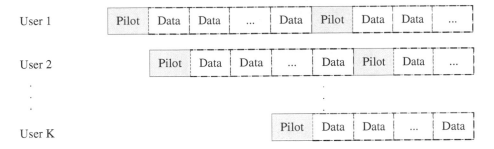

Fig. 2. In OFDMA uplink communications, different users always start to communicate with the base station at different time slots. Thus we suppose all users start to communicate with the base station at different time slots.

In OFDMA uplink communications, different users always start to communicate with the base station at different time slots. Thus we suppose all users start to communicate with the base station at different time slots, as shown in Fig 2. Then, in one OFDM symbol period, only one pilot block which belongs to one user will arrive at the base station. Therefore, estimating the components in the interference matrix is feasible. We also assume that the CFO of each user is quasi static during the pilot block and the following data blocks.

Firstly, making initialization by setting $\mathbf{X}=0$ and $I_L^{(k)} = 0$. To simplify the statement, we suppose all users start to communicate with the base station abide by the user's index order. Thus the first OFDM symbol arrived at the base station is the pilot block belonging to the user with index 0. Then we can set $\mathbf{X}=\mathbf{X^0}$. Because the other users haven't started to communicate with the base station, we can obtain $I_L^{(k)} = 0, (k \neq 0)$. This is the same condition with single user.

Firstly, we set all components in the interference matrix to be 0. Then rewrite formula (9) as

$$\mathbf{Y}=\mathbf{I}\cdot\mathbf{X}+\mathbf{V}$$
$$=\tilde{\mathbf{X}}\cdot\tilde{\mathbf{I}}+\mathbf{V}$$
$$=\tilde{\mathbf{X}}^0 \cdot \mathbf{I}^0 +\mathbf{V}$$
$$=\begin{bmatrix} X_0^0 \cdot H_0^0 & X_1^0 \cdot H_1^0 & \dots & X_{N-1}^0 \cdot H_{N-1}^0 \\ X_1^0 \cdot H_1^0 & X_2^0 \cdot H_2^0 & \dots & X_0^0 \cdot H_0^0 \\ \dots & \dots & \dots & \dots \\ X_{N-1}^0 \cdot H_{N-1}^0 & X_0^0 \cdot H_0^0 & \dots & X_{N-2}^0 \cdot H_{N-2}^0 \end{bmatrix} \cdot \begin{bmatrix} I_0^0 \\ I_1^0 \\ \dots \\ I_{N-1}^0 \end{bmatrix} + \mathbf{V} \qquad (13)$$

where $\mathbf{I^0}=[I^0{}_0,\ I^0{}_1,\ \dots,\ I^0{}_{N-1}]^{\mathrm{T}}$ is the interference vector which is caused by the CFO from the first user in the interference matrix. We assume we already know the channel response by channel estimation. Since this OFDM symbol is the pilot block, the transmitted data on each subcarrier are already know to the receiver. Thus $\tilde{\mathbf{X}}^0$ and its inverse matrix $\widetilde{\mathbf{X}}^{0^{-1}}$ can be easily obtained. Then the interference vector $\mathbf{I}^0$ can be estimated by the inverse matrix $\widetilde{\mathbf{X}}^{0^{-1}}$ as follows

$$\mathbf{I}^0 = \widetilde{\mathbf{X}}^{0^{-1}} \cdot \mathbf{Y}.$$ (14)

After that, we update the interference matrix with the interference vector $\mathbf{I}^0$. In the following OFDM symbols, if the other users don't start to communicate with the base station, the interferences in the following received data blocks can be suppressed by

$$\begin{aligned} Y_{suppressed} &= \mathbf{H}^{-1} \cdot \mathbf{I}^{-1} \cdot \mathbf{Y} \\ &= \mathbf{X} + \mathbf{H}^{-1} \cdot \mathbf{I}^{-1} \cdot \mathbf{V} \end{aligned}$$ (15)

We assume a new user start to communicate with the base station after several OFDM symbols.

To get the interference vector related with this new user's CFO, we can perform as follows.

a) Extract the received symbol vector, which belong to those users whose interference vectors already have been estimated. We ignore the MAI from the new arrived user and suppress the interference (ICI and MAI from those users) by using the formula (15).

b) The suppressed signal is detected and the transmitted data, which belong to those users whose interference vectors have already been estimated, can be obtained.

c) Reconstruct the detected symbol vector $\mathbf{X}^{detect}$, and then calculate the interferences from the detected users by using

$$\boldsymbol{\Phi} = \mathbf{I} \cdot \mathbf{H} \cdot \mathbf{X}^{det\,ect}.$$ (16)

d) Cancel the interferences caused by the detected users by

$$\mathbf{Y}^{New} = \mathbf{Y} - \boldsymbol{\Phi}.$$ (17)

e) Then, the interference vector of the new arrived user can be estimated by performing the same process to estimate the interference vector of the first user.

f) To obtain more accurate estimation results, we can calculate the MAI caused by the new arrived user and remove it from the received signal vector. Then perform the above process a)~f) with several iteration loops.

After obtain the new arrived user's interference vector, we can update the interference matrix with this interference vector and suppress the interference as (15).

When another user starts to communicate with the base station, the interference vector estimation process is same as described above.

When some user stops to communicate with the base station, update the interference matrix by setting the corresponding interference components to be 0.

The algorithm to estimate the interference matrix is list as follows.

- When first user start to communicate with the base station, estimate the interference vector of the first by using formula (13). Then make suppression to the received signal and update the interference matrix with $\mathbf{I}^0$.

- When a new user start to communicate with the base station, estimate the interference vector as a)~f). Then make suppression to the received signal and update the interference matrix with the newly estimated interference vector.
- When some user stops to communicate with the base station, update the interference by the corresponding interference components to be 0.

4 Simulation Results and Discussion

Table 1 shows the simulation parameters. We assume that the normalized frequency offset of each user is a random value uniformly distributed in [-0.1, 0.1], and the multiple CFOs are quasi static during the pilot block and the following 5 data blocks.

Table 1. Simulation Parameters

OFDMA Uplink System	
Modulation scheme	16 QAM
Number of subcarriers/symbol (N)	128
Number of users (K)	2
Subcarrier mapping method	Localized method
CP length	32
Frame size	6
Channel model	AWGN & 802.16 SUI channel model [14]

The pilot sequence used in these simulations is CAZAC (constant amplitude zero autocorrelation) sequence, which is one type of polyphase codes and has many applications in channel estimation because of its good periodic correlation property [15]. Let L to be any positive integer larger than one and k be any number which is relatively to L. Then an example of CAZAC sequence is given as

$$\begin{cases} c_k(n) = e^{j\frac{2\pi k}{L}(n+n\frac{n+1}{2})}, n = 0,1,...,L-1, if\ L\ is\ odd \\ c_k(n) = e^{j\frac{2\pi k}{L}(n+\frac{n^2}{2})}, n = 0,1,...,L-1, if\ L\ is\ even \end{cases}. \quad (18)$$

Then we can get the following simulation results.

Fig. 3 shows the interference components caused by single subcarrier. From this figure, we can see that the interference components caused by single subcarrier on other subcarriers decreases as the distance between the two subcarriers increase. Thus the interference mainly attacks the neighbor subcarriers and localized mapping method is much more robust to MAI than interleaved method.

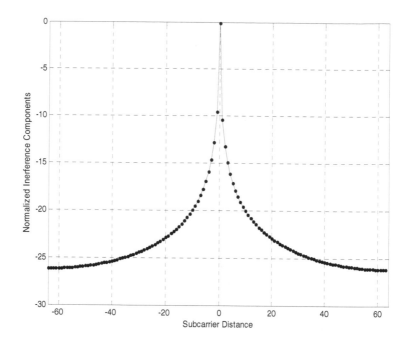

Fig. 3. Interference components caused by single subcarrier

First, let's check the BER performance of proposed method. Fig. 4 shows the BER performance in AWGN channel and Fig. 5 shows the l BER performance in frequency selective fading channel. The channel model used here is the 802.16 SUI-5A model, which is modeled as a tapped-delay ling with 3 non-uniform delay traps. The channel gain of each tap is [0, -5, -10]dB and the delay of each tap is [0, 4, 10]μs respectively. From the simulation results, we can see that with the increase of iteration, the performance of proposed method becomes better.

Then we can compare the BER performance with the method proposed in reference [11] for both the proposed method and the referenced method exploit the inverse matrix. Since the method proposed in reference [11] needs perfect multiple CFOs estimation, we simulate this method in two conditions. One condition is that the multiple CFOs are perfectly estimated and the other condition is that there is a MSE of multiple CFOs estimation about 10^{-4} [16]. Fig. 6 shows the BER performance of the two suppression methods in AWGN channel and Fig. 7 shows the BER performance in frequency selective fading channel. From the simulation results, we can see that when multiple CFOs are perfectly estimated, the referenced method can achieve the best performance. However, perfect estimation is impossible in practical system. When estimation error exists, the performance of referenced method will be highly degraded. Comparing these results, we can see that the proposed method with 5 iterations can achieve better performance than the referenced method with imperfect multiple CFOs estimation.

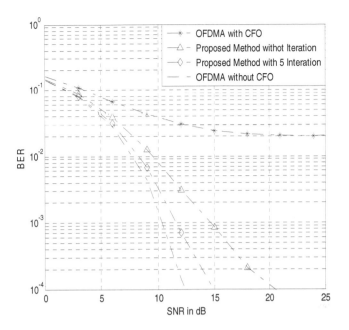

Fig. 4. BER performance of proposed method in AWGN channel

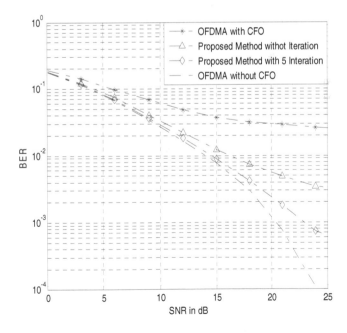

Fig. 5. BER performance of proposed method in frequency selective fading channel

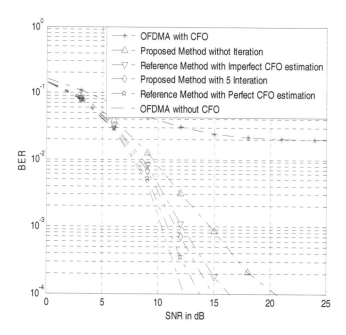

Fig. 6. Comparison of BER performance in AWGN channel

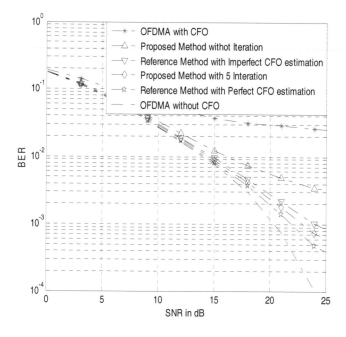

Fig. 7. Comparison of BER performance in frequency selective fading channel

5 Conclusion

In this paper, we have analyzed the interferences generated from multiple CFOs in OFDMA uplink communication system. According to the analysis results, we can see that the received signal will be seriously disturbed and the system performance will be seriously degraded. Also, we can see that the interference matrix is comprised of $K \times N$ different components. However, the rank of the received signal function is N, so it is impossible to get these $K \times N$ components directly. Thus we suppose all users start to communicate with the base station at different time and propose a novel suppression method which is based on block type pilots. Through the received pilot block, we can estimate all components in the interference matrix. Then by reconstructing the interference matrix from the estimation result, we can make suppression to the interferences and finally improve system performance. Simulation results show that the joint suppression algorithm works well in both AWGN and frequency selective fading channel. Compared with other algorithm, the proposed algorithm can achieve better performance when multiple CFOs estimation is imperfect. More accurate algorithm with less complexity should be studied in the future.

Reference

1. IEEE Standard for Local and metropolitan area networks, Part16: Air Interface for Fixed and Mobile Broadband Wireless Access Systems Amendment2: Physical and Medium Access Control Layers for Combined Fixed and Mobile Operation in Licensed Bands. IEEE Std. 802.16e (2005)
2. Morelli, M.: Timing and frequency synchronization for the uplink of an OFDMA system. IEEE Transactions on Communications 52(2), 296–306 (2004)
3. van de Beek, J.J., Borjesson, P.O., Boucheret, M.L., Landstrom, D., Arenas, J.M., Odling, P., Ostberg, C., Wahlqvist, M., Wilson, S.K.: A time and frequency synchronization scheme for multiuser OFDM. IEEE Journal on Selected Areas in Communications 17(11), 1900–1914 (1999)
4. Yanxin, N., Hlaing, M.: Line Search Based Iterative Joint Estimation of Channels and Frequency Offsets for Uplink OFDMA Systems. In: IEEE GLOBECOM 2006, November 2006, pp. 1–5 (2006)
5. Movahedian, M., Ma, Y., Tafazolli, R.: An MUI resilient approach for blind CFO estimation in OFDMA uplink. In: IEEE 19th International Symposium on PIMRC 2008, September 2008, pp. 1–5 (2008)
6. Zhongren, C., Tureli, U., Yu-Dong, Y.: Deterministic multiuser carrier-frequency offset estimation for interleaved OFDMA uplink. IEEE Transactions on Communications 52(9), 1585–1594 (2004)
7. Dai, X.: Carrier frequency offset estimation and correction for OFDMA uplink. IET Communications 1(2), 273–281 (2007)
8. Fantacci, R., Marabissi, D., Papini, S.: Multiuser interference cancellation receivers for OFDMA uplink communications with carrier frequency offset. In: IEEE GLOBECOM 2004, November 2004, vol. 5, pp. 2808–2812 (2004)
9. Manohar, S., Sreedhar, D., Tikiya, V., Chockalingam, A.: Cancellation of Multiuser Interference Due to Carrier Frequency Offsets in Uplink OFDMA. IEEE Transactions on Wireless Communications 6(7), 2560–2571 (2007)

10. Nguyen, H.C., De Carvalho, E., Prasad, R.: Multi-User Interference Cancellation Scheme(s) for Muliple Carrier Frequency Offset Compensation in Uplink OFDMA. In: 2006 IEEE 17th International Symposium on PIMRC 2006, Sept. 2006, pp. 1–5 (2006)
11. Zhongren Cao, U.: Frequency synchronization for generalized OFDMA uplink. In: IEEE GLOBECOM 2004, November 29– December 3, vol. 2, pp. 1071–1075 (2004)
12. Yucek, T., Arslan, H.: Carrier Frequency Offset Compensation with Successive Cancellation in Uplink OFDMA Systems. IEEE Transactions on Wireless Communications 6(10), 3546–3551 (2007)
13. Sun, P., Zhang, L.: A Novel Pilot Aided Joint Carrier Frequency Offset Estimation and Compensation for OFDMA Uplink Systems. In: IEEE VTC Spring 2008, May 2008, pp. 963–967 (2008)
14. Erceg, V., Hari, K.V.S., Smith, M.S., Baum, D.S., et al.: Channel Models for Fixed Wireless Applications. Contribution IEEE 802.16.3c-01/29r1 (Feburary 2001)
15. Wen, Y., Huang, W., Zhang, Z.: CAZAC sequence and its application in LTE random access. In: IEEE Information Theory Workshop 2006, ITW 2006 Chengdu, October 2006, pp. 544–547 (2006)
16. Yonghong, Z., Leyman, A.R.: Pilot-Based Simplified ML and Fast Algorithm for Frequency Offset Estimation in OFDMA Uplink. IEEE Transactions on Vehicular Technology 57(3), 1723–1732 (2008)
17. Goldsmith, A.: Wireless Communications. Stanford University, Stanford (2004)

Capacity of Two-Way Relay Channel*

Shengli Zhang[1,2], Soung Chang Liew[1], Hui Wang[2], and Xiaohui Lin[2]

[1] Department of Information Engineering, The Chinese University of Hong Kong,
Hong Kong, China
[2] Department of Communication Engineering, Shenzhen University, Shenzhen, Chia
slzhang@ie.cuhk.edu.hk, soung@ie.cuhk.edu.hk, wanghsz@szu.edu.cn

Abstract. This paper investigates the capacity of a wireless two-way relay channel in which two end nodes exchange information via a relay node. The capacity is defined in the information-theoretic sense as the maximum information exchange rate between the two end nodes. We give an upper bound of the capacity by applying the cut-set theorem. We prove that this upper bound can be approached in low SNR region using "separated" multiple access for uplinks from the end nodes to the relay in which the data from the end nodes are individually decoded at the relay; and network-coding broadcast for downlinks from the relay to the end nodes in which the relay mixes the information from end nodes before forwarding. We further prove that the capacity is approachable in high SNR region using physical-layer network coding (PNC) multiple access for uplinks, and network-coding broadcast for downlinks. From our proof and observations, we conjecture that the upper bound may be achieved with PNC in all SNR regions.

1 Introduction

The design and analysis of wireless two-way relay channel (TWRC) are attracting increasing attention. Among all the models for TWRC, of greatest interest is the simplest model of three-node TWRC with additive Gaussian noise. This paper focuses on a three-node TWRC system as depicted in Fig. 1. We investigate its maximum

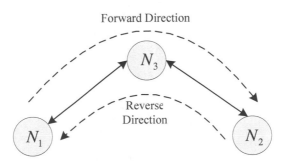

Fig. 1. Three-node two way relay channel

* This work was supported by NSFC projects (Project No. 60902016, 60773203, 60602066) and by a RGC project with Number 414507.

X. Jun Hei and L. Cheung (Eds.): AccessNets 2009, LNICST 37, pp. 219–231, 2010.
© Institute for Computer Sciences, Social-Informatics and Telecommunications Engineering 2010

information exchange rate, defined as the smaller of the forward-direction and re-verse-direction information transfer rates.

The two-way channel without a relay was first studied by Shannon in [1]. The one-way relay channel under various relay strategies has also been widely studied (see [2] and the references therein). As a combination of the two, TWRC is currently drawing much research attention. Ref. [3] gave the achievable rate regions of TWRC when relay protocols borrowed from the one-way relay channel are applied. Under the same relay protocols, [4] derived the rate regions of the TWRC when the nodes are half-duplex and a direct link between the two ends is not available. These strategies that do not exploit network coding cannot achieve the information transfer rate at capacity. Application of network coding is not very fruitful for one-way relay channel. However, applying network coding in TWRC opens up new possibilities.

As shown in [5], broadcasting a network-coded version of the inputs at the relay node holds the promise of significant system-performance improvement. Based on this idea, practical joint network coding and channel coding designs were studied in [6, 7]. Ref. [8] proposed a "physical layer network coding" (PNC) scheme which further improves the transmission efficiency of TWRC. Other transmission schemes inspired by PNC were proposed and analyzed in [9, 10, 11] for TWRC. Besides the works To our knowledge, all the current papers on TWRC focus on the achievable rate regions or bounds under specific transmission strategies. The "ultimate" achievable maximum rate region of TWRC is still an open issue[1].

In contrast to previous work, this paper studies the capacity of TWRC as the maximum information exchange rate under all the possible transmission strategies. In particular, we give an upper bound on symmetric information exchange rate based on the cut-set theorem. We prove that this upper bound is approachable in low SNR region using "separated" multiple-access for uplinks and network-coding broadcast for downlinks. In separated multiple-access [13], the relay node extracts the "complete" information from each of the two nodes; the "separated" information is then combined using network coding [5] for downlink broadcast. In high SNR region, the upper bound is approachable by replacing separated multiple access with PNC multiple access. We conjecture that the upper bound is achievable in all SNR regions with PNC.

The paper is organized as follows. Section 2 introduces the system model studied in this paper. Section 3 gives upper bound of the system capacity. Section 4 and 5 prove the tightness of the upper bound in low SNR and high SNR regions, respectively. Section 6 concludes this paper.

2   System Model

With reference to Fig. 1, nodes N_1 and N_2 exchange information with the help of node N_3. We assume all nodes are half-duplex, i.e., each node can not receive and transmit simultaneously. This is an assumption arising from practical considerations because it is difficult for wireless nodes to remove the strong interference of its own transmitting

---

[1] This paper [22] was independently prepared with the work in [21] almost at the same time. And the proof in this paper is based on LDPC codes rather than lattice codes as in [21].

signal from the received signal. We also assume that there is no direct link between nodes N_1 and N_2. A practical example is satellite communication, wherein two end nodes on the earth can only communicate with each other via a satellite relay.

We assume that the maximum transmission power of node N_i is P_i, and receiver noise is addictive Gaussian with unit variance at all nodes. The path loss is unit constant. By low SNR region, we mean both P_1 and P_2 approach zero, and by high SNR region we mean both P_1 and P_2 approach infinity. We do not consider fading in this paper.

Notations

In this paper, n denotes the Gaussian noise. W_i denote the information packet of node N_i, $i \in \{1,2,3\}$, and $w_i[k] \in \{0,1,\cdots q-1\}, k \in \{0,1\cdots K-1\}$ denote its k-th symbol. The q-ary information symbols are used throughout the paper.

For channel coding, Γ_1, Γ_2 and Γ_3 denote the encoding functions of N_1, N_2, and N_3 respectively. The coded packets of node i is

$$U_i = \Gamma_i(W_i) \quad , \quad i \in \{1,2,3\}$$

Within U_i, $u_i[k] \in \{0,1,\cdots q-1\}, k \in \{0,1\cdots L_i-1\}$ denote its k-th symbol. The coding rate of N_i is therefore K/L_i.

We assume all nodes use the same modulation scheme. X_i denote the modulated packet of N_i, and M denote the modulation mapping:

$$X_i = M(U_i) \quad i \in \{1,2,3\}$$

Within X_i, $x_i[k] \in \{0,1,\cdots q-1\}, \ k \in \{0,1\cdots L_i-1\}$ denote its k-th modulated symbol. Finally, $y_i[k]$ denote the k-th received baseband signal at node N_i.

The capacity of the system is defined as

$$C = \max_{s \in \{all\ possible\ schemes\}} \min\{R_{1,2}(s), R_{2,1}(s)\} \quad (1)$$

where $R_{2,1}(s)$ is the reliable transmission rate from N_2 to N_1 under transmission scheme s, and $R_{1,2}(s)$ is the transmission rate in the opposite direction during the same time under the same transmission scheme.

3 Upper Bound of the TWRC Capacity

The upper bound of the TWRC capacity defined in (1) is given in the following proposition with a cut-set proof.

Proposition 1. For the TWRC model described in the previous section, the capacity defined in (1) is upper-bounded by

$$C \le \frac{1}{2} \frac{\log_2(1 + \min(P_1, P_2)) \cdot \log_2(1 + P_3)}{\log_2(1 + \min(P_1, P_2)) + \log_2(1 + P_3)} \tag{2}$$

where $\frac{1}{2}\log_2(1 + P_i)$ is the Shannon channel capacity for a Gaussian channel with SNR P_i.

Proof: Due to half-duplexity and the lack of a direct link between N_1 and N_2, it is necessary to divide the transmission into two phases, one phase for N_3's reception and the other phase for N_3's transmission. The first phase is referred to as the uplink phase, which includes all the transmissions from node N_1 and/or N_2 to node N_3. Note that there are at most three possible transmission scenarios: N_1 transmits to N_3; N_2 transmits to N_3; or N_1 and N_2 transmit to N_3 simultaneously. In this phase, the maximum reliable transmission rate originating from N_1 is no more than $\frac{1}{2}\log_2(1 + P_1)$. This result is obtained by applying the cut-set theorem where N_1 is regarded as the source set as in [20]. Similarly, the maximum reliable transmission rate from N_2 is no more than $\frac{1}{2}\log_2(1 + P_2)$. Since we are interested in the smaller of the two rates, the transmission rate in the uplink phase is upper bounded by $\frac{1}{2}\log_2(1 + \min(P_1, P_2))$. The second phase is referred as the downlink phase, which includes all the transmissions originating from N_3. According to the Shannon channel capacity, the information transmission rate from N_3 to N_1 and/or N_2 is no more than $\frac{1}{2}\log_2(1 + P_3)$. Besides the transmission rates of the two phases, the final exchange rate also depends on the time allocation. We use t_1 to denote the total time used in the first phase, and $1-t_1$ to denote the total time used in the second phase. Then the final information exchange rate is

$$\min\left\{\frac{t_1}{2}\log_2(1 + \min(P_1, P_2)), \frac{1-t_1}{2}\log_2(1 + P_3)\right\} \tag{3}$$

To maximize the value in (3), obviously we should determine the value of t_1 so that the two arguments in the min function are equal. Doing so yields the upper bound in (2).

4 Approaching the Upper Bound in Low SNR Region

With reference to the proof of *Proposition 1*, we must find a transmission scheme that can approach the upper bounds in both phases to prove the tightness of the upper bound in (2). Let us first consider the downlink phase.

Downlink Phase

Our scheme consists of two steps. The first step is to decide a function $W_3 = f(W_1, W_2)$. After that, we could use a standard capacity approaching channel coding scheme, such as the LDPC code or the Turbo code, to encode the information $W_3 = f(W_1, W_2)$ into U_3 before modulating and broadcasting it to both N_1 and N_2 with a rate approaching $\frac{1}{2}\log_2(1 + P_3)$. Fig.2 shows this transmission strategy from the viewpoint of reception at N_1.

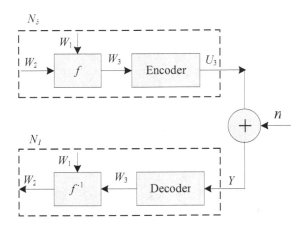

Fig. 2. Reception of downlink transmission at node N_1

Since we use a capacity approaching channel code, N_1 and N_2 can obtain W_3 with an error probability approaching zero as long as the rate of W_3 is no more than $\frac{1}{2}\log_2(1 + P_3)$. The critical issue for the downlink transmission is to find a function f such that the target information W_1 and W_2 can be decoded from W_3 at both end nodes with the same rate of W_3. The requirement can be specified as follows:

Requirement to Satisfy the Downlink Phase Upper Bound

$$H(W_2) = H(W_1) = H(W_3)$$

where W_1 and W_2 are decodable from W_3 at N_2 and N_1 respectively.

With reference to the receiving part in Fig. 2, the interpretation of this requirement is as follows. In order that the transmission rate of W_2 can achieve the upper bound, there should be no information loss during the signal processing to obtain W_2 from W_3. In other words, the entropy of W_2 obtained at N_1 should be equal to that of W_3. To meet this requirement, the following proposition presents the necessary and sufficient conditions that f must satisfy.

Proposition 2: The function f must satisfy both of the following conditions to achieve the upper bound of the downlink phase with the given downlink transmission strategy.

$$H(W_2 \mid W_1, W_3) = 0 \quad H(W_1 \mid W_2, W_3) = 0 \tag{4}$$

$$I(W_3; W_1) = 0 \quad I(W_3; W_2) = 0 \tag{5}$$

Proof: With reference to the receiving part in Fig. 2, we have the following inequalities according to basic Information Theory rules,

$$H(W_2) = H(W_2 \mid W_1) \le H(W_3 \mid W_1) \le H(W_3) \tag{6}$$

The function f must satisfy the inequalities in (6) with equality. The satisfaction of the first inequality $H(W_2 \mid W_1) \le H(W_3 \mid W_1)$ at equality is equivalent to condition (4), as shown below:

$$\begin{aligned}
&H(W_2 \mid W_1) - H(W_3 \mid W_1) \\
&= H(W_2 \mid W_1) - H(W_3 \mid W_1) + H(W_3 \mid W_1, W_2) \\
&= H(W_2 \mid W_1) - I(W_3; W_2 \mid W_1) \\
&= H(W_2 \mid W_1) - H(W_2 \mid W_1) + H(W_2 \mid W_3, W_1) \\
&= H(W_2 \mid W_3, W_1)
\end{aligned} \tag{7}$$

The satisfaction of the second inequality $H(W_3 \mid W_1) \le H(W_3)$ at equality is equivalent condition (5):

$$H(W_3) - H(W_3 \mid W_1) = I(W_3; W_1) \tag{8}$$

When N_2 is considered, we can obtain similar results.

Condition (4) means that f must be reversible when W_1 or W_2 is given. Otherwise, the end nodes cannot recover their counterpart's information from W_3 and their self information. Condition (5) means that the output of f must be probabilistically independent of each of the two input packets alone. Otherwise, the downlink transmission in Fig. 2 is inefficient. Both conditions are needed. For example, the function $f(W_1, W_2) = W_1 + W_2$ satisfies (4) but not (5). On the other hand, $f(W_1, W_2) = W_0$, where W_0 is a random packet, satisfies (5) but not (4). Neither of these functions can achieve the upper bound of the downlink phase. For an f that satisfies both (4) and (5), consider the network coding operation over a finite field, $f(W_1, W_2) = W_1 \oplus W_2$, as in [12].

In summary, in the scheme of Fig. 2 in which the channel coding and signal processing of f are performed separately, the upper bound of the downlink transmission rate can be achieved with a valid f and a capacity-approaching channel code. We refer to such a downlink scheme as network-coding broadcasting. In the remainder of this paper, f denotes a valid function that can achieve the upper bound in the downlink phase.

Uplink Phase

We now consider the uplink phase. We need to find a multiple-access scheme with which we can obtain $f(W_1, W_2)$ with a rate approaching $\frac{1}{2} \log_2(1 + \min(P_1, P_2))$ in the uplink phase. In fact, the separated multiple-access scheme in [13] guarantees that N_3

can obtain both W_1 and W_2 with a rate at least approaching $\frac{1}{2}\log_2(1+\min(P_1,P_2))$ in low SNR region, from which $W_3 = f(W_1,W_2)$ can then be computed.

Proposition 3: In low SNR region, N_3 can obtain both W_1 and W_2 at a rate approaching $\frac{1}{2}\log_2(1+\min(P_1,P_2))$ with the help of the separated multiple-access scheme.

Proof: Without loss of generality, we assume that $L_1 \geq L_2$, which implies $P_1 \leq P_2$. The two end nodes cooperate with each other to transmit at the same time to N_3. Then N_3 decodes W_2 from the received superimposed packet Y_3. Treating N_1's information W_1 as interference, N_3 can reliably decode W_2 with a rate approaching $\frac{1}{2}\log_2(1+P_2/(P_1+1))$. After that, N_3 can decode W_1 after removing the information of W_2 from Y_3. As a result, the reliable transmission rate of W_1 approaches $\frac{1}{2}\log_2(1+P_1)$.

If $P_2/(P_1+1) \geq P_1$, i.e., $P_2 \geq P_1 + P_1^2$, the rate of W_1, which is smaller than that of W_2, approaches $\frac{1}{2}\log_2(1+\min(P_1,P_2))$. On the other hand, if $P_1 \leq P_2 \leq P_1 + P_1^2$, the rate of W_2, which is smaller than that of W_1, can be approximated by

$$\frac{1}{2}\log_2(1+P_2/(P_1+1))$$

$$= \frac{1}{2}\log_2(1+P_1+\frac{P_2-P_1-P_1^2}{P_1+1}) \qquad (9)$$

$$\geq \frac{1}{2}\log_2(1+P_1-\frac{P_1^2}{P_1+1})\xrightarrow{P_1\to 0}\frac{1}{2}\log_2(1+P_1)$$

Hence, *Proposition 3* is proved.

Since we can obtain both W_1 and W_2 at a rate of $\frac{1}{2}\log_2(1+\min(P_1,P_2))$, we can obtain $f(W_1, W_2)$ (e.g., the summation of W_1 and W_2 over a finite field) at the same rate. With the help of separated multiple access and network-coding broadcast, we can approach the upper bound of the TWRC' capacity in (2) in low SNR region. This result indicates that the traditional network coding, which regards network coding as an upper layer operation (i.e., W_1 and W_2 are decoded explicitly at N_3 before $f(W_1, W_2)$ is computed from W_1 and W_2 at the upper layer) is near optimal in low SNR region in TWRC. However, this is not the case in high SNR region.

5   Approaching the Upper Bound in High SNR Region

As for low SNR region, we also need to find a multiple-access scheme that allows N_3 to obtain $f(W_1, W_2)$ with a rate approaching $\frac{1}{2}\log_2(1+\min(P_1,P_2))$ in the uplink phase to prove the tightness of the upper bound in (2). We find that tradition separated multiple access does not work any more. In this section, we show that PNC-based multiple access can approach the upper bound.

For PNC multiple access, we use an f that is fixed during the whole downlink phase, as follows:

$$f(W_1, W_2) = W_1 +_q W_2 = W_1 + W_2 \bmod q \tag{10}$$

where $+_q$ denotes the modulo-q addition (Modulo-q addition of two packets means symbol-wise modulo-q addition). It is easy to verify that the function in (10) satisfies the conditions (4) and (5). Thus, the downlink phase can approach the rate of $\frac{1}{2}\log_2(1 + P_3)$. The following proposition shows that for the uplink phase, N_3 can reliably obtain $W_1 +_q W_2$ with a rate approaching $\frac{1}{2}\log_2(1 + \min(P_1, P_2))$.

Proposition 4: In high SNR region, N_3 can obtain $W_1 +_q W_2$ at a rate approaching $\frac{1}{2}\log_2(1 + \min(P_1, P_2))$ with the PNC scheme depicted in Fig. 3 if the modulo-q LDPC codes can approach the Gaussian channel capacity in high SNR region.

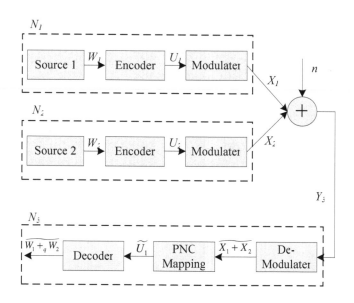

Fig. 3. Transmission and reception diagram of PNC scheme

System Description: Before the proof, let us try to understand the proposed system first. With reference to Fig. 3, let us assume $P_1 \leq P_2$ without loss of generality. The transmission strategy is as follows. We first reduce the transmission power of node N_2

to P_1 so that both end nodes transmit with the same power. We use the same block channel code, which is linear with the operation of modulo-q addition, at the two end nodes. In other words, we have

$$\Gamma_1 = \Gamma_2 = \Gamma$$
$$U_1 +_q U_2 = \Gamma(W_1) +_q \Gamma(W_2) = \Gamma(W_1 +_q W_2) \tag{11}$$

Therefore, the length of U_1 equals the length of U_2. The modulo-q LDPC code, first proposed by G. Gallager in [14], is an example of such a linear coding scheme. We also assume that the q-ary PAM modulation (QAM modulation is also valid in the PNC system) is used at both end nodes, i.e.,

$$X_i = M(U_i) = 2U_i - (q-1) \tag{12}$$

The two end nodes cooperate to transmit so that the two transmitted signals reach node N_3 in synchrony. Therefore, we can denote the k-th received symbol on baseband as

$$y_3[k] = x_1[k] + x_2[k] + n \tag{13}$$

After receiving Y_3, N_3 can obtain an estimation of $X_1 + X_2$, with either hard detection or soft detection, denoted by $\widetilde{X_1 + X_2}$. Although optimal demodulation thresholds could be used to obtain $\widetilde{X_1 + X_2}$ (see [8]), we will show that using the middle value of two adjacent constellation points as the estimation threshold is good enough to prove *Proposition 4*. After that, N_3 will map $\widetilde{X_1 + X_2}$ to the estimation of $U_1 +_q U_2$, denoted by $\widetilde{U_1 +_q U_2}$ with a PNC mapping, as follows

$$\widetilde{U_1 +_q U_2} = (\widetilde{X_1 + X_2})/2 - 1 \bmod q \tag{14}$$

Due to the linearity of Γ, $U_1 +_q U_2$ is the codeword of $W_1 +_q W_2$ as shown in (11). Therefore, we can decode $\widetilde{U_1 +_q U_2}$ with the decoding process corresponding to Γ to obtain an estimation of the target information, denoted by $\widetilde{W_1 +_q W_2}$. Note that W_1 and W_2 are not decoded explicitly in the process to obtain $W_1 +_q W_2$.

A critical assumption in this proposition is that the modulo-q LDPC code can approach the Gaussian channel capacity in high SNR region. This assumption is supported by the following observations. First, [15] proved that modulo-q quantized coset (MQC) LDPC codes can achieve the Shannon capacity of any discrete memoryless channel and the simulation there showed that MQC-LDPC codes can approach the capacity of AWGN channel within a gap of 0.9 dB. Second, for modulo-q LDPC code, the shaping loss (compared to the MQC LDPC) due to the lack of quantization is at most 1.53dB as shown in [16]. Such a fixed SNR loss can be ignored in high SNR region. We now prove *Proposition 4* with the introduced PNC transmission scheme.

Proof: First consider the point-to-point transmission in Fig. 4. Suppose the transmission power of the source is also P_1, and other assumptions are same as in our system

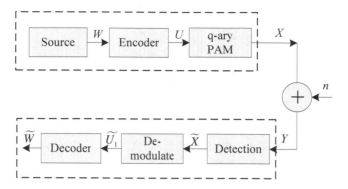

Fig. 4. Point-to-point transmission

model. As shown in [17, Ch5.2], the symbol error rate (SER) before channel decoding is

$$P_q = \Pr(u \neq \tilde{u}) = \Pr(x \neq \tilde{x}) = \frac{q-1}{q}\Pr(|n| \geq d/2) \tag{15}$$

where d is the distance between adjacent constellation points and $\Pr(|n| \geq d/2)$ is the probability that the Gaussian noise will cause a symbol detection error. Since we assume that the coset modulo-q LDPC code with q-ary PAM modulation can approach the Gaussian channel capacity in high SNR region, the SER after decoding, i.e., $\Pr(w \neq \tilde{w})$, will go to zero only if the information rate, determined by the LDPC code rate, does not exceed the Gaussian channel capacity $\frac{1}{2}\log_2(1+P_1)$ in high SNR region.

We now apply the identical coset-LDPC code at N_1 and N_2 in our system of Fig. 3. Note that the coset vector in the point-to-point transmission can be achieved by the two cooperatively designed coset vectors at N_1 and N_2. And we also set the code rate to be the same as that in the point-to-point transmission in Fig. 4. The SER of PNC scheme before decoding is

$$P_{q+} = \Pr((u_1[k]+_q u_2[k]) \neq \overline{(u_1[k]+_q u_2[k])})$$
$$< \Pr((x_1[k]+_q x_2[k]) \neq \overline{(x_1[k]+_q x_2[k])}) \tag{16}$$
$$= \frac{q^2-1}{q^2}\Pr(|n| \geq d/2)$$

where the last line is derived in the paragraph after this proof. As SNR and q go to infinity, we can see that P_{q+} in (16) will go to P_q. Since the same channel encoding and decoding scheme is used, the PNC SER after channel decoding will also go to zero as in the point-to-point system. Because the code rate is same as that of the point-to-point transmission, the information rate of $\overline{W_1 +_q W_2}$, which is equal to that of W_1 and W_2, also approaches $\frac{1}{2}\log_2(1+P_1)$.

SER of two superimposed PAM signal

For a superposition of two synchronized q-ary PAM signals, the new constellation still looks like that of PAM, where the probability of the two end points is $1/q^2$, and the probability of all other constellation points is $1-2/q^2$. Since the two PAM signals have the same transmitting power, the distance between two adjacent constellation points of the superimposed signal is the same as that of the single PAM signal case, denoted by d. The SER of the left and right end points are

$$\text{Pr}_1 = \text{Pr}(n < -d/2) \quad \text{Pr}_2 = \text{Pr}(n > d/2) \qquad (17)$$

where n is the Gaussian noise. The SER of other points is

$$\text{Pr}_3 = \text{Pr}(|n| > d/2) \qquad (18)$$

The overall SER is

$$P = \frac{1}{q^2}\text{Pr}_1 + \frac{1}{q^2}\text{Pr}_2 + \frac{q^2-1}{q^2}\text{Pr}_3 = \frac{q^2-1}{q^2}\text{Pr}(|n| \geq d/2) \qquad (19)$$

Finally, combining the PNC multiple access scheme and network-coding-like broadcasting scheme, the upper bound of the TWRC capacity is approachable in high SNR region.

6 Conclusion

In this paper, we have investigated the capacity of three-node TWRC, in which two end nodes exchange information via a relay node. An upper bound of the capacity has been given, and the tightness of the bound has been proved in the low SNR and high SNR regions.

We conjecture that the high SNR limitation in *Proposition 4* is not necessary for the following reasons. First, we may carefully design the constellation mappings at the two end nodes so that the superimposed signal at the relay can achieve the shaping gain. Second, with reference to the upper bound proof in the last section, we could fix SNR and increase q in (15) and (16). This has the effect of increasing the factor $\text{Pr}(|n| \geq d/2)$ in (15) and (16) similarly. Meanwhile, both the factors $\frac{q-1}{q}$ and $\frac{q^2-1}{q^2}$ approach one. Third, simulation results in [18] suggest that by increasing q in PNC, the achievable rate may be able to approach channel capacity.

This paper has assumed a set-up in which a direct link between the two end nodes is unavailable. We conjecture that this assumption is not necessary for the results we have obtained as long as links are half-duplex (i.e., a node cannot receive and transmit at the same time), and the capacity of the direct link between the two end nodes is no better than half of either of the relay links between the end nodes and the relay node.

The PNC uplink transmission scheme in Fig. 3 can be viewed as a specific scheme for "computation over multiple access channels" first studied in [19]. For the computation over multiple-access channels, the receiving node is interested in a function of the inputs, instead of each individual input. Theoretical results on the capacities of such multiple-access channels for certain functions of inputs have been obtained in [19]. The case of the function as modulo-q addition of the inputs, such as in our PNC scheme in Fig. 3, is first addressed in our paper here.

References

1. Shannon, C.E.: Two-way communication channels. In: Proc. 4th Berkeley Symp. Math. Stat. and Prob., vol. 1, pp. 611–644 (1961)
2. Kramer, G., Gastpar, M., Gupta, P.: Cooperative Strategies and Capacity Theorems for Relay Networks. IEEE Trans. on Inform. Theory 51(9), 3037–3063 (2005)
3. Rankov, B., Wittneben, A.: Achievable rate regions for the two-way relay channel. In: Proc. IEEE Int. Symposium on Inf., Theory, Seattle (2006)
4. Rankov, B., Wittneben, A.: spectral efficient protocols for half duplex fading relay channels. IEEE JSAC 25(2), 379–389 (2007)
5. Wu, Y., Chou, P.A., Kung, S.Y.: Information exchange in wireless networks with network coding and physical-layer broadcast. In: Proc. 39th Annual Conf. Inform. Sci. and Systems, CISS (2005)
6. Hausl, C., Hagenauer, J.: Iterative Network and Channel Decoding for the Two-Way Relay Channel. In: Proc. of IEEE International Conference on Communications (2006)
7. Zhang, S., Zhu, Y., Liew, S.C., Letaief, K.B.: Joint Design of Network Coding and Channel Decoding for Wireless Networks. In: Proc. WCNC 2007, Hong Kong (2007)
8. Zhang, S., Liew, S., Lam, P.: Physical layer network coding. In: ACM Mobicom 2006 (2006)
9. Zhang, S., Liew, S., Lam, P.: Physical layer network coding, http://arxiv.org/ftp/arxiv/papers/0704/0704.2475.pdf
10. Cui, T., Ho, T., Kliewer, J.: Relay strategies for memoryless two way relay channels: performance analysis and optimization. Submitted to ICC 2008 (2008)
11. Dim, S.J., Mitran, P., Tarokh, V.: Performance bounds for bi-directional coded cooperation protocols. In: 27th, ICDCSW, June 2007, p. 83 (2007)
12. Li, S.-Y.R., Yeung, R.W., Cai, N.: Linear network coding. IEEE Trans. on Inform. Theory 49(2), 371–381 (2003)
13. Cover, T., Thomas, J.: Elements of information theory, 2nd edn. Wiley, New York (2006)
14. Gallager, R.G.: Low density parity check codes. MIT Press, Cambridge (1963)
15. Bennatan, A., Burshtein, D.: On the application of LDPC codes to arbitrary discrete memoryless channels. Trans. Inform. Theory 50(3), 417–438 (2004)
16. Forney Jr., G.D., Ungerboeck, G.: Modulation and Coding for Linear Gaussian Channels. IEEE Trans. on Inform. Theory 44, 2384–2415 (1998)
17. Proakis, J.G.: Digital communication, 4th edn. McGraw-Hill Press, New York (2000)
18. Hao, Y., Goecket, D., Ding, Z., Towsley, D., Leung, K.K.: Achievable rates of physical layer network coding schemes on the exchange channel. Submitted to ICC 2008 (2008)
19. Nazer, B., Gastpar, M.: Computation over multiple access channels. IEEE Trans. Inform. Theory 53, 3498–3516 (2007)

20. Wu, Y.: Network coding for multicast. Ph.D thesis, Department of EECS. MIT, Cambridge (January 2006)
21. Nam, W., Chung, S.Y., Lee, Y.H.: Capacity Bounds for Two-Way Relay Channels. In: IEEE International Zurich Seminar on Communications (2008)
22. Zhang, S., Liew, S.: The capacity of two way relay channels (2008), http://arxiv.org/abs/0804.3120

DP Matching Approach for Streaming Contents Detection Using Traffic Pattern

Kazumasa Matsuda[1], Hidehisa Nakayama[2], and Nei Kato[1]

[1] Graduate School of Information Science, Tohoku University
6-3-09 Aza-aoba, Aramaki, Aoba, Sendai, Miyagi, 980-8579, Japan
matsu@it.ecei.tohoku.ac.jp
[2] Department of Electronics and Intelligent Systems, Tohoku Institute of Technology
35-1 Yagiyama-Kasumicho, Taihaku, Sendai, Miyagi, 982-8577, Japan

Abstract. Since the video streaming technology has become widespread, the security of video contents has gained more importance. Our research group previously envisioned a video leakage detection method for streaming contents that makes use of traffic patterns extracted from only traffic volume information obtained from routers. However, as the background traffic increases, packet delay and jitter increase. As a consequence, the detection accuracy decreases. In this paper, we propose a new robust method, which is more resilient to increasing packet delay and jitter by improving the generation process of traffic patterns. In addition, we solve another problem induced by packet loss by using Dynamic Programming (DP) matching. Finally, we evaluate the influence of the background traffic on streaming video detection and discuss the results.

Keywords: content delivery, streaming, traffic pattern, video detection.

1   Introduction

With the rapid advance in the network speed and capacity, streaming technology has become popular recently. Video Delivery Services (e.g., Youtube [1]) help users watch the real-time video streaming more easily. Also, because web conference systems are available arranging, it becomes possible for the company to make their own choices without face-to-face meetings [2], [3]. Therefore, it is employed by many enterprises. On the other hand, we have to take measures against leaking the video streaming traffic because it contains classified information of the company. Generally, these technologies such as protection against confidentiality and author's copyright are called DRM (Digital Rights Management) technology, which can control usage of contents or illegal copying.

Encryption of contents with keys is a basic technique of DRM and it prevents abusive copies and usage of non-licensed users by means of distribution of the decryption key to only licensed users [4]. However, it is possible that the decrypted content is re-distributed to the third person. In recent years, streaming distribution via P2P (Peer to Peer) networks has, indeed, become widespread [5]. Hence, streaming traffic of enterprises' web conferences may be leaked to P2P networks.

The generally way of preventing leakage of streaming traffic to exterior networks is packet filtering on the firewall or the router. In packet filtering, we

X. Jun Hei and L. Cheung (Eds.): AccessNets 2009, LNICST 37, pp. 232–247, 2010.
© Institute for Computer Sciences, Social-Informatics and Telecommunications Engineering 2010

assign destination IP addresses, port numbers or protocol types such as TCP (Transmission Control Protocol) or UDP (User Datagram Protocol) to block the traffic according to the assigned information [6]. However, in case of blocking the streaming traffic by means of conventional packet filtering, it is hard to filter the traffic because the destination address and port number are dynamic. Also, if there are public and secret contents in the streaming server, packet filtering cannot distinguish these contents.

The application filter, which analyzes the packet payloads, is required in order to block any streaming content. However, as traffic volume increases, the load of analysis also increases. For this reason, our research group previously proposed a video content identification method [7]. This method uses the captured traffic volume at the router nearby the distribution server and at the edge router connecting LAN (Local Area Network) and exterior network. Then the matching between these two traffic patterns lets us determine which video is served by the traffic currently on the edge router. This method can filter with relatively low load because of only traffic volume analysis (i.e., without analyzing packet payloads).

The matching requires traffic patterns based on these traffic volumes. However, the generation methods of traffic patterns in conventional schemes employ arrival time of packets. Hence, if packet jitter increases, video detection accuracy decreases due to the mismatching between these two traffic patterns. In this paper, we propose a new generation method of traffic patterns, which is robust against packet delay jitter by means of using packet size information instead of its arriving time. On the other hand, the expansion and contraction of traffic patterns frequently occurs in high packet loss environments. To solve this problem, we employ Dynamic Programming (DP) matching and enable video detection with high accuracy even in a high packet loss environment.

The rest of this paper is organized as follows. In Section 2, we introduce the overview of the video detection system using traffic volume and its usage. Section 3 presents the conventional method of traffic pattern generation, and discusses its inherent problem. In Section 4, we introduce details on the proposed method, which changes the generation method of traffic patterns and uses the DP matching. The performance evaluation of the envisioned method is presented in Section 5. Finally, Section 6 concludes the paper.

2   Video Detection System Using Traffic Volume

2.1   Overview

The bit rates of the Variable Bit Rate (VBR) streaming contents change according to the changes in the contents. When the content is delivered to the user through streaming, the traffic volume observed at the router close to the distribution server and at the edge router represents a unique pattern for each content just as a human fingerprint. By comparing this pattern on the delivery server-side with that on the edge router-side, it is, indeed, possible to detect whether the targeted content in the distribution server is leaking at the edge router or not. Many video session passes through the edge router, hence the edge router side pattern is generated from observing its traffic volume for a short time in contract with the distribution server. In addition, this method can be implemented with a lower computational cost because the traffic patterns matching operations are performed on the management server.

2.2   Overview of Video Detection System

In this section, we introduce two example of video leaking, and present an overview of the proposed system and how to apply the same.

The case of existing public and secret contents. In Fig. 1(a), distribution server S has both a content released to the exterior network and a confidential one, and user $U1$ is receiving a public streaming content. Then, we discuss the

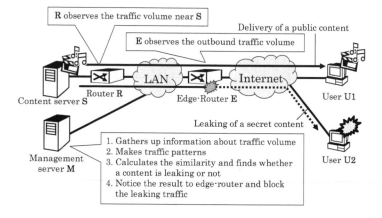

(a) The case of existence of public and secret contents.

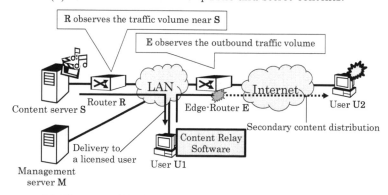

(b) The case of leakage of contents by a licensed user, $U1$.

Fig. 1. The video leakage detection mechanism

case where a confidential content is being leaked to user $U2$ due to misconfiguration of either the distribution server S or the packet filtering mechanism. In the proposed system, router R and edge router E observe distribution server side and outbound traffic volumes from the LAN, respectively. Each observed traffic information is sent to the management server, M. Next, M generates traffic patterns based on traffic volumes and calculates the correlation coefficient. Using this similarity, the system determine whether a confidential content is being leaked or not, and the edge router E prevent a session from getting leaked.

The case of re-distribution by licensed user. Fig. 1(b) shows that distribution server S deliver the contents to licensed user $U1$. Then, if the software which re-distributes the received content to exterior networks such as P2P networks, is installed in user $U1$, $U1$ re-distributes to unlicensed user $U2$. Re-distribution of destination and its port may be changed by the software. Therefore, it is hard to block by packet filtering. In this example, by means of observing router R and edge router E, and by patterns matching, it is possible to block these re-distribution sessions.

2.3   Matching Processes of Traffic Patterns

The outline of comparison of traffic patterns are shown in Fig. 2. The comparison of traffic patterns consists of three steps. First, in step 1, we place a window $(U[slot])$, which snips off a partial patterns X_U from the distribution server side traffic pattern X_S, where U is the length of the edge router side traffic pattern. Next, in step 2, similarity between the partial pattern X_U and the edge router side pattern T_U is calculated. In step 3, the window is moved from left to right by one slot. These three steps are repeated until the window reaches the rightmost part of the the distribution server side pattern, and finally obtains a similarity value of $(S - U + 1)$. When the similarity value is large, it means that the edge router side pattern is similar to the partial pattern found on the distribution server side. In this case, the management server decides that a confidential content is leaking. To decide whether a significantly large value exists or not, this method requires a threshold specific to the considered network setting and streaming dynamic.

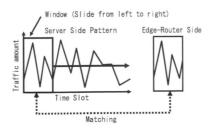

Fig. 2. An example of the comparison of traffic patterns

3   Definition of a Traffic Pattern in a Conventional Method

3.1   The Traffic Pattern Generation and Definition of Similarity

In method our previously proposed [7], the traffic pattern is defined as the volume of traffic for a certain time-slot, $\Delta t[\text{s}]$, and expressed as a N-dimension vector.

$$X = (x_1, x_2, \cdots, x_N)^t, \quad T = N \cdot \Delta t \tag{1}$$

where $T[\text{s}]$ is is the whole length of the traffic pattern and $N[\text{slot}]$ is the number of time slots.

   To detection a leaking, two patterns, X_S and Y_U are generated for the distribution side and the edge router side, respectively. Then X_S and Y_U are matched, i.e., compared. X_S and Y_U have S and Y-dimensions respectively, and $(S > U)$. The similarity between these two patterns are calculated as R_{XY} according to Eq. (2).

$$R_{XY} = \frac{X_U'^t \, Y_U'}{\sqrt{||X_U'||^2 \cdot ||Y_U'||^2}}, \quad -1 < R_{XY} < 1 \tag{2}$$

where X_U is the distribution server side pattern snipped off U-dimension, which is same as that of the edge router side patterns. In addition, X_U' and Y_U' are normalized patterns so that the mean is zero and the valiance is one, as shown in Eq. (3).

$$X_U' = \begin{pmatrix} (x_1 - \bar{x})/s_x \\ (x_2 - \bar{x})/s_x \\ \vdots \\ (x_U - \bar{x})/s_x \end{pmatrix}, Y_U' = \begin{pmatrix} (y_1 - \bar{y})/s_y \\ (y_2 - \bar{y})/s_y \\ \vdots \\ (y_U - \bar{y})/s_y \end{pmatrix} \tag{3}$$

where $\bar{x}$ and s_x denote the mean and standard deviation of the distribution server side pattern, respectively, while $\bar{y}$ and s_y indicate those of the edge router side pattern, respectively.

3.2   Problems Caused by Packet Delay Jitter

Generation method of traffic pattern of conventional method [7] is defined as the volume of traffic for a certain time-slot, as shown in Eq. (1). Then, we discuss the situation that some packets delays exceed Δt. These delayed packets are stored over the slot x_{i+1} instead of the primary slot x_i. Therefore, delay jitter of packet distorts the traffic pattern. As a consequence, the detection accuracy decreases.

4   A Novel Traffic Pattern Based on Packet Size

4.1   Enhancement of Traffic Pattern

Overview. To solve the aforementioned problem related to packet delay jitter, we propose, in this paper, a new generation method of traffic patterns, which is robust against packet delay jitter.

In the envisioned method, the splitting trigger of the traffic pattern receives packets with a certain packet size, instead of time-slot. As a result, the proposed method can produce a traffic pattern with robustness against packet delay jitter and achieves high detection accuracy regardless of a high packet delay jitter environment. This method can make the same traffic pattern between the distribution server and edge router sides unless packet re-ordering or packet loss occurs.

To decide the appropriate packet size, we need to take into account the distribution of packet size. We introduce overview of this survey and results, and decide a certain packet size to split traffic patterns in this section.

The distribution of packet sizes. The bit rates of Variable Bit Rate (VBR) streaming content change according to changes in the contents. Hence each packet size also changes momentarily. Then, if there is variability of packet size, we can split a traffic pattern while receiving a packet having a certain packet size. We connected the distribution server and the user with 1Gbps LAN and delivered six streaming contents, and captured each traffic volume at the router in order to search the distribution of packet sizes. Helix server [8] and Darwin Streaming Server (DSS) [9] were used as the distribution servers in this survey. The result of this survey is shown in Table. 1 and the example of the distribution of packet size is shown in Fig. 3. According to Table. 1, all video contents have variability and similar distributions. Therefore, the proposed method does not depend on content type. Also, according to Fig. 3, there are many packets of MSS (Maximum Segment Size) in both Helix Server and Darwin Streaming Server. If the packet size range of splitting traffic pattern is set around the MSS, the number of packets into each slot becomes extremely low. On the other hand, there are some packets of small size moderately. Packet size range is set to small

Table 1. Average of streaming packet size and variance

Video name	Length	Helix Server		Darwin Streaming Server	
		Ave. of packet size	Variance	Ave. of packet size	Variance
Anime	1m40s	953.5 Bytes	206915	1212.9 Bytes	154573
Documentary 1	1m38s	928.6 Bytes	246853	1253.9 Bytes	136184
Documentary 2	1m43s	940.8 Bytes	217488	1224.8 Bytes	142604
Variety show	2m0s	694.8 Bytes	222917	1268.1 Bytes	115492
Baseball	2m0s	719.4 Bytes	209743	1241.5 Bytes	136110
News	2m0s	710.9 Bytes	218307	1238.8 Bytes	118364

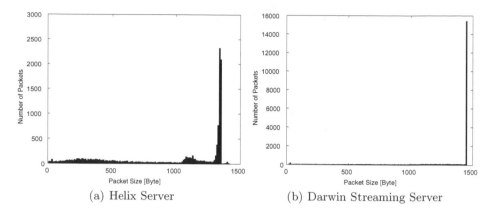

(a) Helix Server   (b) Darwin Streaming Server

Fig. 3. Example of packet size distribution (Anime)

size in the proposed method so that the number of packets into each slot is also moderate.

4.2   Traffic Pattern Matching Using DP Matching

Discussion about matching method. The generation method of traffic patterns which is based on packet size is robust against packet delay jitter. However, if a packet which is separable a traffic pattern is dropped, the traffic pattern is not split by this packet. As a result, traffic patterns between the distribution server and the edge router sides become different.

Fig. 4 shows an example of each traffic pattern based on the same video content, with 1% loss between the distribution server and the edge router. According to Fig. 4, the gap between two traffic patterns was caused by packet loss.

When such a gap in traffic patterns occurs due to packet loss, we can alleviate it by means of expansion and contraction of the pattern on one side so that the matching will be successful. Such a matching technique is called DP (Dynamic Programming) Matching [10], and we adopted this method in our proposed scheme. We introduce how to apply this matching method to the proposed approach in the remainder of this section.

How to apply DP matching. To apply DP matching to the proposed approach, we need to define the distance $d(i, j)$ between a_i and b_j in the distribution server side pattern T and edge router side pattern R, as shown below.

$$\begin{cases} T = a_1 a_2 \cdots a_i \cdots a_I \\ R = b_1 b_2 \cdots b_j \cdots b_J \end{cases} \tag{4}$$

where the server side pattern is snipped off the window which is the same length as the edge router side pattern and the window is moved from left to right by one slot. Hence $(I = J = U)$, where U is the length of edge router side pattern.

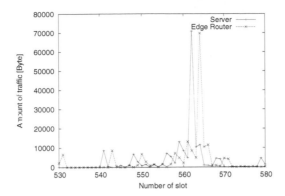

Fig. 4. Server side and edge-router side traffic pattern (loss: 1%)

We describe the cost of displacement to convert from T to R. Each distance of vector between a_i and b_j is defined as $d(i,j) = |a_i - b_j|$. and cost r per gap is added. Finally, T and R are normalized by the number of slots.

When the distance between two vector, $(a_1 a_2 \cdots a_i)$ and $(b_1 b_2 \cdots b_j)$ defined as $g(i,j)$, $D(T,R)$ is given by following recurrence equation because of principle of optimality of dynamic programming.

① Initial condition $g(0,0) = d(0,0)$
  $g(i,0) = g(i-1,0) + r + d(i,0)$
  for $i = 1,2,\cdots,I$
  $g(0,j) = g(0,j-1) + r + d(0,j)$
  for $j = 1,2,\cdots,J$
② Execute ④ about $i = 1,2,\cdots,I$
③ Execute ④ about $j = 1,2,\cdots,J$
④ $g(i,j) = \min \begin{cases} g(i-1,j) + r + d(i,j) \\ g(i-1,j-1) + d(i,j) \\ g(i,j-1) + r + d(i,j) \end{cases}$
⑤ $D(T,R) = g(I,J)/(I+J) = g(U,U)/2U$

The similarity between the server and the edge router sides is calculated as $D(T,R)$. Because the window is moved by one slot while calculating each similarity, conclusive similarity between two patterns is the minimum of each similarity value.

An example of similarity graph using DP matching. Fig. 5 shows the similarity graph using DP matching between two traffic patterns which are based on the same content with packet loss rate 1%. If two traffic patterns are based on the same content, we can find the minimum peak in the similarity graph. Because when the window of the server side pattern corresponds with that of the edge router, the costs of expansion, contraction, and displacement are low.

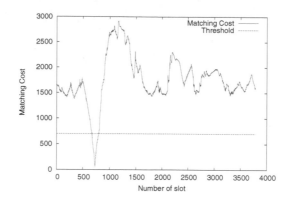

Fig. 5. Example of the DP matching similarity graph

The proposed method sets the threshold to detect this minimum value in order to detect whether the video content is being leaked at the edge router or not.

5   Performance Evaluation

5.1   Overview of the Experiment

To evaluate the feasibility of the proposed method, we conduct experiments about the influence of delay jitter, packet loss, and background traffic on the conventional [7] and the proposed methods. In the proposed method, we consider both the conventional matching (dubbed as P-TRAT) and the DP matching (DP-TRAT) techniques.

Six different contents, namely news, comedy show, anime, live baseball match, and so forth, are distributed from the server to the user, and the corresponding traffic volume of each contents is captured. Then, the traffic patterns are generated from the captured traffic volumes at the content server and also at the user. These traffic patterns are used to compute the similarity. Finally, we confirm the detection accuracy of the proposal approach. Table. 2 shows the experimental environment, and Fig. 6 depicts the topology of the considered network. In addition, NetEm [11] is used in order to produce packet jitter and packet loss. NetEm is a network simulator, which runs on Linux, and can occur jitter, packet loss, or packet re-ordering arbitrarily at a network interface. The background traffic is generated by nuttcp [12], which contains UDP flows from the server to the user.

The user traffic pattern is generated by capturing the whole content volume, and it is snipped off with 2500 packets. According to Fig. 2, observation of the user side traffic is shorter than that of the server side, the user side volume is observed at the whole time and snipped off it changing the snipping window position by 20 points. Finally, we calculate each similarity using the 20 user side

Table 2. Experimental environment

OS	Debian Linux 4.0iKernel v2.6.18j
Sever PC: CPU	Intel Pentium D 3.2 GHz
Client PC: CPU	Intel Core 2 Duo E6600 2.4 GHz
Bridge PC: CPU	Intel Xeon X5450 3.0 GHz
Network card	Intel PRO/1000 MT Server Adapter
Streaming server	Helix Server v11.1.6
Media player	RealPlayer v10.0.9
Video bit-rate	1 Mbps
Traffic observation library	libpcap v0.7.2
Number of packets in userside traffic pattern	2500
Conventional: time slot size	120 ms
P-TRAT, DP-TRAT: threshold of packet size	200 Bytes
Conventional: detection threshold	Chebyshev's inequality
P-TRAT: detection threshold	0.7
DP-TRAT: detection threshold	700

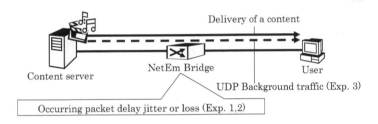

Fig. 6. Consider network topology

traffic generated in the experiment. The average of these similarities is used as result.

The proposed method uses the precision and the recall as indices to verify the performance of the proposed method which are generally used in the validation of performance of the Information Retrieval systems. These indices represent the correctness and the completeness of the detection result, respectively. However, because these indices generally have a trade-off relationship, we also use F-measure, which is a comprehensive measurement to evaluate the performance of our approach. A large value of the F-measure indicates high performance, when it has a large value. These indices are expressed as follows.

$$\text{Precision}: Pr = \frac{C}{A} \times 100 \ [\%] \tag{5}$$

$$\text{Recall}: Re = \frac{C}{W} \times 100 \ [\%] \tag{6}$$

$$\text{F-measure} : F = \frac{2 \times Pr \times Re}{Pr + Re} \, [\%] \tag{7}$$

Here, C is the number of detections number of correct detection decisions (i.e., in terms of discovering an ongoing content-leakage). A is the number of detections, which is declared to be leaking the content, including the false positives. W is the number of actual content-leaks. These indices are calculated by combining all server side and user side patterns. We consider six server side traffic patterns, six user side patterns, and 20 window positions at the user side, thus a total combination of 720 different patterns.

5.2   Evaluation #1: Verification of the Influence of Packet Delay Jitter

Experimental setup. Six different contents are distributed from the server to the user by adding the packet delay jitter via NetEm bridge. The added delay jitter comprises of the following: delay value 200ms and jitter value ($\pm 0 \sim \pm 200$) ms. The jitter is gradually added every 20 ms.

Experimental results. Fig. 7 shows the results of the conducted experiment about precision, recall and F-measure, respectively. As shown in Fig. 7(a) and 7(b), the conventional method is affected by packet jitter and its recall is lower than the proposed method. On the other hand, the proposed method retains 100% F-measures regardless of the packet jitter.

5.3   Evaluation #2: Verification of the Influence of Packet Loss

Experimental setup. In the same way as in the first experiment, six different contents are distributed and the packet loss of $0.1 \sim 10\%$ via NetEm bridge is injected.

Experimental results. Fig. 8 shows the results of these indices. As shown in Fig. 8(a), the precision is retained by each considered method. However, as the packet loss rate increases, the recall of P-TRAT is low with a loss rate exceeding 0.5% (Fig. 8(b)). On the other hand, DP-TRAT achieves high indices regardless of the increasing packet loss rate.

5.4   Evaluation #3: Verification of the Influence of Background Traffic

Experimental setup. In the same way as in the first and second experimental set-ups, six different contents are distributed. At the same time, UDP traffic flows ranging from $0 \sim 500$ Mbps are generated from the server to the user by nuttcp.

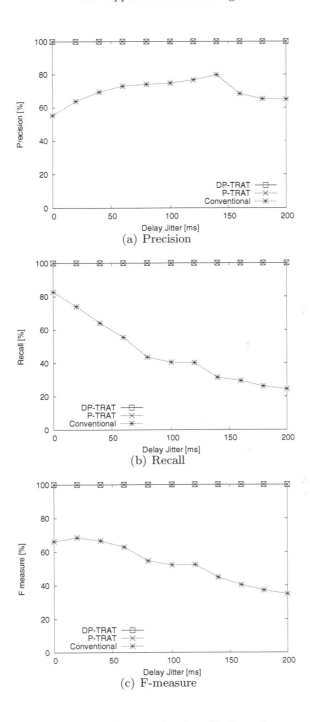

(a) Precision

(b) Recall

(c) F-measure

Fig. 7. Result of the evaluation #1 about jitter

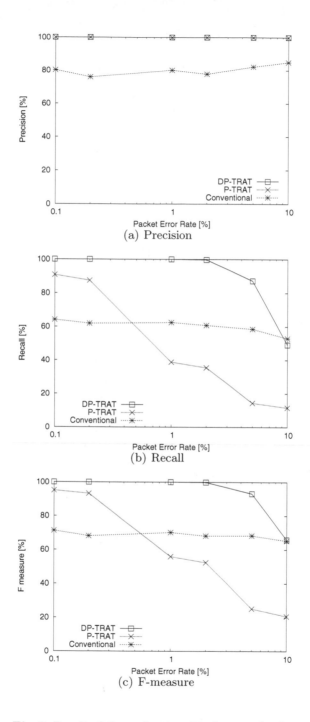

(a) Precision

(b) Recall

(c) F-measure

Fig. 8. Result of the evaluation #2 about packet loss

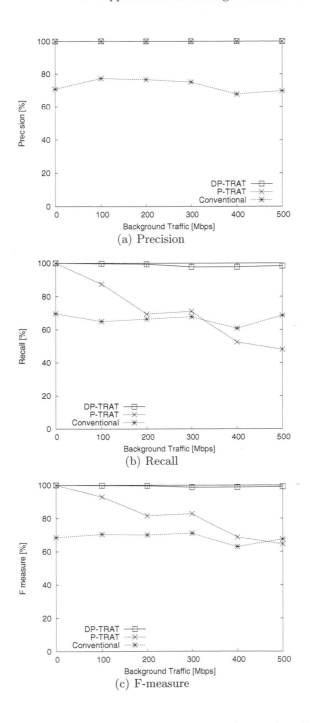

Fig. 9. Result of the evaluation #3 about background traffic

Experimental results. Fig. 9 shows the results of these indices. As shown in Fig. 9(a), each method is precise enough. However, as the background traffic increases, the recall and F-measures of P-TRAT drop. On the other hand, DP-TRAT retains these indices regardless of the increasing background traffic. In addition, the indices obtained through the proposed DP-TRAT are higher than those in the conventional method.

6   Conclusion

In this paper, we proposed a mechanism for effectively detecting the leaks in the streaming contents by observing and correlating the traffic at the distribution server and also at the edge router. This method can be used regardless of the destination IP addresses, port numbers and protocol types since it uses only packet size information. Therefore, this method can deny the session which is not blocked by packet filtering. As a result, this method can be employed as a firewall-aided technique.

We previously envisioned a video leakage detection method for streaming contents that makes use of traffic patterns extracted from only traffic volume information obtained from routers. However, as the packet delay and jitter increase, its detection accuracy significantly decreases. To overcome this issue, we applied the Dynamic Programming (DP) matching scheme in our previously proposed technique by expanding and contracting traffic patterns appropriately. Finally, we evaluated the performance of our enhanced approach under the influence of packet delay, packet loss, and background traffic environment.

References

1. Youtube - Broadcast Yourself, http://www.youtube.com/
2. Yang, Z., Ma, H., Zhang, J.: A dynamic scalable service model for SIP-based video conference. In: Proc. 9th International Conference on Computer Supported Cooperative Work in Design, Coventry, UK, May 2005, vol. 1, pp. 24–26 (2005)
3. Shimakawa, M., Holed, D.P., Tobagi, F.A.: Video-conferencing and Data Traffic over an IEEE 802.11g WLAN using DCF and EDCA. In: Proc. International Conference on Communications (ICC), Seoul, Korea, May 2005, vol. 2, pp. 16–20 (2005)
4. Lin, E.I., Eskicioglu, A.M., Lagendijk, R.L., Delp, E.J.: Advances in Digital Video Content Protection. Proc. IEEE 93(1), 171–183 (2005)
5. Peltotalo, J., Harju, J., Jantunen, A., Saukko, M., Vaatamoinen, L.: Peer-to-Peer Streaming Technology Survey. In: Proc. 7th International Conference on Networking, Cancun, Mexico (April 2008)
6. Zwicky, E.D., Cooper, S., Chapman, D.B.: Building Internet Firewalls, 2nd edn. O'Reilly, Sebastopol (2002)
7. Dobashi, M., Nakayama, H., Kato, N., Nemoto, Y., Jamalipour, A.: Traitor Tracing Technology of Streaming Contents Delivery using Traffic Pattern in Wired/Wireless Environments. In: Proc. IEEE Global Telecommunications Conference, San Francisco, California, USA, November/December (2006)

8. RealNetworks, Product and Services > Media Servers,
    http://www.realnetworks.com/products/media_delivery.html
9. Apple, Open Source - Server - Streaming Server,
    http://developer.apple.com/opensource/server/streaming/
10. Geiger, D., Gupta, A., Costa, L.A., Vlontzos, J.: Dynamic Programming for Detect-
    ing, Tracking, and Matching Deformable Contours. IEEE Transactions on Pattern
    Analysis and Machine Intelligence 17(3), 294–302 (1995)
11. Hemminger, S.: Network Emulation with NetEm. In: Proc. Linux Conference Aus
    tralia, Canberra, Australia (April 2005)
12. The nuttcp development team, http://www.nuttcp.net/

A Linear Precoding Design for Multi-Antenna Multicast Broadcast Services with Limited Feedback

Eddy Chiu and Vincent K.N. Lau

Department of Electronic and Computer Engineering
Hong Kong University of Science and Technology
Clear Water Bay, Kowloon
Hong Kong
eechiua@ust.hk, eeknlau@ee.ust.hk

Abstract. The provision for spectrally efficient multicast broadcast services (MBS) is one of the key functional requirements for next generation wireless communication systems. The challenge inherent to MBS is to ensure that all MBS users can be served, and one effective solution to this problem is to employ MIMO multicast transmit precoding. In previous works on MIMO multicast transmit precoding design, the authors either assumed 1) perfect transmitter-side channel state information (CSIT) or 2) special channel conditions that facilitate precoder design with imperfect CSIT. In this paper, we focus on transmit precoding design for MBS where the CSIT is obtained via limited feedback. In addition, we analyze the average minimum receive signal-noise-ratio (RxSNR) among the MBS users and study the order of growth with respect to the number of MBS users and the number of feedback bits. Finally, we propose a threshold based feedback reduction scheme and study the tradeoff between feedback cost and performance loss.

Keywords: MIMO, transmit precoding, beamforming, multicast, MBS, limited feedback.

1 Introduction

Ubiquitous multimedia multicast broadcast services (MBS) is an integral part of the vision for next generation wireless communication systems [1, Section 7.5] [2]. In multicast transmission, the transmitter sends common information to multiple users, and the transmission rate needs to be adapted to support all the users. However, in a wireless network the MBS users have diverse channel conditions, so the multicast rate can be severely limited by the user with the worst channel. To enhance the spectral efficiency of wireless multicasting, some multi-antenna transmission techniques are proposed in recent literature [3, 4, 5, 6, 7, 8] and references therein. In particular, one effective technique is max-min fair (MMF) transmit precoding (or beamforming) where the multi-antenna

X. Jun Hei and L. Cheung (Eds.): AccessNets 2009, LNICST 37, pp. 248–263, 2010.

base station (BS) scales the transmitted signal with a precoder to enhance the minimum received signal-to-noise ratio (RxSNR) among all the users.

There are two fundamental technical challenges associated with MMF transmit precoding design: first, transmitter-side channel state information (CSIT) of all the MBS users is required; and second, as shown in [3, Appendix I], [9, Section 2], the procoder optimization problem is NP-hard. To address these issues, some prior works proposed precoder designs assuming perfect CSIT or special channel conditions that facilitate precoder design with imperfect CSIT. In [3], given that the BS has perfect CSIT, the authors propose a precoder design that works around the NP-hard nature of the problem via a semi-definite relaxation (SDR) approach and a randomization process. It is shown that this SDR-randomization based algorithm can be solved in polynomial time to produce effective precoders. When the BS has imperfect CSIT, the precoder design needs to suitably account for the CSIT error. In [4], the authors consider transmit precoding design for the case of far-field line-of-sight propagation conditions. By exploiting the special properties of line-of-sight channels, the authors develop a precoder design with approximate knowledge of the user directions. On the other hand, in [6,7] the authors consider transmit precoding design given that the BS is furnished with a channel vector estimate with small Euclidean distance distortion. By adopting robust beamforming concepts, the authors develop a precoder design based on the worst case CSIT error.

In practical communication systems, the channel conditions are substantially different from those considered in the aforementioned prior works. In an urban environment typically there is no line-of-sight channel between the BS and the mobile users [10]. Moreover, when channel reciprocity does not hold as is the case for frequency division duplex (FDD) systems, the BS is commonly provided with CSIT via rate-constrained *limited feedback* from the user [2,11]. There are a number of prior works on limited feedback precoder design for unicast transmission. For example, in [12] the authors model joint power and precoder adaptation of a MIMO link with limited feedback as a vector quantization (VQ) problem and propose a modified Lloyd's algorithm to obtain the optimal solution. On the other hand, in [13] the authors consider the Grassmannian packing approach in MIMO precoder design with limited feedback for single-user systems, whereas in [14,15] the authors consider MIMO precoder design for multi-user systems. However, the limited feedback precoder design for unicast applications in the prior works cannot enhance the worst case user performance and thus are not suitable for MBS scenario.

In this paper, we consider a MIMO MBS system with one BS having N transmit antennas and K MBS users having a single receive antenna. We focus on transmit precoding design to maximize the minimum RxSNR among the MBS users where the CSIT is obtained via limited feedback. Specifically, we have the following emphases:

1. We devise a MIMO transmit precoding design for MBS by means of precoder optimization with limited feedback.

2. We derive a closed-form lower bound for the average minimum RxSNR among the MBS users and study the order of growth with respect to (w.r.t.) the number of MBS users and the number of bits for limited feedback.
3. We devise a threshold-based feedback reduction scheme and study the trade-off between feedback cost and performance loss.

The rest of this paper is organized as follows. In Section 2, we define our system model and problem statement. In Section 3, we introduce our proposed transmit precoding design and, in Section 4, we analyze the system performance. In Section 5, we present our proposed threshold-based feedback reduction scheme. Finally, in Section 6 and Section 7, we provide our numerical simulation results and concluding remarks, respectively.

We adopt the following notations. Θ^N denotes the set of unit vectors in $\mathbb{C}^{N \times 1}$; $\mathbb{R}_+$ denotes the set of nonnegative real numbers; upper and lower case letters denote matrices and vectors, respectively; $(\cdot)^*$, $(\cdot)^T$ and $(\cdot)^\dagger$ denote conjugate, transpose, and Hermitian transpose, respectively; $\text{Tr}(\cdot)$ and $\text{rank}(\cdot)$ denote matrix trace and rank, respectively; $\mathbf{X} \succeq 0$ denotes a positive semi-definite matrix; $\mathbf{I}_N$ denotes an $N \times N$ identity matrix; $\mathbb{E}[\cdot]$ denotes expectation; $\mathcal{CN}(\boldsymbol{\mu}, \boldsymbol{\Sigma})$ denotes complex Gaussian distribution with mean $\boldsymbol{\mu}$ and covariance matrix $\boldsymbol{\Sigma}$; $\mathcal{O}(\cdot)$ denotes the Big O notation, and $\Omega(\cdot)$ denotes the Big Omega notation where $f(n) = \Omega(g(n))$ if there are constants c and n_0 such that $f(n) \geq cg(n) \; \forall n > n_0$; and $\text{Pr}(\cdot)$ denotes the probability of the given event.

2 System Model and Problem Statement

2.1 System Model

We consider a communication system where a BS delivers MBS to K users as shown in Fig. 1. The BS has N transmit antennas, whereas the users have one receive antenna and experience quasi-static Rayleigh flat fading. For simplicity of exposition, in the following we focus on the kth user, whose downlink channel vector is denoted by $\mathbf{h}_{(k)} \in \mathbb{C}^{N \times 1}$. We assume independent and identically distributed (i.i.d.) channels with unit variance such that $\mathbf{h}_{(k)} \sim \mathcal{CN}(0, \mathbf{I}_N)$ and remains unchanged within a fading block. Prior to multicast transmission, the

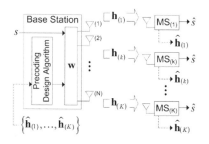

Fig. 1. MIMO MBS system with limited feedback

BS scales the MBS data symbol s with a precoder $\mathbf{w} \in \Theta^N$, and the received symbol is given by $y_{(k)} = \mathbf{h}_{(k)}^T \mathbf{w}^* s + z_{(k)}$, where $z_{(k)}$ is the additive noise with variance N_0. Let $\mathbb{E}[|s|^2] = P$. The instantaneous RxSNR is given by

$$\gamma_{(k)} = \frac{\mathbb{E}[|s|^2]}{\mathbb{E}[|z_{(k)}|^2]} \left|\mathbf{h}_{(k)}^T \mathbf{w}^*\right|^2 = \frac{P}{N_0} \left|\mathbf{h}_{(k)}^T \mathbf{w}^*\right|^2 \tag{1}$$

and we define $\frac{P}{N_0}$ as the transmit SNR (TxSNR). Since the MBS users' channels experience independent fading, the users' RxSNR can be substantially different. The multicast transmission rate is limited by the user with the worst RxSNR. Thus, to enhance the performance of MBS, we are interested for the BS to design the precoder $\mathbf{w}$ to enhance the minimum RxSNR among the users. In order to facilitate the BS with designing $\mathbf{w}$, in each fading block the users provide the BS with CSIT via limited feedback.

2.2   Limited Feedback Scheme

In order to focus on the effects of limited feedback, we make the following assumption.

Assumption 1. *The kth MBS user has perfect knowledge of channel vector $\mathbf{h}_{(k)}$.*

The channel vector of the kth user can be represented as [15, 14]

$$\mathbf{h}_{(k)} = \sqrt{\zeta_{(k)}} \mathbf{g}_{(k)}, \tag{2}$$

where we define $\mathbf{g}_{(k)} = \mathbf{h}_{(k)} / |\mathbf{h}_{(k)}|$ as the *channel direction vector* and $\zeta_{(k)} = |\mathbf{h}_{(k)}|^2$ as the *channel gain*, which are independent. We propose a limited feedback scheme where, for a given channel realization $\mathbf{h}_{(k)}$, the user feeds back to the BS the channel vector estimate

$$\widehat{\mathbf{h}}_{(k)} = \sqrt{q[\mathbf{h}_{(k)}]} \widehat{\mathbf{g}}_{(k)}, \tag{3}$$

which is constituted of a *quantized channel direction vector* $\widehat{\mathbf{g}}_{(k)} \in \Theta^N$ and a *channel quality metric* $q[\mathbf{h}_{(k)}] \in \mathbb{R}_+$ defined as follows.

Quantized channel direction vector. The quantized channel direction vector $\widehat{\mathbf{g}}_{(k)}$ is obtained from $\mathbf{g}_{(k)}$ using a codebook based method. Specifically, let the codebook $\mathcal{A} = \{\mathbf{a}_1, \ldots, \mathbf{a}_{2^b} : \mathbf{a}_i \in \Theta^N\}$ be available to the BS and the MBS users. The user quantizes $\mathbf{g}_{(k)}$ to a codevector in $\mathcal{A}$ according to the maximal squared absolute inner product criterion

$$\widehat{\mathbf{g}}_{(k)} = \arg\max_{\mathbf{a} \in \mathcal{A}} \left|\mathbf{g}_{(k)}^T \mathbf{a}^*\right|^2, \tag{4}$$

and sends the b-bit index corresponding to $\widehat{\mathbf{g}}_{(k)}$ to the BS.

Channel quality metric. The channel quality metric $q[\mathbf{h}_{(k)}]$ encapsulates both the channel gain $\zeta_{(k)}$ and the effects of quantization on $\widehat{\mathbf{g}}_{(k)}$. Since $q[\mathbf{h}_{(k)}]$ is a positive real scalar, it could be accurately represented with a small number of quantization bits. As such, we make the following assumption.

Assumption 2. *We assume the channel quality metric is accurately conveyed from the MBS user to the BS.*

Note that the same assumption that the channel quality is perfectly known to the BS is often made in the literature of SDMA (e.g. [14, 15] and references therein) since the number of bits required for quantizing the channel quality is much less than the number of bits required for quantizing the channel direction vector.

2.3   Problem Formulation

At the BS, given CSIT of the K users $\mathcal{H}_{(K)} = \{\widehat{\mathbf{h}}_{(1)}, \ldots, \widehat{\mathbf{h}}_{(K)}\}$, the BS selects a precoder to maximize the minimum expected RxSNR among the users. Let $\mathbf{w}[\mathcal{H}_{(K)}]$ denote the precoder action for the CSIT realization $\mathcal{H}_{(K)}$ and let $\mathcal{W} = \{\mathbf{w}[\mathcal{H}_{(K)}] \in \Theta^N : \forall \mathcal{H}_{(K)} \in \mathbb{C}^{N \times K}\}$ denote the precoding policy, which is the set of all possible precoder actions for all possible CSIT realizations. The precoder design optimization problem is formally written as:

Problem 1 (Precoder optimization for MBS).

$$\mathcal{W}^\star = \arg \max_{\mathcal{W}} \mathbb{E}\left[\min_{k=1,\ldots,K} \mathbb{E}\left[\gamma_{(k)} \,\middle|\, \mathcal{H}_{(K)}\right]\right].$$

In Problem 1, note that optimization w.r.t. the precoding policy is equivalent to optimization w.r.t. the actions for a given CSIT realization. As a result, Problem 1 is equivalent to

$$\mathbf{w}^\star = \arg \max_{\mathbf{w} \in \Theta^N} \min_{k=1,\ldots,K} \mathbb{E}\left[\gamma_{(k)} \,\middle|\, \mathcal{H}_{(K)}\right] \tag{5}$$

and we shall present a transmit precoding design for obtaining the solution to Problem 1 in the following section.

3   Transmit Precoding Design

To facilitate transmit precoding design with CSIT obtain via limited feedback, we first deduce the expected RxSNR of MBS users given CSIT. After that, we present the solution for precoder optimization for MBS.

3.1 Expected RxSNR of MBS Users Given CSIT

From (1) and (2) the instantaneous RxSNR of the kth user can be expressed as

$$\gamma_{(k)} = \frac{P}{N_0} \zeta_{(k)} \left| \mathbf{g}_{(k)}^T \mathbf{w}^* \right|^2. \tag{6}$$

In Theorem 1, we deduce a lower bound for the expected RxSNR given CSIT and derive the channel quality metric for limited feedback.

Theorem 1 (Lower bound of the average RxSNR). *The expected RxSNR of the kth user given CSIT $\widehat{\mathbf{h}}_{(k)}$ is given by* $\mathbb{E}\left[\gamma_{(k)} | \widehat{\mathbf{h}}_{(k)} \right] \geq \frac{P}{N_0} \left| \widehat{\mathbf{h}}_{(k)}^T \mathbf{w}^* \right|^2 = \frac{P}{N_0} q\left[\mathbf{h}_{(k)} \right] \left| \widehat{\mathbf{g}}_{(k)}^T \mathbf{w}^* \right|^2.$ *The channel quality metric is given by* $q[\mathbf{h}_{(k)}] = \zeta_{(k)} \eta_{(k)},$ *where*

$$\begin{aligned}
\eta_{(k)} &= \frac{1}{\frac{\pi}{2}} \int_0^{\frac{\pi}{2} - \theta_{(k)}} \frac{\cos^2\left(\phi_{(k)} + \theta_{(k)} \right)}{\cos^2\left(\phi_{(k)} \right)} d\phi_{(k)} \\
&= \left(1 - \frac{2}{\pi} \theta_{(k)} \right) \cos\left(2\theta_{(k)} \right) + \frac{2}{\pi} \sin\left(2\theta_{(k)} \right) \left(\ln\left(\sin\left(\theta_{(k)} \right) \right) + \frac{1}{2} \right),
\end{aligned} \tag{7}$$

and $\theta_{(k)} = \arccos|\mathbf{g}_{(k)}^T \widehat{\mathbf{g}}_{(k)}^*|.$

Proof. As per (6), the expected RxSNR of the kth user given $\zeta_{(k)}$ and $\widehat{\mathbf{g}}_{(k)}$ can be expressed as

$$\mathbb{E}\left[\gamma_{(k)} | \zeta_{(k)}, \widehat{\mathbf{g}}_{(k)} \right] = \frac{P}{N_0} \zeta_{(k)} \mathbb{E}\left[\left| \mathbf{g}_{(k)}^T \mathbf{w}^* \right|^2 \Big| \widehat{\mathbf{g}}_{(k)} \right]. \tag{8}$$

We obtain a lower bound for $\mathbb{E}[|\mathbf{g}_{(k)}^T \mathbf{w}^*|^2 | \widehat{\mathbf{g}}_{(k)}]$ as follows. By definition, $\widehat{\mathbf{g}}_{(k)}$ and $\mathbf{g}_{(k)}$ are related by an angle $0 \leq \theta_{(k)} \leq \frac{\pi}{2}$ according to

$$\left| \mathbf{g}_{(k)}^T \widehat{\mathbf{g}}_{(k)}^* \right|^2 = v_{(k)} = \cos^2\left(\theta_{(k)} \right) \tag{9}$$

where $0 \leq v_{(k)} \leq 1$. Similarly, the precoder $\mathbf{w}$ and $\widehat{\mathbf{g}}_{(k)}$ are related by an angle $0 \leq \phi_{(k)} \leq \frac{\pi}{2}$ according to

$$\left| \widehat{\mathbf{g}}_{(k)}^T \mathbf{w}^* \right|^2 = u_{(k)} = \cos^2\left(\phi_{(k)} \right) \tag{10}$$

where $0 \leq u_{(k)} \leq 1$. As illustrated in Fig. 2, $\mathbf{w}_{(k)}$ and $\mathbf{g}_{(k)}$ are related by an angle $\varphi_{(k)}$ according to $\phi_{(k)} - \theta_{(k)} \leq \varphi_{(k)} \leq \phi_{(k)} + \theta_{(k)}$ for $0 \leq \phi_{(k)} - \theta_{(k)}$ and $\phi_{(k)} + \theta_{(k)} \leq \frac{\pi}{2}$ [15]. Equivalently, since $|\mathbf{g}_{(k)}^T \mathbf{w}^*|^2 = \cos^2(\varphi_{(k)})$,

$$\cos^2\left(\phi_{(k)} + \theta_{(k)} \right) \leq \left| \mathbf{g}_{(k)}^T \mathbf{w}^* \right|^2 \leq \cos^2\left(\phi_{(k)} - \theta_{(k)} \right). \tag{11}$$

From (11)

$$\left| \mathbf{g}_{(k)}^T \mathbf{w}^* \right|^2 \geq \begin{cases} \cos^2\left(\phi_{(k)} + \theta_{(k)} \right) & \text{for } 0 \leq \phi_{(k)} < \frac{\pi}{2} - \theta_{(k)} \\ 0 & \text{for } \frac{\pi}{2} - \theta_{(k)} \leq \phi_{(k)} \leq \frac{\pi}{2} \end{cases} \tag{12}$$

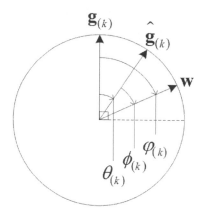

Fig. 2. Quantization model. The angle between $\widehat{\mathbf{g}}_{(k)}$ and $\mathbf{g}_{(k)}$ is $\theta_{(k)}$. The angle between $\mathbf{w}$ and $\widehat{\mathbf{g}}_{(k)}$ is $\phi_{(k)}$. The angle between $\mathbf{w}$ and $\mathbf{g}_{(k)}$ is $\varphi_{(k)}$.

and it follows from (10) that

$$\left| \mathbf{g}_{(k)}^T \mathbf{w}^* \right|^2 \geq \frac{\cos^2 \left(\phi_{(k)} + \theta_{(k)} \right)}{\cos^2 \left(\phi_{(k)} \right)} \left| \widehat{\mathbf{g}}_{(k)}^T \mathbf{w}^* \right|^2 \tag{13}$$

for $0 \leq \phi_{(k)} < \frac{\pi}{2} - \theta_{(k)}$. The average of (13) over $\phi_{(k)}$ gives

$$\mathbb{E}\left[\left| \mathbf{g}_{(k)}^T \mathbf{w}^* \right|^2 \middle| \widehat{\mathbf{g}}_{(k)} \right] \geq \underbrace{\frac{1}{\frac{\pi}{2}} \int_0^{\frac{\pi}{2}-\theta_{(k)}} \frac{\cos^2 \left(\phi_{(k)} + \theta_{(k)} \right)}{\cos^2 \left(\phi_{(k)} \right)} d\phi_{(k)}}_{=\eta_{(k)}} \left| \widehat{\mathbf{g}}_{(k)}^T \mathbf{w}^* \right|^2. \tag{14}$$

Therefore, from (8) and (14) $\mathbb{E}\left[\gamma_{(k)} \middle| \zeta_{(k)}, \widehat{\mathbf{g}}_{(k)} \right] \geq \frac{P}{N_0} \underbrace{\zeta_{(k)} \eta_{(k)}}_{=q[\mathbf{h}_{(k)}]} \left| \widehat{\mathbf{g}}_{(k)}^T \mathbf{w}^* \right|^2$, and it

follows that $\mathbb{E}\left[\gamma_{(k)} \middle| \widehat{\mathbf{h}}_{(k)} \right] \geq \frac{P}{N_0} \left| \widehat{\mathbf{h}}_{(k)}^T \mathbf{w}^* \right|^2 = \frac{P}{N_0} q\left[\mathbf{h}_{(k)} \right] \left| \widehat{\mathbf{g}}_{(k)}^T \mathbf{w}^* \right|^2$.

From Theorem 1, when the BS uses the CSIT of the K MBS users $\mathcal{H}_{(K)}$ to select the precoder $\mathbf{w}$, the expected RxSNR of the kth user satisfies

$$\mathbb{E}\left[\gamma_{(k)} \middle| \mathcal{H}_{(K)} \right] \geq \frac{P}{N_0} \left| \widehat{\mathbf{h}}_{(k)}^T \mathbf{w}^* \right|^2. \tag{15}$$

3.2   Optimization Solution for MBS Precoder Design

To obtain the optimization solution for MBS precoder design, we apply the lower bound for the expected RxSNR of MBS users given CSIT as per (15) to recast the optimization (5) as

$$\mathbf{w}^\star = \frac{P}{N_0} \arg\max_{\mathbf{w} \in \Theta^N} \min_{k=1,\ldots,K} \left| \widehat{\mathbf{h}}_{(k)}^T \mathbf{w}^\star \right|^2. \tag{16}$$

Rewriting (16) in standard form

$$\mathbf{w}^\star = \min_{\substack{\mathbf{w} \in \Theta^N \\ \gamma \in \mathbb{R}_+}} -\gamma$$
$$\text{s.t.} \quad \gamma - \frac{P}{N_0} \left| \widehat{\mathbf{h}}_{(k)}^{T} \mathbf{w}^\star \right|^2 \leq 0, k \in [1, K], \tag{17}$$

we see that this problem is non-convex because the constraints are non-convex. More importantly, this problem is NP-hard as shown in [3, Appendix I], [9, Section 2]. In order to work around the issue of NP-hardness, we employ the SDR-randomization approach [3, 4, 5, 6, 7, 9] to generate an effective precoder solution.

We apply SDR to (17) as follows. Let $\widehat{\mathbf{H}}_{(k)} = \widehat{\mathbf{h}}_{(k)}^* \widehat{\mathbf{h}}_{(k)}^T \in \mathbb{C}^{N \times N}$, and let $\mathbf{W} = \mathbf{w}^* \mathbf{w}^T \in \mathbb{C}^{N \times N}$ which is rank one and positive semidefinite. Thus, (17) can be rewritten as

$$\mathbf{W}^\star = \min_{\substack{\mathbf{W} \in \mathbb{C}^{N \times N} \\ \gamma \in \mathbb{R}_+}} -\gamma$$
$$\text{s.t.} \quad \gamma - \frac{P}{N_0} \text{Tr}\left(\mathbf{W}\widehat{\mathbf{H}}_{(k)}\right) \leq 0, k \in [1, K] \tag{18}$$
$$\text{Tr}(\mathbf{W}) = 1, \mathbf{W} \succeq 0$$
$$\text{rank}(\mathbf{W}) = 1.$$

In this equivalent formulation, the rank-one constraint is non-convex but all other constraints are affine. By SDR, we drop the rank-one constraint and obtain the semidefinite problem (SDP)

$$\widetilde{\mathbf{W}}^\star = \min_{\substack{\mathbf{W} \in \mathbb{C}^{N \times N} \\ t \in \mathbb{R}_+}} -\gamma$$
$$\text{s.t.} \quad \gamma - \frac{P}{N_0} \text{Tr}\left(\mathbf{W}\widehat{\mathbf{H}}_{(k)}\right) \leq 0, k \in [1, K] \tag{19}$$
$$\text{Tr}(\mathbf{W}) = 1$$
$$\mathbf{W} \succeq 0,$$

which can be solved in polynomial time using interior point methods [16, Section 11.6].

Note that if $\text{rank}(\widetilde{\mathbf{W}}^\star) = 1$, then it can be decomposed as $\widetilde{\mathbf{W}}^\star = (\mathbf{w}^\star)^* (\mathbf{w}^\star)^T$ and we obtain as $\mathbf{w}^\star$ the principle eigenvector of $\widetilde{\mathbf{W}}^\star$. Conversely, if $\text{rank}(\widetilde{\mathbf{W}}^\star) \neq 1$, then we obtain an effective solution $\mathbf{w}^\star$ from $\widetilde{\mathbf{W}}^\star$ via the randomization process as follows. Let $\mathbf{Q}\boldsymbol{\Lambda}\mathbf{Q}^\dagger$ denote the eigen-decomposition of $\widetilde{\mathbf{W}}^\star$. By randomization, we generate a set of random candidate precoders in the eigenspaces of $\widetilde{\mathbf{W}}^\star$ and select the *best* solution. Specifically, let $\{\widehat{\mathbf{w}}_{(r)}\}_{r=1}^R$ denote a set of R random unit vectors given by

$$\widehat{\mathbf{w}}_{(r)} = \frac{\mathbf{Q}\boldsymbol{\Lambda}^{\frac{1}{2}}\mathbf{v}_{(r)}}{\left| \mathbf{Q}\boldsymbol{\Lambda}^{\frac{1}{2}}\mathbf{v}_{(r)} \right|}, \quad r = 1, \ldots, R, \tag{20}$$

where $\mathbf{v}_{(r)} \sim \mathcal{CN}(0, \mathbf{I}_N)$. We select as $\mathbf{w}^\star$ the candidate vector that maximizes the minimum expected RxSNR among the MBS users according to

$$\mathbf{w}^\star = \frac{P}{N_0} \arg \max_{\mathbf{w} \in \{\widehat{\mathbf{w}}_{(r)}\}_{r=1}^R} \min_{k=1,\ldots,K} \left| \widehat{\mathbf{h}}_{(k)}^T \mathbf{w}^* \right|^2. \tag{21}$$

Remark 1. We remark that solving the SDP and the randomization process are both of polynomial complexity so the overall SDR-randomization approach is of polynomial complexity.

4   Performance Analysis

In this section, we derive a closed-form lower bound on the average minimum RxSNR among the MBS users based on the proposed transmit precoding design. From the performance lower bound, we study the order of growth of the average minimum RxSNR w.r.t. the number of MBS users K, the number of bits for limited feedback b, and the number of transmit antennas N.

Note that the performance of transmit precoding is lower bounded if the MBS users' channel vectors are orthogonal, and as per [17, Section III-B] a *well-designed* precoder can capture at least a fraction of $\frac{1}{K}$ of each user's channel gain. Thus, using the precoder solution $\mathbf{w}^\star$ obtained as per (16), the minimum expected RxSNR given CSIT among the MBS users is

$$\gamma^\star = \frac{P}{N_0} \min_{k=1,\ldots,K} \left| \widehat{\mathbf{h}}_{(k)}^T (\mathbf{w}^\star)^* \right|^2 \geq \frac{P}{N_0} \frac{1}{K} \min_{k=1,\ldots,K} \left| \widehat{\mathbf{h}}_{(k)} \right|^2.$$

From Theorem 1, $|\widehat{\mathbf{h}}_{(k)}|^2 = q[\mathbf{h}_{(k)}] = \eta_{(k)} \zeta_{(k)}$, so

$$\gamma^\star \geq \frac{P}{N_0} \frac{1}{K} \min_{k=1,\ldots,K} \eta_{(k)} \zeta_{(k)}, \tag{22}$$

where the channel gain $\zeta_{(k)}$ is χ^2 distributed with $2N$ degrees-of-freedom (DOF), and $\eta_{(k)}$ is given in (7).

To analyze the average minimum RxSNR, we first have the following lemmas.

Lemma 1 (Mean of ordered statistics [18, Section 4.6]). *Given K i.i.d. random variables $\{x_{(k)}\}_{k=1}^K$ with cumulative distribution function (CDF) $F_x(x)$, the mean of $\min_{k=1,\ldots,K} x_{(k)}$ grows like*

$$\mu_{x,1:K} = \mathbb{E}\left[\min_{k=1,\ldots,K} x_{(k)}\right] = \mathcal{O}\left(F_x^{-1}\left(\frac{1}{K+1}\right)\right), \tag{23}$$

where $F_x^{-1}(\cdot)$ is the inverse CDF of $\{x_{(k)}\}_{k=1}^K$.

Lemma 2 (Inverse CDF of $\eta_{(k)}$ and $\zeta_{(k)}$). *With N transmit antennas and b bits for limited feedback, the inverse CDF of $\eta_{(k)}$ has the following order of growth*

$$F_\eta^{-1}\left(\frac{1}{K+1}\right) = \mathcal{O}\left(\exp\left(-3\left(1-\left(\frac{1}{K+1}\right)^{\frac{1}{2^b}}\right)^{\frac{1}{2N-1}}\right)\right), \quad (24)$$

and the inverse CDF of $\zeta_{(k)}$ has the following order of growth

$$F_\zeta^{-1}\left(\frac{1}{K+1}\right) = \mathcal{O}\left(\frac{N!}{K+1}\right)^{\frac{1}{N}}. \quad (25)$$

Proof. Please refer to Appendix I.

Based on Lemma 1 and Lemma 2, we summarize in Theorem 2 the lower bound of the average minimum RxSNR among the MBS users.

Theorem 2 (Lower bound on the average RxSNR). *With K MBS users, N transmit antennas and b bits for limited feedback, the closed-form lower bound of the average minimum RxSNR among the MBS users is given by*

$$\begin{aligned}
\mathbb{E}\left[\gamma^\star\right] &\geq \frac{P}{N_0}\frac{1}{K}\mathbb{E}\left[\min_{k=1,\ldots,K}\eta_{(k)}\zeta_{(k)}\right] \geq \frac{P}{N_0}\frac{1}{K}F_\eta^{-1}\left(\frac{1}{K+1}\right)F_\zeta^{-1}\left(\frac{1}{K+1}\right) \\
&= \Omega\left(\frac{P}{N_0}\left(\frac{1}{K}\right)^{1+\frac{1}{N}}(N!)^{\frac{1}{N}}\exp\left(-3\left(1-\left(\frac{1}{K}\right)^{\frac{1}{2^b}}\right)^{\frac{1}{2N-1}}\right)\right).
\end{aligned} \quad (26)$$

Proof. The proof is omitted due to the limited pages.

Remark 2 (Order or growth w.r.t. the number of MBS users, K). From (26), it can be shown that, for fixed b and N, the order of growth of $\mathbb{E}\left[\gamma^\star\right]$ w.r.t. K is $\Omega((\frac{1}{K})^{1+\frac{1}{N}})$. The order of growth relationship is verified by simulation in Fig. 4(a).

Remark 3 (Order or growth w.r.t. the number of feedback bits, b). From (26), it can be shown that, for fixed K and N, the order of growth of $\mathbb{E}\left[\gamma^\star\right]$ w.r.t. b is $\Omega(\exp(-3(1-(\frac{1}{K})^{\frac{1}{2^b}})^{\frac{1}{2N-1}}))$. The order of growth relationship is verified by simulation in Fig. 4(b).

5 Threshold-Based Feedback Reduction Scheme

In the preceding discussion, we formulate the precoder design problem involving feedback of all K MBS users in the system. Intuitively, since the system performance – the minimum RxSNR – is limited by MBS users with the worst channels, some MBS users with strong channels may not need to be considered in the precoder design problem without affecting the system performance. This motivates a threshold-based feedback reduction scheme where the users, based on their channel conditions, selectively feedback to the BS to be considered in the precoder design. As a consequence, we can reduce the system feedback cost. In the threshold-based feedback reduction scheme, the BS broadcasts a common system threshold. Each MBS user locally compares its channel gain with the system threshold and does not attempt to feedback when the channel gain exceeds the system threshold. Based on the CSIT collected from the MBS users that attempt to feedback, the BS solves Problem 1 w.r.t. these users only.

We are interested to quantify the potential performance loss and the feedback cost savings by virtue of the threshold-based feedback reduction scheme. We first have the following lemmas.

Lemma 3 (Distribution of precoder). *Suppose $L \leq K$ MBS users attempt to feedback to the BS and let the CSIT be denoted by $\mathcal{H}_{(L)} = \left\{ \widehat{\boldsymbol{h}}_{(1)}, \ldots, \widehat{\boldsymbol{h}}_{(L)} \right\}$. The precoder solution $\boldsymbol{w}^\star$ w.r.t. these L users is uniformly distributed on Θ^N with randomness induced by CSIT $\mathcal{H}_{(L)}$.*

Proof. The proof is omitted due to the limited pages.

Lemma 4 (Conditional distribution of RxSNR). *Suppose the kth MBS user does not attempt to feedback to the BS and the BS designs the precoder considering all MBS users that feedback. For the kth user, the conditional CDF of the RxSNR $\gamma_{(k)}$, conditioned on channel gain $\zeta_{(k)}$, is given by*

$$Pr\left(\gamma_{(k)} \leq \gamma \,\middle|\, \zeta_{(k)}\right) = 1 - \left(1 - \frac{\gamma}{\frac{P}{N_0}\zeta_{(k)}}\right)^{N-1} \qquad (27)$$

for $\gamma \in [0, \frac{P}{N_0}\zeta_{(k)}]$, where the randomness of $\gamma_{(k)}$ is induced by the CSIT of the users that feedback.

Proof. The proof is omitted due to the limited pages.

Based on Lemma 3 and Lemma 4, we can derive the average performance loss and the average feedback cost savings using the threshold-based feedback reduction scheme. Specifically, with a system threshold ζ_0, the kth MBS user does not attempt to feedback if its channel gain $\zeta_{(k)} > \zeta_0$. The decision of the kth user of not attempting to feedback may or may not cost performance loss. Intuitively, the motivation of the threshold-based scheme is that if a user's instantaneous channel is very strong, it is very likely that this user will not be the "bottleneck user" in the MBS system and hence, there should be no loss of performance even if this user does not feedback. Hence, if the actual instantaneous RxSNR of the kth user $\gamma_{(k)}$ (which depends on the precoder adopted by the BS after considering all the other MBS users that feedback) is larger than is larger than $\frac{P}{N_0}\widehat{\zeta}$ (the best possible RxSNR after precoding), then the decision of not feeding back will not cost any performance loss in the MBS group because the kth user will not be the bottleneck. Otherwise, the decision will cost some performance penalty as the user(s) not feeding back becomes the bottleneck user(s). We define this event as the *miss event*. Theorem 3 summarizes the main results on the probability of miss and the feedback cost.

Theorem 3 (Probability of miss vs. feedback cost). *The system performance loss (quantified by the probability of miss) is given by*

$$Pr\{miss\} \equiv Pr\left(\gamma_{(k)} \leq \frac{P}{N_0}\hat{\zeta}\,\Big|\,\zeta_{(k)} > \zeta_0\right) = 1 - \exp\left(-\zeta_0\right). \tag{28}$$

On the other hand, the probability of feedback is given by

$$Pr\left(\zeta_{(k)} > \zeta_0\right) = 1 - F_\zeta\left(\zeta_0\right), \tag{29}$$

where $F_\zeta\left(\zeta\right)$ is the CDF of the channel gain (cf. (32)). Hence, the average feedback cost (i.e. the average number of users that feedback) is

$$K\,Pr\left(\zeta_{(k)} > \zeta_0\right) = K\left(1 - F_\zeta\left(\zeta_0\right)\right). \tag{30}$$

Proof. The proof is omitted due to the limited pages.

Remark 4. By setting the system threshold to be $\zeta_0 = \mathcal{O}(\ln K)$, we have the average feedback cost $\mathcal{O}((\ln K)^{N-1})$ and the average probability of miss given by $\mathcal{O}(1/K \exp(-\ln(K)/K))$. As a result, to maintain asymptotic optimal performance, the average feedback cost per user is asymptotically negligible.

6   Simulation Results

In this section, we evaluate the performance of the proposed transmit precoding design with numerical results. Specifically, we consider 1) the average minimum RxSNR among MBS users applying the proposed transmit precoding design involving feedback from all MBS users, and 2) the performance of the feedback reduction scheme in terms of the feedback overhead versus the probability of miss.

For the purpose of illustration, in our simulations we assume that the TxSNR is 20dB, up to $K = 30$ MBS users, $b = 10$ or $b = 18$ feedback bits, and up to $N = 9$ transmit antennas. Moreover, we assume that a random codebook [19] is adopted for limited feedback. In order to obtain the precoder solution, during the randomization process at least $R = 100$ candidate vectors are tested.

6.1   Performance Involving Feedback from All MBS Users

In Fig. 3, we compare the average minimum RxSNR with the proposed transmit precoding design, with (baseline 1) transmit precoding with perfect CSIT, and with (baseline 2) no precoding. It can be seen that with the proposed transmit precoding design there is substantial RxSNR gain over no precoding. In particular, there is an RxSNR gain in excess of 5dB given $K = 20$ MBS users, $b = 10$

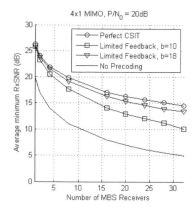

Fig. 3. Average minimum RxSNR using the proposed multicast transmit precoding algorithm. The BS transmits with $N = 4$ antennas and the TxSNR is 20dB.

bits for limited feedback, and $N = 4$ transmit antennas. On the other hand, it can be see that the performance with the proposed transmit precoding design improves with the number of feedback bits and approaches the performance with transmit precoding with perfect CSIT.

In Fig. 4(a) and Fig. 4(b), we illustrate the order of growth of the average minimum RxSNR w.r.t. the number of MBS users and feedback bits, respectively. As per Theorem 2, the average minimum RxSNR scales on the order of $\Omega((\frac{1}{K})^{1+\frac{1}{N}})$ w.r.t. to the number of users as shown in Fig. 4(a) and scales on the order of $\Omega(\exp(-3(1 - (\frac{1}{K})^{\frac{1}{2^b}})^{\frac{1}{2N-1}}))$ w.r.t. to the number of feedback bits as shown in Fig. 4(b).

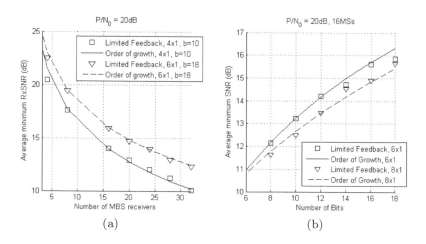

| (a) | (b) |

Fig. 4. Order of growth of average minimum RxSNR w.r.t. (a) the number of MBS users K and (b) the number of feedback bits b.

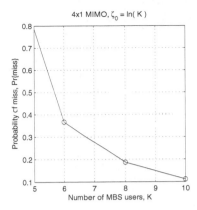

Fig. 5. Probability of miss using the threshold based feedback reduction scheme. The BS transmits with $N = 4$ antennas and the system threshold is $\zeta_0 = \ln(k)$.

6.2   Performance with Feedback Reduction Scheme

In Fig. 5, we show the probability of miss using the threshold based feedback reduction scheme. For the purpose of illustration, we let the BS transmit with $N = 4$ antennas and set the system threshold to be $\zeta_0 = \ln(K)$. As expected, as the number of MBS users K increases, the best possible RxSNR after precoding decreases, and so users with strong instantaneous channels do not have to feedback without affecting system performance.

7   Conclusions

In this paper we consider a MIMO MBS system and propose a transmit precoding design with limited feedback. Specifically, given CSIT obtained via limited feedback, we optimize the precoding policy for enhancing the average minimum RxSNR among MBS users, while suitably accounting for the CSIT error. In order to analyze system performance, we derived a closed-form lower bound and the order of growth expressions for the average minimum RxSNR among the MBS users, and these results agree closely with numerical simulation results. Finally, we further deduce a threshold based feedback reduction scheme, which allows us to effectively reduce system feedback overhead with negligible performance loss.

References

1. IEEE 802.16m system requirements. IEEE 802.16m-07/002r5,
   http://www.ieee802.org/16/tgm/
2. IEEE Standard for Local and Metropolitan Area Networks, Part 16: Air Interface for Fixed and Mobile Broadband Wireless Access Systems, IEEE Std. 802.16e-2005 (2005)

3. Sidiropoulos, N.D., Davidson, T.N., Luo, Z.-Q.: Transmit beamforming for physical-layer multicasting. IEEE Trans. Signal Process. 54, 2239–2251 (2006)
4. Karipidis, E., Sidiropoulos, N.D., Luo, Z.-Q.: Far-field multicast beamforming for uniform linear antenna arrays. IEEE Trans. Signal Process. 55, 4916–4927 (2007)
5. Karipidis, E., Sidiropoulos, N.D., Luo, Z.-Q.: Quality of service and max-min fair transmit beamforming to multiple cochannel multicast groups. IEEE Trans. Signal Process. 56, 1268–1279 (2008)
6. Phany, K.T., Vorobyov, S.A., Sidiropoulos, N.D., Tellambura, C.: Spectrum sharing in wireless networks: A qos-aware secondary multicast approach with worst user performance optimization. In: Proc. IEEE SAM 2008, July 2008, pp. 23–27 (2008)
7. Wajid, I., Gershman, A.B., Vowbyov, S.A., Karanouh, Y.A.: Robust multi-antenna broadcasting with imperfect channel state information. In: Proc. IEEE CAMPSAP 2007, December 2007, pp. 213–216 (2007)
8. Narula, A., Lopez, M.J., Trott, M.D., Wornell, G.W.: Efficient use of side information in multiple-antenna data transmission over fading channels. IEEE J. Sel. Areas Commun. 16, 1423–1436 (1998)
9. Luo, Z.-Q., Sidiropoulous, N.D., Tseng, P., Zhang, S.: Approximation bounds for quadratic optimization with homogeneous quadratic constraints. SIAM J. Optim. 18, 1–28 (2007)
10. IEEE 802.16m evaluation methodology document. IEEE 802.16m-08/004r2, http://www.ieee802.org/16/tgm/
11. Thomas, T.A., Baum, K.L., Sartori, P.: Obtaining channel knowledge for closed-loop multi-stream broadband MIMO-OFDM communications using direct channel feedback. In: Proc. IEEE GLOBECOM 2005, December 2005, pp. 3907–3911 (2005)
12. Lau, V., Liu, Y., Chen, T.-A.: On the design of mimo block-fading channels with feedback-link capacity constraint. IEEE Trans. Commun. 52, 62–70 (2004)
13. Love, D.J., Heath, J.R.W., Strohmer, T.: Grassmannian beamforming for multiple-input multiple-output wireless systems. IEEE Trans. Inf. Theory 49, 2735–2747 (2003)
14. Huang, K., Heath, R.W., Andrews, J.G.: Space division multiple access with a sum feedback rate constraint. IEEE Trans. Signal Process. 55, 3879–3891 (2007)
15. Yoo, T., Jindal, N., Goldsmith, A.: Multi-antenna downlink channels with limited feedback and user selection. IEEE J. Sel. Areas Commun. 25, 1478–1491 (2007)
16. Boyd, S., Vandenberghe, L.: Convex Optimization. Cambridge University Press, Cambridge (2004)
17. Jindal, N., Luo, Z.-Q.: Capacity limits of multiple antenna multicast. In: Proc. IEEE ISIT 2006, July 2006, pp. 1841–(1845)
18. David, H.A.: Order Statistics, 2nd edn. Wiley, New York (1981)
19. Au-Yeung, C.K., Love, D.J.: On the performance of random vector quantization limited feedback beamforming in a MISO system. IEEE Trans. Wireless Commun. 6, 458–462 (2007)
20. Mukkavilli, K.K., Sabharwal, A., Erkip, E., Aazhang, B.: On beamforming with finite rate feedback in multiple-antenna systems. IEEE Trans. Inf. Theory 49, 2562–2579 (2003)

Appendix I: Proof of Lemma 2

Inverse CDF of $\eta_{(k)}$. As per (7), it can be shown that $\eta_{(k)}$ decreases with increasing $\theta_{(k)}$, which is the angle between the channel direction vector $\mathbf{g}_{(k)}$ and the quantized channel direction vector $\widehat{\mathbf{g}}_{(k)}$ obtained via limited feedback. We are interested in obtaining the system performance lower bound, and we assume an upper bound model for $\theta_{(k)}$ where $\dot{\mathbf{g}}_{(k)}$ is obtained using a random codebook [19]. From [19, (11)], the CDF of $\cos^2(\theta_{(k)}) = v_{(k)}$ is given by

$$F_v(v) = \left(1 - (1-v)^{N-1}\right)^{2^b}, \quad v \in [0,1], \tag{31}$$

and the CDF of $\theta_{(k)}$ is given by $F_\theta(\theta) = \Pr\!\left(v \geq \cos^2(\theta)\right) = 1 - \left(1 - \sin^{2(N-1)}(\theta)\right)^{2^b}$, $\theta \in \left[0, \frac{\pi}{2}\right]$. It can be shown that $\eta_{(k)} \approx e^{-3\theta_{(k)}}$, so the CDF of $\eta_{(k)}$ is given by $F_\eta(\eta) = \Pr\!\left(\theta \geq -\frac{\ln(\eta)}{3}\right) = \left(1 - \sin^{2(N-1)}\left(-\frac{\ln(\eta)}{3}\right)\right)^{2^b}$, $\eta \in [0,1)$, and the inverse CDF of $\eta_{(k)}$ is given by $F_\eta^{-1}(q) = \exp\left(-3\arcsin\left(1 - q^{\frac{1}{2^b}}\right)^{\frac{1}{2N-1}}\right)$, $q = \frac{1}{K+1}$. For sufficiently large K, $1 - q^{\frac{1}{2^b}}$ approaches 0. Recall that the Maclaurin series of $\arcsin(x) \approx x$ for small x, and so

$$F_\eta^{-1}(q) = \mathcal{O}\left(\exp\left(-3\left(1 - q^{\frac{1}{2^b}}\right)^{\frac{1}{2N-1}}\right)\right), \quad \text{where } q = \frac{1}{K+1}.$$

Inverse CDF of $\zeta_{(k)}$. The channel gain $\zeta_{(k)}$ is χ^2 distributed with $2N$ DOF, so its CDF is given by

$$F_\zeta(\zeta) = 1 - e^{-\zeta} \sum_{n=0}^{N-1} \frac{\zeta^n}{n!}, \quad \zeta \in [0,\infty). \tag{32}$$

Since $e^\zeta = \sum_{n=0}^{\infty} \frac{\zeta^n}{n!}$, (32) can be rewritten as

$$F_\zeta(\zeta) = 1 - e^{-\zeta}\left(e^\zeta - \sum_{n=N}^{\infty} \frac{\zeta^n}{n!}\right) = e^{-\zeta}\sum_{n=N}^{\infty}\frac{\zeta^n}{n!} \tag{33}$$

For small ζ, we can neglect the higher order terms in (33) to get $F_\zeta(\zeta) = \mathcal{O}\left(\frac{\zeta^N}{N!}\right)$ (cf. [20, (50)]). Let $F_\zeta(\zeta) = \frac{1}{K+1}$ and for sufficiently large K, $F_\zeta^{-1}\left(\frac{1}{K+1}\right) = \mathcal{O}\left(\left(\frac{N!}{K+1}\right)^{\frac{1}{N}}\right)$.

Quantized Beamforming Technique for LTE-Advanced Uplink

Young Ju Kim* and Xun Li

Chungbuk National University
Cheongju, Chungbuk, Republic of Korea
{yjkim,xunli}@cbnu.ac.kr

Abstract. Long term evolution (LTE) standard for uplink transmission is based on single carrier frequency division multiple access (SC-FDMA) to maintain low peak-to-average power ratio (PAPR), which is very valuable for the practical handset design. Recently the usage of codebook-based precoding is thoroughly discussed for the LTE-Advanced (LTE-A) uplink. Among the various precoding schemes, equal gain transmission (EGT) is proposed in this paper because it does not increase any PAPR. Especially, considering nonlinear transmit power amplifier model in uplink, EGT is superior to any other precoding schemes. Theoretical analysis of precoding schemes' PAPR is presented under quasistatic flat fading channel, and link-level bit error rate (BER) is simulated to corroborate the anticipated results.

Keywords: SC-FDMA, LTE-A, uplink, MIMO.

1 Introduction

3rd generation partnership project (3GPP) release 8 standardization, which is called LTE, adopts quite different modulation and multiple access techniques from 3GPP's previous versions such as wideband code division multiple access (WCDMA) and high speed packet access (HSPA) [1][2][3]. Orthogonal frequency division multiple access (OFDMA) and SC-FDMA are employed as downlink and uplink multiple access techniques respectively [4]. Also the notable thing is the fact that SC-FDMA has lower PAPR than OFDMA, which make a small and low cost handset design possible. Meanwhile, the 1st workshop of LTE-A held in Shenzhen, April 2008, proposed advanced key techniques for higher average throughput, cell-edge throughput, and spectrum efficiency, compared to LTE. Then 3GPP approved LTE-A study from June 2008 [5]-[11]. One of the key techniques for LTE-A is applying multi-input multi-output (MIMO) technique for uplink which is a promising technique with many benefits [12][14][15].

When user equipment (UE) moves at a low speed less than 60 km/hr, codebook-based closed-loop MIMO can enhance uplink performances. Conventionally,

---

* "This work was supported by the grant of the Korean Ministry of Education, Science and Technology" (The Regional Core Research Program/Chungbuk BIT Research-Oriented University Consortium).

X. Jun Hei and L. Cheung (Eds.): AccessNets 2009, LNICST 37, pp. 264–275, 2010.

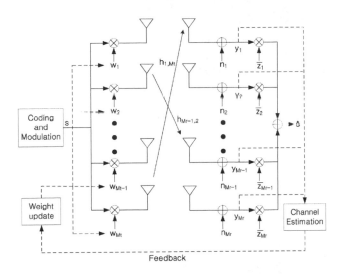

Fig. 1. Block diagram of precoding and combining method in MIMO systems

various codebook design employ maximum ratio transmission (MRT) technique because it shows the optimum received signal-to-noise ratio (SNR) [16]. But in terms of uplink transmission, it can deteriorate PAPR. So in this paper quantized equal gain transmission (EGT) is newly considered for LTE-A uplink because of its perfect PAPR property [17]. Moreover, non-linear transmit power amplifier model is also considered to verify the effect of PAPR in the link-level BER simulations. It can be expected that because MRT-based codebook make the transmit signal level fluctuate, EGT-based codebook outperforms MRT codebook in nonlinear power amplifier channel model.

This paper is organized as follows: Section 2 makes a brief overview of codebook-based precoding scheme. Section 3 describes the precoding method for SC-FDMA system. Section 4 investigates how the PAPR can be obtained in SC-FDMA in quasistatic flat fading channel. In Section 5, we exhibit BER simulation results considering nonlinear transmit amplifier model. Finally, our conclusions are provided in Section 6.

2   Overview of Codebook-Based Precoding

This paper treats closed-loop precoding showing better performance than open-loop precoding in pedestrian channel environment. Closed-loop schemes include explicit and implicit channel state information (CSI) feedback. The explicit CSI feedback is that the quantized channel information is directly delivered to the transmitter by receiver, while implicit one is that the receiver determines and delivers the proper index among the weighting vectors of the codebook which is known by both transmitter and receiver. In WiMAX, multi-rank MRT-based codebooks are proposed when the numbers of transmit antennas are 2,

3 and 4 [18] [19]. LTE release 8 also has MRT-based codebooks for downlink. And codebooks were proposed by some companies for LTE-A uplink [7]. In [17], EGT is also precisely studied by David Love and the generation of EGT-based codebook is also detailed in six steps.

Fig. 1 shows how CSI feedback is performed in precoded MIMO systems. M_t and M_r is the number of transmit antennas and receive antennas, respectively. w is precoding vector, $l(1 \leq l \leq M_t)$ is transmit antenna index, while $k(1 \leq k \leq M_r)$ is receive antenna index. The received signal y_k could be expressed as the following [16] [17]:

$$y_k = \left(\sum_{l=1}^{M_t} h_{k,l} w_l \right) s + n_k, \qquad (1)$$

where $h_{k,l}$ is memoryless fading channel and n_k is AWGN noise at kth receive antenna. The data received by the kth receive antenna, y_k, is multiplied by $\overline{z_k}$. The weighted output of each of the M_r receive antennas is then combined. This formulation allows the equivalent system to be written in matrix form as the following [17]:

$$\hat{s} = \left(z^H H w \right) s + z^H n, \qquad (2)$$

where $\mathbf{w} = [w_1, w_2, \cdots, w_{M_t}]^T$, $\mathbf{z} = [z_1, z_2, \cdots, z_{M_r}]^T$, $\mathbf{n} = [n_1, n_2, \cdots, n_{M_r}]^T$ and $\mathbf{H}$ denotes the $M_r \times M_t$ matrix having coordinate (k, l), which is equal to $h_{k,l}$. Furthermore, $[\cdot]^T$ and $[\cdot]^H$ represent transposition and conjugate transposition, respectively. For the sake of achieving optimum performances, $\mathbf{w}$ and $\mathbf{z}$ should be chosen as a function of the channel estimate to maximize the receive Signal to Noise Ratio (SNR) [16],[20].

The receiver can estimate and send back CSI to the transmitter. But due to a limited feedback channel capacity, it is impossible to send back high precision CSI to the transmitter in most systems. Only quantized CSI or well designed codebook's index within L bits can be sent back. In multiple-input single-output (MISO) system, which can be more easily understood than MIMO, the optimal precoding vector with MRT scheme w_{MRT} is given by [16]:

$$w_{MRT} = \sqrt{M_t} \frac{h^H}{\|h\|_F^2}, \qquad (3)$$

where $h = [h_1, h_2, \cdots, h_{M_t}]$ and $\|\cdot\|_F^2$ represents the Frobenius norm. In case of EGT scheme, the optimal precoding vector w_{EGT} is given by [17]:

$$w_{EGT} = \frac{1}{\sqrt{M_t}} e^{j\theta}, \qquad (4)$$

where

$$\theta \in \arg \max_{\vartheta \in [0, 2\pi)} \left\| H e^{j\vartheta} \right\|. \qquad (5)$$

Texas instruments proposed a Householder-based codebook with potential complexity reduction in [13], whose codebook for Rank 1 transmission with 3 bits feedback is generated by following

$$V_{21}(\theta, \varphi) = \begin{bmatrix} \cos(\theta) \\ \sin(\theta)\exp(j\varphi) \end{bmatrix} \tag{6}$$

where $\theta = \tan^{-1}\{1/3, 3, 3/4, 3/4, 3/4, 4/3, 4/3, 4/3,\}$, and $\varphi = \{0, 0, 0, \pi/3, 2\pi/3, \pi, 4\pi/3, 5\pi/3\}$.

The upper bound of system performance is achievable if $z = Hw/\|Hw\|_2$. In codebook based precoding system with codebook size 2^L, the codebook index k could be determined by following equation

$$k = \arg\max_{1 \leq k \leq 2^L} |Hw(k)|_1 \tag{7}$$

The codebook search algorithm and performance comparison between MRT and EGT with codebook is studied by the authors in [21].

3   Precoding Methods for SC-FDMA Uplink

The basic idea of SC-FDMA could be regarded as discrete fourier transform (DFT)-spread OFDMA, where time domain data symbols are transformed to frequency domain by M-point DFT operation and subcarrier mapping has to be done before going through N-point OFDM modulator, where N is much larger than M. When $Q = N/M$, Q denotes band spreading factor. Users of SC-FDMA system occupy different subcarriers in frequency domain. Thus the overall transmit signal performs like a single carrier signal, PAPR is inherently low at each user equipment compare to the case of OFDMA. Let $\{x_m : m = 0, 1, \cdots, M-1\}$ be data symbols to be modulated. Then, $\{X_k : k = 0, 1, \cdots, M-1\}$ are frequency domain DFT processed samples and $\{y_n : n = 0, 1, \cdots, M-1\}$ represents the OFDM modulated time domain samples. They could be expressed as

$$X_k = \sum_{m=0}^{M-1} x_m e^{-j2\pi\frac{m}{M}k} \tag{8}$$

$$y_n = \frac{1}{N} \sum_{l=1}^{N-1} Y_l e^{j2\pi\frac{n}{N}l}, \tag{9}$$

where $\{Y_l : l = 0, 1, \cdots, N-1\}$ is the frequency domain samples after subcarrier mapping. Interleaved FDMA (IFDMA) and localized FDMA (LFDMA) subcarrier mapping schemes are under consideration as the uplink communications in this paper, which were illustrated in [22]. In IFDMA, DFT transformed signals are allocated over the entire bandwidth with equidistance between occupied subcarriers, whereas consecutive subcarriers are occupied by the DFT outputs in LFDMA. At each user equipment, zeros are occupied in unused subcarriers as the block diagram is shown in Fig. 3. For IFDMA,

$$Y_l = \begin{cases} \widehat{X}_{l/Q}, l = Q \cdot k (0 \leq k \leq M-1) \\ 0, otherwise \end{cases} \tag{10}$$

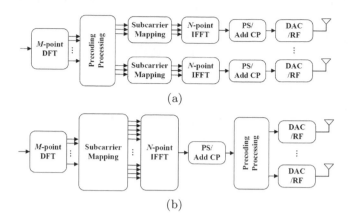

(a)

(b)

Fig. 2. Block diagram of a spatial multiplexing SC-FDMA MIMO system: (a) Precoding in frequency domain, (b) Precoding in time domain

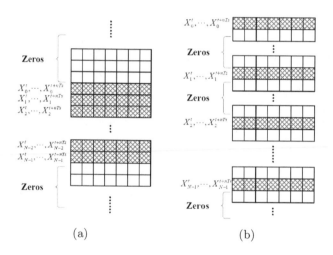

(a)   (b)

Fig. 3. Subcarrier mapping modes: (a) Localized FDMA, (b) Interleaved FDMA

and for LFDMA,

$$Y_l = \begin{cases} \widehat{X}_l, 0 \le l \le M - 1 \\ 0, M \le l \le N - 1 \end{cases},$$ (11)

We have two schemes to implement the precoding operation, precoding in frequency domain as shown in Fig. 2(a), and precoding in timedomain as shown in Fig. 2(b).

In case of precoding in frequency domain, $\{\widehat{X}_l : l = 0, 1, \cdots, M - 1\}$ in (11) are frequency domain precoded samples, and precoding vector $\{W_k : k = 0, 1, \cdots, M - 1\}$ should be determined according to the channel frequency response, $\widehat{X}_k = W_k \cdot X_k$. The transmit samples are OFDM modulated samples $\widehat{y}_n = y_n$.

If the precoding operation is implemented in time domain, $\widehat{X}_l = X_l$. The precoding vector $\{w_n : n = 0, 1, \cdots, N - 1\}$ should be determined according channel impulse response, and the transmit samples after precoding operation becomes $\widehat{y}_n = w_n \cdot y_n$. These two precoding implementations could obtain the same performance if we assume the CSI is perfectly known by the receiver, and ignore the equalization complexity difference between in frequency domain and in time domain. Finally, the transmit samples in time domain could be expressed as the following by substituting (10) and (11) to (9):

$$
\widehat{y}_{n,LFDMA} = \begin{cases} \dfrac{1}{N} \displaystyle\sum_{l=1}^{N-1} W_l X_l e^{j2\pi \frac{n}{N} l}, \text{FD} - \text{precoding} \\[2ex] w_n \dfrac{1}{N} \displaystyle\sum_{l=0}^{N-1} X_l e^{j2\pi \frac{n}{N} l}, \text{TD} - \text{precoding} \end{cases} \tag{12}
$$

$$
\widehat{y}_{n,IFDMA} = \begin{cases} \dfrac{1}{N} \displaystyle\sum_{l=1}^{N-1} W_{l/Q} X_{l/Q} e^{j2\pi \frac{n}{N} l}, \text{FD} - \text{precoding} \\[2ex] w_n \dfrac{1}{N} \displaystyle\sum_{l=0}^{N-1} X_{l/Q} e^{j2\pi \frac{n}{N} l}, \text{TD} - \text{precoding} \end{cases} \tag{13}
$$

4 PAPR of SC-FDMA in Quasistatic Flat Fading Channels

The PAPR of precoded SC-FDMA is analyzed under the quasistatic flat fading channel. Since quasistatic channel means the fading coefficient is constant over a OFDM symbole period, precoded weighting vector is also constant under the period. The PAPR of transmit signal could be expressed as

$$
PAPR = \frac{\max |\widehat{y}_n|^2}{E\left[|\widehat{y}_n|^2\right]} = \frac{\max \left|W_n \widehat{X}_n\right|^2}{E\left[\left|W_n \widehat{X}_n\right|^2\right]}. \tag{14}
$$

Considering flat fading channel, the precoding vector for each subcarrier is equivalent in one OFDM symbol due to the channel is frequency non-selective. Therefore, (13) could be rewritten as

$$
PAPR = \frac{\max \left|W \widehat{X}_n\right|^2}{E\left[\left|W \widehat{X}_n\right|^2\right]} = \frac{|W|^2 \cdot \max \left|\widehat{X}_n\right|^2}{|W|^2 \cdot E\left[\left|\widehat{X}_n\right|^2\right]}. \tag{15}
$$

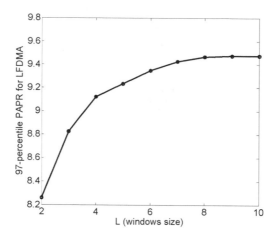

Fig. 4. CCDF curve of PAPR for the obervation window size L

From (14), we could know that it is meaningless to calculate the PAPR in one OFDM symbol. However, it is meaningful to calculate PAPR with several symbols. we set the observation windows size to be L, the new PAPR represents as the following:

$$PAPR = \frac{\max\limits_{0\leq l\leq L-1, 0\leq n\leq N-1} \left| W_l \widehat{X}_{Nl+n} \right|^2}{\frac{1}{L}\cdot\frac{1}{N} \sum\limits_{l=0}^{L-1} \sum\limits_{n=0}^{N-1} \left| W_l \widehat{X}_{Nl+n} \right|^2}. \tag{16}$$

Fig. 4 shows the complementary cululative distribution function (CCDF) result of PAPR with various windows size L using Monte Carlo simulation. The CCDF is the probability that PAPR is higher than a certain PAPR value $PAPR_o$. The souce samples are modulated by QPSK and mapped with LFDMA scheme. The codebook is WiMAX rank 1 codebok which designed for 2 transmit antenna and single user. The observation windows size is increase from 2 to 10. In this simulation, the $PAPR_o$ is determined by the probability is 97-percentage. Another simulation shows the $PAPR_o$ which is determined by the probability is 99.9-percentage in Table 1. Therefore, $L = 10$ would be appropriate to reflect the impact of precoding to PAPR of SC-FDMA system. With this consideration, Fig. 5 shows the CCDF comparison of IFDMA and LFDMA with different codebook, including EGT codebook, MRT codebook (WiMAX), LTE Release 8 downlink codebook, and TI codebook which was proposed by TI company for LTE-A. Raised cosine filter is used at the transmitter for pulse shaping, with over sampling factor is 8 and roll-off factor is 0.5. Fig. 5 shows that SC-FDMA has lowest PAPR with EGT codebook for precoding, and IFDMA mapping scheme outperforms LFDMA mapping scheme.

Table 1. 99.9-percentile PAPR for the observation window size L

L	99.9% PAPR for LFDMA (dB)
2	8.262
4	9.122
6	9.347
8	9.465
10	9.471

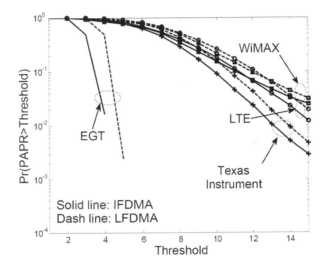

Fig. 5. CCDFs of IFDMA and LFDMA with Raised-cosine roll-off factor $\alpha = 0.5$

5   System Parameters and BER Simulation Results

For this section, we simulated the average probability of bit error with varous codebook. Jakes' model is used as wireless channel with 3km/h and 60km/h of UE's velocity. Perfect channel estimation and ideal synchronization at the receiver is considered, and there is no correlation between transmit antennas and receive antennas since enough antenna space is assumed. The system carrier frequency is 2.0 GHz, symbol rate is 7.68 million symbols/sec which is usually used in LTE-A. PMI related parameters are error-free precoding matrix indicator (PMI) with 1ms delay. We considered $M_r = M_t = 2$. We let the bandwidth expansion factor $Q = 4$, and $M = 512$ and $N = 2048$. Raised-cosine filter is used for pulse shaping with 8x oversampling. More details about simulation parameter are listed in Table 2.

Table 2. Simulation parameters for PAPR and BER

Bandwidth	5MHz
Carrier frequency	2GHz
Data rate	7.68Mbps
Channel for PAPR	Quasistatic Rayleigh fading
Channel for BER	Jakes' model
Tx antenna	2
Modulation	QPSK
Channel estimation	Ideal
DFT size (M)	16/512 (PAPR/BER)
IFFT size (N)	512/2048 (PAPR/BER)
Precoding codebook	EGT/WiMAX/LTE/TI
Oversampling factor	8
Pulse shaping	Raised cosine filter

To approximate the effect of nonlinear power amplifier in the transmitter, we adopt Rapp's model for amplitude conversion which could be represent as

$$g(A) = \frac{A}{(1 + A^{2p})^{1/(2p)}}. \tag{17}$$

Fig. 6 illustrate the relation between amplitude of the normalized input signal A and amplitude of output signal $g(A)$ when the nonlinear characteristic factor $p = 3$. The phase conversion of the power amplifier is neglected in this paper.

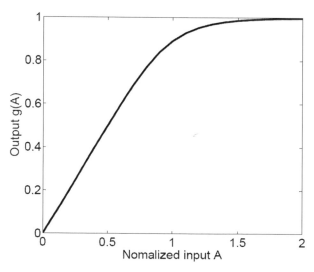

Fig. 6. Input-output relation curve of the Rapp's model when $p = 3$

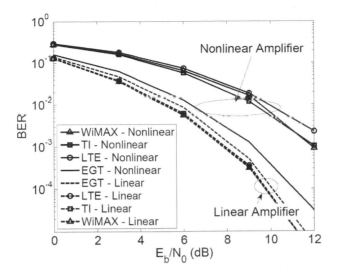

Fig. 7. BER performance of LFDMA with QPSK, velocity is 3km/h

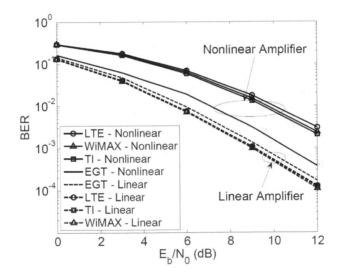

Fig. 8. BER performance of LFDMA with QPSK, velocity is 60km/h

Fig. 7 illustrates the BER performances of LFDMA with different precoding schemes. At the receiver, maximal ratio combining (MRC) scheme is used who provids upper bound receive diversity. Although, when the linear amplifier is considered at the transmitter, EGT scheme performs worse than other code-book almost 1dB. But when the nonlinear amplifier is under consideration, it outperforms other schemes by almost 3dB at a 10^{-3} BER, while other scheme's signal suffering nonlinear power distortion much more seriously. Fig. 8 shows the BER comparison of SC-FDMA system with UE's velocity is 60km/h. Due to feedbacked daley, all BER performances are degraded with high velocity of UEs. However, the performance based on EGT codebook still outperforms other scheme when nonlinear power amplifier is under consideration.

6   Conclusions

In this paper, we have investigated how the precoding schemes impact on the PAPR of SC-FDMA system. Conventional MRT-based methods and newly proposed EGT-based method were carefuly examined. We showed that precoding schemes could increase the PAPR for SC-FDMA signals but EGT does not cause any signal variations. In the BER simulations including non-linear transmit power amplifier model, EGT-based precoding scheme outperforms any other MRT-based ones. In order to maintain the low PAPR advantages of SC-FDMA compared to OFDMA, precoding schems should be cautiously designed, and EGT can be a good technique for LTE-A uplink employing MIMO SC-FDMA.

References

1. Toskala, A., Holma, H., Pajukoski, K., et al.: UTRAN long term evolution in 3GPP. In: Proc. International Symposium on Personal, Indoor and Mobile Radio Communications (PIMRC) 2006, Helsinki, Finland (September 2006)
2. 3rd Generation Partnership Project, http://www.3gpp.org
3. 3rd Generation Partnership Project, 3GPP TS 36.211 - Technical Specification Group Radio Access Network; Evolved Unversal Terrestrial Radio Access (E-UTRA); Physical Channels and Modulation (Release 8) (March 2009)
4. Myung, H.G., Lim, J., Goodman, D.J.: Single Carrier FDMA for Uplink Wireless Transmission. IEEE Vehicular Technology Mag. 1(3), 30–38 (2006)
5. 3GPP TSGRAN1 Chairman, REV-080058, Summaries of LTE-Advanced (April 2008)
6. Panasonic, R1-081791, Technical proposals and considerations for LTE advanced (May 2008)
7. Texas Instruments, R1-081979, Enhancement for LTE-Advanced (May 2008)
8. Alcatel-Lucent, REV-080048, LTE-Advanced candidate technologies, (May 2008)
9. Ericsson, REV-080030, LTE-A technology components (April 2008)
10. NTT DoCoMo, REV-080026, Proposals for LTE-A technologies (April 2008)
11. Nortel, REV-080033, Technical proposals for LTE-A (April 2008)
12. Texas Instrument, R1-082496, Uplink SU-MIMO for E-UTRA (June 2008)
13. Texas Instrument, R1-070271, Precoding Codebook Design for 2 Node-B Antennas (June 2008)
14. Panasonic, R1-082998, Precoding consideration on LTE-Adv uplink (August 2008)
15. Myung, H.G., et al.: Peak power characteristics of single carrier FDMA MIMO precoding system. IEEE VTC (Fall 2007)
16. Lo, T.K.: Maximum ratio transmission. IEEE Trans. Comm. 47(10), 1458–1461 (1999)
17. Love, D.J., Heath, R.W.: Equal gain transmission in multiple-input multiple-output wireless systems. IEEE Trans. Commun. 51(7) (July 2003)

18. IEEE802.16e, Air interface for broadband wireless access systems (June 2008)
19. WiMAX Forum, Mobile WiMAX - Part I: A technical overview and performance evaluation
20. Paulraj, A., Nabar, R., Gore, D.: Introduction to space time wireless communications, pp. 95–96. Cambridge University Press, Cambridge (2003)
21. Park, N.Y., Kim, Y.J., Li, X., Lee, K.S.: A fast index search algorithm for codebook based equal gain transmission beamforming system. In: VTC 2009 (Spring, April 2009)
22. Myung, H.G., Goodman, D.J.: Single Carrier FDMA. Wiley, Chichester (2008)
23. Han, S.H., Lee, J.H.: An overview of peak-to-average power ratio reduction techniques for multicarrier transmission. IEEE Wireless Commun. (April 2005)

Author Index